1986
SEASON
THE COMPLETE HANDBOOK OF
PRO HOCKEY

Super Football Books from SIGNET

1986 SEASON
THE COMPLETE HANDBOOK OF
PRO HOCKEY

EDITED BY ZANDER HOLLANDER

A SIGNET BOOK
NEW AMERICAN LIBRARY

ACKNOWLEDGMENTS

It has been a while since Wayne Gretzky was a nine-year-old in Brantford, Ont., in the year a Boston Bruin named Phil Esposito posted what were then NHL single-season records for goals (76) and points (152). Espo set the stage for the launching of the first edition of *The Complete Handbook of Pro Hockey* in 1971. And this year marks the 15th edition.

One original contributor, Mark Ruskie, is still in our lineup and we salute him along with those who have played roles along the way. We acknowledge the current cast: contributing editor Eric Compton, Hugh Delano, Jay Greenberg, Joe Gergen, Barry Wilner, Jeff Shermack, John Halligan, Richard Rossiter, Phyllis Hollander, Peter Hollander, Steve Wisniewski, Benny Ercolani, Dot Gordineer, Beri Greenwald, the corps at Westchester Book Composition and the NHL team publicity directors.

Zander Hollander

PHOTO CREDITS: Front cover—Paul Bereswell; back cover—Rich Pilling/Focus on Sports; inside photos—Bruce Bennett, Rich Pilling, Scotty Kilpatrick, CBS, UPI and the NHL team photographers.

CONTENTS

Wayne Gretzky's Fear of Flying .... By Joe Gergen   6

Pelle Lindbergh: The Seesaw Life
   Of Young NHL Goalies .... By Jay Greenberg 14

The Officiating Controversy:
   What to Do About It? .... By Barry Wilner 24

Inside the NHL ..... By Hugh Delano and Jay Greenberg 32

Boston Bruins................34   Calgary Flames.............143
Buffalo Sabres 43   Chicago Black Hawks.......153
Hartford Whalers 53   Detroit Red Wings 163
Montreal Canadiens 62   Edmonton Oilers...........172
New Jersey Devils 72   Los Angeles Kings 182
New York Islanders 81   Minnesota North Stars.....192
New York Rangers 93   St. Louis Blues............203
Philadelphia Flyers 103   Toronto Maple Leafs.......213
Pittsburgh Penguins........114   Vancouver Canucks 224
Quebec Nordiques 124   Winnipeg Jets.............234
          Washington Capitals....................133

NHL Statistics...245

All-Time NHL Records 268

NHL Trophy Winners.......................................270

Stanley Cup Winners......................................278

TV/Radio Roundup..281

NHL Schedule...284

Editor's Note: The material herein includes trades and rosters up to final printing deadline.

WAYNE GRETZKY'S FEAR OF FLYING

By JOE GERGEN

Wayne Gretzky became a professional hockey player at 30,000 feet. Perhaps only the Great One himself can fully appreciate the irony. Of all the shooting stars in the National Hockey League, Gretzky is least inclined to flights of fancy.

The man would prefer to remain earthbound for the rest of his natural life. But because of his profession, he constantly is up in the air. And whereas Gretzky remains in control on the ice, he finds himself at the mercy of outside forces on airplanes.

Yet the National Hockey League schedule calls for 80 games each season, excluding playoffs. That's a minimum of 40 flights (and not all non-stop) for the Edmonton Oilers, the northernmost and among the most isolated franchises in the far-flung circuit. For Gretzky, en route to breaking every scoring record in NHL history, the season is measured in takeoffs and landings.

As far back as the spring of 1982, the splendid center underwent hypnosis to alleviate his fear of flying. It was at the suggestion of Rod Phillips, the Oilers' play-by-play broadcaster who had found similar treatment therapeutic several years earlier. "I had to do something," Gretzky said. "I couldn't sleep worrying about my next flight, and I was nervous all day and I wasn't eating right."

According to Gretzky, it helped. But not enough that he was encouraged to return for a second session. Instead, he embarked on another method in recent seasons. Getting up and about.

He prefers not to take his flights sitting down. So, whenever possible, he roams about the plane, jabbers anxiously and attempts to misguide his mind into believing it is on the ground. And when all else fails, he saunters into the cockpit.

These moments are welcomed on Canadian-based airlines, which are not subject to the same regulations as U.S. carriers and on

Fearless Joe Gergen of Newsday *flies everywhere in search of a column.*

Wayne Gretzky is happiest when flying the Stanley Cup.

which a visit with the country's leading sports hero is regarded as a distinct honor. And Gretzky doesn't mind taking a seat where he can see the nerve center of the aircraft. "The pilot," he said, "can reassure me."

Had he come along 20 years earlier, of course, he wouldn't have had to subject himself to such mental torture in pursuit of the puck. The NHL was the last of the major leagues in North America to forsake the train. That's because it was strictly a six-city circuit, the cities stretching no farther west than Chicago and no farther south than New York, until 1967 when expansion opened the west to hockey. This was a decade after pro football and baseball had been lured across the Mississippi.

A 1960 model Gretzky could have traveled almost entirely by rail and fulfilled his duties to the sport. Of course, he would have earned only five figures for his skill, as opposed to the seven-figure contract he renegotiated in 1982. With his business interests and endorsements which at least match his annual hockey salary, Gretzky is a child of the '70s grown into a superstar of the '80s.

By the time he skated into public consciousness, not only was the NHL a coast-to-coast operation but it had a rival in the World Hockey Association. The established league had a ban on signing junior players before they reached the ripe age of 20 but Gretzky and his parents decided he was ready for the pros at 17. So they enlisted an agent, Gus Badali, and set an arbitrary figure of $1.75 million for seven years.

It was Nelson Skalbania, a Vancouver entrepreneur who owned the WHA's Indianapolis Racers, who decided after several meetings that the price was right if not reasonable. He did so while the party was seated in his private plane shuttling over the Canadian Rockies form Vancouver to Edmonton. "Right there, at about 30,000 feet, he told us to sign it," Badali recalled.

Except there really wasn't anything to sign. Among them, all the principals had was a piece of scrap paper. Skalbania handed the paper and a pen to Gretzky and instructed him to write out an agreement by hand. "I had to write it," he said later. "Gus was talking and my dad was too nervous and Mr. Skalbania said he wouldn't write because the figure made him too dizzy."

What happened later was even more dizzying. After eight games in a Racer uniform, Gretzky was sold to the Oilers, where owner Peter Pocklington was better equipped to pay such a handsome salary. And less than three months after that deal, on the occasion of his 18th birthday, the youngster signed a nine-year contract with two six-year options stretching his potential employment to the year 1999. In 1982, the contract was renegotiated, raising Gretzky's salary to $1 million per.

Still, even at the height of his fame and income, Gretzky fears his career may be cut short because of his abhorrence of flying. Should he leave his sport prematurely for that reason, he would not be the first. Only the most famous. Until such time, however, that designation belongs to Jackie Jensen.

Jensen was among the most productive of baseball players, the American League leader in runs batted in for two consecutive seasons before he abruptly announced his retirement from the Boston Red Sox in 1959. He was 32 and in good health. But his life was in turmoil.

He had been a spectacular all-around athlete at the University of California, an All-America in both baseball and football. To outsiders, Jensen was the Golden Boy of the Golden Bears and his marriage to the beautiful Zoe Ann Olsen, a silver medalist in diving at the 1948 Olympics, seemed an extension of his remarkable success on the athletic field. He first reached the major leagues in 1950 when baseball still was confined to the Eastern section of the country and train travel was widespread. By the end of the decade, however, the national pastime had pushed west and flying had become a matter of necessity.

The new dependency was to torment Jensen. Many was the

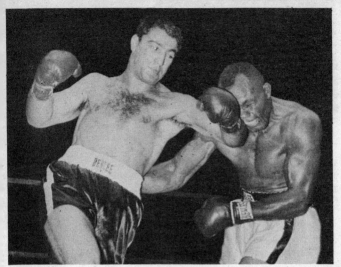

Rocky Marciano (vs. Jersey Joe Walcott) died in air crash.

team flight in which he had to be virtually carried aboard, the victim of a knockout pill. "I would be out when they got me to my seat," he recalled years later. "Then, when the engines started, I'd be wide awake and everybody else on the plane would be sound asleep."

Despite this terrible regimen, however, Jensen drove in more runs than any other player in the AL, including Mickey Mantle and teammate Ted Williams, during his first six years in the Boston outfield. The man also had excellent speed and an outstanding arm and in 1958 he was selected the league's Most Valuable Player. One year later he quit the game for the first time.

Some time later, Jensen would agree with the analysis that the phobia was the result of his disintegrating marriage, that he was using it as a pretext to go home to Nevada and salvage the relationship. So he stayed away from baseball for a year, then attempted a comeback with the Red Sox in 1961. Alas, the time off could not save the marriage. And his fear of flying loomed larger and larger when he returned to the game.

In one instance, he drove 700 miles from Boston to Detroit to avoid a flight. After a month, he left the team and took a train west to keep an appointment with a nightclub hynotist in Las Vegas. Jensen underwent several sessions, then rejoined the team in Los Angeles. Although he finished the season, he was a shadow

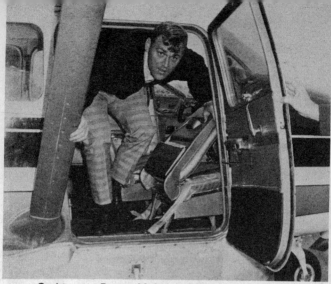

Sad to say, Denny McLain's flying days are over.

of the former all-star, batting .263 and driving in 66 runs. He quit in frustration a second time, and made it stick.

It remains one of the stranger stories in American sports, which has enjoyed a love/hate relationship with the invention of Orville and Wilbur Wright. The ambivalence may be traced back to the crash of a private plane in Kansas in 1931. That plane carried Knute Rockne, the storied football coach at Notre Dame, to his death.

Other national sports heroes have met similar ends in the modern era. Rocky Marciano, who had retired undefeated as heavyweight boxing champion of the world in 1956, also was killed aboard a private plane in 1969. Three years later, only months after he had collected his 3,000th hit in the major leagues, baseball star Roberto Clemente died when his plane bearing aid for stricken earthquake victims in Nicaragua crashed off the coast of Puerto Rico.

Some prominent athletes have taken fate into their own hands by earning their wings. Arnold Palmer ushered golf into the jet age not only with some spectacular triumphs on courses here and in Great Britain but with his assault on the skies, friendly or otherwise. He flew himself from tournament to tournament, upgrading his proficiency rating until he was judged qualified to pilot a 707.

Perhaps the most famous of baseball pilots was Ted Williams, a World War II Marine ace called back into service during the Korean War. In civilian life, however, Williams preferred to leave the flying to others. That was not the case with Bob Feller, the Hall of Fame pitcher who enjoyed taking his Cleveland Indian teammates on flights. And Denny McLain, at the height of a career which would plunge precipitously, reveled in his moments amongst the clouds.

McLain's tragedy would be self-inflicted and humiliating, sentenced to eight years in prison for racketeering, conspiracy and extortion, and another 15 years for the attempted sale of cocaine. But tragedy of the sudden, accidental kind befell Thurman Munson on Aug. 2, 1979, when a private plane he had recently purchased crashed during landing practice near his home in Canton, Ohio. Munson, the 32-year-old catcher and captain of the New York Yankees, was enjoying an off day during the season by indulging in his avid hobby.

Remarkably, there never has been a critical airplane incident involving a professional sports team in this country. College teams haven't been as fortunate. Football teams representing Cal Poly, Wichita State and Marshall all have been decimated. The Marshall crash in the fall of 1970 was particularly devasting. All 75 aboard the chartered flight, including 34 players, the coaching staff and athletic director, perished. When the football program was revived the following season, the team adopted a chilling new tradition. Each time one of their flights landed safely, they would applaud.

More recently, the Evansville University basketball team was wiped out on a chartered flight. Yet, despite flying millions of miles each year, American's professional teams have never met with similar disaster. They all have plans by which to restock stricken franchises, of course, but fortunately they have not had to utilize them.

There was, however, one very, very close call. It occurred in January 1960, in the National Basketball Association, a league just coming to grips with air travel. By the end of the year, the Lakers would be esconced in Los Angeles and routinely flying coast-to-coast on large aircraft. But on this wintry Sunday night, they were headed home to Minneapolis on an old twin-engine DC-3 following a game in St. Louis.

Somewhere over Iowa, the plane ran into a snowstorm, a severe snowstorm. The electrical system died, effectively killing the lights, the radio and the instruments. It was 1:30 in the morning. The pilot and co-pilot provided by Gopher Aviation Company (the Lakers owned the plane) had to lean out the windows in order to see, so powerful was the storm. They saw the lights of a small town later identified as Carroll, Iowa. Silently, almost blindly, they set the plane down in what turned out to be a cornfield blanketed in more than a foot of snow.

Back in Minneapolis, a skinny forward who had been hospitalized for a knee injury heard a radio report that the Lakers' plane was down. Steve Hamilton started crying. "My God," thought the man who would go on to a career as a pitcher with the Yankees and several other clubs, "I'm the only one left."

Miraculously, however, no one on the flight was injured. Those aboard included Tommy Hawkins, Dick Garmaker, Frank Selvy, Rod Hundley and Bob Leonard as well as coach Jim Pollard and a sensational young cornerman named Elgin Baylor, who had broken the one-game scoring record with a 64-point outburst against Boston two months earlier. The Lakers returned to Minneapolis by bus on the morning of Jan. 18 but Baylor was back in the air two days later, en route to the NBA All-Star Game in Philadelphia. Baylor scored 25 points for the West. Not even a frightening airplane scare was going to keep him from his appointed date with the Basketball Hall of Fame.

John Madden was mindful of another 1960 incident whenever he flew. Two years after he played at Cal Poly, a twin-engine craft carrying the football team back from Toledo, Ohio, exploded. Of the 44 people on board, 22 died, including 16 members of the team. Many of those players were friends of Madden.

He had to fly, or course, in his position as a football coach, first as a college assistant, then a pro assistant and, finally, as head coach of the Oakland Raiders. But he didn't have to like it. Madden, like Gretzky does now, paced the aisles, talked and kept himself busy as much as possible. And he thanked the Lord his sport was football, which was played only once a week and required a limited number of flights.

The travel was equally undemanding when Madden was hired as a television analyst after he retired from coaching. But now he no longer was flying on charters among friends and associates. He was on his own and the experience only increased the dread he felt. Finally, on a one-stop flight from Tampa to his home in the San Francisco Bay area, he got off the plane in Houston in a cold sweat and vowed never to fly again. He took a train back to the West Coast.

In that moment of inspiration and perspiration was born something of a national celebrity, a man who traveled all about the country by train and bragged about it, a man who even made a beer commercial expounding on his fear. While the sports world was shooting for the moon, John Madden was riding the rails, just as they did two generations earlier. The man struck a chord with the public and gained far greater fame and fortune than he

John Madden: Most celebrated rider of the rails.

had as a coach of a Super Bowl winner.

Would that Jackie Jensen had that option. Or that the NHL could devise a schedule by which Gretzky might travel in his own private railroad car along the route of the Canadian Pacific from faceoff to faceoff. Alas, times and transportation have changed. If ever an athlete were created for this era, it was Gene Conley, who played both baseball and basketball on the big-league level.

Conley couldn't get enough of travel. So enamored of flying was he, in fact, that one day he got off a team bus stalled in New York traffic, hailed a taxi, found himself at the airport and boarded a flight to Israel. Really, there oughta be a law. At least once in his life, every player should deplane in the Promised Land.

PELLE LINDBERGH: THE SEESAW LIFE OF YOUNG GOALIES

By JAY GREENBERG

This was a shutout sealed with 34 saves and a kiss. Pelle Lindbergh provided the saves and 17,191 lovers and other assorted strangers and hypocrites supplied the kiss.

The scene, as the final minutes of the Flyers' 3-0 shutout of the Islanders in early April counted down, was downright passionate. The fans stood and cheered in an outpouring of warmth and forgiveness we hadn't seen since Richard Gere swept Debra Winger off her feet.

Earlier in the evening, a select panel of writers and sportscasters who cover the Philadelphia Flyers had named Lindbergh the team's Most Valuable Player for the 1984–85 season. He skated out to get the Bobby Clarke Trophy and the fans chanted "Pelle! Pelle! Pelle!" Then he stoned the Islanders, 3-0, playing goal, really about as well as it can be played. Now they were chanting his name again.

Of course none of these same 17,191 persons were within 100 miles of the Spectrum that February night 14 months before.

Not a single one. Nah, had to be a different crowd. If someone would have had a rope and a horse, we would have had one dead Swede on our hands that night.

Lying there flat on his back, the puck behind him and the goal light on, the thought surely must have occurred to Lindbergh to simply not get up.

That way, things could not possibly get any worse. The tying goal had just been mailed bulk rate, in a plain brown package,

---

As hockey writer for the Philadelphia Daily News, *Jay Greenberg has flown with Pelle Lindbergh from the beginning.*

Pelle Lindbergh came back to win the Vezina Trophy.

from center ice by Vancouver's Darcy Rota. But because Lindbergh, who had already allowed two goals between his legs, was at that point trying to hang on to a 5-4 lead, its contents were a greased life preserver with a bomb in it.

Trying to remember everything he had forgotten about goaltending, even doing things by rote failed Pelle. He put his stick down at the side of the goal while trying to make sure he got his skate against the post to guard against the bad bounce.

Of course it came as no surprise to him when that treacherous hop came. The puck hit Lindbergh in the leg and the only reflex left to him was to panic. His feet slid out from under him as the puck crossed the line.

If Lindbergh would have just stayed on his back, waiting for the Zamboni to melt him into the ice, maybe the Flyers could have gotten out of that game with Vancouver with a tie.

But no. Lindbergh covered his eyes for a full second, hoping the ice would open up and swallow him. When it didn't, he got up. The league rule that required the playing of the final 9:21 was both cruel and unusual. And Lindbergh, naked now before fate and 17,001 taunts, faced the music.

It was a dirge. Pelle tried to hang on, getting his stick on a

Moe Lemay drive, his blocker up on another by Tiger Williams and actually kicked in time to save a goal by Patrik Sundstrom. But the Angel of Death, fittingly played by Williams, came rushing toward the Flyer goal with but two minutes left.

Brad Marsh came across and roped Williams before he could get the puck away, but Rota hadn't actually shot on his goal and Williams didn't have to either. Lindbergh left his feet, his pads coming up off the ice for the split second necessary for the puck to find its way through.

It could not possibly get any worse than this. Not for Lindbergh, not for the surly crowd that had, as the 1983–84 season went along, became increasingly disenchanted with coach and GM Bob McCammon. The little creep foreigner on goal was part of the plot to destroy the franchise, that was for sure. Did Lindbergh hear them?

"Yeah," he said. "But I guess they'd heard enough from me, too."

McCammon was asked about alternatives, other than the bench, for his goalie. "I don't know," he said. "There's a plane for Sweden at midnight, but we're not that cruel. No, really, it's pretty obvious we're going to have to do something."

The answer, grasping at straws to be sure, was for Lindbergh to go down and play four American League games at Springfield. He won them all, but it didn't really work. When he came back, at least he wasn't letting them in from center ice anymore, but he was nowhere close to the goaltender who in his rookie 1982–83 season had played in the All-Star Game.

Did it start to come apart the night of that All-Star Game 12 months before at the Nassau Coliseum, when Lindbergh gave up four goals to Wayne Gretsky alone and seven in 30 minutes of play?

No, actually, it began five weeks earlier. Lindbergh, who had just keyed a sweep of a six-game road trip that pushed the Flyers into first place, was playing goal against the Soviets at the Spectrum when he covered a loose puck. A Russian skater jarred his hand, causing a hairline fracture in the navicular bone.

Three weeks later, he returned with a shutout in Los Angeles and seemed ready to pick up where he left off. Two nights before that victory his teammates had savaged his Swedish head with the customary rookie haircut. Pelle didn't like it, but he bit his tongue and went along with the gag.

He then went out into the shooting gallery—that is all that an All-Star game really is—and was torched by Gretzky.

That's what did it. Not the haircut. "It was pretty embarrassing to give up that many goals, with everybody in the league watching,"

Edmonton's Grant Fuhr stood tall in the Cup repeat.

Lindbergh said. He won his next start two nights later, but was shaky. Little by little, the natural began to forget how.

Bob Froese, called up from the minors in Lindbergh's absence, got more and more of the starts. And Pelle, who has always felt he needs a lot of work to be sharp, never quite regained his form of the first half of the season.

A lot of Flyers played worse as the Patrick Division champions went down in a fireball to the fourth-place Rangers in three straight first-round games. But Lindbergh was hardly scintillating.

The night the Rangers completed the sweep with an 8-3 bombing at Madison Square Garden, he dressed in tears. "A lot of people think that the Europeans are over here for the money and we don't really care about winning and losing," he said. "But I feel awful. Just awful."

Actually, he started the next season well. Better, in fact, than did the Flyers, who after a strong first 10 games, began to break down. At first the goals weren't Lindbergh's fault, but he picked up on his teammates' panic. And soon more and more of them were.

McCammon went back to Froese, who continued to do an excellent job. Lindbergh wasn't getting enough work and was soon getting too much advice from too many people. That Vancouver game was the nadir of a two-months-plus stretch running from December to late March in which Lindbergh didn't win a game. His rookie season, in which he compiled a 23-13-3 record with a 2.98 goals-against average, faded to the black of 16-13-3 record and a 4.05 average. And even that was made to look better by his 7-2-1 start.

When the playoffs started, Froese was deservedly the Flyers' goalie.

Pelle went home for the summer to Stockholm with one major decision to make. His country's call for the Canada Cup was upon him and maybe some good stiff international competition would enable him to report to camp with an edge to win his job back.

He decided the opposite. "It's too long a season," he said. "It catches up with you. My first obligation is to win my job back in Philadelphia."

Lindbergh didn't have a great camp last year. But then, as a notorious slow starter, he never really has. However, a new coach, Mike Keenan, without ever really explaining why, put Lindbergh in goal to start the season.

He played well in the opener, a 2-2 tie with Washington. And two nights later he stood on his head as the Flyers, outshot 21-5 by the Caps in the first period, rallied from a 2-0 deficit for 4-2 road victory over the club that five months earlier had put them out of the playoffs in three straight games.

As turning points go, it was as good as any. Both for the Flyers and their goalie. "It just feels so good to be able to hold a team in a game so it can come back to win," Lindbergh said. "It's better than a shutout."

There was, of course, a lot more to it than just one victory. Until the electronic goalie is invented, the old unreliable model still will contain more than 100 moving parts. A lot can go wrong; a lot will go wrong.

A short here causes a hitch there, which causes a glitch somewhere else. By February of the season before, Lindbergh, a Porsche, had an electrical system so thoroughly screwed up that when you turned on his headlights, his doors flew open.

Mechanics, coaches, writers, probably half the International Brotherhood of Electrical Workers, wanted to take Lindbergh apart to get to the bottom of the problem.

That soon became part of the problem. Everybody had an idea and Lindbergh was open—too open—to suggestions.

"The coach and the goaltending coach and the assistant coach were all trying to be helpful and I was trying to be nice and listen to everybody," he said. "Everybody was telling me something different.

"It's like when I first came over here and Jacques Plante [then the Flyers' goaltending coach] tried to give me everything at once. It's too much to think about and you forget what got you here in the first place."

Let's see now, what was that? Oh yeah, Lindbergh's quickness. God put a spectacular set of reflexes on this creature 26 years ago, ones that served him just fine as a prodigy working his way up in the Swedish system. By the age of 20, Lindbergh was the first-string National Team goalie. The Flyers didn't invest a second-round draft choice in 1979 on a guy who was standing there stiff as a board. Yet in all the well-intentioned advice to stand up, play the angles and keep those legs closed, they turned a sports car into a sedan.

Of course he wasn't the first goalie ever to lose it and find it again. Grant Fuhr, who has now won consecutive Stanley Cups for the Oilers, had such a miserable sophomore season that he, like Lindbergh, was sent back to the American League to find himself. Ditto Tom Barrasso, who leaped directly out of a Boston high-school league to win the Vezina Trophy in his first NHL season at Buffalo. When Barrasso started poorly last year, GM-coach Scotty Bowman didn't hesitate to farm the 19-year-old kid to Rochester.

Lindbergh and Fuhr continued to struggle when they came back from the minors, but Barrasso straightened himself right out. The learning curve varies from goalie to goalie, but some down time appears to be almost standard.

"So many of them have the good first year and then start having trouble and they can't fight it," said Calgary's Rejean Lemelin, who had a long minor-league apprenticeship. "They've always had everything and now they don't know what to do and they come apart.

"I learned how to fight back before I got to the NHL; some of these kids have to do that while they're already there. And the pressure of being in the big leagues makes it that much tougher to overcome.

"It should be tougher for some of these kids just to show them that nothing is handed to them, that they have to work for what they get."

Lindbergh did have two years in Maine before the Flyers called him up, so he didn't qualify as the too-much-too-soon spoiled brat in the strictest sense. Still, as he looks back, he admits he didn't handle his down times very well.

He also continues to insist that he can't be as good if he's sharing a net 50-50. When Pelle did go into his one slump of the season last December, Froese was out with a knee injury, and that undoubtedly helped. Keenan isn't a guy to hesitate to make a change. But in this case, the coach had no choice.

Keenan, however, also provided the practice atmosphere to help bring Pelle out of it. "The pattern was that he was getting tired in the third periods," the coach said. "So we just picked up his work load in practice. We like to make corrections through drills in practices. We tell our players, 'This drill is for the goalies.'"

Bernie Parent, the Flyers' goaltending coach, had a word or two of advice, but for the most part he backed off and let Pelle play himself through his problems. Nothing succeeds like success and, the Flyers, a consensus pick to finish fourth in their division in what was perceived to be a rebuilding year, were rolling. And if it ain't broke, you don't fix it.

"Like any athlete who goes into a slump," assistant coach Ted Sator said, "he looks for advice. Anything from snake medicine to faith healers.

"Sooner or later, it all comes back to relying on your natural ability. Pelle's gone back to being the Old Gumper. There's been a laissez-faire approach if anything.

"Last year we were groping for so many reasons why and came up with so many intangibles that we lost Pelle. Maybe we harped so much on his weaknesses that we forgot his strong points.

"We still work with areas that need improvement, but I don't

Farm duty made Buffalo's Tom Barrasso better than ever.

think anybody's tampering with Pelle's style. He's playing with confidence. This guy is a world-class goaltender, no question."

That was in November. Lindbergh went on to prove it. The Flyers went 23-2 down the stretch and raced to the league's best record. The Rangers, those old Flyer nemeses, showed up to play in the first round of the playoffs, but Pelle fought down the knot in his stomach as New York tied the opening game in the final minute and held the fort until Mark Howe's overtime goal gave the Flyers their first playoff victory in 10 games over four years.

Lindbergh let in a bad goal in the third game, allowing the Rangers to get back within a goal early in the third period, but hung tough as the Flyers checked the game away.

Pelle shut out the Islanders twice, including 1-0 in the final game after being touched up for four goals in the preceding one. He had one bad game in the playoffs, the fourth one against Quebec. Lindbergh allowed a goal from the blue line by Dale Hunter and two others he normally gobbles up. As the Flyers flew to Quebec City tied 2-2 in the series, a lot of people were worried about him.

Lindbergh spent the trip reading Mad Magazine (What, him worry?) and listening to a tape that a sports psychologist he has visited a few times gave him. "You can't be great every night," he shrugged.

The Flyers were just awful for two periods the next night, but Lindbergh, in what, considering the circumstances, might have been his best playoff performance of all, held the Nordiques to one goal. His team came back with two third-period goals and the series pivoted again. He finished Quebec off with another shutout in the sixth game.

It was a helluva ride all the way to the finals. Save three more victories against the Oilers, Pelle's season was as complete as that of any NHL goalie since Bernie Parent took the Flyers to their second Stanley Cup in 1975.

Lindbergh led the league in wins (with 40), was third in goals-against average (3.02), and was second in save percentage (.889). His 83 games, playoff and regular season combined, were the second most in league history.

When a particular rupture in the quadriceps tendon in his right leg put him out of the playoffs with but one game to go, his playoff record was 12-6 with a 2.50 goals-against average. Included were three shutouts. In June he was named the winner of the Vezina Trophy as the league's top goaltender.

The TV camera lights were on. Reporters surrounding Lindbergh in the minutes following his 1-0 shutout that eliminated the Islanders, were scribbling notes.

In the crowd, Pelle spotted a guy who had chronicled it all, from his draft day in 1979, to his mangled attempts at English when he showed up at his first Flyer camp, to his request to be traded when the Flyers didn't immediately promote him after being named the Most Valuable Player in the American League, to his rookie triumphs, to his fall, to his redemption.

Lindbergh's face lit up. "How did you like that?" he asked. "I think it was a little bit better than that Vancouver game, don't you?"

Lindbergh defends against Islander John Tonelli.

The Officiating Controversy: What To Do About It?

By BARRY WILNER

Exhibit A

A seething Michel Bergeron storms into the interview room and summons the press corps to his private screening area to see tapes of several incidents in his Nordiques' playoff loss to the Philadelphia Flyers.

Bergeron is annoyed that referee Kerry Fraser had nullified a goal in the final minutes by Michel Goulet which would have tied the fifth game of the Wales Conference final. Fraser had ruled—correctly—that Goulet had directed the puck into the net with his skate.

But it was the rugged treatment Philadelphia's Ed Hospodar had given Quebec stars Peter and Anton Stastny that really enrages Bergeron. His tapes show Hospodar spearing Peter and cross-checking Anton in the back of the neck. Fraser and his linesmen did not see either incident because they occurred behind the play.

But when Peter viciously retaliated with a cross-check to Hospodar's face, Fraser handed out a major penalty to the Nordique.

"Fraser is supposed to be one of the best referees in the NHL," says Bergeron. "If that is true, why did he ignore these things?"

Exhibit B

The Edmonton Oilers have been thoroughly thrashed by the Flyers in Game 1 of the Stanley Cup finals on a steamy night in the Spectrum. The ice is as choppy as the North Atlantic and as slushy as a Manhattan street crossing the day after a snowstorm. The Oilers' play is just as messy.

Barry Wilner calls 'em as he sees 'em as hockey editor for the Associated Press.

Andy Van Hellemond is one of NHL's top referees.

Yet, after the game, Oilers' boss Glen Sather is ranting and raving about referee Andy Van Hellemond just as much as he is complaining about the conditions.

Sather takes exception to the number of power plays Van Hellemond awarded to Philadelphia (seven), including a 5-on-3 during which the Flyers opened the scoring, while Edmonton had only three manpower advantages.

"The refereeing?" Sather snaps in response to a query. "It was as good as the ice."

Exhibit C

Washington's Mike Gartner circles the New York Islanders' net in the second overtime of Game 2 of their Stanley Cup series. He stuffs home a wraparound shot seconds after Capitals' forward Greg Adams has collided with goalie Kelly Hrudey. Referee Don Koharski, who is in position, lets the goal stand and the Islanders go wild. Led by Coach Al Arbour, who actually bumps Koharski while questioning the call, the Islanders surround Koharski, who holds his ground.

The next day, Arbour is fined for his actions. Bergeron also is fined later in the spring. Sather escapes punishment, mainly because his verbal attack was relatively mild and did not involve any histrionics.

Ah, the life of an NHL referee. Good pay, extensive travel, first-rate hotels. And criticism, complaints and catcalls wherever he goes.

"I think to be an official, you have to accept the fact that your decisions will be criticized one way or the other all the time," says Fraser, one of the league's best referees. "In the best of times, you will only be 50 percent right in the eyes of the viewers, who are either cheering one team or the other and not seeing things impartially. It is the nature of the sport and the beast, as far as the fan is concerned.

"You either accept it or get out of the profession and into selling shoes . . . or something else that does not provide the controversy."

Yes, the controversy. It's always there with game officials. What can be done about it? Are the NHL refs and linesmen up to snuff? Will rules changes help them perform better? Is the game too fast and frantic for the present setup of one referee and two linesmen?

In any examination of hockey officiating, it must be mentioned that the requirements of the job have become increasingly difficult. One referee, Bryan Lewis (who worked the Cup finals last spring along with Fraser and Andy Van Hellemond because they were the highest-rated refs in the league), notes that "the players are getting bigger, faster and more creative and teams are doing more things with the puck. A good referee has to cover more of the ice at a faster pace."

Linesman Ron Foyt admits that "NHL hockey has changed so much that our jobs are different each year and different than they ever were before." Or at least the emphasis placed on positioning, speed and endurance has increased every year.

Adds Fraser, "Games have gone from almost barbaric and brutal violence 10 years ago to now, when you are looking at a highly skilled player coming into the league. Teams are faster, guys are bigger and better at handling the puck and shooting."

And the referees and linesmen? Are they measuring up? And what can be done about it if they aren't?

One member of the NHL's officiating hierarchy was appalled by some of the things he saw game officials doing on the ice last season. In his off-the-record comments, he expressed "serious concern" about the physical conditioning of some refs and linesmen and wondered "if we need to get rid of some of these guys."

"When there is a clear-cut infraction or a decision needs to be made right away and [the referee] is out of position . . . consistently out of position . . . we have to think about whether he can keep up," he said. "I don't care who he is, how many years he has [in the NHL] . . . if he can't do the job anymore, get rid of him. I think we have a few guys, referees and linesmen, who fall into that category."

From a fan's viewpoint, the only good referee is the one who works a game the fan's team wins. The only good linesman is one who allows a hometown favorite to beat up on a visitor.

More than in any other sport, the officials are blamed in hockey for a home team's failure.

Van Hellemond, who in the 1981–82 season was struck by Boston's Terry O'Reilly and Philadelphia's Paul Holmgren, directly leading to an "abuse of officials rule" which carries a 20-game suspension, stresses that he and his peers play no favorites.

"If your job requires that you do something specific, you do it," explains Van Hellemond. "Our job demands impartiality and I know it has never been a problem for me to be impartial.

"If a referee at any time tried to play favorites, I think it would be easy to tell. Besides, it would be foolish. We all hold a dedication to the game, we all have a special feeling about hockey, just like the players and the coaches and the fans. The better job we do, the better the game."

Adds Fraser, "We should not be thought upon as the enemy. All we are are impartial judges; we don't care who wins and loses. We can very often be used as a scapegoat; a player takes a bad penalty or there is bad coaching, that tends to be the referee's fault in too many eyes."

But the referees are at fault in many instances, too. Too few of them can keep up with the action, though the good ones make up for it by always being in the correct position to view a play. Some are arrogant—a complaint once made of Fraser and Van Hellemond but no longer heard—and carry an air of omnipotence. Some, even on their best nights, are in over their heads in the NHL.

For instance, the league has four referees who are at least 40 years old. Gordie Howe aside, no skater has come close to remaining in the NHL for extended play at that age. Not surprisingly, of those four—Lewis, Ron Wicks, Bob Myers and Dave Newell— only the latter is considered acceptable by a majority of coaches and players.

Of the linesmen, some appear to be frustrated refs who like nothing better than to make an impact on the game in ways other than calling lines, dropping pucks on faceoffs and breaking up altercations. Others are terribly inconsistent on offsides calls and a few seem to regard the puck as priceless—they take eons to drop it on faceoffs.

"It gets pretty frustrating when they don't want to drop the puck," says Montreal center Bobby Smith. "You see so many [centers] thrown out [on faceoffs] because of it.

"How patient do they expect us to be?"

By far the noisiest and most pointed complaints have come regarding the inconsistency on penalty calls. Simply stated, coaches and players are asking why a hooking, holding or tripping infraction is a penalty early in the game and not later on. Why does it take a near-felony to get a call in the final period, especially in a playoff game?

The critics have a point.

"When I see a clear tripping or holding in the last five or 10 minutes and the referee doesn't react, I want to go right down there and ask him myself, 'Why not?'" says an NHL officiating supervisor. "A penalty is a penalty, all the time."

"All we ask is that they be consistent," says Arbour. "Let the players know what kind of game it's going to be, what will be accepted and what will get them sent to the box. And stick with that. Not many referees do."

Indeed, for every Fraser, Van Hellemond, Koharski and Ron Hoggarth—the guys who stick to the same style throughout a

Ref has his perch in this mid-'50s shot.

game—there is a Myers, Wicks, Denis Morel or Ron Fournier, who look like they're calling two different games.

"My vantage point will dictate what kind of official I am," says Fraser. "I gain a lot of self-satisfaction when players know they will get a fair game and tell me so.

"I try to remember that if it is a penalty, it must be called. It's in the rule book. I didn't commit it, the player did and he must be penalized for it, regardless of the time of game, score or situation."

When the league perceives a problem regarding its game officials, it has a system of procedure to correct the ill. But the NHL doesn't feel the refereeing or line-calling is causing much trouble.

"There are always the odd incidents and they get isolated and draw a lot of attention," says John McCauley, the league's assistant director of officiating and a former referee. "But I have to say the overall picture has been good. We have methods for formal requests of review when a controversy arises. We do listen to a lot of complaints but most of them come out of frustration when someone's team loses a big game or feels it lost because of a decision by an official.

"We don't feel we have people who have a problem with conditioning, but if we did find that, we would monitor it, especially if it involved a weight gain, which an official seems prone to sometimes. We would test his conditioning and get him on a program to upgrade it, if necessary.

"As for the teaching aspect, if a fellow has consistent problems, we will call him in for a lot of one-on-one conversations, let him look at tapes and show him why he should have handled it another way. We have supervisors at the games for that reason, as observers. They'll talk to the official, ask why he did or didn't make a call, especially if he did see it. If he didn't see it, why not? Was he in the right position?"

So what can be done about the officiating? Will the NHL ever have a full supply of the Frasers, Van Hellemonds, Koharskis and Hoggarths, guys who take control of the game from the outset and hold onto it through consistency and respect? And linesmen like Ray Scapinello, Ron Finn, Kevin Collins and Wayne Bonney, about whom you rarely hear a disparaging word?

Or will the NHL always have second-rate officials along with those top-of-the-heap performers?

"You can't get the public to understand the situation an official is in," says McCauley. "They take into account their teams and their players only. They only see the act from one side and they only see it through their biased judgment."

One suggestion McCauley expects the NHL Board of Governors to consider seriously in the near future is adopting a two-referee system.

"The game is very fast now and players tend to take advantage because a referee has to go with the flow and can't see everything," he explains. "One of the safeguards we have now is for linesmen to make certain calls as a deterrent to sticking incidents.

"Any type of change that would improve the officiating, we would have to look at. If they feel the system is inadequate, they will do something. But how many years have we used this system without it falling apart?"

Fraser thinks a two-ref format is a loser.

"Everything I've heard is that the biggest knock against us is inconsistency," he says. "No two people ever think alike, which would make a two-referee system very difficult. They may adjust to one another if they stay together a long time, which I guess would be a possibility. But we have to try to be consistent in ourselves, make the calls come automatic."

Another suggestion has been that the linesmen be allowed to call more penalties. Again, however, consistency would be a problem.

The use of instant replays has its supporters among the officials. Fraser says replays "would prove us right almost 100 percent of the time." McCauley admits that placing a supervisor in a press box with a replay monitor in front of him and a communications system with the on-ice officials could work and should, like anything else, be considered if it can be proven as a positive move.

Rules changes to increase punishment for violent incidents could make the officiating task a lot easier because it might cut down on stick-swinging.

"I'm all for tougher legislation on stick fouls," says Fraser. "It's the only way we are going to eliminate it, so whatever they propose, I'm all for it."

Van Hellemond notes that it is crucial that if such changes were made, they must be enforced.

"If it becomes a rule for stick infractions that it is a major penalty, we have to make sure we treat it that way," he says.

Several referees said they see sticking penalties—slashing, high-sticking, cross-checking, spearing—as the major problem they face. It was suggested by a few officials that a player be ejected for more than one stick infraction major in a game and the player be suspended if he gets thrown out of three games for sticking penalties. In other words, give it the same treatment as fighting.

The key, however, lies in the understanding of the duties and pressure of each performer's job. The players and coaches and GMs must have a stronger grasp of what an official goes through. The officials have to concentrate on calling the action the same way from the first faceoff to the final buzzer. And they must be willing to consult with each other, make quick but accurate decisions and explain precisely how they arrived at their calls.

"I wish one of them would be on the other side," says Glen Sather, "and see how some of them try to explain what happened. Maybe then they would understand us."

The critical word, says Fraser, is communication.

"There is a great deal we can improve on," he says. "We have to communicate more away from the game. They have to understand as coaches what we go through and we have to understand what they are going through. We have to come to a common ground through communication.

"I think we must work something out that is beneficial to the game—meetings, seminars with each other, to air the problems and discuss things that bother them and us.

"You can never solve anything when two people are emotional and you are in a no-win situation."

INSIDE THE NHL

BY HUGH DELANO and JAY GREENBERG

PREDICTED ORDER OF FINISH

Adams	Patrick	Smythe	Norris
Quebec	Philadelphia	Edmonton	Chicago
Buffalo	Washington	Winnipeg	Minnesota
Montreal	N.Y. Islanders	Calgary	St. Louis
Hartford	N.Y. Rangers	Los Angeles	Detroit
Boston	New Jersey	Vancouver	Toronto
	Pittsburgh		

Stanley Cup: Edmonton

"Edmonton is an awesome champion in its prime and I don't see anyone beating or knocking out Edmonton right now," said veteran coach Tom McVie. "Edmonton's won two Stanley Cups in a row. They're like an army that keeps coming at you.

"They're young, deep in talent. They've got the best scorer [Wayne Gretzky] and the best defenseman [Paul Coffey]. They've got a smart coach [Glen Sather] and a great goaltender [Grant Fuhr]. They're fast and they're strong. They are capable of keeping the Stanley Cup for the next few years."

That's what you call a dynasty.

"We haven't won four or five Cups yet but I would think this is the start of a dynasty for us," agreed Coffey after the Oilers repeated by whipping Philadelphia in five games last May.

"We have to be rated as good as any team that's ever won two Cups in a row," said Gretzky.

Joe Mullen, one of the best right wings in the NHL, believes

Hugh Delano of the New York Post *wrote the Adams and Smythe divisions and Jay Greenberg of the Philadelphia* Daily News *covered the Patrick and Norris. Delano wrote the introduction after a faceoff with Greenberg.*

its possible the Oilers and Flyers will clash again in the 1986 Stanley Cup playoff final.

"I think there's a good chance it will happen," said Mullen. "Philadelphia made it to the final with a very young team and could do it again. But I don't know if Philadelphia will be No. 1 in points again. Edmonton is getting stronger, especially defensively."

As usual, there have been a number of coaching changes for the 1985-86 season.

No new coach will be under greater pressure than Ted Sator. The little-known Sator, a man without NHL head-coaching experience, becomes the Rangers' ninth coach since 1973. He was a Flyers' assistant coach last season. The troubled Rangers have gone longer without winning a championship than any team in major-league sports. They last won the Stanley Cup in 1940.

Tom Watt faces a difficult job. He is Vancouver's new coach, replacing coach Harry Neale, who resumed coaching after Bill LaForge was fired after only 20 games last season. And now Neale winds up as the Red Wings' coach. Former NHL defenseman Jim Schoenfeld is Buffalo's new coach, replacing Scotty Bowman, the most successful coach in NHL history. Bowman will devote his full attention to his GM job. Former NHL forward Butch Goring is Boston's new coach and GM Bob Pulford starts his first full season as Chicago coach, having taken over last season when Orval Tessier was dismissed. And ex-Islander Lorne Henning gets his chance behind the North Stars' bench.

Some familiar faces will be missing. Defenseman Brad Park retired after 17 seasons with the Rangers, Boston and Detroit. Right wing Terry O'Reilly called it quits after 14 years in a Bruins' uniform. Left wing Steve Shutt, traded last season from Montreal to Los Angeles, has left hockey. Guy Lafleur, who scored 518 career goals, announced his retirement early last season after 14 glorious seasons with Montreal.

But time marches on, and so likely will Edmonton—unless there's a surprise that shuffles our predicted (not guaranteed) order of finish.

BOSTON BRUINS

TEAM DIRECTORY; Pres.-Gov.: Paul A. Mooney; GM: Harry Sinden; Asst. GM: Tom Johnson; Dir. Pub. Rel.: Nate Greenberg; Coach: Butch Goring. Home ice: Boston Garden (14,451; 195' × 83'). Colors: Gold, black and white. Training camp: Danvers, Mass.

SCOUTING REPORT

OFFENSE: The Bruins don't score goals the way they used to. They scored their fewest goals in 15 years last season, and their once-potent power play ranked a poor 15th in the NHL.

The absence of Barry Pederson had a lot to do with the offensive decline. The talented center missed most of last season because of an arm injury. Now he's presumed healthy again.

Right wing Rick Middleton was healthy last season but experienced his first disappointing season. He must regain his scoring touch or the Bruins' attack will sputter again as it did in 1984–85. The addition last season of left wing Charlie Simmer from Los Angeles helped. Simmer led the Bruins with 33 goals. Keith Crowder, Ken Linseman, Tom Fergus and newcomer Dave Reid are some of Boston's more prominent forwards. Defensemen Ray Bourque and Mike O'Connell play vital offensive roles.

The Bruins still pound visiting teams with fierce forechecking pressure in their small Boston Garden rink. But one of their best grinders and cornermen will not be there. Terry O'Reilly has retired and the Bruins will miss his inspirational play.

DEFENSE: The offensive-minded Bourque is perhaps hockey's best all-around defenseman. And O'Connell is a good two-way defenseman, skilled at shot-blocking and rushing with the puck.

Big Gord Kluzak, a former No. 1 draft choice, missed all last season following a training camp knee injury and ensuing surgery. He'll return but how effective he will be remains to be seen.

Mike Milbury, a dynamic bodychecker and team leader, retired unexpectedly after last season to become assistant coach. His presence on the ice will be missed. There is not much quality depth among the defensemen. Michael Thelven, a defenseman from Sweden, should be a welcome addition.

Goaltending is a question mark. Pete Peeters, who is one of hockey's better goalies, did not have a good 1984-85. He relinquished his starting job late in the season and in the playoffs to Doug Keans. Boston allowed its most goals since 1961-62.

Two-way defenseman Ray Bourque topped Bruins in scoring.

OUTLOOK: The Bruins slipped to fourth place in the Adams Division, recording their fewest points in 18 years. They have a new coach, Butch Goring, who never has coached and who retired as a player after last season. This could be a difficult year for Boston.

BRUIN PROFILES

RAY BOURQUE 24 5-11 205   **Defenseman**
Became first defenseman to lead Bruins' scoring since Bobby Orr in 1974-75 . . . Set career high with 66 assists . . . Led NHL de-

BRUIN ROSTER

No.	Player	Pos.	Ht.	Wt.	Born	1984-85	G	A	Pts.	PIM
33	John Blum	D	6-3	205	10-8-59/Detroit	Boston	3	13	16	263
7	Raymond Bourque	D	5-11	205	12-28-60/Montreal	Boston	20	66	86	53
12	Lyndon Byers	RW	6-1	185	2-29-64/Saskatoon, Sask.	Boston	3	8	11	41
						Hershey	4	6	10	55
32	Russ Courtnall	LW	5-11	165	6-18-62/Victoria, B.C.	Boston	12	16	28	82
						Hershey	8	4	12	4
18	Keith Crowder	RW	6-0	195	1-6-59/Windsor, Ont.	Boston	32	38	70	152
34	Brian Curran	D	6-4	220	11-5-63/Toronto	Boston	0	1	1	158
						Hershey	0	0	0	19
29	Dave Donnelly	LW	6-1	190	2-2-63/Edmonton	Boston	6	8	14	46
						Hershey	11	6	17	28
28	Tom Fergus	C	6-0	200	6-16-62/Chicago	Boston	30	43	73	75
14	Mike Gillis	RW-C	6-1	195	12-1-58/Toronto	Injured	–	–	–	–
	Dean Jenkins	RW	6-0	190	11-21-59/Billerica, Man.	Hershey	14	32	46	135
33	Greg Johnston	RW	6-1	200	1-14-65/Barrie, Ont.	Hershey	1	0	1	0
						Boston	0	0	0	0
						Toronto (OHL)	22	28	50	55
11	Steve Kasper	LW	5-8	160	9-28-61/Montreal	Boston	16	24	40	33
6	Gord Kluzak	D	6-4	210	3-6-64/Climax, Sask.	Injured	–	–	–	–
	Doug Kostynski	C	6-1	170	2-23-63/Castlegar, B.C.	Hershey	17	27	44	26
						Boston	0	0	0	2
13	Ken Linseman	C	5-11	175	8-11-58/Kingston, Ont.	Boston	25	49	74	126
12	Morris Lukowich	RW	5-9	175	6-1-56/Speers, Sask.	Winn.-Bos.	10	17	27	52
17	Nevin Markwart	LW	5-10	170	12-9-64/Toronto	Boston	0	4	4	136
						Hershey	13	18	31	79
16	Rick Middleton	RW	5-11	175	12-4-53/Toronto	Boston	30	46	76	6
	Doug Morrison	C	5-11	175	2-1-60/Vancouver	Hershey	28	25	53	25
						Boston	0	0	0	2
20	Mike O'Connell	D	5-9	185	11-25-55/Chicago	Boston	15	40	55	64
	Dave Pasin	RW	6-1	185	7-8-66/Edmonton	Prince Albert	64	52	116	88
10	Barry Pederson	C	5-11	185	3-13-61/Big River, Sask.	Boston	4	8	12	10
	Ray Podloski	C	6-2	190	1-5-66/Edmonton	Portland	63	75	138	41
36	Dave Reid	LW	6-1	210	5-15-64/Toronto	Boston	14	13	27	27
						Hershey	10	14	24	6
23	Charlie Simmer	LW	6-3	210	3-20-54/Terrace Bay, Ont.	L.A.-Boston	34	30	64	39
21	Frank Simonetti	D				Hershey	0	6	6	14
						Boston	1	5	6	26
25	Louis Sleigher	RW	5-11	195	10-23-58/Nouvelle, Que.	Que.-Bos.	13	21	34	45
27	Mats Thelin	D	5-10	185	3-30-61/Sweden	Boston	5	13	18	78

No.	Player	Pos.	Ht.	Wt.	Born		GP	GA	SO	Avg.
31	Doug Keans	G	5-7	185	1-7-58/Pembroke, Ont.	Boston	25	82	1	3.29
	Cleon Deskalakis	G	5-9	175	9-29-62/Boston	Boston	8	24	0	4.98
						Hershey	30	119	3	4.42
1	Pete Peeters	G	6-0	185	8-1-57/Edmonton	Boston	51	172	1	3.47

fensemen with 332 shots on goal, second only to overall league-leader Wayne Gretzky's 358 shots ... Has powerful shot from blue line and is outstanding shooter-passer as power play point man ... Firmly established as one of best all-around defensemen in NHL ... Born Dec. 28, 1960, in Montreal ... Doesn't make many mistakes as a defender ... Skates as well as many forwards ... Strongest part of his game is leading rush up the ice to put Bruins on the attack ... Won Calder Trophy as Rookie of the Year and was named to first All-Star team in 1979-80.

Year	Club	GP	G	A	Pts.
1979-80	Boston	80	17	48	65
1980-81	Boston	67	27	29	56
1981-82	Boston	65	17	49	66
1982-83	Boston	65	22	51	73
1983-84	Boston	78	31	65	96
1984-85	Boston	73	20	66	86
	Totals	428	134	308	442

RICK MIDDLETON 31 5-11 175   Right Wing

Did not have an outstanding season by his high standards ... Goal and point production was his lowest in eight years ... Eleven-year veteran still ranks as one of best all-around right wings in NHL ... Needs 10 goals to reach 400 for his career ... Ranks among highest career scorers in Bruins' history ... Outstanding defensive forward and penalty-killer as well as scoring threat ... Born Dec. 4, 1953, in Toronto ... Rival defensemen rate him as toughest man to stop one-on-one ... Fast, flashy, fun to watch ... Nicknamed "Nifty" or "Wheels" for his slick, quick passing and skating ... Former 50-goal, 100-point scorer ... Rangers still look foolish for trading him to Bruins in 1976 for fading veteran Ken Hodge.

Year	Club	GP	G	A	Pts.
1974-75	New York R	47	22	18	40
1975-76	New York R	77	24	26	50
1976-77	Boston	72	20	22	42
1977-78	Boston	79	25	35	60
1978-79	Boston	71	38	48	86
1979-80	Boston	80	40	52	92
1980-81	Boston	80	44	59	103
1981-82	Boston	75	51	43	94
1982-83	Boston	80	49	47	96
1983-84	Boston	80	47	58	105
1984-85	Boston	80	30	46	76
	Totals	821	390	454	844

KEN LINSEMAN 27 5-11 175   Center

Has perfect personality and style of play for Bruins and their small
Boston Garden rink . . . Plays feisty, aggressive hockey . . . Most
opponents dislike his persistent play but respect his ability . . .
Nicknamed "Rat" . . . Once fined and suspended for biting an opponent on ear . . . Gained his reputation for nasty, pesky play with
Flyers . . . Has almost 1,000 penalty minutes in NHL career . . .
Born Aug. 11, 1958, in Kingston, Ont. . . . GM Harry Sinden was
criticized when he traded popular Mike Krushelnyski to Edmonton
for Linseman on June 21, 1984 . . . Boston fans quickly learned
to appreciate his intense style of play . . . Works hard every shift,
every game . . . Clever playmaking center.

Year	Club	GP	G	A	Pts.
1977-78	Birmingham (WHA) ..	71	38	38	76
1978-79	Philadelphia	30	5	20	25
1979-80	Philadelphia	80	22	57	79
1980-81	Philadelphia	51	17	30	47
1981-82	Philadelphia	79	24	68	92
1982-83	Edmonton..........	72	33	42	75
1983-84	Edmonton..........	72	18	49	67
1984-85	Boston	74	25	49	74
	NHL Totals	458	144	315	459
	WHA Totals	71	38	38	76

MIKE O'CONNELL 29 5-9 185   Defenseman

One of hockey's most underrated defensemen . . . Does good job
in both ends of ice . . . Capable of scoring goals and stopping them
from being scored against Bruins with solid defensive play . . .
Has scored 47 goals in last three seasons . . . Excels as shot-blocker
and with penalty-killing and power-play units . . . Started NHL
career with Chicago . . . Born Nov. 29, 1955, in Chicago but grew
up in Cohasset, Mass. . . . Bruins first interested in O'Connell when
he was 13-year-old playing in Boston South Shore Hockey League
. . . Starred in Boston scholastic hockey at Archbishop Williams
High . . . Outstanding team player . . . Son of Tommy O'Connell,
former Cleveland Browns' quarterback.

Year	Club	GP	G	A	Pts.
1977-78	Chicago	6	1	1	2
1978-79	Chicago	48	4	22	26
1979-80	Chicago	78	8	22	30
1980-81	Chi-Buf............	82	15	38	53
1981-82	Boston	80	5	34	39
1982-83	Boston	80	14	39	53
1983-84	Boston	75	18	42	60
1984-85	Boston	78	15	40	55
	Totals	527	80	238	318

CHARLIE SIMMER 31 6-3 210   Left Wing

Bruins gave up 1985 No. 1 draft choice on Oct. 23, 1984, to acquire big high-scorer from Los Angeles ... Turned out to be a smart move by GM Harry Sinden ... Simmer scored 33 goals, 63 points in 63 games ... Scored 12 power-play goals, five game-winners ... Had best shooting percentage on Bruins, scoring on 26.2 percent of shots ... Twice scored 56 goals for Kings, leading NHL goal-scorers in 1979-80 ... Starred on King's Triple Crown Line with Marcel Dionne and Dave Taylor ... Born March 30, 1954, in Terrace Bay, Ont. ... Not overly fast but deadly as a scorer on rebounds and close-range shots ... Career hampered by knee surgery in 1975-76 ... Set modern NHL record by scoring goals in 13 consecutive games for Kings in 1979-80.

Year	Club	GP	G	A	Pts.
1974-75	California	35	8	13	21
1975-76	California	21	1	1	2
1976-77	Cleveland	24	2	0	2
1977-78	Los Angeles	3	0	0	0
1978-79	Los Angeles	38	21	27	48
1979-80	Los Angeles	64	56	45	101
1980-81	Los Angeles	65	56	49	105
1981-82	Los Angeles	50	15	24	39
1982-83	Los Angeles	80	29	51	80
1983-84	Los Angeles	79	44	48	92
1984-85	LA-Bos	68	34	30	64
	Totals	527	266	288	554

KEITH CROWDER 26 6-0 195   Right Wing

Just right for Bruins' small home rink ... Plays hard-driving, hard-hitting game ... Forechecks with gusto ... Doesn't back down from anyone and averages more than 100 penalty minutes a season ... Good cornerman who seldom fails to finish his check ... Born Jan. 6, 1959, in Windsor, Ont. ... Set a Boston record with 43 penalty minutes in one game in 1981 ... Brother of former Bruin Bruce Crowder, who retired last season ... Started pro career in 1978-79 with Birmingham Bulls of WHA ... Fifth-highest scorer on Bruins last season.

Year	Club	GP	G	A	Pts.
1978-79	Birmingham (WHA)	5	1	0	1
1980-81	Boston	47	13	12	25
1981-82	Boston	71	23	21	44
1982-83	Boston	74	35	39	74
1983-84	Boston	63	24	28	52
1984-85	Boston	79	32	38	70
	NHL Totals	334	127	138	265
	WHA Totals	5	1	0	1

BARRY PEDERSON 24 5-11 185 Center

One of the NHL's best young centers begins a comeback this season
... Played only 22 games last season and underwent arm surgery
on Jan. 11, 1985... His absence from lineup hurt Bruins badly
... "He's one of the best all-around centers in the game," said
Jean Ratelle, Bruins' assistant coach and former star center for
Rangers... Scored 92 points as rookie in 1981-82... Led Bruins
in scoring with 107 and 116 points next two seasons... Born
March 13, 1961, in Big River, Sask.... Formed effective one-
two scoring punch on line with Rick Middleton... Outstanding
stick-handler, playmaker, penalty-killer... Ranks among best in
NHL at winning faceoffs.

Year	Club	GP	G	A	Pts.
1980-81	Boston	9	1	4	5
1981-82	Boston	80	44	48	92
1982-83	Boston	77	46	61	107
1983-84	Boston	80	39	77	116
1984-85	Boston	22	4	8	12
	Totals	268	134	198	322

TOM FERGUS 23 6-0 200 Center

Had his best of four NHL seasons with Bruins in 1984-85...
Established career highs with 30 goals, 43 assists, 73 points...
Has good moves offensively, especially around the net, and has
developed into a reliable defensive center... Doesn't draw a lot
of penalties but still plays a hard-driving, aggressive game and
can't be pushed around... Good at digging out puck in corners,
along boards, behind the net... Born June 16, 1962, in Chicago
... Has done well for player chosen 60th in 1980 entry draft...
Grew up in Montreal and lives in St. George, Ont.... As a young
hockey player, the Bruins were his favorite team.

Year	Club	GP	G	A	Pts.
1981-82	Boston	61	15	24	39
1982-83	Boston	80	28	35	63
1983-84	Boston	69	25	36	61
1984-85	Boston	79	30	43	73
	Totals	289	98	138	236

PETE PEETERS 28 6-0 185 Goaltender

Last season is one he would like to forget... Had his poorest
record (19-26-4) and worst goals-against average (3.47) since
trade from the Flyers in 1978-79... Developed a propensity for
nagging injuries and lost his starting job to Doug Keans in playoffs... His best season was his first with Bruins following trade

with Philadelphia for defenseman Brad McCrimmon . . . Compiled 40-11-9 record, led league with eight shutouts and 2.36 average and won Vezina Trophy in 1982-83 . . . Born Aug. 1, 1957, in Edmonton . . . Hoping to regain his form this season . . . Can be moody at times . . . Has outstanding career won-lost-tied record of 163-90-29 but has encountered difficulty winning in playoffs.

Year	Club	GP	GA	SO	Avg.
1978-79	Philadelphia	5	16	0	3.43
1979-80	Philadelphia	40	108	1	2.73
1980-81	Philadelphia	40	115	2	2.96
1981-82	Philadelphia	44	160	0	3.71
1982-83	Boston	62	142	8	2.36
1983-84	Boston	50	151	0	3.16
1984-85	Boston	51	172	1	3.47
	Totals	292	864	12	3.05

GORD KLUZAK 21 6-4 210   Defenseman

Missed entire 1984-85 season following knee injury on Oct. 7, 1984, in training-camp exhibition game . . . Injury happened when he was bodychecked by Devils' Dave Lewis, who specializes in delivering hard but clean hits . . . This will be his comeback season . . . "He's fine and we expect a great season from him," said Bruins' GM Harry Sinden . . . Born March 4, 1964, in Climax, Sask. . . . Was first player selected in 1982 draft . . . Struggled during rookie season but made significant progress in second season . . . Bobby Orr was his childhood hero . . . Not fast but has good moves for big man . . . Has potential to become one of league's top defensemen.

Year	Club	GP	G	A	Pts.
1982-83	Boston	70	1	6	7
1983-84	Boston	80	10	27	37
1984-85	Boston		Injured		
	Totals	150	11	33	44

COACH BUTCH GORING: Surprise selection as Bruins' new coach . . . Had only joined Bruins last season in deal with Islanders . . . "He gave us the spark and spirit we needed on the ice and I feel he'll do the same thing as coach," said GM Harry Sinden, who coached Bruins after firing Gerry Cheevers as coach last season . . . Has the qualities to become a good NHL coach in time . . . Was playing assistant coach with Islanders . . .

Born Nov. 22, 1949, in St. Boniface, Man. . . . Hustling 16-year NHL veteran center . . . Best known as defensive specialist and penalty-killer . . . Spent first 11 NHL seasons with Los Angeles . . . Helped Islanders win four consecutive Stanley Cups . . . Voted 1981 playoff MVP . . . Do you know his first name? It's Robert but he's always been known as "Butch" . . . "Butch Goring is hockey's Pete Rose. He's Charlie Hustle," former Ranger goalie Steve Baker once said of Goring's playing style.

MOST COLORFUL PLAYER

Do bears sleep in the woods? Does Loni Anderson have a nice figure? Is Bruce Springsteen The Boss?

The answers are as easy as saying Bobby Orr is the best and most colorful player in Bruins' history.

Who knows how much more greatness he could have achieved if his surgically-repaired knees had not forced him into premature retirement in 1978 at age 30 after only 12 seasons?

From the moment he played his first game in 1966 with the Bruins as an 18-year-old with a blond crewcut, Orr was an instant star. He revolutioned hockey as a rushing defenseman who could— and often did—outscore most forwards. There was nothing he could not do—and do twice as well and seemingly twice as easily— as other players. Although he did not have a colorful personality, he was hockey's most exciting player, even after he left the Bruins, played on bad knees and ended his career with Chicago.

No. 4 now lives in the New England area, where he still is a sports hero, with his wife and children. At 37, he's a successful businessman deeply involved in promoting a program to lessen the stress and pressure and put the fun back into sports for boys and girls.

ALL-TIME BRUIN LEADERS

GOALS: Phil Esposito, 76, 1970-71
ASSISTS: Bobby Orr, 102, 1970-71
POINTS: Phil Esposito, 152, 1970-71
SHUTOUTS: Hal Winkler, 15, 1927-28

BUFFALO SABRES

TEAM DIRECTORY: Chairman: Seymour H. Knox III; Pres.: Northrup R. Knox; GM: Scotty Bowman; Dir. Pub. Rel.: Gerry Helper; Coach: Jim Schoenfeld. Home ice: Memorial Auditorium (16,433; 196' × 85'). Colors: Blue, white and gold. Training camp: Lake Placid and Buffalo, N.Y.

SCOUTING REPORT

OFFENSE: Oh, how the Sabres could use a goal-scorer like Mike Bossy. Or skaters with the swift, clever moves of Mark Pavelich or Dale Hawerchuk.

The offensive edge of the Sabres needs sharpening. Veteran Gilbert Perreault can't be expected to carry the offense on his back forever. The Sabres need more speed, more scoring snipers among their forwards.

Ageless Gil Perreault embarks on 15th Sabre season.

John Tucker, a promising young forward, could help solve the problem this season. Buffalo has good big forwards who are capable goal-scorers: Mike Foligno, Dave Andreychuk and Sean McKenna. It has hustling, hard-working forwards who are willing to check and excel defensively: Craig Ramsay, Ric Seiling, Brent Peterson. Newcomers such as Paul Cyr and Mal Davis show promise but Buffalo needs a game-breaking scorer. It may be necessary for Phil Housley to be moved from defense to forward. The young American-born athlete has played forward before. He could add much-needed speed and finesse up front to give the Sabres' offense a sharper cutting edge.

DEFENSE: No problem here. The Sabres play as well without the puck as any team in hockey. That's typical of teams run by Scotty Bowman . . . good checking, proper positional play in all three zones, devotion to defensive duty. It's a system new coach Jim Schoenfeld, a former defenseman, should feel comfortable with.

Peterson, Craig Ramsay and Seiling are three of the most persistent defensive forwards in the league. The corps of defensemen is one of the best in the NHL: Mike Ramsey, Bill Hajt, Dave Maloney, Lindy Ruff, Hannu Virta, Housley and Dave Fenyves. Virta, a fast skater, and Housley are noted for their offensive skills as defensemen.

Bowman made another of his many wise moves last season when he traded with the Rangers for Maloney. Not only did Maloney excel in tandem with Ramsey, his intense style of play and enthusiasm gave the Sabres a mental lift. But Maloney opted to retire. Hajt is an excellent defensive defenseman. Ramsey excels in all areas and is especially adept at blocking shots and taking rival forwards out of the play.

The Sabres had the best defensive record in the NHL last season. Additionally, they were No. 1 in penalty-killing, a Bowman-coached team trademark. The goaltending is in good hands with Tom Barrasso and his backup, Bob Sauve. Because Buffalo plays so well defensively as a team, Barrasso and Sauve faced the fewest shots in the NHL last season.

OUTLOOK: Fifteen seasons in the NHL, most of them good ones. Always a contender but never a champion. Somehow people expect more than they get from the Sabres.

There's probably no better GM in the NHL than the demanding Bowman. He knows talent and he knows how to acquire it by making clever trades and draft choices. With Bowman running the show, the Sabres always will be a contender. With a few more goal-scorers, they may eventually win a Stanley Cup.

SABRE ROSTER

No.	Player	Pos.	Ht.	Wt.	Born	1984-85	G	A	Pts.	PIM
25	Dave Andreychuk	C	6-3	200	9-29-63/Hamilton, Ont.	Buffalo	31	30	61	54
8	Real Cloutier	RW	5-10	185	7-30-56/St. Emile, Que.	Buffalo	0	0	0	0
						Rochester	4	3	7	0
	Adam Creighton	C	6-5	202	6-2-65/Burlington, Ont.	Buffalo	2	8	10	33
						Rochester	5	3	8	2
						Ottawa	4	14	18	23
	Randy Cunneyworth		6-0	177	5-10-61/Etobichoke, Ont.	Rochester	30	38	68	148
18	Paul Cyr	LW	5-11	185	10-31-83/Pt. Alberoni, B.C.	Buffalo	22	24	46	63
29	Mal Davis	LW	5-11	180	10-10-56/Lockeport, N.S.	Buffalo	17	9	26	26
						Rochester	4	4	8	14
31	Dave Fenyves	D	5-11	188	4-29-60/Dunnville, Ont.	Buffalo	1	8	9	27
						Rochester	0	3	3	8
17	Mike Foligno	RW	6-2	195	1-29-59/Sudbury, Ont.	Buffalo	27	29	56	154
24	Bill Hajt	D	6-3	205	11-1-51/Borden, Sask.	Buffalo	5	13	18	14
9	Gilles Hamel	RW	6-0	183	12-15-57/Asbestoes, Que.	Buffalo	18	30	48	36
6	Phil Housley	D	5-10	180	5-9-64/St. Paul, Minn.	Buffalo	16	53	69	28
	Val James	D	6-2	203	2-14-57/Ocala, Fla.	Rochester	1	4	5	70
	Timo Jutila	D	5-7	175	12-24-63/Finland	Rochester	13	30	43	29
						Buffalo	1	5	6	13
44	Jerry Korab	D	6-3	218	9-15-48/Sault Ste. Marie, Ont.	Buffalo	1	6	7	29
						Rochester	1	2	3	6
32	Normand Lacombe	RW	5-11	205	10-18-64/Pierrefonds, Que.	Buffalo	2	4	6	25
						Rochester	13	16	29	33
12	Sean McKenna	C	6-0	186	3-17-62/Asbestoes, Que.	Buffalo	20	16	36	41
14	Mike Moller	RW	6-0	189	6-16-62/Red Deer, Alta.	Buffalo	0	2	2	0
23	Gates Orlando	RW	5-8	175	11-13-62/La Salle, Que.	Buffalo	3	6	9	6
						Rochester	26	30	56	62
11	Gil Perreault	C	6-0	202	11-13-50/Victoriaville, Que.	Buffalo	30	53	56	62
20	Brent Peterson	C	6-0	190	2-15-58/Calgary	Buffalo	12	22	34	47
27	Larry Playfair	D	6-4	202	6-23-58/Calgary	Buffalo	3	14	17	157
10	Craig Ramsay	RW	5-10	175	3-17-51/Toronto	Buffalo	12	21	33	16
5	Mike Ramsey	D	6-3	190	12-3-60/Minneapolis	Buffalo	8	22	30	102
4	Mark Renaud	D	5-11	180	2-21-59/Windsor, Ont.	Rochester	8	34	42	56
	Geordie Robertson	C	6-0	163	8-1-59/Victoria, B.C.	Rochester	27	48	75	91
22	Lindy Ruff	LW-D	6-2	190	2-17-60/Warburg, Alta.	Buffalo	13	11	24	45
16	Ric Seiling	RW	5-11	178	12-15-57/Elmira, Ont.	Buffalo	16	15	31	86
7	John Tucker	C	6-0	184	9-29-64/Windsor, Ont.	Buffalo	22	27	49	21
21	Claude Verret	C	5-10	164	4-20-63/Lachine, Que.	Buffalo	0	0	0	0
						Rochester	40	53	93	12
3	Hannu Virta	D	6-0	176	3-22-63/Finland	Buffalo	1	23	24	16

No.	Player	Pos.	Ht.	Wt.	Born	1984-85	GP	GA	SO	Avg.
30	Tom Barrasso	G	6-3	195	3-31-65/Boston	Buffalo	54	144	5	2.66
						Rochester	5	6	1	1.35
1	Jacques Cloutier	G	5-7	155	1-3-60/Noranda, Que.	Buffalo	1	4	0	3.69
						Rochester	14	36	0	2.69
28	Bob Sauve	G	5-8	165	6-17-55/St. Genevieve, Que.	Buffalo	27	84	0	3.22
	Vince Tremblay	G	5-11	185	10-21-59/Quebec City, Que.	Buffalo	33	115	0	3.81

SABRE PROFILES

GIL PERREAULT 34 6-0 202   **Center**

An original Sabre ... No. 1 selection in NHL draft in 1970 when Buffalo entered the NHL ... Led Sabres in scoring for 11th time in 15 years last season ... Needs only 18 goals to become one of the few players in NHL history to score 500 or more career goals ... Has slowed down some with passage of time but still is graceful skater and puckhandler who excels with one-on-one fast-break moves ... Born Nov. 13, 1950, in Victoriaville, Que. ... Won Rookie-of-Year honors in 1970-71 ... Has been an All-Star center ... Outstanding playmaker ... Has developed into better defensive forward under coaching of Scotty Bowman ... Ranks among NHL career leaders with 768 assists.

Year	Club	GP	G	A	Pts.
1970-71	Buffalo	78	38	34	72
1971-72	Buffalo	76	26	48	74
1972-73	Buffalo	78	28	60	88
1973-74	Buffalo	55	18	33	51
1974-75	Buffalo	68	39	57	96
1975-76	Buffalo	80	44	69	113
1976-77	Buffalo	80	39	56	95
1977-78	Buffalo	79	41	48	89
1978-79	Buffalo	79	27	58	85
1979-80	Buffalo	80	40	66	106
1980-81	Buffalo	56	20	39	59
1981-82	Buffalo	62	31	42	73
1982-83	Buffalo	77	30	46	76
1983-84	Buffalo	73	31	59	90
1984-85	Buffalo	78	30	53	83
	Totals	1099	482	768	1250

JOHN TUCKER 22 6-0 185   **Center**

A cracked ankle bone caused this bright prospect to miss 16 games, but he showed enough to indicate he's on the way to a solid career ... He registered 22 goals, 27 assists in his rookie season after two stints with the Sabres in 1983-84 ... "He has great hands and a knack of slipping and sliding away from people and staying open," said his Kitchener coach, Tom Barrett. "He shakes a check real quickly and does it naturally." ... GM Scotty Bowman likes his confidence and the fact that he sets high standards for himself ... Born Sept. 29, 1964, in Windsor, Ont., this six-foot center was Player of the Year in the Ontario Hockey League in 1983-84, when he scored 100 points and led his team to the Memorial Cup Finals ... He was the first of two second-round picks (31st overall) in the 1983 entry draft in which the Sabres' first-rounders were Tom Barrasso, Normand Lacombe and Adam Creighton . . . Sabres figure they ended up with the equivalent of four first-rounders . . . Recorded his first NHL hat trick against Toronto on April Fool's Day, 1984.

Year	Club	GP	G	A	Pts.
1983-84	Buffalo	21	12	4	16
1884-85	Buffalo	64	22	27	49
	Totals	85	34	31	65

PHIL HOUSLEY 21 5-10 180   Defenseman

Well-established after three seasons as one of the best young players in game . . . Sabres' first choice in 1982 draft . . . Like goaltending teammate Tom Barrasso, he moved directly from high-school hockey into NHL stardom . . . Starred at South St. Paul High School, Minn. . . . Former Ranger coach Herb Brooks predicted Housley would become NHL star . . . Born March 9, 1964, in St. Paul . . . Became youngest defenseman to score 30 or more goals in 1983-84 . . . Outstanding rushing defenseman . . . Occasionally has tendency to over-handle puck and commit giveaways . . . Has been used by Sabres as center and does a good job winning faceoffs.

Year	Club	GP	G	A	Pts.
1982-83	Buffalo	77	19	47	66
1983-84	Buffalo	75	31	46	77
1984-85	Buffalo	73	16	53	69
	Totals	225	66	146	212

DAVE ANDREYCHUK 22 6-3 200   Center

Like Flyers' Tim Kerr, a dangerous power forward . . . Uses size and strength effectively to establish position near net . . . Skates with power and knows how to fight through checks and maintain possession of puck . . . At his best on power plays . . . Capable of digging puck free behind net or in corners to set up teammates' shots . . . Born Sept. 29, 1963, in Hamilton, Ont. . . . Has accurate wrist shot from slot or faceoff circles but gets many of goals on close-in shots or on rebounds ... Opposing defensemen have difficulty neutralizing him ... Strong on skates with good balance and seldom is knocked down or taken out of play with routine bodycheck.

Year	Club	GP	G	A	Pts.
1982-83	Buffalo	43	14	23	37
1983-84	Buffalo	78	38	42	80
1984-85	Buffalo	64	31	30	61
	Totals	185	83	95	178

MIKE FOLIGNO 26 6-2 195   Right Wing

Detroit made a mistake by trading him to Sabres in 1981 ... Husky right wing plays aggressively and with great enthusiasm ... Fans at the Aud enjoy watching his goal-scoring dance ... Has scored 101 goals in four years with Sabres ... Always battles hard for puck in corners and along boards ... Uses size and strength well to ward off checks by opposing defensemen when Sabres are on the attack ... Born Jan. 29, 1959, in Sudbury, Ont. ... Plays a good game as defensive forward and always checks closely ... Not afraid to fight when he feels it's necessary ... Has accumulated 936 penalty minutes in NHL career, an average of 156 a season.

Year	Club	GP	G	A	Pts.
1979-80	Detroit	80	36	35	71
1980-81	Detroit	80	28	35	63
1981-82	Det-Buf	82	33	44	77
1982-83	Buffalo	66	22	25	47
1983-84	Buffalo	70	32	31	63
1984-85	Buffalo	77	27	29	56
	Totals	455	178	199	377

MIKE RAMSEY 24 6-3 190   Defenseman

One of the best shot-blocking defensemen in NHL ... American-born athlete played for gold-medal winning 1980 U.S. Olympic team ... Sabres chose him as their No. 1 draft pick in 1979 when he played for University of Minnesota ... Plays a robust game on defense ... Hits hards and makes accurate breakout passes to forwards ... Born Dec. 3, 1960, in Minneapolis ... Formed outstanding defensive tandem last season with Dave Maloney ... Has good sense of anticipation and reads enemy plays well ... Outstanding bodychecker ... Sabres have him on ice for most critical late-game situations ... Makes few mistakes.

Year	Club	GP	G	A	Pts.
1979-80	Buffalo	13	1	6	7
1980-81	Buffalo	72	3	14	17
1981-82	Buffalo	80	7	23	30
1982-83	Buffalo	77	8	30	38
1983-84	Buffalo	72	9	22	31
1984-85	Buffalo	79	8	22	30
	Totals	393	36	117	153

BILL HAJT 33 6-3 205   **Defenseman**

Best all-around season in NHL was spoiled when he was sidelined with shoulder separation on Feb. 9, 1985 ... Was chosen to play in All-Star Game but injury prevented him from playing ... A defensive defenseman who does not shoot or score often but makes vital contributions with his strong defensive play ... Has been a Sabre for 12 seasons ... Born Nov. 18, 1951, in Borden, Sask. ... Injuries have hampered him throughout his NHL career ... May have set NHL record for shortest retirement—five days ... Announced he was retiring as player during 1983-84 training camp, then changed his mind and rejoined team ... Seldom caught out of position.

Year	Club	GP	G	A	Pts.
1973-74	Buffalo	6	0	2	2
1974-75	Buffalo	76	3	26	29
1975-76	Buffalo	80	6	21	27
1976-77	Buffalo	79	6	20	26
1977-78	Buffalo	76	4	18	22
1978-79	Buffalo	40	3	8	11
1979-80	Buffalo	75	4	12	16
1980-81	Buffalo	68	2	19	21
1981-82	Buffalo	65	2	9	11
1982-83	Buffalo	72	3	12	15
1983-84	Buffalo	79	3	24	27
1984-85	Buffalo	57	5	13	18
	Totals	773	41	184	225

TOM BARRASSO 20 6-3 195   **Goaltender**

Best young goalie to surface in NHL since former Montreal star Ken Dryden ... Some believe he's the best goalie in hockey ... Moved directly from Massachusetts' Acton-Boxboro High School into NHL in 1983-84 ... Became an immediate sensation ... Won Vezina Trophy as NHL's leading goalie and selected as Rookie of the Year ... Sent to minor leagues briefly after slow start last season ... Rejoined Sabres and had another brilliant season ... His 2.66 goals-against average was best in NHL ... Led NHL with five shutouts ... Born March 31, 1965, in Boston ... Named to first All-Star team as a rookie ... Has two-season record of 51-30-13 with seven shutouts ... Plays with supreme confidence in his ability ... Has size and quickness ... Gives up few bad goals.

Year	Club	GP	GA	SO	Avg.
1983-84	Buffalo	42	117	2	2.84
1984-85	Buffalo	54	144	5	2.66
	Totals	96	261	7	2.74

BRENT PETERSON 27 6-0 190   **Center**

Not a great scorer but is one of NHL's most underrated all-around centers ... Usually assigned to check opponents' best offensive center ... Credited with doing outstanding job neutralizing such outstanding centers as Wayne Gretzky, Bryan Trottier, Dale Hawerchuk and Peter Stastny ... A dedicated team player and gifted penalty-killer ... Born Feb. 15, 1958, in Calgary, Alberta ... You'll usually see him on ice in critical situations late in game because of his defensive ability ... Started NHL career with Detroit ... One of the best faceoff winners in NHL.

Year	Club	GP	G	A	Pts.
1978-79	Detroit	5	0	0	0
1979-80	Detroit	18	1	2	3
1980-81	Detroit	53	6	18	24
1981-82	Det-Buf.	61	10	5	15
1982-83	Buffalo	75	13	24	37
1983-84	Buffalo	70	9	12	21
1984-85	Buffalo	74	12	22	34
	Totals	356	51	83	134

CRAIG RAMSAY 34 5-10 175   **Left Wing**

Classy old pro ... Enters 15th NHL season ... Has been a valuable Sabres' left wing since 1971-72 ... One of hockey's most outstanding defensive forwards and penalty-killers ... Did not miss playing in a game for eight consecutive seasons...His streak of playing in 776 consecutive games from 1973-74 to 1982-83 is one of the longest in NHL history...Serves as Sabres' playing assistant coach...Born March 17, 1951, in Weston, Ont....Has scored 27 shorthanded goals in NHL career...Smart, hard-working player...Although best known for defensive skill, he has scored 252 goals in 1,070 NHL games.

Year	Club	GP	G	A	Pts.
1971-72	Buffalo	57	6	10	16
1972-73	Buffalo	76	11	17	28
1973-74	Buffalo	78	20	26	46
1974-75	Buffalo	80	26	38	64
1975-76	Buffalo	80	22	49	71
1976-77	Buffalo	80	20	41	61
1977-78	Buffalo	80	28	43	71
1978-79	Buffalo	80	26	31	57
1979-80	Buffalo	80	21	39	60
1980-81	Buffalo	80	24	35	59
1981-82	Buffalo	80	16	35	51
1982-83	Buffalo	64	11	18	29
1983-84	Buffalo	76	9	17	26
1984-85	Buffalo	79	12	21	33
	Totals	1070	252	420	672

COACH JIM SCHOENFELD: Surprising choice to succeed Scott Bowman as Sabres' coach...Bowman has more coaching wins (718-301-207) than any man in NHL history and will devote full time to job as general manager...Schoenfeld spent 10 years with Sabres' as rock-hard, shot-blocking defenseman...Always a dedicated, hard-working player, popular with Buffalo fans...Played two seasons with Detroit, one with Boston before rejoining Sabres...Playing career often hampered by injuries...Was Sabres' captain at 22...Born Sept. 4, 1952, in Galt, Ont....Made successful coaching debut in 1984-85 with Sabres' Rochester American League farm team...He started with 11-game winning streak and had 17-6-2 record when Buffalo reactivated him as a defenseman...Should make a good coach...Believes attitude of players is vital to success.

MOST COLORFUL PLAYER

Gilbert Perreault does not project the off-ice image of a colorful player. He was quiet and reserved, almost to the point of shyness, when he joined the Sabres in 1970 at 19, the first player chosen in the draft. He has not changed much in his 15 glorious seasons with the Sabres. He's still quiet and reserved, not quite so shy but essentially a private person who prefers to avoid the public spotlight.

Perreault still does most of his talking on ice with a stick, a puck, a pair of skates. Mention the name Buffalo Sabres and people throughout hockey think first of one man: Gilbert Perreault. He always has been colorful and exciting to watch on the ice. He has survived the greatest test of excellence: the test of time.

Now on the sunset side of his career, he still plays at a high skill level. The tall, graceful center holds virtually all of Buffalo's scoring records. And he still is an exciting performer. "When I'm not playing, Gil Perreault is a player I love to watch," says New Jersey Devils' goalie Glenn (Chico) Resch.

ALL-TIME SABRE LEADERS

GOALS: Danny Gare, 56, 1979-80
ASSISTS: Gil Perreault, 69, 1975-76
POINTS: Gil Perreault, 113, 1975-76
SHUTOUTS: Don Edwards, 5, 1977-78
                Tom Barrasso, 5, 1984-85

HARTFORD WHALERS

TEAM DIRECTORY; Chairman/Managing Gen. Partner: Howard Baldwin; Pres.-GM: Emile Francis; Dir. Pub. Rel.: Phil Langan; Coach: Jack Evans. Home ice: Hartford Civic Center (15,000; 200′ × 85′). Colors: Green, blue and white. Training camp: Hartford, Ct.

SCOUTING REPORT

OFFENSE: This is the Whalers' biggest problem.

"There's no doubt about it . . . we have to score more goals," said Emile (The Cat) Francis, team president and GM.

Ron Francis (no relation to Emile) is an outstanding young center who has superstar potential and plays hard every game. But he's capable of scoring more than the 24 goals he scored last season. Fifty-seven assists indicates his playmaking ability. Hart-

Ron Francis is still in quest of first 100-point season.

ford must find adequate wingers to play on Francis' line to bring out his best abilities.

Sylvain Turgeon is one of the best shooters in the NHL. Injuries hampered his play last season but he still led the Whalers with 31 goals. He has the potential to score 40 or more goals. Hartford made a good trade in the offseason by acquiring winger Jorgen Pettersson from St. Louis. Used properly, he's capable of scoring 35 or 40 goals.

Husky Ray Neufeld and Greg Malone are prominent forwards. Torrie Robertson is an aggressive hard-driving forward who was penalized for 337 minutes. Bobby Crawford scored 36 goals in 1983-84 but missed most of last season with a knee injury. If he regains his health and scoring touch, it will help the Whalers' attack. Three young forwards who could help are Dave Tippett, Kevin Dineen and Dean Evason, who was acquired from Washington.

Risto Siltanen, a fast-skating defenseman with a hard shot from the blue line, is Hartford's best offensive defenseman.

DEFENSE: The addition of veteran Mike Liut from St. Louis should improve the Whalers' goaltending, which wasn't so bad in the past with Greg Millen, who was traded to St. Louis.

Former Ranger Steve Weeks played well in the second half of the season. Hartford believes Liut and Weeks will give it a quality goaltending tandem.

The defense corps is not great but it's not all that bad. The problem is that it lacks mobility, except for Siltanen, and depth. Hartford's defensemen need more backchecking help from the forwards.

Joel Quenneville was Hartford's most consistent defenseman last season. Rugged Chris Kotsopoulos has developed into a good defenseman but was hampered by injuries in 1984-85. Siltanen has improved his play in the defensive zone. Sylvain Cote is a promising young defenseman. Ulf Samuelsson had a good rookie season and showed a knack for shot-blocking. The key to the defense this season could be Scot Kleinendorst. The former Ranger has the quick hands, quick feet and skating and passing ability to become a good NHL defenseman.

Hartford has a good penalty-killer and defensive forward in veteran Mike Zuke. The Whalers' penalty-killing was the fourth best in the league last season.

OUTLOOK: A poor start hurt the Whalers last season. They improved in the second half and their 30 wins were the most they've had since entering the NHL six years ago. They are grad-

WHALER ROSTER

No.	Player	Pos.	Ht.	Wt.	Born	1984-85	G	A	Pts.	PIM
31	Dan Bourbonnais	LW	5-11	180	3-6-62/Winnipeg	Binghamton	13	22	35	17
28	Pat Boutette	RW	5-8	175	3-1-52/Windsor, Ont.	Pitt.-Hart.	7	11	18	75
						Binghamton	8	17	25	10
34	Jack Brownschidle	D	6-1	180	10-2-55/Buffalo, N.Y.	Hartford	1	4	5	5
						Binghamton	4	17	21	8
21	Sylvain Cote	D	6-0	175	1-19-66/Quebec City, Que.	Hartford	3	9	12	17
25	Bobby Crawford	RW	5-11	180	4-6-59/Belleville, Ont.	Hartford	14	14	28	8
18	Mike Crombeen	RW	5-11	192	7-16-57/Sarnia, Ont.	Hartford	4	7	11	16
						Binghamton	2	1	3	0
	Kevin Dineen	LW	5-10	186	10-28-63/Quebec City, Que.	Hartford	25	16	41	120
						Binghamton	15	8	23	41
4	Richie Dunn	D	6-0	192	5-12-57/Boston	Hartford	1	4	5	2
						Binghamton	9	39	48	43
12	Dean Evason	C	5-9	172	8-22-64/Flin Flon, Man.	Wash.-Hart.	3	4	7	2
						Binghamton	27	49	76	38
11	Paul Fenton	LW	5-11	180	12-22-59/Springfield, Mass.	Hartford	7	5	12	10
						Binghamton	26	21	47	18
26	Ray Ferraro	C	5-10	165	8-23-64/Trail, B.C.	Hartford	11	17	28	40
						Binghamton	20	13	33	29
10	Ron Francis	C	6-2	195	3-1-63/Sault Ste. Marie, Ont.	Hartford	24	57	81	66
33	Mark Fusco	D	5-9	180	3-12-61/Woburn, Mass.	Hartford	3	8	11	40
	Mike Hoffman	LW	5-11	186	2-26-63/Cambridge, Mass.	Hartford	0	0	0	0
						Binghamton	19	26	45	95
27	Marty Howe	D	6-1	195	2-18-54/Detroit	Hartford	1	1	2	10
						Binghamton	7	12	19	22
	Randy Gilhen	LW	5-11	188	1-13-63/Winnipeg	Binghamton	3	3	6	9
35	Scot Kleinendorst	D	6-3	205	1-16-60/Grand Rapids, Minn.	Hartford	1	8	9	69
						Binghamton	3	7	10	42
24	Chris Kotsopoulos	D	6-3	215	11-27-58/Toronto	Hartford	5	3	8	53
	Paul Lawless	LW	5-11	181	7-2-64/Scarborough, Ont.	Hartford	1	1	2	0
						Salt Lake City	49	48	97	14
	Brent Loney	D	6-0½	165	5-25-64/Cornwall, Ont.	Binghamton	0	0	0	0
						Ham.-Oshawa	24	24	48	40
36	Paul MacDermid	RW	6-1	209	4-14-63/Chesley, Ont.	Hartford	4	7	11	29
						Binghamton	9	31	40	87
	Dave MacLean	RW	6-0	190	1-12-65/Brantford, Ont.	Belleville	64	90	154	41
14	Greg Malone	C	6-0	190	3-8-56/Fredericton, N.B.	Hartford	22	39	61	67
	Dana Murzyn	D	6-3	200	12-9-66/Calgary	Calgary (WHL)	32	60	92	233
17	Ray Neufeld	RW	6-3	210	4-13-59/St. Boniface, Man.	Hartford	27	35	62	129
6	Mark Paterson	D	6-0	195	2-22-64/Nepean, Ont.	Hartford	1	3	4	24
						Binghamton	2	18	20	74
	Jorgen Pettersson	LW	6-2	185	7-11-56/Sweden	St. Louis	23	32	55	20
38	Randy Pierce	RW	6-0	180	11-23-57/Arnprior, Ont.	Hartford	3	2	5	8
						Binghamton	6	10	16	45
3	Joel Quenneville	D	6-0	190	9-15-58/Windsor, Ont.	Hartford	6	16	22	96
32	Torrie Robertson	LW	5-11	184	8-2-61/Victoria, B.C.	Hartford	11	30	41	337
5	Ulf Samuelsson	D	6-1	195	3-26-64/Sweden	Hartford	2	6	8	83
						Binghamton	5	11	16	92
	Brad Shaw	D	5-10	184	4-28-64/Kitchener, Ont.	Binghamton	1	10	11	4
8	Risto Siltanen	D	5-9	180	10-31-58/Finland	Hartford	12	33	45	30
15	Dave Tippett	C	5-10	175	8-25-61/Moosomin, Sask.	Hartford	7	12	19	12
16	Sylvain Turgeon	C	6-0	190	1-17-65/Noranda, Que.	Hartford	31	31	62	67
20	Mike Zuke	C	6-0	180	4-16-54/Sault Ste. Marie, Ont.	Hartford	4	12	16	12

No.	Player	Pos.	Ht.	Wt.	Born		GP	GA	SO	Avg.
1	Mike Liut	G	6-2	195	1-7-56/Weston, Ont.	Hart.-St. L.	44	156	2	3.60
	Pete Sidorkiewicz	G	5-9	165	6-29-63/Poland	Binghamton	45	137	3	3.05
	Ed Staniowski	G	5-9	170	7-7-55/Moose Jaw, Sask.	Hartford	1	1	0	3.30
						Binghamton	10	44	0	4.31
31	Steve Weeks	G	5-11	165	6-30-58/Scarborough, Ont.	Hartford	24	92	2	3.79
						Binghamton	5	13	0	2.57

ually improving but their chances of gaining a playoff position are not good because they play in a difficult division. To do it, they'll have to score more goals and win more games on home ice.

WHALER PROFILES

RON FRANCIS 22 6-2 195   Center
Not related to Whalers' GM Emile (The Cat) Francis . . . This could be the year he joins elite ranks of 100-point scorers . . . Whalers still trying to find ideal linemates to bring out the best in Francis' scoring and playmaking abilities . . . Led low-scoring Whalers with 81 points last season but had poor minus-23 record . . . Born March 1, 1963, in Sault Ste. Marie, Ont. . . . Hartford's team captain . . . Has perfect size and ability to develop into one of hockey's best centers . . . Plays with determination . . . Hustles every time he's on ice.

Year	Club	GP	G	A	Pts.
1981-82	Hartford	59	25	43	68
1982-83	Hartford	79	31	59	90
1983-84	Hartford	72	23	60	83
1984-85	Hartford	80	24	57	81
	Totals	290	103	219	322

GREG MALONE 29 6-0 190   Center
Spent first seven NHL seasons with Pittsburgh . . . A 35-goal scorer for Penguins in 1978–79 . . . Was Whalers' fourth-highest scorer last season . . . Shared team leadership with three game-winning goals . . . Was voted Hartford's unsung hero after 1983–84 season . . . Born March 8, 1956, in Chatham, N.B. . . . Scored three goals, two assists when Whalers whipped Edmonton, 11-0, on Feb. 12, 1984 . . . Veteran center is a good playmaker and checker . . . Older brother of Jim Malone, Rangers' No.1 draft choice in 1980 who never reached the NHL.

Year	Club	GP	G	A	Pts.
1976-77	Pittsburgh	66	18	19	37
1977-78	Pittsburgh	78	18	43	61
1978-79	Pittsburgh	80	35	30	65
1979-80	Pittsburgh	51	19	32	51
1980-81	Pittsburgh	62	21	29	50
1981-82	Pittsburgh	78	15	24	39
1982-83	Pittsburgh	80	17	44	61
1983-84	Hartford	78	17	37	54
1984-85	Hartford	76	22	39	61
	Totals	649	182	297	479

RISTO SILTANEN 26 5-9 180   **Defenseman**

An offensive defenseman...His style of play is similar to that of
the Rangers' Reijo Ruotsalainen...Flashy skater with slick, quick
speed...Defensive part of his game still is vulnerable but it's
better than it used to be...Often leads Whalers' rush up the ice
with clever puck-handling...Born Oct. 31, 1958, in Manta, Finland...Stocky, compact player with low center of gravity which
makes it difficult for opponents to dislodge puck...Played four
seasons for Edmonton...Has powerful shot from blue line...
Twenty of his 27 goals in two seasons with Whalers have been
scored on power plays.

Year	Club	GP	G	A	Pts.
1978-79	Edmonton (WHA)	20	3	4	7
1979-80	Edmonton..........	64	6	29	35
1980-81	Edmonton..........	79	17	36	53
1981-82	Edmonton..........	63	15	48	63
1982-83	Hartford	74	5	25	30
1983-84	Hartford	75	15	38	53
1984-85	Hartford	76	12	33	45
	NHL Totals	431	70	209	279
	WHA Totals	20	3	4	7

STEVE WEEKS 27 5-11 165   **Goaltender**

Started slowly but finished with a flourish in first season with
Whalers...Demoted to minor leagues after starting season with
2-8-1 record...Regained his confidence and was promoted from
minors to Hartford...Was 8-4-1 in final 13 decisions, including
two shutouts for team with poor defensive record ...Born
June 30, 1958, in Scarborough, Ont....Once hailed as one of
many "Ranger goalies of the future"...Compiled 42-33-14 record
in parts of four seasons with Rangers but was traded to Whalers
in 1984..."Considering the situation with the Rangers, I think it
was a good move for me," said Weeks...Has soft-spoken, low-
key personality but inwardly is a fierce competitor...Technically
sound goalie...Expected to share goaltending this season with
newly acquired Mike Liut.

Year	Club	GP	GA	SO	Avg.
1980-81	New York R.........	1	2	0	2.00
1981-82	New York R.........	49	179	1	3.77
1982-83	New York R.........	18	68	0	3.92
1983-84	New York R.........	26	90	0	3.97
1984-85	Hartford	24	92	2	3.79
	Totals	118	431	3	3.82

JOEL QUENNEVILLE 27 6-0 190   Defenseman

Whalers' most consistently effective defenseman last season...
Never has experienced the pleasure of playing for a strong team
... Started NHL career with Toronto and was traded to Colorado
... Team then moved to New Jersey... Was traded from New
Jersey to Calgary in June 1983, and one month later was traded
to Hartford... Born Sept. 15, 1958, in Windsor, Ont... Doesn't
rush with puck often... Prefers to let forwards handle the offensive part of the game... A steady defensive defenseman... Good
at breaking up enemy plays in defensive end of ice... Voted Hartford's most valuable defenseman in 1983–84.

Year	Club	GP	G	A	Pts.
1978-79	Toronto............	61	2	9	11
1979-80	Tor-Col............	67	6	11	17
1980-81	Colorado	71	10	24	34
1981-82	Colorado	64	5	10	15
1982-83	New Jersey	74	5	12	17
1983-84	Hartford...........	80	5	8	13
1984-85	Hartford...........	79	6	16	22
	Totals.............	496	39	90	129

MIKE LIUT 29 6-2 195   Goaltender

Joined Whalers on Feb. 22, 1985, in controversial trade with St.
Louis made by GM Emile Francis... Hartford traded goalie Greg
Millen and forward Mark Johnson to Blues for Liut.... Whalers
later received forward Jorgen Pettersson from St. Louis... Many
Hartford fans and media people criticized trade... "I'd make that
deal again any day of the week," said Francis. "With Liut and
Steve Weeks, we've got great goaltending now."... Born Jan. 7,
1956, in Weston, Ont.... Played better than 4-7-1 record, 3.04
average indicates after joining Hartford last season... An All-Star
goalie for Blues in 1981... Played college hockey at Bowling
Green... Has NHL career goaltending record of 155-140-53.

Year	Club	GP	GA	SO	Avg.
1979-80	St. Louis	64	194	2	3.18
1980-81	St. Louis	61	199	1	3.34
1981-82	St. Louis	64	250	2	4.06
1982-83	St. Louis	68	235	1	3.72
1983-84	St. Louis	58	197	3	3.45
1984-85	St L-Hart	44	156	2	3.60
	Totals.............	359	1231	11	3.56

CHRIS KOTSOPOULOS 27 6-3 215   Defenseman

Broken foot and injured knee limited aggressive defenseman to
only 33 games last season... "We missed him a lot because he's

become one of our best defensemen," said coach Jack (Tex) Evans ...Feisty player dislikes Rangers for trading him in 1981... Rangers claimed Kotsopoulos was overweight, didn't have the mobility to fit into their plans..."I've showed them they made a mistake trading me," said Kotsopoulos... Born Nov. 27, 1958, in Scarborough, Ont.... Lost almost 30 pounds after joining Whalers and his play improved...Reached NHL the hard way ...Was overlooked in draft...Then-Ranger coach Fred Shero signed him as a free agent...Good passer with hard shot from blue line...Plays a mean, hard-hitting game.

Year	Club	GP	G	A	Pts.
1980-81	New York R	54	4	12	16
1981-82	Hartford	68	13	20	33
1982-83	Hartford	68	6	24	30
1983-84	Hartford	72	5	13	18
1984-85	Hartford	33	5	3	8
	Totals	295	33	72	105

JORGEN PETTERSSON 29 6-2 185   Left Wing
The Cat got his man—again!... Emile Francis made a personal scouting trip to Sweden in 1980 to bring back Pettersson to play for St. Louis, where Francis was GM...Francis, now Hartford GM, traded goalie Greg Millen and forward Mark Johnson to St. Louis last season for "future considerations"...Pettersson was the "future consideration" Francis wanted from St. Louis..."Emile made a smart deal. Pettersson can score 40 goals for Hartford," said Boston assistant GM Tom Johnson...Born July 11, 1956, in Gothenburg, Sweden...Has outstanding shot...Scored 138 goals in first four seasons with St. Louis.

Year	Club	GP	G	A	Pts.
1980-81	St Louis	62	37	36	73
1981-82	St Louis	77	38	31	69
1982-83	St Louis	74	35	38	73
1983-84	St Louis	77	28	34	62
1984-85	St Louis	75	23	32	55
	Totals	365	161	171	332

RAY NEUFELD 26 6-3 210   Right Wing
Has put together three consistently good seasons with Whalers... Husky performer who always plays forceful, aggressive hockey ...Likes to hit and willing to use his fists when provoked...Not an outstanding skater but has worked hard to upgrade his level of skating ability...Born April 15, 1959, in St. Boniface, Man....

Hartford drafted him in 1979 . . . Spent three years in minor leagues before he won a job as an NHL regular . . . Helps Hartford the most with his rugged style of play in corners or behind the net.

Year	Club	GP	G	A	Pts.
1979-80	Hartford	8	1	0	1
1980-81	Hartford	52	5	10	15
1981-82	Hartford	19	4	3	7
1982-83	Hartford	80	26	31	57
1983-84	Hartford	80	27	42	69
1984-85	Hartford	76	27	35	62
	Totals	315	90	121	211

SYLVAIN TURGEON 20 6-0 190   Center

Has sizzling, rapidly-released shot from faceoff circles, slot or blue line . . . Can score with wrist shots or slap shots . . . Missed 16 games with injuries last season but still scored 62 points in 64 games . . . "He can shoot the puck as well as anyone in the league," said GM Emile Francis, who made Turgeon Whalers' No. 1 draft pick in 1983 . . . Had 40-goal season as rookie . . . Born Jan. 17, 1965, in Noranda, Que. . . . NHL scouts first recognized his skill and pro potential when he was an 11-year-old midget-league player in Quebec . . . Dangerous on power plays . . . Has 29 power-play goals in two NHL seasons.

Year	Club	GP	G	A	Pts.
1983-84	Hartford	76	40	32	72
1984-85	Hartford	64	31	31	62
	Totals	140	71	63	134

COACH JACK EVANS: Best known as "Tex" . . . That's been his nickname since he was a rough, tough Ranger defenseman in the 1940s and '50s . . . Tall, stoic chap . . . Doesn't say a lot but what he says usually makes good sense . . . Believes in the old values of hard work . . . Will not tolerate players who cruise and float, fail to hustle and hit . . . Played 24 years of pro hockey and was a feared fighter who piled up 989 penalty minutes in 752 NHL games . . . One of his Ranger teammates was Fred Shero

...Another was Emile Francis, Whalers' president and general manager...A man's man...Born April 21, 1928, in Morriston, South Wales...Played for 1961 Stanley Cup champion Chicago Black Hawks...Compiled 230-143-23 record as coach of Central League Salt Lake City Eagles for five years...Had 102-171-47 record as coach of lowly California Golden Seals and Cleveland Barons...Hartford is 58-83-19 in his two seasons as coach... "Jack Evans will be my coach as long as I'm here," Francis says of rumors that Evans may be replaced as coach.

MOST COLORFUL PLAYER

John McKenzie was a short, stocky forward with a round, moon face. His nickname was "Pie." As in Pie Face. But there was no cream puff in his style of play. He inspired teammates and intimidated opponents with his feisty, rough, tough, vigorous style of play.

Some rival players and fans said he was a dirty player.

So be it. Pie McKenzie cared more about winning and playing the game the only way he knew: hard and tough. He took a special delight in challenging and fighting physically bigger players. He embarrassed quite a few of them by outpunching them.

He was a leader of the Big Bad Bruins who won Stanley Cups in 1970 and 1972. He previously played for Chicago, Detroit and the Rangers in an NHL career starting in 1965. When the World Hockey Association was organized, he left the Bruins and joined the New England Whalers, later to become the NHL Hartford Whalers.

Pie McKenzie became an instant hockey hero in Hartford for his robust, colorful style of play. He retired in 1979, the year before the Whalers entered the NHL, but fans at Hartford Civic Center still delight in recalling the way he played for them in the WHA. As an NHL player, McKenzie scored 206 goals and received 917 penalty minutes.

ALL-TIME WHALER LEADERS

GOALS: Blaine Stoughton, 56, 1979-80
ASSISTS: Mark Howe, 65, 1978-79
　　　　　　Mike Rogers, 65, 1980-81
POINTS: Mark Howe, 107, 1978-79
SHUTOUTS: Al Smith, 3, 1972-73
　　　　　　　Louis Levasseur, 3, 1977-78

MONTREAL CANADIENS

TEAM DIRECTORY: Pres.: Ron Corey; GM: Serge Savard; Dir. Player Development: Andre Boudrias; Dir. Player Personnel: Jacques Lemaire; Dir. Pub. Rel.: Claude Mouton; Coach: Jean Perron. Home ice: Montreal Forum (16,074; 200′ × 85″). Training camp: Montreal.

SCOUTING REPORT

OFFENSE: It's not what it used to be. The Canadiens were known as the Flying Frenchmen throughout their glory years of the past. Now they are the Checking Frenchmen.

Chicago-born Chris Chelios led Canadiens in assists.

Jacques Lemaire was partially responsible. His system of play dictated a tight-checking, team-defense style. One reason he emphasized defense was because he knew his team no longer had a lot of gifted goal-scorers.

By playing conservatively and cautiously, Montreal won many low-scoring games and led the Adams Division in 1984-85. But lack of firepower led to playoff elimination. And now Lemaire has resigned, replaced by his assistant, Jean Perron.

Montreal's best offensive weapon isn't even French or Canadian. Slick, quick Mats Naslund is from Sweden. He scored 42 goals last season. Next came Mario Tremblay with 31. After that, most opponents didn't have to worry much. Bobby Smith and Ryan Walter have not lived up to expectations as goal-scorers. Nor has Ron Flockhart, who has the speed and moves to be more of a scoring threat. Alfie Turcotte, a young prospect, is being counted upon to provide some scoring punch. Bob Gainey, Lucien DeBlois and Pierre Mondou are steady and hard-working but they are not Guy Lafleur, Steve Shutt or Yvon Cournoyer of yesteryear.

Guy Carbonneau is one of the best defensive forwards in the NHL, an outstanding faceoff man normally assigned to check the opposition's best center. He has the capability to score more goals but it's often negated by his defensive role. Two of last season's rookie defensemen, Chris Chelios and Tom Kurvers, played well offensively.

DEFENSE: The Canadiens had the fourth-best defensive record in the NHL last season, allowing the second-fewest shots on goal.

Larry Robinson has slowed down somewhat as a defenseman but still is a quality player and on-ice leader, at his best during pressure situations. Chelios, Kurvers and another rookie defenseman, Czechoslovakian Petr Svoboda, all performed at a high level last season. Svoboda could develop into one of the league's best offensive defensemen this season. Big Craig Ludwig and veteran Rick Green, who excels as a shot-blocker, give the Canadiens strength behind their blue line.

Montreal seems set in goal for the future with Steve Penney, sensational as a rookie in the 1984 playoffs. He had some shaky moments in last season's playoffs, notably on long shots and rebounds. Doug Soetaert did a fine job as No. 2 goalie but his job appears in jeopardy. The Canadiens want to bring in rookie Patrick Roy.

OUTLOOK: The Canadiens surprised a lot of people last season. They bounced back with a first-place finish after a 1983-84 season in which they experienced their first losing record since 1951.

CANADIEN ROSTER

No.	Player	Pos.	Ht.	Wt.	Born	1984-85	G	A	Pts.	PIM
12	Serge Boisvert	RW	5-9	172	6-1-59/Drummondville, Que.	Montreal	2	2	4	0
						Sherbrooke	38	41	79	8
	Graeme Bonar	C-RW	6-3	205	1-21-66/Toronto	Sault Ste. Marie	66	71	137	93
21	Guy Carbonneau	C	5-11	175	3-18-60/Sept Isles, Que.	Montreal	23	34	57	43
2	Kent Carlson	D	6-3	200	1-11-62/Concord, N.H.	Montreal	1	1	2	33
						Sherbrooke	1	4	5	7
	Jose Charbonneau	RW	6-0	193	11-2-66/Ferme Neuve, Que.	Drummondville	34	40	74	90
24	Chris Chelios	D	6-1	190	1-25-62/Chicago	Montreal	9	55	64	87
	Shayne Corson	C	6-0	175	8-13-66/Barrie, Ont.	Hamilton	27	63	90	154
27	Lucien DeBlois	RW	5-11	205	6-21-57/Joliette, Que.	Montreal	12	11	23	20
29	Rob Flockhart	C	5-11	174	10-10-60/Smithers, B.C.	Pitt.-Mont.	10	17	27	18
23	Bob Gainey	LW	6-1	200	12-13-53/Peterborough, Ont.	Montreal	19	13	32	40
	Gaston Gingras	D	6-0	191	2-13-59/North Bay, Ont.	Toronto	0	2	2	0
						Sher.-St. C.	10	26	36	19
5	Rick Green	D	6-3	202	2-20-56/Belleville, Ont.	Montreal	1	18	19	30
	Alain Heroux	C	6-3	190	5-20-64/Terrebonne, Que.	Sherbrooke	7	11	18	20
18	Tom Kurvers	D	5-10	180	10-14-62/Minneapolis	Montreal	10	35	45	30
32	Claude Lemieux	C	6-0	215	7-16-65/Buckingham, Que.	Montreal	0	1	1	7
						Verdun	58	66	124	152
17	Craig Ludwig	D	6-2	204	3-15-61/Eagle River, Wis.	Montreal	5	14	19	90
35	Mike McPhee	C	6-2	205	2-14-60/Sydney, N.S.	Montreal	17	22	39	120
	Sergio Momesso	C	6-3	202	9-4-65/Montreal	Shawinigan	56	90	146	216
6	Pierre Mondou	RW-C	5-10	185	11-27-55/Sorel, Que.	Montreal	18	39	57	21
26	Mats Naslund	RW	5-7	160	10-31-59/Sweden	Montreal	42	37	79	14
3	Ric Natress	D	6-2	208	5-25-62/Hamilton, Ont.	Montreal	0	1	1	2
						Sherbrooke	8	40	48	37
31	John Newberry	C	6-1	185	4-8-62/Port Alberni, B.C.	Montreal	0	4	4	6
						Sherbrooke	23	40	63	30
30	Chris Nilan	RW	6-0	200	2-9-58/Boston	Montreal	21	16	37	358
22	Stephane Richer	C	6-0	190	6-7-66/Buckingham, Que.	Chicoutimi	61	59	130	71
						Montreal	0	0	0	0
						Sherbrooke	0	0	0	0
19	Larry Robinson	D	6-3	220	6-2-51/Marvelville, Ont.	Montreal	14	33	47	44
15	Bobby Smith	C	6-4	210	2-12-58/North Sydney, N.S.	Montreal	16	40	56	59
25	Petr Svoboda	D	6-0	167	2-14-66/Czechoslovakia	Montreal	4	27	31	65
34	Jeff Teal	RW	6-3	206	5-30-60/Edina, Minn.	Montreal	0	1	1	0
						Sherbrooke	18	24	42	16
14	Mario Tremblay	RW	6-0	190	9-2-56/Montreal	Montreal	31	35	66	120
8	Alfie Turcotte	C	5-9	170	1-15-65/Gary, Ind.	Montreal	8	16	24	35
11	Ryan Walter	C	6-0	195	4-23-58/New Westminster, B.C.	Montreal	19	19	38	59

No.	Player	Pos.	Ht.	Wt.	Born		GP	GA	SO	Avg.
	Greg Moffett	G	5-11	175	4-1-59/Bath, Me.	Sherbrooke	41	162	1	4.11
37	Steve Penney	G	6-1	190	2-2-61/Ste. Foy, Que.	Montreal	54	167	1	3.08
33	Patrick Roy	G	6-0	164	10-5-55/Quebec, Que.	Montreal	1	0	0	0.00
						Sherbrooke	1	4	0	4.00
						Granby	44	228	0	5.55
1	Doug Soetaert	G	6-0	185	4-21-55/Edmonton	Montreal	28	91	0	3.40

They are well-coached, well-disciplined and play outstanding team defense. They need more offense. The team which as won the Stanley Cup more times (22) than any team in NHL history may have trouble preventing Quebec from finishing first in the Adams Division this season.

CANADIEN PROFILES

MATS NASLUND 26 5-7 160   Left Wing

Has the darting, lightning-fast speed of a sprinter, making him one of swiftest men in hockey . . . Small winger had finest NHL season in 1984-85 when he led Canadiens in scoring . . . Scored dramatic goal for 1-0 playoff conquest of Bruins . . . Has the ability to slip past defenders and head for net on give-and-go plays . . . Born Oct. 31, 1959, in Timra, Sweden . . . Scored eight game-winning goals last season . . . Impressive 23.5 percent of his shots resulted in goals . . . Does better than adequate job as checker.

Year	Club	GP	G	A	Pts.
1982-83	Montreal	74	26	45	71
1983-84	Montreal	77	29	35	64
1984-85	Montreal	80	42	37	79
	Totals	231	97	117	214

PIERRE MONDOU 29 5-10 185   Center

A model of consistency for nine years with Montreal . . . Was Canadiens' second draft pick in 1975 . . . Has three 30-or-more-goal seasons to his credit . . . Would score more goals if he took more shots . . . Good playmaking center . . . Most of his goals and big plays come at crucial times . . . Has scored 25 game-winning goals in NHL career . . . Born Nov. 27, 1955, in Sorel, Que. . . . Needs six goals to reach 200 for his career . . . Suffered career-threatening injury last season when struck in eye by opponent's stick.

Year	Club	GP	G	A	Pts.
1977-78	Montreal	71	19	30	49
1978-79	Montreal	77	31	41	72
1979-80	Montreal	75	30	36	66
1980-81	Montreal	57	17	24	41
1981-82	Montreal	73	35	33	68
1982-83	Montreal	76	29	37	66
1983-84	Montreal	52	15	22	37
1984-85	Montreal	67	18	39	57
	Totals	548	194	262	456

MARIO TREMBLAY 29 6-0 190   **Right Wing**

Used mainly as checking forward in early stages of 11-season career with Canadiens... Has developed into capable goal-scorer ... Strong, fast, tough... Excellent in corners and in "jungle warfare" in slot and close to net... Has 988 penalty minutes in NHL career... Born Sept. 2, 1956, in Alma, Que.... Became proficient power-play scorer last season when he led Montreal with 14 man-advantage goals... Plus-22 record was among best by Montreal forwards... Plays with determination and well-known for always giving second effort.

Year	Club	GP	G	A	Pts.
1974-75	Montreal............	63	21	18	39
1975-76	Montreal............	71	11	16	27
1976-77	Montreal............	74	18	28	46
1977-78	Montreal............	56	10	14	24
1978-79	Montreal............	76	30	29	59
1979-80	Montreal............	77	16	26	42
1980-81	Montreal............	77	25	38	63
1981-82	Montreal............	80	33	40	73
1982-83	Montreal............	80	30	37	67
1983-84	Montreal............	67	14	25	39
1984-85	Montreal............	75	31	35	66
	Totals............	796	239	306	545

CHRIS CHELIOS 23 6-1 190   **Defenseman**

Proved he was ready to become solid NHL defenseman with strong all-around performance in 1984 playoffs... Led Canadiens with 55 assists last season as rookie... American-born athlete played college hockey for University of Wisconsin... Was member of 1984 U.S. Olympic team coached by Brooklyn-born Lou Vairo, New Jersey Devils' assistant coach... Born Jan. 25, 1962, in Chicago... Moves puck effectively with passing and rushing ability... Makes smooth breakout passes to forwards from defensive zone... Has hard shot from blue line and finds forwards with scoring passes as pointman on offense... A potential All-Star defenseman.

Year	Club	GP	G	A	Pts.
1983-84	Montreal............	12	0	2	2
1984-85	Montreal............	74	9	55	64
	Totals............	86	9	57	66

GUY CARBONNEAU 25 5-11 175   Center

Says he gets as much satisfaction from making good defensive plays as he does scoring goals... Many opposing players believe he is the best defensive center in NHL... Almost always wins more faceoffs than he loses... Assigned to check the opposition's highest-scoring center and always does a fine job... Born March 28, 1960, in Sept Isles, Que.... Forechecks and backchecks with gusto... Reads enemy attacking plays well and often breaks them up to give Canadiens possession of puck... A gifted penalty-killer... Scored four of his 23 goals in shorthanded situations last season... Has scored 16 shorthanded goals in three seasons with Montreal.

Year	Club	GP	G	A	Pts.
1980-81	Montreal	2	0	1	1
1982-83	Montreal	77	18	29	47
1983-84	Montreal	78	24	30	54
1984-85	Montreal	79	23	34	57
	Totals	236	65	94	159

LARRY ROBINSON 34 6-3 220   Denfenseman

Not quite so dynamic a player as he once was but still ranks among leading defensemen in NHL... Thirteen-year veteran... Former winner of Norris Trophy as NHL's best defenseman... Was playoff MVP in 1979 when Canadiens won Stanley Cup... Doesn't fight much anymore because opponents know he's hard to handle when provoked... Born June 2, 1951, in Winchester, Ont.... Has scored 155 goals in his career... Led Montreal with plus-32 record last season... Gets most of his points on assists because of passing ability... Born and raised on a farm... One of the best team leaders in NHL.

Year	Club	GP	G	A	Pts.
1972-73	Montreal	36	2	4	6
1973-74	Montreal	78	6	20	26
1974-75	Montreal	80	14	47	61
1975-76	Montreal	80	10	30	40
1976-77	Montreal	77	19	66	85
1977-78	Montreal	80	13	52	65
1978-79	Montreal	67	16	45	61
1979-80	Montreal	72	14	61	75
1980-81	Montreal	65	12	38	50
1981-82	Montreal	71	12	47	59
1982-83	Montreal	71	14	49	63
1983-84	Montreal	74	9	34	43
1984-85	Montreal	76	14	33	47
	Totals	927	155	526	681

STEVE PENNEY 24 6-1 190   Goaltender

Became an instant hero in Montreal Forum during 1984 playoffs
... Made many remarkable saves en route to 2.20 goals-against
average, three shutouts ... Spent four years in minor leagues before he finally made it as a successful NHL goalie ... Was not
quite so sensational in last season's playoff ... Had difficulty con-
trolling rebounds, gave up several bad goals on routine long shots
... Criticized for misplaying shot which enabled arch-rival Quebec
to eliminate Canadiens from playoffs ... Born Feb. 2, 1961, in
Ste. Foy, Que. ... Had impressive 26-18-8 record for low-scoring
Canadiens last season ... Played in 54 of 80 games ... He and
Doug Soetaert formed good goaltending tandem last season.

Year	Club	GP	GA	SO	Avg.
1983-84	Montreal.............	4	19	0	4.75
1984-85	Montreal...........	54	167	1	3.08
	Totals.............	58	186	1	3.19

TOM KURVERS 23 5-10 180   Defenseman

A pleasant surprise as a rookie ... Won job as defenseman and
played with the poise of a veteran ... American-born athlete excelled for four seasons in college hockey at the University of
Minnesota-Duluth ... Montreal drafted him in 10th round in 1981
... Canadiens knew he had potential to play in NHL but did not
expect him to develop so quickly ... Born Sept. 14, 1962, in
Minneapolis ... Devils' assistant coach Lou Vairo predicts he'll
be a consistently good NHL defenseman for years to come ...
Three of his 10 goals last season won games.

Year	Club	GP	G	A	Pts.
1984-85	Montreal...........	75	10	35	45

BOB GAINEY 31 6-1 200   Left Wing

Montreal's captain ... Twelve-year veteran ... One of hockey's
best defensive forwards and clutch players ... Has won Frank Selke
Trophy four times as best defensive forward in NHL ... Closing

in on 200 career goals and 1,000 career games ... Born Dec. 13, 1953, in Peterborough, Ont. ... Although never a dominating scorer in junior hockey, Montreal chose him first in 1973 draft because of his marvelous defensive ability ... Has had three 20-goal seasons ... A dedicated worker who does his job in all areas of rink ... Scored 16 points in 16 games when Montreal won Stanley Cup in 1979 and was named winner of Conn Smythe Trophy as playoff MVP.

Year	Club	GP	G	A	Pts.
1973-74	Montreal	66	3	7	10
1974-75	Montreal	80	17	20	37
1975-76	Montreal	78	15	13	28
1976-77	Montreal	80	14	19	33
1977-78	Montreal	66	15	16	31
1978-79	Montreal	79	20	18	38
1979-80	Montreal	64	14	19	33
1980-81	Montreal	78	23	24	47
1981-82	Montreal	79	21	24	45
1982-83	Montreal	80	12	18	30
1983-84	Montreal	77	17	22	39
1984-85	Montreal	79	19	13	32
	Totals	906	190	213	403

BOBBY SMITH 27 6-4 210   Center

First player drafted in 1978 ... Had brilliant 114-point season in 1981-82 for Minnesota ... Has never reached that scoring plateau again ... North Stars traded him to Montreal in 1983 ... Goal production declined to career low of 16 last season ... Has long skating stride, long reach ... Good puck-handler and passer but is capable of scoring more goals and points than he has scored in recent seasons ... With his talent, it's a mystery why he faded after playing so well in first four seasons with North Stars ... Born Feb. 12, 1958, in North Sydney, N.S. ... Two more goals will give him 200 for NHL career ... Scored 69 goals, 192 points in final season of junior hockey for Ottawa in 1977-78 ... Critics say he needs to play with greater intensity.

Year	Club	GP	G	A	Pts.
1978-79	Minnesota	80	30	44	74
1979-80	Minnesota	61	27	56	83
1980-81	Minnesota	78	29	64	93
1981-82	Minnesota	80	43	71	114
1982-83	Minnesota	77	24	53	77
1983-84	Minn-Mont	80	29	43	72
1984-85	Montreal	65	16	40	56
	Totals	521	198	371	569

Captain Bob Gainey has won Selke Trophy four times.

COACH JEAN PERRON: Jacques Lemaire shocked the hockey community when he resigned last summer, explaining, "When I went home to relax, whether we won or lost, I couldn't relax. I kept thinking about what I should do to win the next game. I'm not saying it's too much pressure—it's just a thing I don't want to do."... It's a cinch that the 39-year-old Jean Perron, Lemaire's replacement, won't relax either...A native of Sherbrooke, Que., born Oct. 5, 1946, Perron has had only one year in the NHL, as Lemaire's assistant, but he brings impressive credentials to his challenging post...He's a graduate of the University of Sherbrooke, where he played wing and majored in physical education...While obtaining his master's degree at Michigan State, he was an assistant hockey coach... From 1973-83 he was head coach at the University of Moncton, where he was once Coach of the Year...He was assistant coach of Canada's 1984 Olympic team before joining the Canadiens... He's regarded as a strong technical coach, a good communicator and motivator, and is liked by the players.

MOST COLORFUL PLAYER

No team in the NHL has been so consistently successful for so long or had so many outstanding and colorful players as the Montreal Canadiens.

But one man stands above the rest: Maurice Richard...The Rocket.

"For sheer ability and being colorful, no one could touch the Rocket...not when he played, not now," said Tom Johnson, a Hall of Fame defenseman as a Canadien and now the Boston Bruins' assistant general manager.

The Rocket was the Babe Ruth of Canada. He was to hockey what Wilt Chamberlain was to pro basketball or what Jimmy Brown was to pro football. From 1942 to 1960, he scored 544 goals, including a sensational 50 in 50 games in 1944-45, a feat unheard-of at the time. Goalies actually feared him. He had burning, deep-set eyes and a hot temper to match. From the blue line to the net, he was almost unstoppable. Not only did he score goals, he played a mean, emotional game, and he was feared as a fist-fighter. He's 64 now, still an imposing figure, works in Montreal and is a member of the Hockey Hall of Fame.

There was only one Rocket Richard. There never will be another like him.

ALL-TIME CANADIEN LEADERS

GOALS: Steve Shutt, 60, 1976-77
            Guy Lafleur, 60, 1977-78
ASSISTS: Pete Mahovlich, 82, 1974-75
POINTS: Guy Lafleur, 136, 1976-77
SHUTOUTS: George Hainsworth, 22, 1928-29

NEW JERSEY DEVILS

TEAM DIRECTORY: Owner: John McMullen; VP-Operations/GM: Max McNab; Dir. Player Personnel: Marshall Johnston; Dir. Pub. Rel.: Larry Brooks; Coach: Doug Carpenter. Home ice: Byrne Meadowlands Arena (19,040; 200′ × 85′). Colors: White, red and green.

SCOUTING REPORT

OFFENSE: Actually the Devils don't play the game too badly until, inevitably, the time comes to shoot. You know the statue of Venus de Milo, the goddess without arms? That's New Jersey.

It appears the Devils did fine with Kirk Muller, the second player taken in last year's draft. He had a solid 54-point rookie

Youngsters Kirk Muller (27) and Bruce Driver give Devils hope.

season as an 18-year-old and, as advertised, is strong in every facet of the game.

Improved young wingers like Aaron Broten, Paul Gagne and Doug Sulliman will get you 20 goals, as will veteran Mel Bridgman. Alas, there's no one big wheel to build an offense around, but the Devils were organized by rookie coach Doug Carpenter and they worked.

Veteran Don Lever, the club's leading scorer the year before, slumped badly last season, but it's just as well. It's time the Devils get on with it and play the kids. It looks like they've got a good one in Greg Adams, signed as a free agent out Northern Arizona University. He scored 21 points after being called up for the final 36 games.

Pat Verbeek is an irritating force who slipped last year. John MacLean, a high No. 1 pick in 1983, has so far been a big disappointment.

DEFENSE: It's old with Bob Lorimer, Bob Hoffmeyer, Dave Lewis and Phil Russell. And more than a little slow, too.

The bright spot was rookie Bruce Driver. The disappointment was Joe Cirella, a No. 1 pick while the club was in Colorado who had shown promise the year before. Dave Pichette, a waiver-draft pickup from St. Louis, started well, but slumped in the second half. Uli Hiemer, the West German import, showed flashes. Sometimes it takes a year for European players to get their feet on the ground.

New Jersey, with the third pick in the entry draft, claimed a defenseman, Craig Wolanin, whom they feel can immediately upgrade their defense.

Chico Resch, 37, one of the team's new links to respectability in its first three seasons in the Meadowlands, is signed for another year, buying the Devils time to develop a young goalie better than the departed Hannu Kamppuri. They like Chris Terreri, who stood on his head to take Providence College to the NCAA finals. Craig Billington, the club's No. 2 pick in 1984, is a fine prospect, but is probably at least a year away.

OUTLOOK: The Devils moved up 13 points last year, thanks to hard work, organization and the infusion of some kids who were at least better than what they had before.

But other than Muller, and perhaps Driver, there's just not enough base to expect any immediate, dramatic improvement. Too many recent high draft picks—Rocky Trottier, Ken Daneyko, John MacLean—appear to have been blown.

The Devils will make you work for your two points, but hang in there and you'll get them.

DEVIL ROSTER

No.	Player	Pos.	Ht.	Wt.	Born	1984-85	G	A	Pts.	PIM
24	Greg Adams	C	6-2	185	8-1-63/Nelson, B.C.	New Jersey	12	9	21	14
						Maine	15	20	35	12
	Michel Bolduc	D	6-3	210	3-13-61/Ange Gardien, Que.	Maine-Fred.	1	16	17	160
18	Mel Bridgman	C	6-0	190	4-28-55/Victoria, B.C.	New Jersey	22	39	61	105
10	Aaron Broten	RW	5-10	175	11-14-60/Roseau, Minn.	New Jersey	22	35	57	38
7	Murray Brumwell	D	6-1	190	3-31-60/Calgary	Maine	8	31	39	52
14	Rich Chernomaz	RW	5-9	175	9-1-63/Selkirk, Man.	New Jersey	0	2	2	2
						Maine	17	34	51	64
2	Joe Cirella	D	6-2	193	5-9-63/Hamilton, Ont.	New Jersey	6	18	24	143
3	Ken Daneyko	D	6-0	193	4-16-64/Windsor, Ont.	New Jersey	0	0	0	10
						Maine	4	9	13	206
23	Don Dietrich	D	6-1	195	4-5-61/Deloraine, Man.	Maine	6	21	27	36
	Bruce Driver	D	6-0	185	4-29-62/Toronto	New Jersey	9	23	32	36
	Shawn Evans	D	6-2	193	9-7-65/Kingston, Ont.	Peterborough	16	83	99	78
	Greg Evtushevski	C	5-8	181	5-4-65/St. Paul, Alta.	Kamloops	47	93	140	167
	Chris Felix	D	5-10	179	5-27-64/Bramalea, Ont.	Sault Ste. Marie	29	72	101	85
	Larry Floyd	C	5-8	177	5-1-61/Peterborough, Ont.	Maine	30	51	81	24
17	Paul Gagne	LW	5-10	180	2-6-62/Iroquois Falls, Ont.	New Jersey	24	19	43	28
6	Alan Hepple	D	5-9	203	8-16-83/England	Maine	7	17	24	125
						New Jersey	0	0	0	0
28	Uli Hiemer	D	6-1	190	9-21-62/West Germany	New Jersey	5	24	29	70
20	Tim Higgins	RW	6-0	181	2-7-58/Ottawa, Ont.	New Jersey	19	29	48	30
21	Bob Hoffmeyer	D	6-0	182	7-27-55/Dodsland, Sask.	New Jersey	1	6	7	65
9	Don Lever	LW	5-11	175	11-14-52/S. Porcupine, Ont.	New Jersey	10	8	18	31
25	Dave Lewis	D	6-2	205	7-3-53/Kindersley, Sask.	New Jersey	3	9	12	78
4	Bob Lorimer	D	6-0	190	8-25-53/Toronto	New Jersey	2	6	8	35
29	Jan Ludwig	RW	5-10	187	9-17-61/Czechoslovakia	New Jersey	12	19	31	53
15	John MacLean	RW	6-0	193	11-20-64/Oshawa, Ont.	New Jersey	13	20	33	44
14	Kevin Maxwell	C	5-9	165	3-30-60/Edmonton	Maine	25	21	46	70
11	Gary McAdam	RW	5-11	175	12-31-55/Smith Falls, Ont.	Maine	32	20	52	39
						New Jersey	1	1	2	0
16	Rick Meagher	C	5-10	175	11-4-53/Belleville, Ont.	New Jersey	11	20	31	22
32	Glen Merkosky	C	5-10	175	8-4-60/Edmonton	Maine	38	38	76	19
27	Kirk Muller	C	5-11	185	2-8-66/Kingston, Ont.	New Jersey	17	37	54	69
8	Dave Pichette	D	6-3	190	2-4-60/Grand Falls, N.S.	New Jersey	17	40	57	41
5	Rich Preston	RW	6-0	185	5-22-52/Regina, Sask.	New Jersey	12	15	27	26
	Phil Russell	D	6-2	200	7-21-52/Edmonton	New Jersey	4	16	20	110
	Bud Stefanski	C	5-10	170	4-28-55/S. Porcupine, Ont.	Maine	19	34	53	67
	Al Stewart	LW	6-0	175	1-31-64/Grande Center, Alta.	Maine	8	11	19	241
22	Doug Sulliman	LW	5-9	195	8-29-59/Glace Bay, N.S.	New Jersey	22	16	38	4
26	Rocky Trottier	C	5-11	185	4-11-64/Climax, Sask.	New Jersey	5	3	8	2
						Maine	17	16	33	4
	Steve Tsujiura	C	5-5	165	2-28-62/Coaldale, Alta.	Maine	28	38	66	40
12	Pat Verbeek	RW	5-9	191	5-24-64/Sarnia, Ont.	New Jersey	15	18	33	162
	Mitch Wilson	LW	5-9	190	2-15-62/Calgary	New Jersey	0	2	2	21
						Maine	6	3	9	220
	Craig Wolanin	D	6-3	188	7-27-67/Warren, Mich.	Kitchener	5	16	21	95

	Player	Pos.	Ht.	Wt.	Born		GP	GA	SO	Avg.
	Craig Billington	G	5-10	150	9-11-66/London, Ont.	Belleville	47	180	1	4.25
	Alain Chevrier	G	5-10	160	4-23-61	Fort Wayne	56	–	3	3.60
	Shawn MacKenzie	G	5-7	155	8-22-62/Bedford, Sask.	Maine	24	70	3	3.35
	Kirk McLean	G	6-0	177	6-26-66/Willowdale, Ont.	Oshawa	47	143	1	3.32
1	Glenn Resch	G	5-9	165	4-17-48/Regina, Sask.	New Jersey	51	200	0	4.16
	Sam St. Laurent	G	5-10	185	2-16-59/Arrida, Que.	Maine	55	168	4	3.11
	Chris Terreri	G	5-9	155	11-15-64/Providence, R.I.	Prov. Coll.	33	–	–	3.55

DEVIL PROFILES

GLENN RESCH 37 5-9 165   Goaltender

Still Chico after all these years...Another fine season keeping the Devils in a lot of games while waiting for management to get this team some more players...One of the game's goodwill ambassadors and still one of its better goalies...Forever a student and theorist about the game..."If I wasn't always talking," he once said, "I wouldn't know what to say."...Has been granted U.S. citizenship...Represented his adopted country in last fall's Canada Cup...After eight years of sharing the Islander goal with Bill Smith, he was traded, along with Steve Tambellini, to the Colorado Rockies for Mike McEwen and Jari Kaarela in 1981... Collector of sports memorabilia...Twice a second-team NHL All-Star...Winner of the Bill Masterton Trophy in 1982 for perseverence, sportsmanship and dedication to hockey... Born July 10, 1948, in Moose Jaw, Sask.

Year	Club	GP	GA	SO	Avg.
1973-74	New York I	2	6	0	3.00
1974-75	New York I	25	59	3	2.47
1975-76	New York I	44	88	7	2.07
1976-77	New York I	46	103	4	2.28
1977-78	New York I	45	112	3	2.55
1978-79	New York I	43	106	2	2.50
1979-80	New York I	45	132	3	3.04
1980-81	NYI-Col	40	121	3	3.20
1981-82	Colorado	61	230	0	4.03
1982-83	New Jersey	65	242	0	3.98
1983-84	New Jersey	51	184	1	4.18
1984-85	New Jersey	51	200	0	4.16
	Totals	518	1583	26	3.25

MEL BRIDGMAN 30 6-0 190   Center

Devils' captain and leading scorer last season...Criticized for not supplying leadership on a young, struggling team his first season at New Jersey, responded better last year...Not as physical as in his young Philadelphia days when he was known as one of the NHL's best fighters, but a workmanlike player who supplies toughness and gets his share of points...Very strong on faceoffs ...First player taken in the 1975 draft...Flyers traded him to Calgary in 1981 for Brad Marsh...Not a favorite of Flames' coach Bob Johnson, who wanted to rebuild that team with youth and speed...So the Flames sent him to the Devils after the 1982-83 season with Phil Russell for Steve Tambellini and Joel Quenneville . . . As good with a buck as he is with a puck. Very much into investments . . . Born April 28, 1955, in Trenton, Ont.

Year	Club	GP	G	A	Pts.
1975-76	Philadelphia	80	23	27	50
1976-77	Philadelphia	70	19	38	57
1977-78	Philadelphia	76	16	32	48
1978-79	Philadelphia	76	24	35	59
1979-80	Philadelphia	74	16	31	47
1980-81	Philadelphia	77	14	37	51
1981-82	Phil-Calg	72	33	54	87
1982-83	Calgary	79	19	31	50
1983-84	New Jersey	79	23	38	61
1984-85	New Jersey	80	22	39	61
	Totals	763	209	362	571

AARON BROTEN 24 5-10 175   Left Wing

Bounced back from a disappointing sophomore season . . . Applied his talent more regularly than in the past . . . Good skills, intelligent playmaker . . . Sixth-round choice in 1980 . . . Played well for Team USA in the 1984 Canada Cup, scoring a key goal in a 3-2 victory over Czechoslovakia . . . Older brother, Neal, plays for the North Stars and younger brother, Paul, has been drafted by the Rangers . . . Born Nov. 14, 1960, in Roseau, Minnesota.

Year	Club	GP	G	A	Pts.
1981-82	Colorado	58	15	24	39
1982-83	New Jersey	73	16	39	55
1984-85	New Jersey	80	22	35	57
	Totals	211	53	98	151

DAVE PICHETTE 25 6-3 190   Defenseman

Valuable pickup in last October's waiver draft from St. Louis . . . Became the player last year who had shown so much promise when he came up with Quebec in 1982. Scored the winning goal in the Nordiques' seventh-game victory over Boston in the 1982 quarterfinals . . . Rangy, good offensive skills that were badly needed by a team that generally can't shoot straight . . . Hard worker, but prone to mistakes . . . Originally signed as a free agent by the

Nordiques after junior career with the hometown Remparts...
Born Feb. 4, 1960, in Grand Falls, Newfoundland.

Year	Club	GP	G	A	Pts.
1980-81	Quebec............	46	4	16	20
1981-82	Quebec............	67	7	30	37
1982-83	Quebec............	53	3	21	24
1983-84	Que-St L	46	2	18	20
1984-85	New Jersey	71	17	40	57
	Totals............	283	33	125	158

KIRK MULLER 19 5-11 185   Center

The Devils' building block...First choice in the 1984 draft
(second overall)...Not flashy, but solid in every way...Shows
leadership qualities...Decent offensive numbers in rookie year
and should get better..."You've got to shoot him to stop him,"
Devils' assistant coach Lou Vairo said...Shy, but no lack of confidence when he steps onto the ice...Member of the 1984
Canadian Olympic Team...Played junior hockey with Guelph...
Born Feb. 8, 1966, in Kingston, Ont.

Year	Club	GP	G	A	Pts.
1984-85	New Jersey	80	17	37	54

GREG ADAMS 22 6-2 185   Center

Scored 12 goals and 9 assists in 36 games after being recalled
from Maine...Good speed, smart, looks like he'll be a player
...Devils would like to put 10-20 more pounds on him...Signed
as a free agent out of Northern Arizona University in 1984...
Born Aug. 1, 1963, in Nelson. B.C.

Year	Club	GP	G	A	Pts.
1984-85	New Jersey	36	12	9	21

PAUL GAGNE 23 5-10 180   Left Wing

Finally healthy, he began to live up to his promise last year
...Being the Devils' leading goal-scorer is like being named
the best ski-jumper in the Sahara, but somebody has to be it...
First-round choice in 1980...Finished strong in 1982-83, but suffered a groin pull at training camp the next season and never
hit stride...100-point scorer with Windsor of the OHL...Lives
in Iroquois Falls, Ont., where he was born Feb. 6, 1962.

Year	Club	GP	G	A	Pts.
1980-81	Colorado	61	25	16	41
1981-82	Colorado	59	10	12	22
1982-83	New Jersey	53	14	15	29
1983-84	New Jersey	66	14	18	32
1984-85	New Jersey	79	24	19	43
	Totals	318	87	80	167

BRUCE DRIVER 23 6-0 185   Defenseman

Had excellent rookie year...A real key to the Devils' modest
improvement...Should be solid NHL player for a lot of years
...Sixth-round choice in 1981, he joined the Devils after playing
for the Canadian Olympic Team at Sarajevo...First-team WCHA
All-Star and a member of the NCAA all-tournament team while
at the University of Wisconsin...Had four assists in Devils'
8-3 victory over Quebec in December...Born April 29, 1962,
in Toronto.

Year	Club	GP	G	A	Pts.
1983-84	New Jersey	4	0	2	2
1984-85	New Jersey	67	9	23	32
	Totals	71	9	25	34

DOUG SULLIMAN 26 5-9 195   Right Wing

Nice pickup for the Devils after being let go by Hartford...
Rebounded from 19-point season in 1983-84 to get 38 last year
...Good defensive player, very aggressive for his size...First-
round pick by the Rangers in 1979, went to the Whalers along
with Chris Kotsopoulos and Gerry McDonald in the Mike Rogers

deal . . . Attended the University of Waterloo . . . Born Aug. 29, 1959, in Glace Bay, Nova Scotia.

Year	Club	GP	G	A	Pts.
1979-80	New York R	31	4	7	11
1980-81	New York R	32	4	1	5
1981-82	Hartford	77	29	40	69
1982-83	Hartford	77	22	19	41
1983-84	Hartford	67	6	13	19
1984-85	New Jersey	57	22	16	38
	Totals	341	87	96	183

PAT VERBEEK 21 5-9 190   Center

Aggressive, chippy, irritant . . . Disappointing scoring year, slipped back from 47 points as a rookie to 33 last season . . . Third-round choice in 1982 draft . . . Played junior in Sudbury . . . Good shot, but lacks size and speed to become a top-notch scorer . . . Gives it all he has, which catches your eye on a chronic losing team . . . Born May 24, 1964, in Sarnia, Ont.

Year	Club	GP	G	A	Pts.
1982-83	New Jersey	6	3	2	5
1983-84	New Jersey	79	20	27	47
1984-85	New Jersey	78	15	18	33
	Totals	163	38	47	85

COACH DOUG CARPENTER: Did a fine job in his rookie year as the Devils improved 13 points on their 1983-84 record . . . Replaced Tommy McVie, who turned down a short-term contract and decided to return to the team's farm club at Maine . . . Coached Toronto's AHL team at St. Catharines but was passed over for the Leafs' job that went to assistant coach Dan Maloney . . . Good teacher, cool and accomplished in making moves behind the bench . . . Reserved, cautious with the media . . . Extremely dedicated, gives the impression of loving his job . . . Coached Team Canada to an upset victory over the Soviets and a silver medal in World Championships in April . . . Won the Memorial

Cup, the junior hockey championship, when he coached at Cornwall, Ont. His competitors in the three-team final were Regina's Bryan Murray, now with Washington, and Mike Keenan, now with Philadelphia . . . Never advanced beyond the Eastern and International Leagues as a player . . . Holds degree from Loyola University in Montreal . . . Born July 1, 1942, in Cornwall, Ont.

MOST COLORFUL PLAYER

Though many a former Devil general manager would turn red at the mention of the numerous bungled trades since this franchise began as the Kansas City Scouts in 1974, let's face it. The only color in the complexion of the Scouts-Rockies-Devils has been grey.

The acrobatic Doug Favell entertained, thrilled and disappointed during the Denver years. And how can we forget exciting Scouts like Jim McElmury and Gary Coalter?

So, you've got to go with Chico Resch. Whatever personality this organization has demonstrated as it struggles back from the disastrous moves that sent it to New Jersey in 1982 emanates from its bubbly veteran goaltender. It's a people business and Chico loves mankind.

The Bryne Meadowlands Arena faithful adore Resch, with good reason. Bouncy, effervescent, kind and considerate, he has been this team's link to respectability and an ambassador off the ice.

ALL-TIME DEVIL LEADERS

GOALS: Wilf Paiement, 41, 1976-77
ASSISTS: Wilf Paiement, 56, 1977-78
POINTS: Wilf Paiement, 87, 1977-78
SHUTOUTS: Doug Favell, 1, 1977-78
             Bill Oleschuk, 1, 1978-79
             Bill McKenzie, 1, 1979-80
             Glenn Resch, 1, 1983-84
             Ron Low, 1, 1984-85

NEW YORK ISLANDERS

TEAM DIRECTORY: Chairman of the Board: John Pickett; Pres.-GM: Bill Torrey; Dir. Pub. Rel.: Les Wagner; Coach: Al Arbour. Home ice: Nassau Coliseum (15,861; 200′ × 85′). Colors: White, blue and orange. Training camp: Hicksville, N.Y.

SCOUTING REPORT

OFFENSE: The Islanders were beginning a transition even as

Nobody could keep Brent Sutter from a 100-point season.

they won their last Stanley Cup in 1983. They're really into it now.

Brent Sutter emerged as a 100-point scorer last year. If Bryan Trottier is really in decline, Sutter looks like an entirely worthy heir apparent. Patrick Flatley and Greg Gilbert, who were missed in the playoffs, are two fine cornermen and workers and will be essential as Clark Gillies, Bob Bourne and Bob Nystrom fade toward retirement.

Twenty-year-old Pat LaFontaine never quite bounced back from a midseason bout with mononucleois, but still scored 54 points in 67 games. There's still no reason to believe he's not going to be the slick, 100-point centerman the Islanders expect.

As long as Mike Bossy and John Tonelli are still at their peaks, the Islanders shouldn't have any trouble scoring goals.

DEFENSE: Much more worrisome. Here and there, Denis Potvin reaches back for his former greatness, but night-in, night-out, he can't be what he was. If Ken Morrow's knees don't hold up or if he has truly lost a step, and if Tomas Jonsson, Paul Boutilier and Gord Dineen don't develop more consistency than they've shown so far, the Islanders are going to give up a lot of goals. The game has changed. They have to upgrade their speed not just on defense, but all over the ice.

The Isles will take a long look at Gerald Diduck, the club's No. 1 pick in 1983, try to get another good year out of Stefan Persson and hope for the best.

It looks like the Islanders do have the guy in goal to replace Billy Smith—Kelly Hrudey. Hrudey had his rookie ups and downs, but was outstanding when the 34-year-old Smith broke down in the Flyer series.

OUTLOOK: The glory days are now clearly past. The Isles reached back for a hurrah in the Washington series, but the old guys looked too old and the young guys too young as the Flyers' superior speed and drive wore them down in five games.

Bill Torrey remained loyal to his veterans, but not to a fault. LaFontaine, Flatley, Gilbert, Jonsson, Hrudey and Roger Kortko all look like comers. Despite picking at the bottom, the Islanders' last few drafts look pretty good. Tonelli and Bossy are going to keep them a factor while the rebuilding continues. And if Trottier bounces back, then a challenge of the Flyers and Caps is not out of the question.

But, realistically, it looks like it's going to take the Isles at least a year or two to become real contenders again.

ISLANDER ROSTER

No.	Player	Pos.	Ht.	Wt.	Born	1984-85	G	A	Pts.	PIM
22	Mike Bossy	RW	6-0	185	1-22-57/Montreal	Islanders	58	59	117	38
14	Bob Bourne	C-RW	6-3	200	6-11-54/Kindersley, Sask.	Islanders	8	12	20	51
4	Paul Boutilier	D	6-0	190	5-3-63/Sydney, N.S.	Islanders	12	23	35	90
2	Gord Dineen	D	5-11	180	9-21-62/Toronto	Islanders	1	12	13	89
						Springfield	1	8	9	46
29	Gerald Diduck	D	6-2	195	4-6-65/Edmonton	Islanders	2	8	10	80
8	Pat Flatley	RW	6-2	195	10-3-63/Toronto, Ont.	Islanders	20	31	51	104
17	Greg Gilbert	LW	6-1	194	1-22-62/Mississauga, Ont.	Islanders	13	25	38	36
9	Clark Gillies	LW	6-3	215	4-4-54/Moose Jaw, Sask.	Islanders	15	17	32	73
20	Mats Hallin	LW	6-2	202	3-19-58/Sweden	Islanders	5	0	5	50
57	Mark Hamway	LW	6-0	185	8-9-61/Detroit	Springfield	29	34	63	29
						Islanders	0	2	2	2
25	Ron Handy	LW	5-10	174	1-15-63/Toronto	Springfield	29	35	64	38
46	Scott Howson	LW	5-11	165	4-9-60/Toronto	Islanders	4	1	5	2
						Springfield	20	40	60	31
3	Tomas Jonsson	D	5-10	176	4-12-60/Sweden	Islanders	16	34	50	58
33	Allan Kerr	LW	5-10	181	3-28-64/Hazelton, B.C.	Islanders	3	1	4	24
						Springfield	32	27	59	140
	Derek King	LW	6-2	220	2-11-67/Hamilton, Ont.	Sault Ste. Marie	35	38	73	106
11	Roger Kortko	C	5-10	182	2-1-63/Hofford, Sask.	Islanders	2	9	11	9
						Springfield	8	30	38	6
16	Pat LaFontaine	C	5-9	170	2-20-65/St. Louis	Islanders	19	35	54	32
26	Dave Langevin	D		215	5-15-54/St. Paul, Minn.	Islanders	0	13	13	35
	Ken Leiter	D	6-1	195	4-19-61/Detroit	Islanders	0	2	2	2
						Springfield	3	12	15	12
6	Ken Morrow	D	6-4	205	10-17-56/Davison, Mich.	Islanders	1	7	8	14
23	Bob Nystrom	RW	6-1	200	10-10-52/Sweden	Islanders	2	5	7	58
7	Stefan Persson	D	6-1	189	12-22-54/Sweden	Islanders	3	19	22	30
5	Denis Potvin	D	6-0	205	10-29-53/Ottawa, Ont.	Islanders	17	51	68	96
	Vern Smith	D	6-1½	195	5-30-64/Lethbridge, Alta.	Islanders	0	0	0	0
						Springfield	6	20	26	115
21	Brent Sutter	C	5-11	175	6-10-62/Viking, Alta.	Islanders	42	60	102	51
12	Duane Sutter	RW	6-1	189	3-6-60/Viking, Alta.	Islanders	17	24	41	172
27	John Tonelli	LW	6-1	200	3-23-57/Hamilton, Ont.	Islanders	42	58	100	95
19	Bryan Trottier	C	5-11	195	7-17-56/Val Marie, Sask.	Islanders	28	31	59	47
	Monte Trottier	C	5-8	160	8-25-61/Val Marie, Sask.	Springfield	6	12	18	40

No.	Player	Pos.	Ht.	Wt.	Born		GP	GA	SO	Avg.
30	Kelly Hrudey	G	5-10	180	1-13-61/Edmonton	Islanders	41	141	2	3.62
	Todd Lumbard	G	6-0	185	8-31-63/Brandon, Man.	Springfield	6	35	0	6.03
	Lorne Molleken	G	6-1	190	6-11-56/Regina, Sask.	Springfield	34	129	1	4.37
31	Billy Smith	G	5-10	185	12-12-50/Perth, Ont.	Islanders	37	133	0	3.82

ISLANDER PROFILES

BILLY SMITH 34 5-10 185   **Goaltender**

Though his regular-season statistics are little better than ordinary, the four Stanley Cup rings on his fingers make him one of the all-time greats . . . Phenomenal 88-36 playoff record . . . Permitted two goals or less in 11 of 21 playoff games in 1983-84 as the Oilers brought an end to the Islanders' run of four straight Cups . . . When he brought an 86-point Islander team out of a 2-0 hole to a first-round victory over Washington last spring, it looked like Smitty was going to do it again, but the Flyers scored five goals on him in the pivotal Game Three of the quarterfinals and coach Al Arbour went with Kelly Hrudey the final two games of the five-game Flyer victory . . . Born December 12, 1950, in Perth, Ont. . . . An original Islander, taken from Los Angeles in the 1972 expansion draft . . . One of the game's great characters and one of its most hated personnages . . . His stickwork has been continually villified, but in the last few years he has mellowed both on and off the ice . . . Rails on about forwards crowding his crease and has appointed himself a one-man vigilante to take care of it . . . "I'm willing to die by the sword," he once said. "I've already told my wife that my career is going to end when sooner or later, somebody gets through. But before then a lot of guys are going to fall." . . . Honest, to a fault . . . Much better with reporters than earlier in his career, when he suffered in comparison to the bubbly Chico Resch. "If people take the time to know me, they find out I'm not a bad guy," he says . . . In fact, the New York hockey writers gave him their annual Good Guy Award in 1984. "Even my kids," Smith said, "aren't going to believe this."

Year	Club	GP	GA	SO	Avg.
1971-72	Los Angeles	5	23	0	4.60
1972-73	New York I	37	147	0	4.16
1973-74	New York I	46	134	0	3.07
1974-75	New York I	58	156	3	2.78
1975-76	New York I	39	98	3	2.61
1976-77	New York I	36	87	2	2.50
1977-78	New York I	38	95	2	2.65
1978-79	New York I	40	108	1	2.87
1979-80	New York I	38	104	2	2.95
1980-81	New York I	41	129	2	3.28
1981-82	New York I	46	133	0	2.97
1982-83	New York I	41	112	1	2.87
1983-84	New York I	42	130	2	3.42
1984-85	New York I	37	133	0	3.82
	Totals	544	1589	18	3.07

DENIS POTVIN 31 6-0 200   **Defenseman**

Three-time Norris Trophy winner and a certain future Hall of Famer... Superb offensive player with devastating slap and wrist shots... Pinpoint passer and key to one of the game's all-time great power plays... Reached back for his former brilliance in the Washington series last April, but overall did not have a good season... His age is beginning to catch up with him... Taking medication for hypertension, which manifested itself in the form of leg cramps in the 1984 playoffs... Had the star's ego in his early years, was not popular with his teammates. But he mellowed and they learned how to accept him. "I think people mistake my honesty for arrogance," he said... He was given the captaincy before the Islanders' first Stanley Cup year, 1980... Born October 29, 1953, in Ottawa, Ont.... First player taken in the 1973 draft... GM Bill Torrey turned down a nine-player offer from Montreal for the rights to draft him... Always a very willing interview, even after bad press from his public divorce hearing in 1983... Married for the second time a year ago... Active in charity work.

Year	Club	GP	G	A	Pts.
1973-74	New York I	77	17	37	54
1974-75	New York I	79	21	55	76
1975-76	New York I	78	31	67	98
1976-77	New York I	80	25	55	80
1977-78	New York I	80	30	64	94
1978-79	New York I	73	31	70	101
1979-80	New York I	31	8	33	41
1980-81	New York I	74	20	56	76
1981-82	New York I	60	24	37	61
1982-83	New York I	69	12	54	66
1983-84	New York I	78	22	63	85
1984-85	New York I	77	17	51	68
	Totals	856	258	642	900

KELLY HRUDEY 24 5-10 180   **Goaltender**

Heir apparent to Billy Smith, now that No. 2 man Roland Melanson has been traded to Minnesota... Very satisfactory rookie season, played well in his three playoff appearances... Islanders' second-round choice in 1980 out of Medicine Hat, where he was a second-team Western League All-Star... Quick, standup style ... As Smith nears twilight, it appears the Islanders are still in good shape in goal... Born January 13, 1961, in Edmonton... Quit hockey after being cut from a midget team at age 16... Walked on with the Medicine Hat juniors after being sent a form letter inviting him to camp and was stunned to make the team. "I really had no confidence in my ability," he said. "I'd always felt that teams took me because they had no one else." . . . First-team All-Star in the Central League for two years while awaiting the Islanders' call-up . . . "I'm just having fun out there," he says. "I never feel like I'm under any pressure. I mean, it's important to us, but it is just a game."

Year	Club	GP	GA	SO	Avg.
1983-84	New York I	12	28	0	3.14
1984-85	New York I	41	141	2	3.62
	Totals	53	169	2	3.53

KEN MORROW 28 6-4 205   Defenseman

Quickly became the best pure defensive defenseman in the NHL after joining the Islanders from the 1980 U.S. Gold Medal Olympic Team . . . Missed most of last season following a serious knee operation . . . Was brought along slowly and helped out down the stretch but was obviously not himself in the playoffs . . . There's good reason to worry about his future . . . "I realize I can't put my eggs in one basket anymore," he said. "During the time I couldn't play, I found out there are other things in life. I have two girls, you know." . . . Enormous upper-body strength, especially smart player . . . Born October 17, 1956, in Flint, Mich. . . . Great fourth-round draft pick in 1976 out of Bowling Green University . . . Stepped right in after the Olympics, freeing GM Bill Torrey to deal Dave Lewis to L.A. for Butch Goring. It was a trade that put the Islanders over the top . . . The only hockey player ever to win an Olympic gold medal and a Stanley Cup the same year . . . Scored the dramatic overtime goal that lifted the Islanders past the Rangers in the first round in 1984, climaxing one of the most exciting games ever played . . . Quiet, unassuming, friendly like a puppy dog off the ice . . . Nickname: "Wolfman." . . . In the limousine business with teammate Clark Gillies.

Year	Club	GP	G	A	Pts.
1979-80	New York I	18	0	3	3
1980-81	New York I	80	2	11	13
1981-82	New York I	75	1	18	19
1982-83	New York I	79	5	11	16
1983-84	New York I	63	3	11	14
1984-85	New York I	15	1	7	8
	Totals	330	12	61	73

BRYAN TROTTIER 29 5-11 195   Center

One of the all-time greats could be at the crossroads . . . His 59 points last year in 68 games represented the fewest in 10 NHL seasons . . . Bothered by a lot of nagging injuries, the worst of which appears to be a lower back problem . . . He bounced back to key the Islander comeback from a 2-0 deficit against Washington, but was largely ineffective as the Flyers put the Islanders out of the playoffs . . . For a five-year stretch from 1979-84, he was inarguably the best all-around player in the NHL . . . Excellent playmaker, incredibly sturdy on his skates, physical and smart . . . One of the finest ever at faceoffs . . . Two-time winner of the Hart Trophy as the league's Most Valuable Player . . . Rookie of the Year in 1975-76 . . . Also won the Conn Smythe Trophy as the Most Valuable Player in the 1980 playoffs . . . Soft-spoken and impassive off the ice, fierce and unyielding on it . . . His stubborn streak was exemplified by his decision to become an American citizen and play for Team USA in the 1984 Canada Cup. Took criticism from his best friend and long-time linemate, Mike Bossy, and was booed heavily in Canadian rinks throughout the tournament . . . Born July 17, 1956, in Val Marie, Sask. . . . Second-round pick in 1974 as an underage junior . . . Played a final junior year at Lethbridge before turning pro . . . Married, two children, very involved in charity work.

Year	Club	GP	G	A	Pts.
1975-76	New York I	80	32	63	95
1976-77	New York I	76	30	42	72
1977-78	New York I	77	46	77	123
1978-79	New York I	76	47	87	134
1979-80	New York I	78	42	62	104
1980-81	New York I	73	31	72	103
1981-82	New York I	80	50	79	129
1982-83	New York I	80	34	55	89
1983-84	New York I	68	40	71	111
1984-85	New York I	68	28	31	59
	Totals	756	380	639	1019

MIKE BOSSY 28 6-0 185   Right Wing

On a pace to become the greatest goal scorer in league history, if he decides to play long enough . . . Will become the 11th player to pass 500 this year and will do it in his eighth season. . . . It took Gordie Howe 26 to set the record of 801. Nobody above Bossy on the all-time list has played less than 13 years . . . Four times a first-team All-Star, two times a second-teamer . . . Deft puck-handler with as great a sense around the net as anyone who has ever played the game . . . Has also worked hard to become a fine defensive player as well . . . "I think the biggest asset of being successful is not being afraid to be successful," he said . . . Aloof and sensitive in his early years, he has more than proven himself to be a great team man . . . Has long planned to leave hockey after the 1987-88 season, convinced he will have had enough by then . . . Has parlayed his estimated $600,000-a-year salary with many investments, all of which he enjoys handling by himself . . . Born January 22, 1957, in Montreal, the sixth of ten children . . . Passed over by 14 teams in the 1977 draft because teams didn't think he would check . . . One of three players to score 50 goals in his rookie year. Has scored 60 three times and holds the NHL mark of eight straight plus-50 seasons.

Year	Club	GP	G	A	Pts.
1977-78	New York I	73	53	38	91
1978-79	New York I	80	69	57	126
1979-80	New York I	75	51	41	92
1980-81	New York I	79	68	51	119
1981-82	New York I	80	64	83	147
1982-83	New York I	79	60	58	118
1983-84	New York I	67	51	67	118
1984-85	New York I	76	58	59	117
	Totals	609	474	454	928

JOHN TONELLI 28 6-1 200   Left Wing

Long one of the NHL's hardest working and effective two-way left wings . . . Had his best offensive season last year . . . Playing most of the season with Brent Sutter and Mike Bossy, Tonelli scored 100 points for the first time in his career . . . Named the Most Valuable Player in the 1984 Canada Cup and the key to the 3-2 overtime victory over the Soviets that made that championship possible. He set up the winning goal in that semifinal game, which many observers think was the best single match ever played . . . Has a history of scoring important goals. With the Isles on the ropes against Pittsburgh in the 1982 first-round series, he tied the deciding game in the final minutes and then won it in overtime . . . Two years later, with the Isles down 1-0 and facing elimination at the hands of the Rangers, his goal early in the third period tied the score and the Islanders went on to win 4-1, then take the fifth contest in overtime . . . Tireless worker, one of the league's best cornermen . . . "I've always had to work hard to get places because I don't have a lot of talent," he said. "I love being around the rink. I look forward to every game, to putting on the uniform. I really love it." Born March 23, 1957, in Hamilton, Ont. . . . Turned professional as a 19-year-old with the WHA Houston Aeros . . .

When his contract ran out after three seasons there, he joined the Islanders, who had made him their second-round choice in 1977.

Year	Club	GP	G	A	Pts.
1975-76	Houston (WHA)	79	17	14	31
1976-77	Houston (WHA)	80	24	31	55
1977-78	Houston (WHA)	65	23	41	64
1978-79	New York I	73	17	39	56
1979-80	New York I	77	14	30	44
1980-81	New York I	70	20	32	52
1981-82	New York I	80	35	58	93
1982-83	New York I	76	31	40	71
1983-84	New York I	73	27	40	67
1984-85	New York I	80	42	58	100
	NHL Totals	529	186	297	483
	WHA Totals	224	64	86	150

BRENT SUTTER 23 5-11 175   Center

The heir apparent to Bryan Trottier as the Islanders gradually turn over a new order ... Emerged as a 102-point scorer last year as Al Arbour played him mostly with Mike Bossy and John Tonelli ... The fourth of the six Sutter brothers to make the NHL ... Two years younger than his teammate, Duane ... Relentless worker and forechecker with fine ability around the net. Nicknamed "Pup", which grew out of Duane's "Dog" moniker ... Really came into his own with a fine performance for Team Canada last fall ... Seventeenth player taken in the 1980 draft despite the fact that he was still playing in a Tier II league ... Born June 11, 1962, in Viking, Alta. ... Teamed briefly with brothers Rich and Ron (now with Philadelphia) on a line at Lethbridge, before the Islanders recalled him midway through the 1981-82 season ... He made an immediate impact as the Islanders rolled up a league-record 15-game winning streak.

Year	Club	GP	G	A	Pts.
1980-81	New York I.	3	2	2	4
1981-82	New York I.	43	21	22	43
1982-83	New York I.	80	21	19	40
1983-84	New York I.	69	34	15	49
1984-85	New York I.	72	42	60	102
	Totals	267	120	118	238

PATRICK FLATLEY 22 6-2 195   Right Wing

As the core of their championship teams begins to fray with age, the Islanders are still coming up with good ones that should keep them a factor for years to come. Flatley is a good example ...

Has all the tools to be a solid performer for years to come... Joined the Islanders after playing for Canada in the 1984 Olympics and made an immediate impact... Scored nine goals and six assists in 21 games and was a lifesaver as the hobbled Islanders nonetheless made it to the finals for the fifth straight year... Followed up with 51 points last year, his full rookie season... Very physical, his shoulder check put Barry Beck out of the 1984 playoffs... Excellent shot and good playmaking potential... Suffered a broken hand in the Washington series last spring and was sorely missed as the Isles went down to Philadelphia... "We weren't too old," Denis Potvin said. "We just lost our youth. Flats and Greg Gilbert [knee surgery] would have made a big difference."... Born October 3, 1963, in Toronto... Islanders' first-round pick in 1982 after his freshman season at the University of Wisconsin... Led the Badgers to the NCAA championship in his sophomore season before joining the Olympic team... Journalism major in school.... Prefers Patrick to the shortened Pat... Single and already a very popular player on a team with a lot of holdovers from the dynasty.

Year	Club	GP	G	A	Pts.
1983-84	New York I	16	2	7	9
1984-85	New York I	78	20	31	51
	Totals	94	22	38	60

BOB BOURNE 31 6-3 200　　　　　　　　　　**Left Wing**

Steady, effective veteran who had a great deal to do with the Islanders' four championships... Missed a lot of the 1984 playoffs with a shoulder separation, then suffered severed hand tendons via a skate cut in January... He returned for the playoffs, but couldn't be effective... Still one of the fastest skaters in the league ... Not blessed with great hands, but always got his 20 goals and his 50-60 points.... One of the nicest, and most quotable personalities in the league... An inspiration as he has skated with the burden of his son, Jeffrey, being born with Spina Bifida... One of GM Bill Torrey's great steals. Originally a third-round draft choice by the Kansas City Scouts in 1974, Torrey gave up Bart Crashley and the rights to Larry Hornung for Bourne after Kansas City refused to come up with the money to sign him... Drafted by the Houston Astros, played a year of minor-league baseball before deciding upon hockey.... Born June 21, 1954, in Netherhill, Sask.

Year	Club	GP	G	A	Pts.
1974-75	New York I.........	77	16	23	39
1975-76	New York I.........	14	2	3	5
1976-77	New York I.........	75	16	19	35
1977-78	New York I.........	80	30	33	63
1978-79	New York I.........	80	30	31	61
1979-80	New York I.........	73	15	25	40
1980-81	New York I.........	78	35	41	76
1981-82	New York I.........	76	27	26	53
1982-83	New York I.........	77	20	42	62
1983-84	New York I.........	78	22	34	56
1984-85	New York I.........	44	8	12	20
	Totals.............	752	221	289	510

COACH AL ARBOUR: Fourteenth season behind the Islander bench...A certain Hall of Famer, with 545 regular-season and 113 playoff victories. The latter mark is second on the all-time list behind Buffalo's Scotty Bowman...Took over an expansion franchise in only its second year, had the Islanders in the playoffs by their third season and, of course, won four Stanley Cups... Widely recognized as a great teacher and motivator, but still underrated as innovator...Designed the best power play in NHL history...Never afraid to tinker with new ways to bring out the best in his players. Last year he had the players write postgame notes on their thoughts and performances...As good as anybody manipulating a bench...Like all the best, has an excellent sense of when to push players and when to back off... Job has worn on him the last few years. After the 1983 finals, he was hospitalized for exhaustion. Even his wife thought last year would be his final one...His decision to return was a relief to his players. "I'd be scared to death to play for anybody else," Bob Bourne said. "He knows me too well, knows what motivates me." ...Says he is invigorated by the new talent the Islanders are infusing and is too young to take the upstairs job he has been promised...Has turned over more of the practice duties to assistant and heir apparent, Brian Kilrea...Born November 1, 1932, in Sudbury, Ont., where he maintains an offseason residence... Fine defenseman in his 12 years in the NHL, played on three Cup winners . . . Finished up in St. Louis, where he got his first coaching job . . . Fired there twice, he took a scouting job with Atlanta before Isles GM Bill Torrey hired him. Nicknamed "Radar," both for his all-knowing ways and his glasses.

MOST COLORFUL PLAYER

Of course it was only proper that Bob Nystrom scored the goal that gave the Islanders their first Stanley Cup in 1980.

Since becoming their third-round choice in their very first draft in 1972, Nystrom had been the Nassau Coliseum fans' favorite. He was, first of all, combative and valorous. What's more, his own career curve mirrored that of the team.

Overmatched, like the 12-60-6 expansion team, during an 11-game trial as a rough-around-the-edges 20-year-old in 1972-73. He plugged away to 21 goals in his full rookie year as the overachievers improved 26 points the following year. The team became a contender as Nystrom established himself as a solid 20-goal winger and character player. Then there were the severe disappointments as the Islanders, not quite good enough, began to be perceived as playoff chokers, with Nystrom being roasted for a perceived lack of the belligerence on a team labeled unjustifiably meek.

The deliverance came in 1980, with Nystrom scoring six playoff goals, including one in a key semifinal game against Buffalo, then the Stanley Cup winner in Game Six against the Flyers. There were three more years of regular-season ups and downs, with Nystrom and the Islanders always at their best in April and May when they had to be.

As he enters his 14th NHL season, Nystrom has said he would retire, rather than accept a trade. It's probably the way it should be.

ALL-TIME ISLANDER LEADERS

GOALS: Mike Bossy, 69, 1978-79
ASSISTS: Bryan Trottier, 87, 1978-79
POINTS: Mike Bossy, 147, 1981-82
SHUTOUTS: Glenn Resch, 7, 1975-76

NEW YORK RANGERS

TEAM DIRECTORY: Pres.: John H. Krumpe; VP-GM: Craig Patrick; Dir. Pub. Rel.: Vince Casey; Coach: Ted Sator. Home ice: Madison Square Garden (17,500; 200′ × 85′). Colors: Blue, red and white. Training camp: Rye, N.Y.

SCOUTING REPORT

OFFENSE: When your leading scorer is a defenseman, it tells you something. When he is also minus-27, it tells you a little more.

That's not completely fair. Reijo Ruotsalainen played part of the season on left wing. So did a lot of people as the Rangers, who suffered crippling injuries, a growing dislike for coach Herb Brooks and just some of that same old it's-New York-and-who-cares-until-the-playoffs attitude, set a club record for losses.

Of course, they're not that bad. Practically the same team

At least Glen Hanlon was a bright spot for the Rangers.

finished with 93 points the year before. But they obviously have some work to do.

Mark Pavelich missed 32 games and never hit his stride. There's no reason to expect he won't bounce back, but the club's other two supposed top centers, Pierre Larouche and Mike Rogers, are in the age-30 neighborhood and coming off disinterested seasons.

Right wing looks reasonably bleak with the retirement of Anders Hedberg. Left wing, with the exception of Don Maloney, doesn't look much better. The Rangers have a lot of young Swedish forwards—Peter Sundstrom, Tomas Sandstrom, Jan Erixon—with talent but it's going to be hard for them to become driving forces if the Rangers can't surround them with enough good old North American grit.

Stephen Patrick, George McPhee, Bob Brooke and Mark Osborne are plugging types. You just wonder whether they are good enough to make a difference.

DEFENSE: It's better than the 345 goals allowed last year—16th in the league—would indicate. Barry Beck labored with a very sore shoulder for most of the season. James Patrick had his rookie woes, but remains an excellent prospect. Ruotsalainen can be dazzling, so the hell with his defense—just let him go. And Tom Laidlaw had a very steady year.

That's a pretty good four. It could be five if Willie Huber underwent a personality transplant, but that's an old story. Grant Ledyard and Steve Richmond might be here. Then again they might not be if Terry Carkner, the club's No. 1 pick in 1984, is ready.

Goalie Glen Hanlon had a pretty good season, despite all that was going on around him. In flashes, rookie backup John Vanbiesbrouck looked like he can do a job.

OUTLOOK: Some recent mediocre drafting appears to be catching up with this club. Chris Kontos, a No. 1 in 1982, looks like a complete bust and Dave Gagner, No. 1 in 1983, appears a little smallish to be a force. Except for James Patrick, about all the good young talent the Rangers have turned over the last few years is European in nature.

GM Craig Patrick says he has some good collegians picked in later rounds coming in the next few years. But after last year's disaster, the pressure is on for him to show some immediate improvement or be gone.

The Flyers, Capitals and Islanders all look much better. And the Rangers look like a .500 team at best.

RANGER ROSTER

No.	Player	Pos.	Ht.	Wt.	Born	1984-85	G	A	Pts.	PIM
14	Mike Allison	C	6-0	200	3-28-61/St. Francis, Ont.	Rangers	9	15	24	17
21	Mike Backman	RW	5-10	175	1-2-53/Halifax, N.S.	New Haven	10	36	46	120
5	Barry Beck	D	6-3	215	6-3-57/Vancouver	Ranger	7	19	26	65
18	Mike Blaisdell	RW	6-1	195	1-18-60/Regina, Sask.	Rangers	1	0	1	11
						New Haven	21	23	44	41
13	Bob Brooke	LW	6-2	207	12-18-60/Melrose, Mass.	Rangers	7	9	16	79
	Terry Carkner	D	6-3	197	3-7-66/Winchester, Ont.	Peterborough	14	47	61	125
33	Andre Dore	D	6-2	200	2-11-58/Montreal	Rangers	0	7	7	35
						New Haven	3	22	24	48
20	Jan Erixon	LW	6-0	190	7-8-62/Sweden	Rangers	7	22	29	33
22	Nick Fotiu	LW	6-2	210	5-25-52/Staten Is., N.Y.	Rangers	4	7	11	54
8	Robbie Ftorek	C	5-8	160	1-2-52/Needham, Mass.	Rangers	9	10	19	35
						New Haven	9	17	26	30
9	Dave Gagner	C	5-10	182	12-11-64/Chatham, Ont.	Rangers	6	6	12	16
						New Haven	13	20	33	23
4	Ron Greschner	D	6-2	205	12-23-54/Goodsoil, Sask.	Rangers	16	29	45	42
26	Randy Heath	LW	5-8	162	11-11-64/Vancouver	Rangers	2	3	5	15
						New Haven	23	26	49	29
	Raimo Helminen	C	6-0	183	3-11-64/Finland	Ilves, Fin.	21	36	57	20
27	Willie Huber	D	6-5	228	1-15-58/West Germany	Rangers	3	11	14	55
23	Chris Kontos	C	6-1	196	12-10-63/Toronto	Rangers	4	8	12	24
						New Haven	19	24	43	30
2	Tom Laidlaw	D	6-2	215	4-15-58/Brampton, Ont.	Rangers	1	11	12	52
19	Pierre Larouche	C	5-11	175	11-16-55/Teschereau, Que.	Rangers	24	36	60	8
	Grant Ledyard	D	6-2	190	11-19-61/Winnipeg	Rangers	8	12	20	53
						New Haven	6	20	26	18
	Jim Malone	C	6-1	190	2-20-62/Chatham, Ont.	Fredericton	0	2	2	9
12	Don Maloney	LW	6-1	190	9-5-58/Kitchener, Ont.	Rangers	11	16	27	32
37	George McPhee	LW	5-9	170	7-2-58/Guelph, Ont.	Rangers	12	15	27	139
						New Haven	2	2	4	13
40	Kelly Miller	C	5-11	185	3-3-63/Detroit	Rangers	0	2	2	2
						Mich. St. U.	27	23	50	21
	Gerry Minor	C	5-8	178	10-27-58/Regina, Sask.	N.S.-N.H.	15	39	54	23
19	Mark Osborne	LW	6-1	185	8-13-61/Toronto	Rangers	4	4	8	33
	Larry Patey	C	6-1	185	2-17-53/Toronto	Rangers	0	1	1	12
						New Haven	14	14	28	43
3	James Patrick	D	6-2	185	6-14-63/Winnipeg	Rangers	8	28	36	71
11	Steve Patrick	RW	6-4	206	2-4-61/Winnipeg	Buff.-Rang.	13	20	33	67
16	Mark Pavelich	C.	5-8	170	2-28-58/Everleth, Minn.	Rangers	14	31	45	29
41	Steve Richmond	D	6-1	205	12-11-59/Chicago	Rangers	0	5	5	90
						New Haven	3	10	13	122
17	Mike Rogers	C	5-9	170	10-24-54/Calgary	Rangers	26	38	64	24
29	Reijo Ruotsalainen	D	5-8	170	4-4-60/Winnipeg	Rangers	28	45	73	32
28	Tomas Sandstrom	RW	6-2	200	9-4-64/Sweden	Rangers	29	29	58	51
	Brent Sapergia	C	5-11	190	12-16-62/Moose Jaw, Sask.	Salt Lake City	47	47	94	36
25	Peter Sundstrom	LW	6-0	180	12-14-61/Sweden	Rangers	18	25	43	34
	Vesa Salo	D	6-3	180	4-17-65/Finland	Lukko, Fin.	12	9	21	20
21	Simo Saarinen	D	5-10	170	2-10-63/Finland	Rangers	0	0	0	8
	Gordon Walker	RW	6-0	185	1-21-65/Castlegar, B.C.	Kamloops	67	67	134	76
24	Jim Wiemer	D	6-4	197	1-9-61/Sudbury, Ont.	Buff.-Rang.	7	5	12	34
						Roch.-N.H.	10	36	46	63

No.	Player	Pos.	Ht.	Wt.	Born		GP	GA	SO	Avg.
1	Glen Hanlon	G	6-0	185	2-20-57/Brandon, Man.	Rangers	44	175	9	4.18
	Mario Proulx	G	5-11	180	11-19-61/Drummondville, Que.	New Haven	5	19	0	4.87
						Toledo	12	0	0	5.24
35	Ron Scott	G	5-8	155	7-21-60/Guelph, Ont.	New Haven	36	130	0	3.81
34	John Vanbiesbrouck	G	5-7	165	9-4-63/Detroit, Mich.	Rangers	42	166	1	4.22

RANGER PROFILES

DON MALONEY 27 6-1 190   Left Wing

Missed 43 games last year with a broken ankle suffered in a collision with New Jersey's Bruce Driver . . . It was a struggle to return to the form that has made him one of the league's top triers and cornermen, but, as always, he was one of the Rangers' best players in the playoffs . . . Scored two goals to force an overtime in Game One of the series against the heavily-favored Flyers . . . Disappointed about the trade of his older brother, Dave, to Buffalo last year, but bit his tongue. "When some people lost confidence in him," Don said, "it was hard to play." . . . Second-round pick, out of Kitchener, by the Rangers in 1978 . . . Most Valuable Player of the 1984 All-Star Game . . . Voracious reader, dabbles with a home computer . . . One of the game's most outgoing friendly persons . . . Nickname: "Big Frame," "Bugsy" . . . Born Sept. 5, 1958, in Lindsay, Ont.

Year	Club	GP	G	A	Pts.
1978-79	New York R	28	9	17	26
1979-80	New York R	79	25	48	73
1980-81	New York R	61	29	23	52
1981-82	New York R	54	22	36	58
1982-83	New York R	78	29	40	69
1983-84	New York R	79	24	42	66
1984-85	New York R	37	11	16	27
	Totals	410	149	222	371

BARRY BECK 28 6-3 215   Defenseman

That he managed to play 56 games last year is a tribute to his character . . . Suffered shoulder problems all year long and returned to play in the playoffs despite the fact a chunk of bone had broken off . . . Underwent surgery the week following the Rangers' elimination . . . Has not quite achieved the star status predicted but has been a fine performer for eight NHL seasons . . . Second player taken in the 1977 draft (by Colorado), traded to the Rangers for six players in 1979 . . . Devastating body-checker and fine defensive defenseman, but has never scored like expected . . . Nickname "Bubba" . . . Intelligent, articulate, but has a temper . . . One of the many reasons that built up to the firing of Brooks was the Ranger coach calling Beck a "coward" in front of his teammates. He blew up, overturning a stick rack at practice when news of the incident hit the papers . . . Brooks denied using that term, Beck tried to downplay it. He was diplomatic when Brooks was fired, but he couldn't have been unhappy . . . Somewhat the street tough as a kid growing up in Vancouver, where he was born June 3, 1957, he now spends a lot of his time working with disadvantaged youths.

Year	Club	GP	G	A	Pts.
1977-78	Colorado	75	22	38	60
1978-79	Colorado	63	14	28	42
1979-80	Col-NYR	71	15	50	65
1980-81	New York R	75	11	23	34
1981-82	New York R	60	9	29	38
1982-83	New York R	66	12	22	34
1983-84	New York R	72	9	27	36
1984-85	New York R	56	7	19	26
	Totals	538	99	236	335

JAMES PATRICK 22 6-2 185   Defenseman

Eye-opening start after signing with the Rangers following the Sarejevo Olympics, but generally disappointing rookie year... Still, a likely future star... No. 1 pick in 1981, one of the few non-European Ranger choices who hasn't been a wash... Completed his college eligibility at the University of North Dakota before playing for the Canadian Olympic Team... First-team All-American at North Dakota... "He was well worth the wait," said former Ranger coach Herb Brooks. "He's a very intelligent young man. The elevator goes all the way up on this kid. He's good enough that I can't screw him up"... Still, it was Patrick's mediocre rookie season that was one of the factors that sent Brooks packing... Brother of Stephen, whom the Rangers acquired from Buffalo in the Dave Maloney deal last year... Father, Stephen, played 13 years of Canadian professional football with the Winnipeg Blue Bombers and was later a member of Parliament... Mobile, should score points... Rangers want him to bulk up another 10 pounds... Born June 14, 1963, in Winnipeg.

Year	Club	GP	G	A	Pts.
1983-84	New York R.........	12	1	7	8
1984-85	New York R.........	75	8	28	36
	Totals	87	9	35	44

TOMAS SANDSTROM 21 6-2 200   Right Wing

Maybe the only bright light of a disastrous Ranger season... Rookie scored 29 goals and 28 assists and was named the team's MVP... Divided his time almost equally on both sides as injuries forced a lot of juggling . . . Second-round pick in the 1982 draft . . . Born Sept. 4, 1964, in Finland, but family moved to Fagersta, Sweden, where he made his hockey debut . . . Great shot, hard worker . . . A skilled carpenter . . . Voted best player in the World Junior Championships in 1982.

Year	Club	GP	G	A	Pts.
1984-85	New York R.........	74	29	29	58

MARK PAVELICH 27 5-8 170   Center

Durable, dynamic performer in his first three Rangers seasons but, like so many Rangers, had a discouraging 1984-85 . . . Missed 32 games with a broken wrist . . . Came on a little down the stretch, but was totally shut down in the Rangers' three-game sweep by the Flyers . . . Star of the 1980 U.S. Olympic gold medal team . . . Overlooked by NHL because of his size during his career at the University of Minnesota-Duluth . . . Signed as a free agent at the urging of Olympic, and later Ranger, coach Herb Brooks . . . Played a year in Switzerland until the Rangers hired Brooks . . . The Rangers will have to find a new right wing for him with the retirement of Anders Hedberg . . . Spends his entire offseason with his first love, fishing, near his home in Eveleth, Minnesota, where he was born Feb. 28, 1958 . . . Turned down a Canada Cup invitation for that reason . . . Co-holder of the Ranger one-game goal-scoring record, five.

Year	Club	GP	G	A	Pts.
1981-82	New York R	79	33	43	76
1982-83	New York R	78	37	38	75
1983-84	New York R	77	29	53	82
1984-85	New York R	48	14	31	45
	Totals	282	113	165	278

REIJO RUOTSALAINEN 25 5-8 170   Defenseman

Probably the fastest skater in the NHL . . . Lateral speed is so unbelievable, he must be playing with illegal thighs . . . Dynamic shot . . . Ran up his best point total (73) of his four-year NHL career last season, but was still a minus 27 . . . Lack of size hampers his defensive play . . . Was at his best in the 1982 and 1983 playoffs when he tore up the Flyers . . . Herb Brooks built a lot of his offense

around Rexy, using circling patterns at center ice which enabled
him to roar in behind the play and catch defensemen flat-footed
... Not as effective and often caught up ice when the Rangers
went back to playing straight up-and-down hockey... Had two
goals in the playoffs, but gave away the puck for the Flyers'
overtime goal in Game One... Sixth-round choice in 1980...
Born April 1, 1960, in Oulu, Finland, a village near the Arctic
Circle... Shy, a road roommate of Pavelich.

Year	Club	GP	G	A	Pts.
1981-82	New York R	78	18	38	56
1982-83	New York R	77	16	53	69
1983-84	New York R	74	20	39	59
1984-85	New York R	80	28	45	73
	Totals	309	82	175	257

PETER SUNDSTROM 23 6-0 180   Right Wing

Twin brother of the Canucks' Patrik, but admits the two are not
especially close... Miserable sophomore season, he was one of
the few key Rangers who was healthy enough to produce. But
still a guy the club hopes to build around... Inseparable from
linemate and countryman Jan Erixon... They each own pacers in
Sweden... Third-round choice in 1981... "I'm still learning," he
says. "Smaller rinks, faster play here is a factor. We will adjust
and play better."... Born Dec. 14, 1961, in Skelleftea, Sweden.

Year	Club	GP	G	A	Pts.
1983-84	New York R	77	22	22	44
1984-85	New York R	76	18	25	43
	Totals	153	40	47	87

GLEN HANLON 28 6-0 185   Goaltender

Had a solid season, considering all that was going on in front of
him, but a disappointing playoff... Flyers' Tim Kerr scored four
goals in one period on Hanlon in the third game, and he was pulled
... Outstanding in the 1984 playoffs when the Rangers came within
an overtime goal of eliminating the four-time champion Islanders
... Calmed down from his intense, injury-filled, early days in
Vancouver. "I was so out of control that maybe it contributed to

my injuries," he said . . . So did off-ice accidents. He once fell off the roof of his home and hooked himself in the eye fly-casting . . . Lost his Vancouver job to Richard Brodeur and was traded to St. Louis in 1982. The Rangers got him along with Vaclav Nedomansky for Andre Dore in January 1983 . . . Fourth-round choice by the Canucks in 1977 . . . Born Feb. 20, 1957, in Brandon, Man.

Year	Club	GP	GA	SO	Avg.
1977-78	Vancouver	4	9	0	2.70
1978-79	Vancouver	31	94	3	3.10
1979-80	Vancouver	57	193	0	3.47
1980-81	Vancouver	17	59	1	4.44
1981-82	Van-StL	30	114	1	4.06
1982-83	StL-NYR	35	117	0	3.81
1983-84	New York R	50	166	1	3.51
1984-85	New York R	44	175	0	4.18
	Totals	268	925	6	3.70

TOM LAIDLAW 27 6-2 215   Defenseman

Solid 1984-85 season through trying times and one of the better Rangers in the playoffs . . . Stand-up defenseman, stand-up guy . . . Seventh-round pick out of Northern Michigan University in 1978 . . . The 19 games he missed last year were his only absences of his five year Ranger career . . . Single, inseparable from his golden retriever "Buck." . . . Born April 15, 1958, in Brampton, Ont. . . . Likes country music and driving his jeep.

Year	Club	GP	G	A	Pts.
1980-81	New York R	80	6	23	29
1981-82	New York R	79	3	18	21
1982-83	New York R	80	0	10	10
1983-84	New York R	79	3	15	18
1984-85	New York R	61	1	11	12
	Totals	379	13	77	90

MIKE ALLISON 24 6-0 200   Center

Suffered a knee injury and was lost for the season following only 31 games . . . Has fought an injury jinx throughout his career, but when healthy has been an effective performer . . . Rangers are still counting on him . . . Not particularly fast, but a plugger, his type was missed on a team that may have become over-Europeanized . . . Scored his first NHL goal on his first shift and first shot in 1980 . . . Born March 28, 1961, in Fort Francis, Ont., where he built a log cabin on an island he owns...Practical joker and locker-room pepper-pot...Second-round choice in 1980.

Year	Club	GP	G	A	Pts.
1980-81	New York R.........	75	26	38	64
1981-82	New York R.........	48	7	15	22
1982-83	New York R.........	39	11	9	20
1983-84	New York R.........	45	8	12	20
1984-85	New York R.........	31	9	15	24
	Totals............	238	61	89	150

COACH TED SATOR: Named Ranger coach in June...Served as an assistant coach with Philadelphia the last two years after coaching five years in Sweden ..."He is an intelligent, articulate, very organized young man," Ranger GM Craig Patrick said. "I have absolutely no question he can be decisive enough to handle standing behind an NHL bench."...Turned down the likely offer of the Minnesota North Stars to take on the Rangers..."I've never coached a losing team in my life," he said, "and I don't intend to start now."...Born Nov. 18, 1949, in Utica, N.Y....Played at Bowling Green University and very briefly for the New York Raiders of the WHA before a knee injury ended his playing career...Returned to Bowling Green to earn a master's degree in exercise physiology...His job in Sweden grew out of his attendance at a European camp seminar...In five years he won five championships with Rogle, a First Division team...But it was his reputation as a power-skating instructor on the summer camp circuit that brought him to the Flyers...Recommended by Michigan State coach Ron Mason to then-Flyer coach Bob McCammon, who wanted a skating instructor for a rookie camp in 1983...McCammon, impressed, put Sator on retainer as a European scout and made plans to hire him as an assistant the following year.

MOST COLORFUL PLAYER

Lou Fontinato was the NHL's quintessential tough guy of the 1950's. Strong as a gorilla and seemingly as short-tempered, he terrorized the league and became a New York hero.

Among his triumphs was a bloodying of Maurice Richard, the fiery Montreal star. Fontinato unquestionably ruled the roost of NHL bad guys until the fateful night at Madison Square Garden in 1957 when he ran into Gordie Howe.

The Red Wing legend had nearly sliced the Ranger bull's ear off earlier that season. So when Fontinato saw Howe squaring off with the Rangers' Eddie Shack, he wasted no time.

As usual, Leapin' Louie started quickly, before Howe could see him coming. Gordie took several blows that would have knocked down a horse, but he only staggered backwards to see who had come at him.

Then Howe started jabbing lefts off Fontinato's face. The Ranger tried to counter with some body punches, but Howe drilled him time after time. When it was over, Fontinato's nose was at a right angle from his face, which dripped with blood.

The picture taken of him leaving the ice is still one of the most famous and chilling in the history of the game. And Fontinato, having suffered his first career defeat, was never the same.

His ego as smashed as his face, Fontinato's play deteriorated until he was traded to Montreal in 1961, where his career ended due to a broken neck suffered in a Vic Hadfield check.

ALL-TIME RANGER LEADERS

GOALS: Vic Hadfield, 50, 1971-72
ASSISTS: Mike Rogers, 65, 1981-82
POINTS: Jean Ratelle, 109, 1971-72
SHUTOUTS: John Roach, 13, 1928-29

PHILADELPHIA FLYERS

TEAM DIRECTORY: Chairman Exec. Comm.: Edward Snider; Chairman of the Board: Joseph Scott; Pres.: Jay Snider; Exec. VP: Keith Allen; GM: Bobby Clarke; Dir. Scouting-Asst. GM: Gary Darling; Dir. Press Rel.: Rodger Gottlieb; Coach: Mike Keenan. Home ice: The Spectrum (17,147; 200′ × 85′). Colors: Orange and white. Training camps: Voorhees, N.J., and Philadelphia.

SCOUTING REPORT

OFFENSE: When Tim Kerr's knee broke down against Edmonton in the finals, the need for another big scorer was obvious. Then again, everybody needs another big scorer against the Oilers and

Tim Kerr posted three four-goal games, five hat tricks.

they're hard to find in a trade. Yet so many of the Flyers' first- and second-year forwards showed so much promise a year ago, their management has reason to hope that another two years could mean a 10-15 goal difference for a lot of these kids.

Maybe Todd Bergen, who has a big shot, but a laconic style, will be the answer. Two of the kids, Peter Zezel and Murray Craven, have great offensive potential. Zezel, with outstanding playmaking skills, had 61 points in 65 games his rookie year. Craven, who does everything well at the callow age of 20, scored 26 goals in his first full season and could, in time, get 40.

The Flyers look deep everywhere and quick in most places. Take center, for instance. Dave Poulin, their captain and leader, scored at a point-a-game clip and time after time during their remarkable stretch drive, made the big play at the critical time. Zezel has 100-point potential. They don't come much more valuable than Ron Sutter, who at 21 is already a superior defensive player and will score more as he matures.

Left wing, with 96-point man Brian Propp, Craven and Derrick Smith, is symbolic of the Flyers' new-found quickness. Right wing, with Kerr, the hulking goal machine, the talented Ilkka Sinsalo and the hardrock Rick Tocchet has all the prerequisite parts.

DEFENSE: Almost all the young forwards had their ups and downs as the Flyers, a consensus pick to finish fourth in the Patrick Division a year ago, soared to the league's best record. The club's real strength, and the reason it got to the Stanley Cup finals, was the consistency of its defense. A team couldn't ask for anything more than Mark Howe, Brad Marsh, Doug Crossman and Brad McCrimmon gave the Flyers night-in, night-out under relentless playoff pressure.

Howe has forsaken his offense to take absolute control in the Flyer end. During the playoffs he was all but flawless. Marsh blocked shots and moved bodies and was a tower of strength, Crossman, who started the season slowly, cooly moved the puck out of trouble. And McCrimmon, until lost with a shoulder separation in the fourth semifinal game, played a season worthy of All-Star consideration.

Perhaps if they had McCrimmon, the Flyers would have extended the Oilers past five games. So depth is always a concern. Especially with Howe turning 30, Philadelphia could probably could use one more guy. Ed Hospodar is a bouncer who played well in stretches, Thomas Eriksson a superior skater and puckhandler whose talent must be unlocked.

Pelle Lindbergh was the best goalie in the league last year. Bob

FLYER ROSTER

No.	Player	Pos.	Ht.	Wt.	Born	1984-85	G	A	Pts.	PIM
	Ray Allison	RW	5-9	178	3-4-59/Cranbrook, B.C.	Philadelphia	1	1	2	2
						Hershey	17	22	39	61
7	Bill Barber	LW	6-0	190	7-11-52/Colander, Ont.	Injured	–	–	–	–
19	Todd Bergen	LW	6-3	190	7-11-63/Prince Albert, Sask.	Philadelphia	11	5	16	4
						Hershey	20	19	39	2
21	Dave Brown	RW	6-5	205	10-12-62/Saskatoon, Sask.	Philadelphia	3	6	9	163
18	Lindsay Carson	C	6-2	190	11-21-60/Oxbow, Sask.	Philadelphia	20	19	39	123
32	Murray Craven	C	6-1	170	7-20-64/Medicine Hat, Alta.	Philadelphia	26	35	61	30
3	Doug Crossman	D	6-2	190	6-13-60/Peterborough, Ont.	Philadelphia	4	33	37	65
	Per-Erik Eklund	C	5-10	170	—/Sweden	Sweden	16	33	49	–
6	Tom Eriksson	D	6-2	182	10-16-59/Sweden	Philadelphia	10	29	39	36
34	Ross Fitzpatrick	LW	6-0	195	10-7-60/Peniction, B.C.	Philadelphia	1	0	1	0
						Hershey	26	15	41	8
39	Paul Guay	RW	6-0	193	9-2-63/N. Smithfield, R.I.	Philadelphia	0	1	1	0
						Hershey	23	30	53	123
11	Len Hachborn	C	5-10	175	9-9-61/Brantford, Ont.	Philadelphia	5	17	22	23
						Hershey	6	7	13	14
17	Ed Hospodar	D-RW	6-2	200	2-5-59/Bowling Green, Ohio	Philadelphia	3	4	7	130
2	Mark Howe	D	5-11	190	5-28-55/Detroit	Philadelphia	18	39	57	31
12	Tim Kerr	C	6-3	225	1-5-60/Windsor, Ont.	Philadelphia	54	44	98	57
8	Brad Marsh	D	6-3	220	3-31-58/London, Ont.	Philadelphia	2	18	20	91
10	Brad McCrimmon	D	5-11	186	3-29-59/Dodsland, Sask.	Philadelphia	8	35	43	81
28	Joe Paterson	LW-C	6-1	208	6-25-60/Calgary	Philadelphia	0	0	0	31
						Hershey	26	27	53	173
20	Dave Poulin	C	5-11	180	12-17-58/Timmins, Ont.	Philadelphia	30	44	74	59
26	Brian Propp	LW	5-10	190	2-15-59/Neudorf, Sask.	Philadelphia	43	53	96	43
23	Ilkka Sinisalo	LW	6-1	190	7-10-58/Finland	Philadelphia	36	37	73	16
24	Derrick Smith	LW	6-1	190	1-22-65/Scarborough, Ont.	Philadelphia	17	22	39	31
	Steve Smith	D	5-10½	210	4-4-63/Trenton, Ont.	Philadelphia	0	0	0	7
						Hershey	10	20	30	83
15	Rich Sutter	RW	5-11	170	12-2-63/Viking, Alta.	Philadelphia	6	10	16	89
						Hershey	3	7	10	14
14	Ron Sutter	C	5-11	175	12-2-63/Viking, Alta.	Philadelphia	16	29	45	94
	Darryl Stanley	D	6-2	200	12-2-62/Winnipeg	Hershey	0	7	7	33
22	Rick Tocchet	RW	6-0	195	4-9-64/Scarborough, Ont.	Philadelphia	14	25	39	181
	Tim Young	C	6-1	192	2-22-55/Scarborough, Ont.	Philadelphia	2	6	8	12
						Hershey	19	29	48	56
25	Peter Zezel	C	5-11	195	4-22-65/Toronto	Philadelphia	15	46	61	26

No.	Player	Pos.	Ht.	Wt.	Born	1984-85	GP	GA	SO	Avg.
35	Bob Froese	G	5-11	178	6-30-58/St. Catharines, Ont.	Philadelphia	17	37	1	2.41
						Hershey	4	15	0	3.67
	Ron Hextall	G	6-1	175	5-3-64/Winnipeg	Hershey	11	34	0	3.68
33	Darren Jensen	G	5-8	165	5-27-60/Cresto, B.C.	Hershey	39	150	1	3.98
						Philadelphia	1	7	0	7.00
31	Pelle Lindbergh	G	5-9	166	3-24-59/Sweden	Philadelphia	65	194	2	3.02

Froese, who was outstanding when Lindbergh came unglued in his sophomore season, is better than many team's first-stringers.

OUTLOOK: Excellent, with every reason to expect a second-straight trip to the finals.

FLYER PROFILES

PELLE LINDBERGH 26 5-9 166   **Goaltender**
Blossomed, in his third NHL season, into one of the best in the game . . . Led the league in wins (40) and was third in goals-against average (3.02) and second in save percentage (.899) . . . Bounced back from a disastrous sophomore season in which he lost his No. 1 job to Bob Froese . . . Fact that Froese was injured when Lindbergh hit his one slump of the season in December was a big help . . . So was the Flyers learning from their mistakes of over-coaching their goalies in the past . . . An exceptional athlete, as quick as any goalie in the history of the game . . . Has improved his positioning and cut down on his rebounds . . . Named the Flyers' Most Valuable Player last year . . . Recorded three shutouts in the playoffs, including a 1-0 job that clinched the series as the Flyers eliminated the Islanders in five games . . . Born May 24, 1959, in Stockholm . . . The first European goalie to make it big in the NHL . . . Second-round pick in 1979 draft . . . Member of Sweden's 1980 bronze-medal team at the Lake Placid Olympics . . . His friendly manner and shoulder shrugs notwithstanding, a competitor and a battler . . . Likes fast, expensive cars.

Year	Club	GP	GA	SO	Avg.
1981-82	Philadelphia	8	35	0	4.38
1982-83	Philadelphia	40	116	3	2.98
1983-84	Philadelphia	36	135	1	4.05
1984-85	Philadelphia	65	194	2	3.02
	Totals	149	480	6	3.32

TIM KERR 25 6-3 225   **Right Wing**
Recorded his second consecutive 54-goal season last year . . . Superior hand speed and impossible to move out from in front of the net . . . One of the greatest free-agent finds in NHL history . . . Signed as an underage player after a shortened, six-round draft in

1979. . . . Hampered by a series of injuries his second and third years in the NHL, but really busted out in 1983-84 . . . Recorded the fastest four goals by one player in Stanley Cup history as the Flyers completed first-round sweep of the Rangers . . . Had five hat tricks and three four-goal games last season despite missing six games with injuries . . . Signed a five-year, $250,000-a-year contract before last season. "The way I look at it, it doesn't put more pressure on me," he said. "If they expect me to score, all that means is they'll give me more ice time to do it." . . . Strong on faceoffs. Not the quickest guy in the league from a standing start, but moves well for a big man . . . Born Jan. 5, 1960, in Windsor, Ont. . . . Suffered a right-knee ligament strain and was able to play in only three of the Flyers' final 11 playoff games.

Year	Club	GP	G	A	Pts.
1980-81	Philadelphia	68	22	23	45
1981-82	Philadelphia	61	21	30	51
1982-83	Philadelphia	24	11	8	19
1983-84	Philadelphia	79	54	39	93
1984-85	Philadelphia	74	54	44	98
	Totals	306	162	144	306

MARK HOWE 30 5-11 190   Defenseman

One of the NHL's best . . . The Flyers expected him to score more when they acquired him from Hartford in the three-way deal that sent Ken Linseman to Edmonton and Risto Siltanen to the Whalers, but they are not complaining . . . Very effective defensively, his speed and ability to move the puck is a lifeline for the Flyers out of their own end . . . Lived down his reputation of never playing well in the playoffs with an outstanding performance last spring . . . Scored the overtime goal in Game One against the Rangers that ended the Flyers' three-year, nine-game string of playoff futility . . . Was on his way to his best season in 1980-81 with the Whalers when he suffered a career-threatening puncture wound in his rectum while crashing into a goal post . . . Son of Gordie, the Red Wing Hall of Famer and Mr. Hockey . . . Broke in as an 18-year-old with his brother Marty and dad on the WHA Houston Aeros. Traded to Hartford before the Whalers were admitted to the NHL in 1979 . . . Runnerup for the Norris Trophy in his first Flyer season, 1982-83 . . . Played on US silver-medal team in the 1972 Olympics as a 16-year-old . . . Extensive investments in real estate . . . Says his greatest hockey thrill was being at the Detroit Olympia the night his dad passed Maurice Richard to become the NHL's all-time leading goal scorer . . . Nagged by knee, back and shoulder problems in recent years, plays his best when he complains the most . . . Born May 28, 1955, in Detroit.

Year	Club	GP	G	A	Pts.
1973-74	Houston (WHA)	76	38	41	79
1974-75	Houston (WHA)	74	36	40	76
1975-76	Houston (WHA)	72	39	37	76
1976-77	Houston (WHA)	57	23	52	75
1977-78	New England (WHA)	70	30	61	91
1978-79	New England (WHA)	77	42	65	107
1979-80	Hartford	74	24	56	80
1980-81	Hartford	63	19	46	65
1981-82	Hartford	76	8	45	53
1982-83	Philadelphia	76	20	47	67
1983-84	Philadelphia	71	19	34	53
1984-85	Philadelphia	73	18	39	57
	NHL Totals	433	108	267	375
	WHA Totals	426	208	296	504

BRAD MARSH 27 6-3 220   **Defenseman**
Had his best and most consistent season of his seven in the NHL in 1984-85 . . . "His heart," said GM Bobby Clarke, "is as big as his feet." . . . Sound defensive defenseman and one of the NHL's top shot-blockers . . . Has elevated the clutch-and-grab tactic to a science . . . Awkward skater, but not as slow as he looks . . . A throwback to an earlier age, yet still highly effective . . . Former captain of the Calgary Flames, who traded him to the Flyers for Mel Bridgman in 1981 . . . Coming off an up-and-down season in 1983-84 and beset by personal problems, he was passed over for the Flyer captaincy upon Clarke's retirement in favor of Dave Poulin. But Poulin said Marsh was very helpful in his adjustment to a leadership role . . . Maybe the most popular player on the team, both with his teammates and fans . . . One of the nicest men in the game . . . First-round pick by the Flames in 1978 out of the London Knights . . . Born March 31, 1958, in London, Ont.

Year	Club	GP	G	A	Pts.
1978-79	Atlanta	80	0	19	19
1979-80	Atlanta	80	2	9	11
1980-81	Calgary	80	1	12	13
1981-82	Calg-Phil	83	2	23	25
1982-83	Philadelphia	68	2	11	13
1983-84	Philadelphia	77	3	14	17
1984-85	Philadelphia	77	2	18	20
	Totals	545	12	106	118

BRIAN PROPP 26 5-10 190   **Left Wing**
One of the best at his position in the game . . . Consistent 40-goal scorer and much underrated defensively . . . Challenged to provide

leadership by the absence of Clarke, Bill Barber and Darryl Sittler, and he responded. Recorded new career highs in goals and assists last year, but more importantly, he played better than ever in big games . . . Still quiet, but has come a long way from the shy rookie who would look at the floor when you said hello . . . Born Feb. 15, 1959, in Lanisan, Sask. . . . Only survivor from the Flyer team that went to the finals in 1980 . . . Another Flyer who found redemption from the three straight years of playoff failures, although with Tim Kerr out, he failed to pick up the scoring load in the finals . . . Had a hat trick against the Islanders in the quarterfinals . . . Has represented the Flyers in the All-Star Game four times in his six seasons.

Year	Club	GP	G	A	Pts.
1979-80	Philadelphia	80	34	41	75
1980-81	Philadelphia	79	26	40	66
1981-82	Philadelphia	80	44	47	91
1982-83	Philadelphia	80	40	42	82
1983-84	Philadelphia	79	39	53	92
1984-85	Philadelphia	76	43	53	96
	Totals	474	226	276	502

BRAD McCRIMMON 26 5-11 186   **Defenseman**

His 1982 acquisition from Boston in the trade that sent goalie Peter Peeters to the Bruins looked like a mistake until last season . . . As Peeters, the 1983 Vezina Trophy winner, faltered, McCrimmon came on . . . Had shown flashes in his first two seasons, but last year became a game-in, game-out force . . . Slimmed down 10 pounds, put personal problems behind him and responded to the increased ice time new coach Mike Keenan gave him . . . Regained the confidence with the puck that made him a 98-point junior and first-round draft choice in 1979 and vastly improved himself as a one-on-one defender . . . His playoffs ended during the semifinals when he separated a shoulder when checked into the boards by Quebec's Wilf Paiement . . . Nicknamed "The Beast" . . . Voted the Flyers' best defenseman last season . . . Born March 23, 1959, in Dodsland, Sask.

Year	Club	GP	G	A	Pts.
1979-80	Boston	72	5	11	16
1980-81	Boston	78	11	18	29
1981-82	Boston	78	1	8	9
1982-83	Philadelphia	79	4	21	25
1983-84	Philadelphia	71	0	24	24
1984-85	Philadelphia	66	8	35	43
	Totals	444	29	117	146

DAVE POULIN 26 5-11 180   Center

Named Flyer captain in only his second NHL season... Fine leader... Not a superior playmaker, but his speed makes things happen and he's an excellent defensive player besides... Played his best hockey down the stretch, when the Flyers went on a 16-1 tear to overtake Washington and win the Patrick Division. Game after game he scored or set up the big goal at a pivotal time ... Missed eight games of last year's playoffs with a knee sprain and struggled in the finals while playing with a cracked rib... Overlooked in the draft after a fine career at Notre Dame University ... Accepted a one-year contract with Rogle, a Swedish minor-league team... "I had just gotten married," he said. "We looked at it as a honeymoon."... Was considering several opportunities to go into business when the Flyers, upon the recommendation of Rogle coach Ted Sator (who was on his way to an assistant coaching job with Philadelphia) signed him... Scored on his first shot of his first NHL game... Articulate spokesman, bears a resemblance to Steve Garvey both in looks and manner. "The highest compliment I can give him," said Mike Keenan, "is that he is filling the shoes of Bobby Clarke as the Flyers' leader."... Born December 17, 1958, in Timmins, Ont.

Year	Club	GP	G	A	Pts.
1982-83	Philadelphia	2	2	0	2
1983-84	Philadelphia	73	31	45	76
1984-85	Philadelphia	73	30	44	74
	Totals	148	63	89	152

ILKKA SINISALO 27 6-1 190   Right Wing

Has steadily improved from a 15-goal scorer as a rookie to 36 in his fourth NHL season... Dynamic shot, quick off the wing, there may be only two handfuls of talents in the league with more natural ability... Once considered a defensive disaster, he became a penalty-killer, with more checking responsibilities... He also scored more important goals in big games than ever before... Born July 19, 1958, in Valeakoski, Finland... Was a late bloomer in the Finnish program... Signed as a free agent by Philadelphia in February 1981 when he was 22 years old... Scored his first NHL goal on a penalty shot... Suffered a shoulder bruise when hit by Edmonton's Paul Coffey early in the finals and was ineffective as the Oilers went on to win in five games... Polite, though not exactly locquacious with the media, but his teammates report an excellent sense of humor... Close friend of the Oilers' Jari Kurri.

Year	Club	GP	G	A	Pts.
1981-82	Philadelphia	66	15	22	37
1982-83	Philadelphia	61	21	29	50
1983-84	Philadelphia	73	29	17	46
1984-85	Philadelphia	70	36	37	73
	Totals	270	101	105	206

DOUG CROSSMAN 25 6-2 190   Defenseman

A key member of the Flyers' four-man defensive rotation during the playoffs... Smart, very good with the puck... Played disappointingly in the first year-and-a-half after being acquired from Chicago for Behn Wilson, but came on strong after January... Flyers had some injuries at the time and Mike Keenan turned to Crossman more often. "I'm playing better because I'm playing more," he said. "That's just about all there is to it. We played with four most of the time in Chicago. You have to prove yourself here, I accept that. I'm glad it's worked out."... Born June 30, 1960, in Peterborough, Ont.... Black Hawks' sixth-round pick in 1979... Had a 116-point season his final junior season in Ottawa and made the Black Hawks after only one season in the AHL ... Not the most rugged guy in the world, his real strength is his cool under pressure... A very eligible bachelor.

Year	Club	GP	G	A	Pts.
1980-81	Chicago	9	0	2	2
1981-82	Chicago	70	12	28	40
1982-83	Chicago	80	13	40	53
1983-84	Philadelphia	78	7	28	35
1984-85	Philadelphia	80	4	33	37
	Totals	317	36	131	167

RON SUTTER 21 5-11 175   Center

Had as much to do with the Flyers reaching the finals as anyone ... Night after night he ground away against the opposition's top center... Outstanding against Bryan Trottier, Mark Pavelich and Peter Stastny in the first three rounds of the playoffs and held Wayne Gretzky to one point in the two Spectrum games that Mike Keenan was able to have the last line change.... Has all the dogged traits that have put five of his brothers in the NHL, plus a set of hands that should eventually make him an 80-90 point scorer... Keenan put him in a defensive role from the beginning of the season. The kid was not exactly thrilled at first, but eventually grew to enjoy it... A constant lobbyist for more playing time for his twin brother Rich, a Flyer right wing... Born December 2, 1963, in Viking, Alta., 30 minutes after Richie... Fourth player taken in the 1982 draft. Rich went six rounds later to Pittsburgh. Flyers traded three players and dropped down five places in the 1984 draft to reunite the twins 15 months later... "Ron wasn't ready for us to put pressure on him to score points," Keenan said. "He's an excellent defensive player for his age and that was the way to use him. I'm sure he'll score more as he goes along."

Year	Club	GP	G	A	Pts.
1982-83	Philadelphia	10	1	1	2
1983-84	Philadelphia	79	19	32	51
1984-85	Philadelphia	73	16	29	45
	Totals	162	36	62	98

COACH MIKE KEENAN: Outstanding job in his rookie year, taking a team with 12 first- and second-year players to the Stanley Cup finals... Named Coach of the Year by *The Sporting News*... A taskmaster with the sense not to push too hard on tight players... Very cool and adept behind the bench... A stickler for details, all the way down to postgame meals for the players and separate water bottles during practices... Extremely intense, so far not very good copy, particularly after games ... "Presence is the best way to describe him," captain Dave Poulin says. "He can be all things to different persons. It reminds me of what they used to say about Vince Lombardi. You'll take a lot of criticism for just one pat on the back from Mike Keenan."... Born October 21, 1949, in Toronto... Played defense at St. Lawrence University, the University of Toronto and one year with the Roanoke Valley Rebels of the Southern Hockey League before going back to Toronto to teach school... His first coaching job was with the high-school lacrosse team. It won the championship, as did several Junior B teams he coached part time... Got a junior

A job in Peterborough and took the Petes to the Memorial Cup final in his only season...The next stop was Rochester of the American League, where he won the title in his third season... Seeing little chance for advancement in the Buffalo organization, he took the University of Toronto coaching job for a season (yeah, he won the championship there, too) before the Flyers hired him to replace Bob McCammon...Married, one daughter...Does have another side...Enjoys music, used to sing with a group of college chums named Nik and the Nice Guys.

MOST COLORFUL PLAYER

Dave Schultz was truly one of the most reviled villains in the history of the NHL. Soft-spoken and a bundle of insecurities off the ice, "The Hammer" underwent a major personality change when the puck was dropped. He fought anybody and everybody as the Flyers rose to power and consecutive Stanley Cups in 1974 and 1975.

Hard work, discipline and the skills of Bobby Clarke, Rick MacLeish and Bernie Parent won for the Flyers, but terror played no small part in their success. Coach Fred Shero said that it was Schultz who transformed the Flyers' personality from a meek, run-of-the-mill expansion team to one that was capable of winning important games on the road.

His was, depending upon your viewpoint, either a colorful or repulsive act. Undeterred by the absence of rules that later prevented the Flyers from turning one-on-one bouts into gang warfare, Schultz challenged anybody and everybody.

His 2,294 penalty minutes, liberally padded with misconducts from his post-fight histrionics, still rank second on the NHL's all-time list. Several of the NHL's rule changes can be directly credited to his behavior.

Schultz played nine seasons in the NHL. Traded to Los Angeles in 1976, he moved on to Pittsburgh and Buffalo before retiring.

ALL-TIME FLYER LEADERS

GOALS: Reggie Leach, 61, 1975-76
ASSISTS: Bobby Clarke, 89, 1974-75, 1975-76
POINTS: Bobby Clarke, 119, 1975-76
SHUTOUTS: Bernie Parent, 12, 1973-74, 1974-75

PITTSBURGH PENGUINS

TEAM DIRECTORY: Owner: Edward DeBartolo; GM: Eddie Johnston; Dir. Player Personnel: Ken Schinkel; Dir. Media Relations: Terry Schiffhauer; Coach: Bob Berry. Home ice: Civic Arena (16,033; 200′ × 85′). Colors: Black and gold. Training camp: Pittsburgh.

SCOUTING REPORT

OFFENSE: Mario Lemieux scored 100 points in his rookie year without a top-notch winger to play with. That tells you how good the kid is going to be. It also tells you what kind of shape this franchise is in.

For half the season, journeyman rookie Warren Young did fine with Lemieux, but he slumped so badly in the second half that one began to suspect there really was a good reason he was buried in the minors all those years. And now he's signed with Detroit.

Lemieux wound up playing with Gary Rissling and Jim McGeough. So you might say a winger, either side, any size, any shape, is a top Penguin priority. Actually, about five of them are needed, but in Pittsburgh, they know by now not to be greedy.

Adding Lemieux to Mike Bullard, who scored 51 goals in 1983-84, figured to make an excellent one-two, up-the-middle punch. But Bullard's production fell way off. With no other bona fide major-league talent, save possibly Doug Shedden, up front, the Penguins, who were only two games under .500 in mid-January, wound up improving only eight points on their sick 45 of the season before.

The irony is that just as Lemieux planted his skates and began to become more and more dominant, the rest of the Penguins were coming apart. There was no depth, and at the end, not much spirit. But at least the cornerstone, Lemieux, was in.

Troy Loney, a hulking left wing, may provide some badly-needed grit if he is skilled enough. John Chabot can be a good third-center type if he keeps his head on straight. The Penguins like both Roger Belanger, a late first-rounder in the 1984 draft, and Mark Teevens, a fourth-rounder who scored well in the OHL last year. Let's just say that they will be given every opportunity to win a job.

DEFENSE: Doug Bodger, the Penguins' second No. 1 draft pick, is going to be a good one. His play, too, fell off during the second half, but that's not unusual for an 18-year-old.

Otherwise, GM Eddie Johnston kept close watch on the waiver

Rookie of the Year Mario Lemieux scored 100 points.

wire. Until January, it looked like E.J. had really upgraded the Penguins' defense. Moe Mantha, who came with the pick that was used for Bodger in the Randy Carlyle deal with Winnipeg, gave Pittsburgh someone who could move the puck and Randy Hillier, picked up from Boston, had a pretty decent season.

Teams were no longer scoring at will on the Penguins. But 385 goals against, 20th worst in the league, indicates a lot of scoring. The goaltending, which Denis Herron had handled heroically

PENGUIN ROSTER

No.	Player	Pos.	Ht.	Wt.	Born	1984-85	G	A	Pts.	PIM
26	Wayne Babych	RW	5-11	191	6-6-58/Edmonton	Pittsburgh	20	34	54	35
24	Roger Belanger	C	6-0	188	12-1-65/Welland, Ont.	Pittsburgh	3	5	8	32
						Hamilton	3	3	6	0
33	Doug Bodger	D	6-2	200	6-18-66/Cheraimus, B.C.	Pittsburgh	5	26	31	67
	Phil Bourque	D	6-0	179	6-8-62/Chelmsford, Mass.	Baltimore	6	15	21	164
	Andy Brickley	LW	6-0	190	8-9-61/Melrose, Mass.	Pittsburgh	7	15	22	10
						Baltimore	13	14	27	8
22	Mike Bullard	C	5-10	185	3-10-61/Ottawa, Ont.	Pittsburgh	32	31	63	75
	Ted Bulley	LW	6-1	192	3-25-55/Windsor, Ont.	Baltimore	9	11	20	125
7	Rod Buskas	D	6-1	197	1-7-61/Wetaskiwin, Alta.	Pittsburgh	2	7	9	191
	John Chabot	C	6-2	195	5-18-62/Summerside, PEI	Mont.-Pitt.	9	51	60	14
27	Todd Charlesworth	D	6-1	191	3-22-65/Ottawa, Ont.	Pittsburgh	1	8	9	31
	Dean DeFazio	LW	5-11	185	4-16-63/Ottawa, Ont.	Baltimore	10	17	27	88
10	Bob Errey	LW	5-10	183	9-21-64/Montreal	Pittsburgh	0	2	2	7
						Baltimore	17	24	41	14
2	Greg Fox	D	6-2	190	8-12-53/Port McNeill, B.C.	Pittsburgh	2	5	7	26
						Baltimore	3	14	17	38
	Steve Gatzos	RW	5-11	182	6-22-61/Toronto	Pittsburgh	0	2	2	2
						Baltimore	26	13	39	55
13	Jim Hamilton	RW	6-0	180	1-18-57/Barrie, Ont.	Pittsburgh	2	1	3	0
						Baltimore	5	6	11	24
32	Dave Hannan	C	5-10	173	11-26-61/Sudbury, Ont.	Pittsburgh	6	7	13	43
						Baltimore	20	25	45	91
	Randy Hillier	D	6-0	180	3-20-60/Toronto	Pittsburgh	2	19	21	56
6	Greg Hotham	D	5-11	185	3-8-56/London, Ont.	Pittsburgh	0	2	2	4
						Baltimore	4	27	31	43
28	Tim Hrynewich	LW	5-11	187	10-2-63/Leamington, Ont.	Baltimore	4	3	7	31
19	Arto Javanainen	LW	6-3	183	4-8-59/Finland	Pittsburgh	4	1	5	2
						Baltimore	26	29	55	15
12	Mitch Lamoureaux	C	5-6	185	8-22-62/Ottawa, Ont.	Pittsburgh	11	8	19	53
						Baltimore	10	14	24	34
66	Mario Lemieux	C	6-4	200	10-5-65/Montreal	Pittsburgh	43	57	100	54
11	Troy Loney	LW	6-3	215	9-21-63/Bow Island, Alta.	Pittsburgh	10	8	18	59
						Baltimore	4	26	30	25
20	Moe Mantha	D	6-2	195	1-21-61/Lakewood, Ohio	Pittsburgh	11	40	51	54
5	Bryan Maxwell	D	6-2	198	9-7-55/North Bay, Ont.	Pittsburgh	0	8	8	57
						Baltimore	0	0	0	2
25	Kevin McCarthy	D	5-11	185	7-14-57/Winnipeg	Pittsburgh	9	10	19	30
	Joe McDonnell	D	6-2	195	5-11-61/Kitchener, Ont.	Pittsburgh	2	9	11	20
						Baltimore	7	27	34	22
16	Jim McGeough	LW	5-8	170	4-13-63/Regina, Sask.	Wash.-Pitt.	3	4	7	16
						Binghamton	32	21	53	26
4	Marty McSorley	D	6-1	189	5-18-63/Hamilton, Ont.	Pittsburgh	0	0	0	15
						Baltimore	6	24	30	154
	Tom O'Regan	C	5-10	182	12-29-61/Cambridge, Mass.	Baltimore	28	28	56	62
15	Gary Rissling	LW	5-9	175	8-1-56/Saskatoon, Sask.	Pittsburgh	10	9	19	209
						Baltimore	9	17	26	60
18	Tom Roulston	C	6-1	185	11-20-57/Winnipeg	Baltimore	31	39	70	48
	Mike Rowe	D	6-1	212	3-8-65/Kingston, Ont.	Pittsburgh	0	0	0	7
						Toronto (OHL)	17	34	51	202
	Grant Sasser	C	5-10	185	2-13-64/Portland, Ore.	Baltimore	5	7	12	12
3	Norm Schmidt	D	5-11	190	1-24-63/Sault Ste. Marie, Ont.	Baltimore	0	22	22	31
14	Dough Sheddan	C	6-0	185	4-26-61/Wallaceburg, Ont.	Pittsburgh	35	32	67	30
	Craig Simpson	C	6-2	185	2-15-67/London, Ont.	Mich. St. U.	31	53	84	—
	Mark Teevens	RW	6-0	178	6-17-66/Ottawa, Ont.	Peterborough	43	90	133	70
	Tim Tookey	LW	5-11	180	8-29-60/Edmonton	Baltimore	25	43	68	74
23	Wally Weir	D	6-2	205	6-3-54/Verdun, Que.	Que.-Pitt.	2	6	8	90
	Bennett Wolf	D	6-3	205	10-23-59/Kitchener, Ont.	Baltimore	0	8	8	285

No.	Player	Pos.	Ht.	Wt.	Born		GP	GA	SO	Avg.
29	Michel Dion	G	5-10	184	2-11-54/Granby, Que.	Pittsburgh	10	43	0	4.67
						Baltimore	21	65	0	3.49
31	Brian Ford	G	5-10	170	9-22-61/Edmonton	Pittsburgh	8	48	0	6.30
						Baltimore	6	21	0	3.47
1	Denis Herron	G	5-11	165	6-18-52/Chambly, Que.	Pittsburgh	42	170	1	4.65

when the club really hit the pits the season before, was not especially good last year. Coach Bob Berry turned more to rookie Roberto Romano, but at the end of the year Romano turned away from the Penguins. Saying his heart wasn't in a hockey career, he announced plans to retire. Johnston was trying to talk him out of it at press time.

OUTLOOK: The team is still in Pittsburgh. Lemieux looks like solid gold. Bodger looks like the kind of guy you can build a defense around. Attendance was up 3,000 per game. If center Craig Simpson, the third player taken in this year's draft, can make an immediate impact, the Penguins may be able to play an entire season of respectable hockey.

They still need a lot—is a goalie, three defensemen and about six forwards enough for you?—but the worst should be over. The organization is starting to look to Europe, is accepting Frenchmen and was even throwing some money at this year's class of college free agents.

They know not to expect too much too soon in Pittsburgh. Just little improvement and a lot of Mario may save the sport yet in the city.

PENGUIN PROFILES

MARIO LEMIEUX 20 6-4 200 Center

The franchise . . . Recorded the third-best rookie season in NHL history . . . The critics sniped all year long about his lazy streak and supposed attitude problem, but this was a 19-year-old kid who scored 43 goals and 57 assists for a weak team without a top-notch complementing winger . . . Criticized coach Bob Berry when he didn't feel he played enough or against the right line matchup . . . Was called the "laziest player in the league" by Canadian TV commentator Don Cherry . . . Picked up his intensity level as the season went along and became more and more dominant . . . The worst thing the Penguins could do is make his occasional outbursts of verbiage an issue. They have to hitch their buggy to this work-horse or the franchise will find a home in another city . . . Has the star's ego, has to get his points, but the losing bothers him . . . It's easy to forget this man-child is so young . . . Considered a future NHL superstar since he was 16 years old, he broke every Quebec League scoring record with the Laval Voisins . . . "He was so superior to the players he was playing with that it took away from his game," Berry says . . . Wears No. 66, Wayne

Gretzky's 99 upside down. "I don't want to be compared to Gretzky, just related," he says. "Also, it's good for publicity." ... Became the highest-paid rookie in NHL history ... Named the Most Valuable Player in the 1985 All-Star Game ... Born Oct. 5, 1965, in Montreal ... Won Calder Trophy as Rookie of the Year.

Year	Club	GP	G	A	Pts.
1984-85	Pittsburgh	73	43	57	100

DENIS HERRON 33 5-11 165   Goaltender

Generally did not play as well last year as when the team was absolutely defenseless in front of him in 1983-84, but he had his moments ... Still the best the Penguins have ... In his third tour of duty with Pittsburgh, which traded him to Kansas City in 1975 and Montreal in 1979 ... Personable veteran of 12 NHL seasons ... Shared the Vezina Trophy when with Montreal in 1980 ... Emaciated build ... Earlier in his career he went on milkshake diet to bulk up, but developed kidney stones and gave up ... Born June 18, 1952, in Chambly, Que.

Year	Club	GP	GA	SO	Avg.
1972-73	Pittsburgh	18	55	2	3.41
1973-74	Pittsburgh	5	18	0	4.15
1974-75	Pitt-KC	25	91	0	3.93
1975-76	Kansas City	64	243	0	4.03
1976-77	Pittsburgh	34	94	1	2.94
1977-78	Pittsburgh	60	210	0	3.57
1978-79	Pittsburgh	56	180	0	3.37
1979-80	Montreal	34	80	0	2.51
1980-81	Montreal	25	67	1	3.50
1981-82	Montreal	27	68	3	2.64
1982-83	Pittsburgh	31	151	1	5.31
1983-84	Pittsburgh	38	138	1	4.08
1984-85	Pittsburgh	42	170	1	4.65
	Totals	459	1565	10	3.69

DOUG BODGER 19 6-2 200   Defenseman

Penguins' second first-round pick in the 1984 draft and another excellent one ... Tailed off after an excellent start, but is quality goods ... A player the Penguins can build their defense around ... Strong, mobile, good playmaker, he'll get better as the team around him improves ... Broke 90 points twice in two years with Kamloops of Western League ... Acquired as part of deal sending Randy Carlyle to Winnipeg for Jets' first-round choice in '84 entry draft and Moe Mantha ... Born June 18, 1966, in Chermainus, B.C.

Year	Club	GP	G	A	Pts.
1984-85	Pittsburgh	65	5	26	31

MIKE BULLARD 24 5-10 185   Center

Gifted goal scorer, had 51 in 1983-84, but slid back to 32 last year as the trade rumors swirled ... Suspended in 1984 for breaking curfew ... Penguins are worried about his lack of off-ice discipline ... First choice (ninth overall) in 1980 draft ... Scored 150 points in predraft season at Brantford ... Holds club record for goals by a rookie (36) ... Most notable goal was the one that broke the Islanders' 15-game winning streak in February 1982 ... Born March 10, 1961, in Ottawa.

Year	Club	GP	G	A	Pts.
1980-81	Pittsburgh	15	1	2	3
1981-82	Pittsburgh	75	36	27	63
1982-83	Pittsburgh	57	22	22	44
1983-84	Pittsburgh	76	51	41	92
1984-85	Pittsburgh	68	32	31	63
	Totals	291	142	123	265

JOHN CHABOT 23 6-2 195   Center

Excellent addition last year in a November trade that sent Ron Flockhart to Montreal ... Rangy, good checker and scorer, too ... Like a lot of Penguins, his play deteriorated in the second half of the season ... Canadiens' third pick in the 1980 draft ... Led the Quebec League in assists in 1981-82 ... Played one year on the Habs' farm at Nova Scotia before being promoted to the parent team... Played for coach Bob Berry with the Canadiens, and Berry pushed for him when Montreal inquired about Flockhart... Born May 18, 1962, in Summerside, P.E.I.

Year	Club	GP	G	A	Pts.
1983-84	Montreal............	56	18	25	43
1984-85	Mont-Pitt..........	77	9	51	60
	Totals.............	133	27	76	103

MOE MANTHA 24 6-2 195   Defenseman

Upgraded the Penguin defense after being acquired from Winnipeg ... Moves the puck well, but not the most intense player in the league... Slumped in the second half. This is a recording... Father, Moe Sr., a former NHL defenseman, is a member of Canadian parliament... An American, he was born Jan. 21, 1961, in Lakewood, Ohio, when his dad was playing for the Cleveland Barons... Was the throw-in on the deal that sent Randy Carlyle to Winnipeg for the No. 1 pick the Pens used for Doug Bodger ... Second-round pick by the Jets in 1980.

Year	Club	GP	G	A	Pts.
1980-81	Winnipeg...........	58	2	23	25
1981-82	Winnipeg..........	25	0	12	12
1982-83	Winnipeg.........	21	2	7	9
1983-84	Winnipeg..........	72	16	38	54
1984-85	Pittsburgh.........	71	11	40	51
	Totals.............	247	31	120	151

DOUG SHEDDEN 24 6-0 185   Right Wing

Missed 13 games in 1983-84 with a broken wrist and struggled much of the rest of the season... Bounced back to score 35 goals last year... Good wrist shot but not particularly aggressive or physical... Fifth-round pick in 1980... Led team in scoring in 1982-83... Only true goal-scoring winger the Penguins have... Wasn't used much with Lemieux because of defensive shortcomings ... Had one of the worst minuses in the league last year, 50 ... Born April 19, 1961, in Wallaceburg, Ont.

Year	Club	GP	G	A	Pts.
1981-82	Pittsburgh	38	10	15	25
1982-83	Pittsburgh	80	24	43	67
1984-85	Pittsburgh	80	35	32	67
	Totals	198	69	90	159

RANDY HILLIER 25 6-0 180   **Defenseman**
Gives the Penguins a steady hand as they try to upgrade their defense ... Acquired from Boston for a fourth-round draft pick in 1984 ... He got his first shot in the NHL early in 1982 when the Bruins called him up as a replacement for an injured Mike Milbury ... Missed time last year with two separate shoulder injuries ... More nights than not, he did a competent job ... Played junior hockey in Sudbury ... Fourth-round pick by Boston in 1980 ... Born March 30, 1960, in Toronto.

Year	Club	GP	G	A	Pts.
1981-82	Boston	25	0	8	8
1982-83	Boston	70	0	10	10
1983-84	Boston	69	3	12	15
1984-85	Pittsburgh	45	2	19	21
	Totals	209	5	49	54

TROY LONEY 22 6-3 215   **Left Wing**
One of the few Penguins who continued to play hard as the team came apart the last two months of the season ... Big and strong and appeared to be developing a modicum of touch around the net ... Third-round pick in 1982 ... Played on a junior line at Lethbridge, Alberta with the Flyers' Rich and Ron Sutter ... Character player and these are in short supply in Pittsburgh ... So, almost since the franchise's birth, have been left wings ... This is a guy the club is really counting on ... Born Sept. 21, 1963, on Bow Island, Alta.

Year	Club	GP	G	A	Pts.
1983-84	Pittsburgh	13	0	0	0
1984-85	Pittsburgh	46	10	8	18
	Totals	59	10	8	18

COACH BOB BERRY: Signed on with the Penguins after being fired by Montreal late in the 1983-84 season ... Began NHL coaching career with Los Angeles, took the Kings to a surprising 43-24-13 record in 1980-81 ... Unable to get along with then-Kings GM George Maguire, he quit to take the Canadiens' job ... Came up in the Canadien organization but played the bulk of his nine NHL seasons in Los Angeles ... Began his coaching career with the Kings' AHL farm team in Springfield, Mass ... Disciplinarian, no-nonsense type ... Seemed to appreciate the less pressurized atmosphere in Pittsburgh but was frustrated by several attitude problems left over from a long-time loser ... A native of Montreal, he was born Nov. 29, 1943.

MOST COLORFUL PLAYER

Until Mario Lemieux came along, this franchise has never had a true drawing card. But it did have its share of personalities.

None was any stronger than Bryan Watson. A hard worker of modest skills, he asked no quarter and gave none over 16 NHL seasons. With 2,212 penalty minutes, he still ranks third on the NHL's all-time list of badmen.

Watson played in six different cities before hanging it up in 1978, but his best years were with the Penguins. He was a leader on the 1969-70 club, one of the few who captured the city's imagination. He helped the Penguins, who had not made the playoffs their first two years in the NHL, to a second-place Western Division finish, a first-round sweep of Oakland and a hard-fought six-game loss to heavily favored St. Louis in the semifinals.

Penguin lore is a little more than a short story, but Watson's ongoing battles with St. Louis' Plager brothers would regularly fill the Civic Arena when the Blues visited.

"Bugsy" started more on-ice riots than he finished and his scarred face suggested that he lost more battles than he won, but he was not deterred by failure. "I try hard, that's all," he would say.

All the while he represented his teams and the league in an exemplary fashion off the ice, donating countless hours to working with the mentally retarded.

ALL-TIME PENGUIN LEADERS

GOALS: Rick Kehoe, 55, 1980-81
ASSISTS: Syl Apps, 67, 1975-76
  Randy Carlyle, 67, 1980-81
POINTS: Pierre Larouche, 111, 1975-76
SHUTOUTS: Les Binkley, 6, 1967-68

Rick Kehoe retired with Penguins' single-season goal mark.

QUEBEC NORDIQUES

TEAM DIRECTORY; Pres.: Marcel Aubut; GM: Maurice Filion; Dir. Communications: Bernard Brisset; Coach: Michel Bergeron. Home ice: Quebec Coliseum (15,153; 200′ × 85′). Training camp: Quebec City.

SCOUTING REPORT

OFFENSE: Next to Edmonton, no team scares opponents with a high-powered offense as much as the Nordiques.

Quebec has every ingredient needed to score goals: skating speed, accurate shooting, players who work beautifully together, and spectacular passing.

Michel Goulet had third 50-goal season in a row.

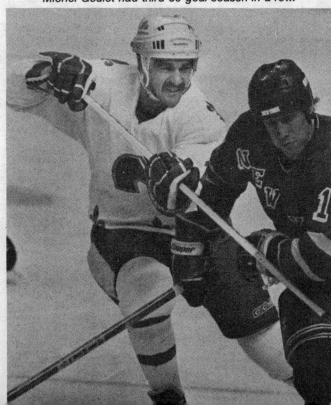

So why did Quebec's potentially overpowering power play malfunction so often last season? It ranked a mediocre 17th in the 21-team NHL. With the offense the Nordiques have, they should rank near the top in power-play efficiency.

One of the reasons for the power-play failure is the lack of a gifted pointman among their defensemen to direct the power-play attack, a player with the skills of Boston's Ray Bourque, the Islanders' Denis Potvin, a defenseman like Edmonton's Paul Coffey. A young defenseman, Bruce Bell, showed promise as a power-play pointman last season. The acquisition of Brad Maxwell from Minnesota helped, too.

Peter Stastny and Michel Goulet are two of the most dominant scorers in the NHL. Stastny's brother, Anton, is another scoring threat. The third Stastny brother, Marian, had a disappointing 1984-85 season and was waived. J.F. Sauve has the speed to develop into another game-breaking goal-scorer. Brent Ashton was a throw-in when the Nordiques acquired Maxwell from Minnesota. Ashton proved his scoring ability had been underestimated by his previous teams, New Jersey and Minnesota, as he became a consistent goal-scorer once he put on a Quebec uniform.

American-born Mark Kumpel established himself last season. Alain Cote, one of the best defensive forwards and backcheckers in the NHL, proved in the playoffs he can score goals, too.

DEFENSE: Quebec once had to score six, seven or even eight goals to win a game. It was all-offense, no defense with Quebec. The scores often resembled baseball or lacrosse scores.

That changed last season. Coach Michel Bergeron insisted that the Nordiques check as well as score goals. They did. They surrendered 275 goals, their lowest goals-against total since entering the NHL six years ago. They reduced giveaways which often led to opponents' scoring chances. It was a team effort, team defense, the forwards as well as defensemen concentrating harder on preventing opponents from scoring.

Pat Price had his best season as an NHL defenseman, blocking shots and bodychecking with gusto. Mario Marois, Randy Moller, Normand Rochefort, Maxwell and Bell helped give the Nordiques a better unit of defensemen.

The goaltending was improved, too, with rookie Mario (Goose) Gosselin. He took over from veteran No. 1 goalie Daniel Bouchard and established himself as one of the NHL's best young goalies.

OUTLOOK: Quebec always had the offense. Now it has the defense. The Nordiques look like the best team in the Adams Division this season.

NORDIQUE ROSTER

No.	Player	Pos.	Ht.	Wt.	Born	1984-85	G	A	Pts.	PIM
9	Brent Ashton	LW	6-1	210	5-18-60/Saskatoon, Sask.	Minn.-Que.	31	31	62	53
6	Bruce Bell	D	5-11	180	2-15-65/Toronto	Quebec	6	31	37	44
19	Alain Cote	LW	5-10	205	5-3-47/Matone, Que.	Quebec	13	22	35	31
2	Gord Donnelly	D	6-3	195	4-5-62/Montreal	Quebec	0	0	0	33
						Fredericton	1	5	6	134
24	Jean-Marc Gaulin	LW	6-1	185	3-3-62/West Germany	Quebec	3	3	6	8
						Fredericton	10	9	19	32
23	Paul Gillis	C	5-11	191	12-31-63/Toronto	Quebec	14	28	42	168
16	Michel Goulet	LW	6-1	185	4-21-60/Perihonqua, Que.	Quebec	55	40	95	55
12	Wayne Groulx	C	5-9	176	2-2-65/Welland, Ont.	Quebec	0	0	0	0
						Sault Ste. Marie	59	85	144	102
32	Dale Hunter	C	5-9	190	7-31-60/Oil Springs, Ont.	Quebec	20	52	72	209
	Mike Hough	RW	6-1	190	2-6-63/Montreal	Fredericton	21	27	48	49
17	Mark Kumpel	RW	6-0	190	3-7-61/Wakefield, Mass.	Quebec	8	7	15	26
						Fredericton	9	6	15	17
	Dave Latta	LW	6-0	181	1-3-67/Thunder Bay, Ont.	Kitchener	38	27	65	26
14	Alain Lemieux	C	6-0	185	5-29-61/Montreal	St. L.-Que.	15	13	28	12
10	Jim Mann	RW	6-0	200	4-17-59/Montreal	Quebec	0	4	4	54
						Fredericton	4	4	8	97
22	Mario Marois	D	5-11	190	12-15-57/Lovette, Que.	Quebec	66	37	43	91
4	Brad Maxwell	D	6-2	197	7-7-57/Brandon, Man.	Quebec	10	31	41	172
21	Randy Moller	D	6-2	205	8-30-63/Calgary	Quebec	7	22	29	120
27	Wilf Paiement	RW	6-1	210	10-16-55/Earlton, Ont.	Quebec	23	28	51	165
7	Pat Price	D	6-2	195	3-24-55/Nelson, B.C.	Quebec	1	26	27	118
5	Normand Rochefort	D	6-1	200	1-28-61/Three Rivers, Que.	Quebec	3	21	24	74
15	J.F. Sauve	C	5-6	175	1-23-60/St. Genevieve, Que.	Quebec	13	29	42	21
11	Andre Savard	C	6-0	180	2-9-53/Tamiskaming, Que.	Quebec	9	10	19	8
20	Anton Stastny	LW	6-0	185	8-5-59/Czechoslovakia	Quebec	38	42	80	30
26	Peter Stastny	C	6-1	195	9-18-56/Czechoslovakia	Quebec	32	68	100	95
	Trevor Stienberg	RW	6-1	180	5-13-66/Moscow, Ont.	Guel.-Lon.	16	23	39	83
	Tom Thornbury	D	5-11	175	3-17-63/Lindsay, Ont.	Balt.-Fred.	15	28	43	47
25	Blake Wesley	D	6-1	200	7-10-59/Red Deer, Alta.	Quebec	0	2	2	28
						Fredericton	3	4	7	80

No.	Player	Pos.	Ht.	Wt.	Born		GP	GA	SO	Avg.
35	Danny Bouchard	G	6-0	190	12-12-50/Val D'Or, Que.	Quebec	30	103	0	3.44
33	Mario Gosselin	G	5-8	160	6-15-63/Thetford, Mines, Que.	Quebec	35	109	1	3.34
30	Clint Malarchuk	G	5-10	170	5-1-61/Edmonton	Fredericton	56	198	2	3.55
1	Richard Sevigny	G	5-8	172	4-11-57/Montreal	Quebec	20	62	1	3.37

NORDIQUE PROFILES

PETER STASTNY 29 6-1 195   Center
"All you have to do is look at him on ice, see the way he moves, watch all the things he does and you know he's a hockey player—a great one," said former star Gordie Howe...Has scored 100 or more in each of five NHL seasons since defecting from his native Czechoslovakia..."With the puck, he's the most dangerous player in the game in the offensive zone," said former Ranger coach Herb Brooks...Born Sept. 18, 1956, in Bratislava, Czechoslovakia ...Has become a Canadian citizen...Exceptional skater, puck-handler, shooter...Classic center who makes difficult plays look easy.

Year	Club	GP	G	A	Pts.
1980-81	Quebec............	77	39	70	109
1981-82	Quebec............	80	46	93	139
1982-83	Quebec............	75	47	77	124
1983-84	Quebec............	80	46	73	119
1984-85	Quebec............	75	32	68	100
	Totals............	387	210	381	591

MICHEL GOULET 25 6-1 185   Left Wing
Has scored 57, 56, 55 goals in last three seasons...Best left wing in NHL...Led Nordiques with 17 power-play goals last season, six winning goals, second only to Peter Stastny's nine game-winning shots...Made pro debut at 18 with WHA Birmingham Bulls...An NHL All-Star...Born April 21, 1960, in Peribonqua, Quebec...A threat to score from almost any position inside offensive zone...Has quick wrist shot...Scores many goals from close to net...Able to break free from defenders and drive to net for shots...Injury prevented him from registering third straight 100-point season in 1984–85.

Year	Club	GP	G	A	Pts.
1978-79	Birmingham (WHA) ..	78	28	30	58
1979-80	Quebec............	77	22	32	54
1980-81	Quebec............	76	32	39	71
1981-82	Quebec............	80	42	42	84
1982-83	Quebec............	80	57	48	105
1983-84	Quebec............	75	56	65	121
1984-85	Quebec............	69	55	40	95
	NHL Totals.........	457	264	266	530
	WHA Totals	78	28	30	58

ANTON STASTNY 26 6-0 185   Left Wing

Left wing brother of Peter Stastny had strong 80-point season in 1984–85 after subpar 1983–84 . . . Plays with emotion . . . Skates with several changes of speed—all fast . . . Like brothers Peter and Marian, he defected from Czechoslovakia to play hockey in North America . . . Born Aug. 5, 1959, in Bratislava, Czechoslovakia . . . Has averaged point-a-game since entering NHL in 1980 . . . Capable of playing effectively in straight-ahead, up-and-down style of play or weaving, criss-crossing European style . . . Smart player who knows how to get himself in perfect position for shots and passes.

Year	Club	GP	G	A	Pts.
1980-81	Quebec............	80	39	46	85
1981-82	Quebec............	68	26	46	72
1982-83	Quebec............	79	32	60	92
1983-84	Quebec............	69	25	37	62
1984-85	Quebec............	79	38	42	80
	Totals............	375	160	231	391

BRENT ASHTON 25 6-1 210   Left Wing

Nordiques never expected husky left wing would do what he did after trade last season with Minnesota . . . Defenseman Brad Maxwell was player Nordiques wanted most in trade . . . Ashton was a throw-in . . . Became a goal-scoring machine: 27 goals, 24 assists, 51 points in 49 games in Quebec light-blue-and-white uniform . . . Vancouver Canucks, New Jersey Devils, Minnesota North Stars know now they made mistake by failing to recognize Ashton's ability as scorer . . . North Stars mistakenly limited his role to spare forward and checker . . . Born May 18, 1960, in Saskatoon, Sask. . . . Next goal will be 100th of his NHL career.

Year	Club	GP	G	A	Pts.
1979-80	Vanouver	47	5	14	19
1980-81	Vancouver	77	18	11	29
1981-82	Colorado	80	24	36	60
1982-83	New Jersey	76	14	19	33
1983-84	Minnesota	68	7	10	17
1984-85	Minn-Que..........	78	31	31	62
	Totals............	426	99	121	220

WILF PAIEMENT 29 6-1 210   Right Wing

Made NHL debut as 18-year-old right wing with old Kansas City Scouts in 1974 . . . Still going strong . . . Plays fiercely aggressive hockey . . . Willing to fight . . . Does not hesitate to use his stick

on various parts of rivals' bodies ... Two-time 40-goal scorer ...
Has scored 323 goals, spent 1,452 minutes in NHL penalty boxes
... Born Oct. 16, 1955, in Earlton, Ont. ... One of the strongest
players in NHL ... Doesn't mind playing in heavy traffic in slot
or close to net ... An old-school hockey player who combines
skill with toughness and highly competitive attitude.

Year	Club	GP	G	A	Pts.
1974-75	Kansas City	78	26	13	39
1975-76	Kansas City	57	21	22	43
1976-77	Colorado	78	41	40	81
1977-78	Colorado	80	31	56	87
1978-79	Colorado	65	24	36	60
1979-80	Col-Tor	75	30	44	74
1980-81	Toronto	77	40	57	97
1981-82	Tor-Que	77	25	46	71
1982-83	Quebec	80	26	38	64
1983-84	Quebec	80	39	37	76
1984-85	Quebec	68	23	28	51
	Totals	815	326	417	743

DALE HUNTER 25 5-9 190   Center

Brothers Dave and Mark play for Edmonton and Montreal, respectively ... A grinder who gets results the old-fashioned way—
by hard work ... Tough, two-fisted approach to hockey has resulted in 1,145 penalty minutes in first five NHL seasons ...
Durable player who has missed playing in only three games (a
suspension) in five NHL seasons ... Born July 31, 1960, in Pe-
trolia, Ont. ... Strong forechecker ... Good play-making center
not afraid to take a hit to make a play ... Willing to give and take
considerable body contact ... Plays with super-charged emotion.

Year	Club	GP	G	A	Pts.
1980-81	Quebec	80	19	44	63
1981-82	Quebec	80	22	50	72
1982-83	Quebec	80	17	46	63
1983-84	Quebec	77	24	55	79
1984-85	Quebec	80	20	52	72
	Totals	397	102	247	349

MARIO MAROIS 27 5-11 190   Defenseman

One of many players who have excelled for other teams after being
traded by New York Rangers ... Has learned to control his temper,
play with discipline, reduce tendency for committing needless

penalties . . . Named Quebec captain in 1983 . . . Equalled personal scoring high last season with 43 points . . . Cut down on penalty minutes but still plays an aggressive game . . . Born Dec. 15, 1957, in Ancienne Lorette, Que. . . . Good-natured athlete off the ice . . . Has 1,007 penalty minutes in nine years in NHL . . . Credits former defenseman Carol Vadnais for helping him improve his game when they were Ranger teammates.

Year	Club	GP	G	A	Pts.
1977-78	New York R	8	1	1	2
1978-79	New York R	71	5	26	31
1979-80	New York R	79	8	23	31
1980-81	NYR-Van-Que	69	5	21	26
1981-82	Quebec	71	11	32	43
1982-83	Quebec	36	2	12	14
1983-84	Quebec	80	13	36	49
1984-85	Quebec	76	6	37	43
	Totals	490	51	188	239

PAT PRICE 30 6-2 195   **Defenseman**

Finally developed into valuable defenseman and gained recognition for his play last season . . . "He's made himself into a pretty good defenseman," said legendary Gordie Howe . . . Had an outstanding playoff last season as shot-blocking defensive defenseman . . . Set up goal which enabled Nordiques to clinch playoff series with arch-rival Montreal . . . Born March 24, 1955, in Nelson, B.C. . . . Hard-hitter . . . Not unwilling to mix it up and fight . . . Played for Islanders, Edmonton, Pittsburgh before joining Quebec . . . Nicknamed "Pricy" and "Woodchuck" . . . Friendly, outgoing athlete . . . Not afraid to speak his mind . . . One of the best media interviews in NHL.

Year	Club	GP	G	A	Pts.
1974-75	Vancouver (WHA)	69	5	29	34
1975-76	New York I	4	0	2	2
1976-77	New York I	71	3	22	25
1977-78	New York I	52	2	10	12
1978-79	New York I	55	3	11	14
1979-80	Edmonton	75	11	21	32
1980-81	Edmonton	59	8	24	32
1980-81	Pittsburgh	13	0	10	10
1981-82	Pittsburgh	77	7	31	38
1982-83	Pittsburgh	38	1	11	12
1982-83	Quebec	14	1	2	3
1983-84	Quebec	72	3	25	28
1984-85	Quebec	60	0	23	23
	NHL Totals	590	39	192	231
	WHA Totals	69	5	29	34

MARIO GOSSELIN 22 5-8 160 **Goaltender**

"Goose" . . . Took No. 1 goaltending job away from veteran Daniel Bouchard last season . . . Staged a superb goaltending performance in playoffs . . . Colorful personality off the ice . . . Colorful, acrobatic style of goaltending . . . Plays angles well and leaves little open net for shooters trying to place puck . . . Works himself up to highly competitive state of mind before game . . . Likes to regard game as a personal challenge between two goalies . . . Born June 15, 1963, in Thetford Mines, Que. . . . Played for 1984 Canadian Olympic team in Sarajevo . . . Shut out St. Louis on Feb. 26, 1984, in first NHL game.

Year	Club	GP	GA	SO	Avg.
1983-84	Quebec............	3	3	1	1.21
1984-85	Quebec............	35	109	1	3.34
	Totals............	36	112	2	3.19

ALAIN COTE 28 5-10 205 **Left Wing**

One of hockey's best defensive players . . . If there were an All-Star backchecking team, he'd be on it . . . Picks up the man he's assigned the instant the opposing team goes on the attack . . . Stays close to him from one end of the ice to the other . . . "In my mind, he's the best defensive forward in the league," said teammate Pat Price . . . Born May 3, 1957, in Matane, Que. . . . Career with Nordiques dates to 1977 in WHA . . . Seldom gets the recognition he deserves outside of Quebec . . . Could be the best penalty-killing forward in hockey . . . Sacrifices personal glory as goal-scorer for welfare of team . . . Scored several important goals in last season's playoffs.

Year	Club	GP	G	A	Pts.
1977-78	Quebec (WHA)	27	3	5	8
1978-79	Quebec (WHA)	79	14	13	27
1979-80	Quebec............	41	5	11	16
1980-81	Quebec............	51	8	18	26
1981-82	Quebec............	79	15	16	31
1982-83	Quebec............	79	12	28	40
1983-84	Quebec............	77	19	24	43
1984-85	Quebec............	80	13	22	35
	NHL Totals	407	72	119	191
	WHA Totals	106	17	18	35

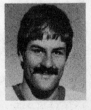

COACH MICHEL BERGERON: Le Tigre of Quebec . . . Nick-named "Tiger" for his bold, intense coaching personality . . . Has developed running feud with Jacques Lemaire, coach of arch-rival Canadiens . . . Not afraid to speak his mind when he dislikes other teams' tactics or a referee's decision . . . Always chews gum behind the bench . . . Glib and sometimes outrageous in his postgame chats with media . . . Born June 12, 1946, in Montreal . . . Coaching peers respect his tactical moves . . . Able to make effectively quick adjustments in strategy during games . . . Has turned all-offensive, no-defense Nordiques into hard-working defensive team . . . Has not had a losing record in five seasons as Quebec coach . . . His teams have 179-152-63 record . . . "We think he has outstanding qualities in every area of coaching," says Nordiques' team president Marcel Aubut. "He's a great motivator of players."

MOST COLORFUL PLAYER

Gordie Howe was watching the Quebec Nordiques in pregame warmups before a playoff game last season. He kept his eyes trained on the player wearing No. 26.

"You can tell he's a hockey player just by looking at him, the way he stands, the way he moves, the way he makes all the little things look so easy to do," said Howe.

Howe, the highest scorer in hockey history, was talking about Peter Stastny, the Nordiques' marvelously gifted center who defected from his native Czechoslovakia to come to North America to play hockey.

"Peter's the perfect hockey player," said teammate Pat Price. "Watch him and you'll see greatness in everything he does and how hockey should be played."

ALL-TIME NORDIQUE LEADERS

GOALS: Real Cloutier, 75, 1978-79
ASSISTS: Peter Stastny, 93, 1981-82
POINTS: Marc Tardif, 154, 1977-78
SHUTOUTS: Richard Brodeur, 3, 1978-79
Jim Corsi, 3, 1978-79

WASHINGTON CAPITALS

TEAM DIRECTORY: Chairman-Pres.: Abe Pollin; VP/GM: David Poile; Dir. Pub. Rel.: Lou Corletto; Coach: Bryan Murray. Home ice: Capital Centre (18,130; 200′ × 85′). Colors: Red, white and blue. Training camp: Washington, D.C.

SCOUTING REPORT

OFFENSE: Two real gamebreakers and a cast of thousands who get their points off transition mistakes. Still, it wasn't enough to get past the Islanders in the first round last year. So GM David Poile continues his search for the two forwards who are probably needed to put his team over the top.

The Caps could use one big, grinding forward plus another one who can put the puck in the net 40 times a year. Mike Gartner, who scored 50 goals last year and Bob Carpenter, who emerged as one of the league's best centers, are as dynamic as they come.

Bob Carpenter: First U.S. player to score 50 goals.

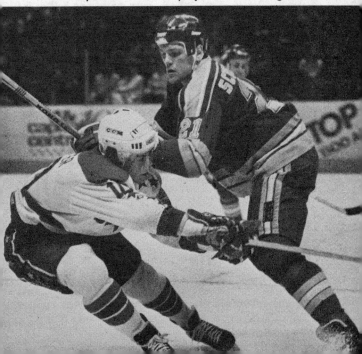

If Bengt Gustafsson, who missed 29 games last year, is healthy, it will help.

Dave Christian didn't quite have the year he had in 1983-84, but has that two-way effectiveness and quickness that has become this club's trademark. So do Craig Laughlin, Alan Haworth and Gaeten Duchesne, but it appears Washington has progressed as far as it can with these kinds of guys. They are all fine complimenting players, but to get past the Flyers and Oilers, the Caps need a couple more heavyweights.

DEFENSE: Very good. Rod Langway, a two-time Norris Trophy winner, is a tower of strength and leadership and 21-year-old Scott Stevens is entering his fourth season, already one of the best in the league.

Larry Murphy doesn't score like he did in his rookie year in Los Angeles, but has become a much more effective player both ways. The Caps got a pretty good year out of Darren Veitch and the team concept made Timo Blomqvust and retread Mike McEwen functional. Kevin Hatcher, the No. 1 pick in 1983, is a fine prospect who should upgrade this group even further.

Goalie Pat Riggin slumped badly over the second half of the season and the feeling persists the Caps are looking for something better. They've gotten good mileage out of Al Jensen the last three years when he's been healthy.

A lot of teams make do with a lot worse in goal, but a good reason the Flyers overhauled the Caps down the stretch was that Washington didn't have a Pelle Lindbergh.

OUTLOOK: The Caps might be the third-best team in the league, but the Flyers have come so far so fast, it's going to be hard for Washington to get out of the divisional playoffs.

All the moves Poile has made in his three years running this team have been the right ones. But without a blue-chip scoring prospect in the organization, the next step will prove to be the most difficult.

CAPITAL PROFILES

BOBBY CARPENTER 22 6-1 190   **Center**
Blossomed into a full-fledged star in 1984-85 . . . Became the first American player ever to score 50 goals . . . Highly-touted prep star at St. John's of Danvers, Mass., subject of a *Sports Illustrated* cover story before his draft year . . . Third player taken in the 1981

CAPITAL ROSTER

No.	Player	Pos.	Ht.	Wt.	Born	1984-85	G	A	Pts.	PIM
22	Greg Adams	LW	6-1	190	5-31-80/Duncan, B.C.	Binghamton	9	16	25	58
						Washington	6	12	18	72
19	Peter Andersson	D	6-2	200	3-2-61/Sweden	Washington	0	10	10	21
						Binghamton	2	3	5	6
17	Timo Blomqvist	D	6-0	198	1-23-61/Finland	Washington	1	4	5	51
10	Bob Carpenter	C	6-1	190	7-13-63/Beverley, Mass.	Washington	53	42	95	87
	Marc Chorney	D	6-0	200	11-8-59/Edmonton	Binghamton	4	25	29	38
27	Dave Christian	C	5-11	170	5-12-59/Warroad, Minn.	Washington	26	43	69	14
12	Glen Currie	C	6-2	180	7-18-58/Montreal	Washington	1	5	6	19
						Binghamton	1	5	6	6
14	Gaetan Duchesne	LW	5-11	195	7-11-62/Quebec City, Que.	Washington	15	23	38	32
24	Bryan Erickson	LW	5-9	170	3-7-60/Roseau, Minn.	Washington	15	13	28	23
						Binghamton	6	11	17	8
32	Lou Franceschetti	LW	5-11	180	3-28-58/Toronto	Washington	4	7	11	45
						Binghamton	29	43	72	75
11	Mike Gartner	RW	6-0	185	10-29-59/Ottawa, Ont.	Washington	50	52	102	71
16	Bengt Gustafsson	C	6-0	190	3-23-58/Sweden	Washington	14	29	43	8
23	Bob Gould	RW	5-11	195	9-2-57/Petrolia, Ont.	Washington	14	19	33	69
4	Kevin Hatcher	D	6-3	183	9-9-66/Sterling Hgts., Mich.	Washington	1	0	1	0
						North Bay	26	37	63	75
15	Alan Haworth	LW	5-10	188	9-11-60/Drummondville, Que.	Washington	23	26	49	48
21	Andre Hidi	C	6-2	203	6-5-60/Toronto	Washington	2	1	3	9
						Binghamton	12	17	29	57
25	Doug Jarvis	C	5-9	170	3-24-55/Brantford, Ont.	Washington	9	28	37	32
	Dave Jensen	LW	5-10	180	8-19-65/Needham, Mass.	Hartford	0	4	4	6
						Binghamton	8	9	17	2
5	Rod Langway	D	6-3	215	5-3-57/Taiwan	Washington	4	22	26	54
18	Craig Laughlin	RW	5-11	198	9-19-57/Toronto	Washington	16	34	50	38
34	Mikko Leinenen	RW	6-0	175	7-15-55/Finland	Washington	0	1	1	2
2	Mike McEwen	D	6-1	185	8-10-56/Hornepayne, Ont.	Washington	11	27	38	42
						Binghamton	2	10	12	14
8	Larry Murphy	D	6-0	200	3-8-61/Scarborough, Ont.	Washington	13	42	55	51
	Graeme Nicolson	D	6-0	188	1-13-58/North Bay, Ont.	Binghamton	3	9	12	53
20	Gary Sampson	RW	6-0	190	8-24-59/Atkokan, Ont.	Washington	10	15	25	13
						Binghamton	2	2	4	2
	Mike Siltala	LW	5-9	170	8-5-63/Toronto	Binghamton	42	36	78	53
3	Scott Stevens	D	5-11	200	4-1-64/Kitchener, Ont.	Washington	21	44	65	221
28	Mark Taylor	C	5-11	190	6-1-58/Vancouver	Pitt.-Wash.	8	11	19	21
6	Darren Veitch	D	6-0	188	4-24-60/Saskatoon, Sask.	Washington	3	18	21	37

No.	Player	Pos.	Ht.	Wt.	Born	1984-85	GP	GA	SO	Avg.
35	Al Jensen	G	5-10	180	11-27-58/Hamilton, Ont.	Washington	14	34	1	2.54
						Binghamton	3	9	0	3.00
31	Bob Mason	G	6-1	180	4-22-61/International Falls, Ont.	Washington	12	31	1	2.81
						Binghamton	20	58	1	3.31
1	Pat Riggin	G	5-9	170	5-26-59/Kincardine, Ont.	Washington	57	168	2	2.98

draft, the highest an American had ever been selected... Turned down a scholarship at Providence University to immediately turn pro... Played 80 games as an 18-year-old and scored 67 points on a bad team... When Bryan Murray took over as coach, he moved Carpenter to left wing and cut back on his ice time. "He wasn't a star," Murray said. "He was a kid. So the first thing I did was take him off the big line and make defensive responsibilities easier."... Carpenter didn't like it, said so, but Murray continued to bring him along slowly... Finally last year, his fourth in the NHL, the streaky center became a night-in, night-out force ... Has filled out 16 pounds since coming into the NHL... Has not missed a game in his four seasons in the league... Greatly improved defensively... Born July 13, 1963, in Beverly, Mass.

Year	Club	GP	G	A	Pts.
1981-82	Washington	80	32	35	67
1982-83	Washington	80	32	37	69
1983-84	Washington	80	28	40	68
1984-85	Washington	80	50	52	102
	Totals	320	142	164	306

BENGT GUSTAFFSON 27 6-0 190   Right Wing

Extraordinarily talented performer whose production last year was limited by a series of injuries... Missed 29 games... Magician with the puck, strong defensive player... Born March 23, 1958, in Karlskoga, Sweden... Caps' fourth pick in 1978, but didn't turn pro right away and eventually signed a contract and played with Edmonton of WHA... Caps appealed to the league office when the Oilers joined the NHL in 1979, and despite the fact that Edmonton had made Gustaffson one of their two protected players (as called for in the merger agreement), the Caps were awarded his services... Fine performance in the 1984 Canada Cup as Sweden won a surprising berth in the finals... Scored five goals in a game against Philadelphia in 1984.

Year	Club	GP	G	A	Pts.
1979-80	Washington	80	22	38	60
1980-81	Washington	72	21	34	55
1981-82	Washington	70	26	34	60
1982-83	Washington	67	22	42	64
1983-84	Washington	69	32	43	75
1984-85	Washington	51	14	29	43
	Totals	409	137	220	357

MIKE GARTNER 25 6-0 185   Right Wing

One of the NHL's flashiest and most effective goal-scorers . . . Reached 50 last year for the first time in his six NHL seasons . . . Dynamic presence cutting off the wing, excellent speed and bazooka shot . . . Fourth player taken in the 1979 draft after turning pro at age 19 with Cincinnati of the WHA . . . Takes a hit and gives one as well . . . Articulate spokesman . . . Member of the Felowship of Christian Athletes . . . He and Carpenter were the first building blocks that turned a sorry franchise into a power . . . Member of the Canada's 1984 Canada Cup championship team . . . Born Oct. 29, 1959, in Ottawa.

Year	Club	GP	G	A	Pts.
1978-79	Cincinnati(WHA)	78	27	25	52
1979-80	Washington	77	36	32	68
1980-81	Washington	80	48	46	94
1981-82	Washington	80	35	45	80
1982-83	Washington	73	38	38	76
1983-84	Washington	80	40	45	85
1984-85	Washington	80	50	52	102
	NHL Totals	470	247	258	505
	WHA Totals	78	28	25	52

SCOTT STEVENS 21 5-11 200   Defenseman

Fast moving into the top handful of defenseman in the league . . . Devastating bodychecker, one of the strongest players in the NHL . . . Murray used him up front on the power play last year and Stevens scored 65 points . . . Fierce competitor, gradually learning to control his temper . . . A frequent opposition tactic has been to goad Stevens into retaliatory penalties . . . Fifth player taken in the 1982 draft after starring for the Memorial Cup champion Kitchener Rangers, he made the jump into the NHL at age 18 . . . Perhaps overshadowed a bit by Langway when it comes trophy and All-Star time, but his time is clearly coming . . . Incredible hulk and a friendly one . . . A very eligible bachelor . . . Born April 1, 1964, in Kitchener, Ont.

Year	Club	GP	G	A	Pts.
1982-83	Washington	77	9	16	25
1983-84	Washington	78	13	32	45
1984-85	Washington	80	21	44	65
	Totals	235	43	92	135

ROD LANGWAY 28 6-3 215   Defenseman

The heart and soul of the Caps . . . One of the most effective players and leaders in professional sports . . . His acquisition from Montreal in September 1982 turned the franchise around . . . Winner of the Norris Trophy as the league's best defenseman in 1983 and 1984 . . . Generally conceded he did not quite have the big year last season, but he still rated Norris Trophy consideration . . . Tremendous strength and endurance . . . A Navy brat, he was born May 3, 1957, in Taiwan . . . The Langway family settled in Randolph, Mass., when Rod was five . . . Heavily recruited football prep star, he attended the University of New Hampshire because they agreed to let him play both sports . . . Second-round pick in 1977 by Montreal . . . Underpaid and bled by unfavorable tax system, the American in Quebec threatened to retire unless traded and Canadiens complied, sending Langway, Doug Jarvis, Craig Laughlin and Brian Engblom to the Caps for Rick Green and Ryan Walter. "It wasn't the Montreal tradition at work," GM Dave Poile said about team's rise to third place that season. "It was Rod Langway. How can you not win when your best players are also your hardest workers?"

Year	Club	GP	G	A	Pts.
1977-78	Birmingham (WHA) ..	52	3	18	21
1978-79	Montreal............	45	3	4	7
1979-80	Montreal............	77	7	29	36
1980-81	Montreal............	80	11	34	45
1981-82	Montreal............	66	5	34	39
1982-83	Washington	80	3	29	32
1983-84	Washington	80	9	24	33
1984-85	Washington	79	4	22	26
	NHL Totals	507	42	176	218
	WHA Totals	52	3	18	21

DAVE CHRISTIAN 26 5-11 170   Center

Of the Warroad, Minn., Christians . . . Offspring of the family synonymous with U.S. hockey . . . His father, Bill,, and uncle, Roger, starred for the team that won the Olympic gold medal at Squaw Valley in 1960 . . . Family business remains a major supplier of sticks to the NHL . . . Played at the University of North Dakota and on the 1980 Olympic champions . . . Second-round pick by Winnipeg in 1979, he joined the Jets after Lake Placid and played three full seasons there . . . Traded to the Caps for a No. 1 draft choice in part because of a salary dispute . . . Versatile performer, quick, a good puck-handler and in Winnipeg also played some defense and wing . . . Good defensive player . . . Did not play quite as well last year as in his first Washington season and had

a disappointing playoff as the Caps fell again to the Islanders . . .
Born May 12, 1959, in Warroad.

Year	Club	GP	G	A	Pts.
1979-80	Winnipeg	15	8	10	18
1980-81	Winnipeg	80	28	43	71
1981-82	Winnipeg	80	25	51	76
1982-83	Winnipeg	55	18	26	44
1983-84	Washington	80	29	52	81
1984-85	Washington	80	26	43	69
	Totals	390	134	225	359

LARRY MURPHY 24 6-0 200   Defenseman

Offensive-oriented defenseman when he broke in with Los Angeles, he is gradually learning the Caps' defensive way of doing
things . . . Much improved in 1984-85 . . . His points are down (he
averaged 70 in three years with the Kings,) but his effectiveness
is up . . . Had a lot to do with the Caps' power-play improvement
last year, which was the big reason they traded for him . . . Fifth
player taken in the 1980 draft . . . Acquired early in the 1983-84
season for Brian Engblom and Ken Houston . . . Set an NHL record
for most assists and points by a rookie defenseman in 1980-81 . . .
Career was going backwards in losing situation in L.A. and he
gladly exchanged the sun for the chance to play on a contender
. . . Born March 8, 1961, in Scarborough, Ont.

Year	Club	GP	G	A	Pts.
1980-81	Los Angeles	80	16	60	76
1981-82	Los Angeles	79	22	44	66
1982-83	Los Angeles	77	14	48	62
1983-84	LA-Wash	78	13	36	49
1984-85	Washington	79	13	42	55
	Totals	393	78	230	308

PAT RIGGIN 26 5-9 170   Goaltender

Shouldered the Caps' goaltending load after Al Jensen suffered
back and knee problems . . . His numbers (2.98 goals-against average) were better than his performance . . . He didn't win a game
between the All-Star break and the final two weeks of the season
. . . Played in two playoff games, winning one, 4-3, in overtime
and losing the deciding fifth game to the Islanders, 2-1 . . . Second-
round pick by Atlanta in 1979, traded to Washington in 1982 . . .
Caps' GM Dave Poile, then Calgary's assistant GM, had a hand
in that decision, then inherited Riggin when he got the Caps' job
three months later . . . Career of highs and lows, not the greatest

team man in the world, and there's little secret the Caps are looking for something better . . . Father, Dennis, played goal for the Detroit Red Wings in the 1950s . . . Born May 26, 1959, in Kincardine, Ont.

Year	Club	GP	GA	SO	Avg.
1978-79	Birmingham (WHA) ..	46	158	1	3.78
1979-80	Atlanta	25	73	2	3.20
1980-81	Calgary.	42	154	0	3.83
1981-82	Calgary.	52	207	2	4.23
1982-83	Washington	38	121	0	3.36
1983-84	Washington	41	102	4	2.66
1984-85	Washington	57	168	2	2.88
	NHL Totals	255	825	10	3.40
	WHA Totals	46	158	1	3.78

AL JENSEN 26 5-10 180   **Goaltender**
Hampered by physical problems, he played only 14 games last year, but got three starts in the playoffs . . . Workmanlike, unspectacular veteran . . . Fine 1983-84 season (25-13-3, 2.91 goals-against average) but Riggin had to take over when back problems knocked him out . . . Second-round pick by Detroit in 1978, his minor-league work earned him only one start with the Red Wings . . . Acquired by the Caps in 1981 for Mark Lofthouse and little by little earned the No. 1 job . . . His back problems remain a real concern . . . Born Nov. 27, 1958, in Hamilton, Ont.

Year	Club	GP	GA	SO	Avg.
1980-81	Detroit	1	7	0	7.00
1981-82	Washington	26	81	0	3.81
1982-83	Washington	40	135	1	3.44
1983-84	Washington	43	117	4	2.91
1984-85	Washington	14	34	1	2.54
	Totals	124	374	6	3.25

DOUG JARVIS 30 5-9 170   **Center**
Incredibly, has not missed a game in 10 seasons in the league . . . "It wouldn't upset me to see the streak [second longest in the league behind Buffalo's Craig Ramsay] end," he said. "But it would upset me to not dress for a game. I like to play." . . . Valuable checking center and faceoff man . . . "He's probably the most consistent player in the game," Rod Langway says . . . Played on four Stanley Cup winners at Montreal . . . Student of the game, practically functions as an assistant coach, helping Bryan and Terry Murray to evaluate game tapes . . . The 1984 winner of the Frank Selke Trophy as the league's top defensive center . . . "Doug Jarvis epitomizes what the Capitals are all about," Bryan Murray said.

"He has an incredible work ethic."... Born March 24, 1955, in Brantford, Ont.

Year	Club	GP	G	A	Pts.
1975-76	Montreal	80	5	30	35
1976-77	Montreal	80	16	22	38
1977-78	Montreal	80	11	28	39
1978-79	Montreal	80	10	13	23
1979-80	Montreal	80	13	11	24
1980-81	Montreal	80	16	22	38
1981-82	Montreal	80	20	28	48
1982-83	Washington	80	8	22	30
1983-84	Washington	80	13	29	42
1984-85	Washington	80	9	28	37
	Totals	800	121	233	354

COACH BRYAN MURRAY: One of the NHL's best... Named Coach of the Year in 1984... Patient teacher, doesn't try to fit round pegs into square holes ... Getting Langway and Jarvis enabled him to build a defensive-oriented team, so that's the way he went... One of the most notorious referee baiters and bench jockies in the league... Owns a bar in Shawville, Que., where he was born Dec. 5, 1942... Physical education teacher in the high school there, he coached Tier II teams on the side. He won several championships, but it took a while for a major junior team to notice... He interviewed for the Peterborough job, but lost it to Mike Keenan, now the Philadelphia coach... Soon after, he was offered the job at Regina, Sask. Murray left his family for a year to take a shot at it, and took the Pats to the Memorial Cup ... The two opposing coaches in that tournament were Keenan and Cornwall's Doug Carpenter, who now coaches New Jersey ... The Caps hired Murray to coach their Hershey farm club the next year... The following November, they fired Gary Green and promoted Murray... His brother, Terry, who finished up his career with the Caps, stayed on to assist him.

MOST COLORFUL PLAYER

When the infant Capitals wrapped themselves in an American flag to hide their expansion nakedness in 1984, it didn't give them instant color.

Nor respectability either. It took nine seasons for the Caps to go from tedious to teeming. They didn't make the playoffs until 1983 because of the absence of character. And in the interim, they could have used a character or two to make them more interesting. So, for the lack of anybody else, we'll go with Hartland Monahan. A hard-charging right wing of limited skill, his shots, which always went off the Capital Centre glass, delighted the Caps' fans. Admittedly, those who came out to watch those teams were an easily entertained lot.

This may have been the only player in NHL history picked up on waivers who was introduced at a press conference. (Hartland read from a prepared statement.)

He scored 40 goals and 56 assists in two seasons with the Capitals, but he left his mark on the franchise in two other ways. In 1978 the Caps managed to unload him to Pittsburgh for a No. 1 draft choice, truly one of the greatest steals in the history of the NHL.

The other mark he left was on the throat of a Washington newspaperman during a team flight. Disturbed at the writer's reference to him as an "enigma", Monahan charged the scribe and began strangling him.

"The only enigma on this team," Monahan screamed, pointing at black left wing Mike Marson, "is right there."

It turns out Hartland wasn't much better with a dictionary than with a hockey stick. But the Caps remember him fondly.

ALL-TIME CAPITAL LEADERS

GOALS: Dennis Maruk, 60, 1981-82
ASSISTS: Dennis Maruk, 76, 1981-82
POINTS: Dennis Maruk, 136, 1981-82
SHUTOUTS: Al Jensen, 4, 1983-84
              Pat Riggin, 4, 1983-84

CALGARY FLAMES

TEAM DIRECTORY: Pres.-GM: Cliff Fletcher; Asst. to Pres.: Al Coates; Asst. GM: Al MacNeil; Dir. Pub. Rel.: Rick Skaggs; Coach: Bob Johnson. Home ice: Olympic Saddledome (16,683; 200' × 85'). Colors: Red, white and gold. Training camp: Calgary.

SCOUTING REPORT

OFFENSE: The Flames may regret trading leading scorer Kent Nilsson to Minnesota for draft choices June 15, 1985. They unloaded the Swedish center because of his failure to play well in the playoffs and because coach Bob Johnson questioned Nilsson's work ethics and lack of intensity.

Nilsson, however, was the one Calgary player opposing teams feared most. The Flames must find a replacement or develop more scorers this season to fill the void.

With or without Nilsson, the Flames are an explosive team with size and speed among their forwards. Their 363 goals were second only to Edmonton's 401 and their power play was third best in the NHL. Finland's Hakan Loob scored 37 goals, sharing the goal-scoring lead with the departed Nilsson. Rookie Carey Wilson had an outstanding rookie season. Calgary has other fine forwards in Eddy Beers, Dan Quinn, Richard Kromm, Jim Peplinski and Colin Patterson. Injuries reduced veteran Lanny McDonald's goal-scoring effectiveness last season. A healthy McDonald in 1985-86 could compensate for the absence of Nilsson.

Paul Reinhart and Al MacInnis, who has the hardest shot in the NHL, are scoring defensemen who add to the Flames' scoring power.

DEFENSE: Calgary's overall defensive play does not match its scoring ability.

The penalty-killing must be improved this season. It was dreadful last season when the Flames ranked 18th. And their power play had flaws; it allowed 22 shorthanded goals, most in the NHL.

Reinhart is one of the best all-around defensemen in the NHL. He can score from the blue line and he can prevent opponents from scoring with strong defensive play. MacInnis must improve the level of his defensive play. The remainder of the defense corps is only average: Paul Baxter, Kari Eloranta, Jamie Macoun and Steve Konroyd. The Flames need more forwards who will backcheck and help out as team defense players.

Reggie Lemelin has developed into a quality goaltender, capable of playing most of the games and doing a good job. If Lemelin falters, Flames will have problems in goal. They traded veteran Don Edwards to Toronto after last season and enter 1985-86 without a proven No. 2 goalie. Rookies Mark D'Amour and Mike Vernon, along with college rookie Rich Kosti, will contend for a position as Lemelin's goaltending partner.

Calgary's first selection in the 1985 draft was Chris Biotti, an 18-year-old high school defenseman from Massachusetts. He'll attend Harvard before becoming a pro player.

OUTLOOK: The Flames are well-managed by veteran Cliff Fletcher and well-coached by Johnson. Their 94 points last season were the most they've had since entering the NHL in 1972-73 as the Atlanta Flames. They must improve defensively to advance closer to Edmonton in the Smythe Division.

FLAME PROFILES

PAUL REINHART 25 5-11 205   **Defenseman**
Husky, poised veteran defenseman who can do it all . . . Respected team leader . . . Strong defensively when rival team has the puck . . . Scored 23 goals, 69 points last season . . . Once scored 51 goals as a junior hockey defenseman . . . Strong skater with powerful shot . . . Makes few mistakes . . . Born Jan. 8, 1960, in Kitchener, Ont. . . . Made remarkable recovery from serious back injury which limited him to only 27 games in 1983–84 . . . Scored six goals, 17 points in 11 playoff games and played center as well as defense . . . Scored 12 power-play goals, five winning goals last season . . . Scored on 13.3 percent of his shots, impressive figure for defenseman who takes most shots from long range.

Year	Club	GP	G	A	Pts.
1979-80	Atlanta	79	9	38	47
1980-81	Calgary.	74	18	49	67
1981-82	Calgary.	62	13	48	61
1982-83	Calgary.	78	17	58	75
1983-84	Calgary.	27	6	15	21
1984-85	Calgary.	75	23	46	69
	Totals	395	86	254	340

FLAME ROSTER

No.	Player	Pos.	Ht.	Wt.	Born	1984-85	G	A	Pts.	PIM
4	Paul Baxter	D	5-11	194	10-25-55/Winnipeg	Calgary	5	14	19	126
27	Ed Beers	LW	6-2	195	10-12-59/Merritt, B.C.	Calgary	28	40	68	94
21	Perry Berezan	C	6-1	178	12-25-64/Edmonton	Calgary	3	2	5	4
28	Charles Bourgeois	D	6-3	204	11-11-59/Moncton, N.B.	Calgary	2	10	12	134
26	Steve Bozek	C	5-11	186	11-26-60/Castlegar, B.C.	Calgary	13	22	35	6
	Brian Bradley	C	5-10	179	1-21-65/Kitchener, Ont.	London	27	49	76	22
6	Gino Cavallini	LW	6-2	215	11-24-62/Toronto	Calgary	6	10	16	14
						Moncton	29	19	48.	28
25	Yves Courteau	RW	5-10	183	4-35-64/Cote des Neiges, Que.	Calgary	1	4	5	4
						Moncton	19	21	40	32
	Bruce Eakin	C	5-10	180	9-28-62/Winnipeg	Moncton	35	48	83	60
7	Mike Eaves	C	5-10	180	6-10-56/Denver	Calgary	14	29	43	10
20	Kari Eloranta	D	6-2	200	4-29-56/Finland	Calgary	2	11	13	39
18	Dave Hindmarch	LW	5-11	182	10-15-58/Vancouver	Injured	–	–	–	–
19	Tim Hunter	RW	6-1	186	9-10-60/Calgary	Calgary	11	11	22	259
16	Jim Jackson	RW	5-8	181	2-1-60/Oshawa, Ont.	Calgary	1	4	5	0
						Moncton	2	5	7	6
3	Steve Konroyd	D	6-1	195	2-10-61/Scarborough, Ont.	Calgary	3	23	26	73
22	Richard Kromm	LW	5-11	190	3-29-64/Trail, B.C.	Calgary	20	32	52	32
	Mark Lamb	C	5-9	167	8-3-64/Swift Current, Sask.	Moncton	23	49	72	53
12	Hakan Loob	LW	5-9	180	7-3-60/Kalstad, Swe.	Calgary	37	35	72	14
2	Al MacInnis	D	6-1	185	7-11-63/Inverness, N.B.	Calgary	14	52	66	75
34	Jamie Macoun	D	6-2	197	8-17-61/Newmarket, Ont.	Calgary	9	30	39	67
9	Lanny McDonald	RW	6-0	195	2-16-53/Hanna, Alta.	Calgary	19	18	37	36
29	Joel Otto	C	6-4	220	10-29-61/St. Cloud, Minn.	Calgary	4	8	12	30
						Moncton	27	36	63	89
11	Colin Patterson	RW	6-2	195	5-11-60/Rexdale, Ont.	Calgary	22	21	43	5
24	Jim Peplinski	RW	6-3	209	10-24-60/Renfrew, Ont.	Calgary	16	29	45	111
10	Dan Quinn	C	5-10	172	6-1-65/Ottawa, Ont.	Calgary	20	38	58	22
23	Paul Reinhart	D	5-11	205	1-8-60/Kitchener, Ont.	Calgary	23	46	69	18
8	Doug Risebrough	C	5-11	180	1-29-54/Kitchener, Ont.	Calgary	7	5	12	49
	Gary Roberts	LW	6-2	185	5-23-66/Whitby, Ont.	Moncton	4	2	6	7
5	Neil Sheehy	D	6-2	215	2-9-60/Ft. Francis, Ont.	Calgary	3	4	7	109
						Moncton	6	9	15	101
	Mario Simioni	C	6-1	200	4-1-63/Toronto	Moncton	4	8	12	6
	Tony Stiles	D	6-0	200	8-12-59/Carstairs, Alta.	Moncton	5	9	14	46
15	Steve Tambellini	C	6-0	190	5-14-58/Trail, B.C.	Calgary	19	10	29	4
						Moncton	2	5	7	0
	Mickey Volcan	D	6-0	190	3-3-62/Edmonton	Moncton	8	14	22	44
33	Carey Wilson	C	6-2	205	5-19-62/Winnipeg	Calgary	24	48	72	27

No.	Player	Pos.	Ht.	Wt.	Born	1984-85	GP	GA	SO	Avg.
	Mark D'Amour	G	5-9	185	4-29-61/Sudbury, Ont.	Moncton	37	115	0	3.36
31	Rejean Lemelin	G	5-11	170	11-19-54/Sherbrooke, Que.	Calgary	56	183	1	3.46
35	Mike Vernon	G	5-9	160	2-24-63/Calgary	Moncton	41	134	0	3.92

Flames are counting on a healthy Lanny McDonald.

CAREY WILSON 23 6-2 205   **Center**
Scored 72 points in impressive rookie season... Centered Dice
Line (uniform numbers 11, 22, 33) with Richard Kromm and Colin
Patterson... Starred for 1984 Canadian Olympic team... Scored
goal on first shot in first NHL game against Philadelphia in 1984
... Born May 19, 1962, in Winnipeg, Man.... Originally drafted
by Chicago in 1980... Black Hawks traded him to Flames in 1982
for Denis Cyr... Finished third among Flames' scorers last season
... Played hockey and studied biochemistry and medicine at
Dartmouth.

Year	Club	GP	G	A	Pts.
1983-84	Calgary............	15	2	5	7
1984-85	Calgary............	74	24	48	72
	Totals.............	89	26	53	79

HAKAN LOOB 25 5-9 180   **Right Wing**
Swift Swedish right wing has given many opponents a "Loob Job"
since entering NHL in 1982... Scored 30 goals, 55 points in
rookie season... Raised scoring figures to 37 goals, 72 points last
season... Scored five game-winning goals... Small but shifty
and difficult for opponents to check... Has ability to accelerate
rapidly and break free from defenders... Born July 3, 1960, in
Karlstad, Sweden... Scored 42 goals in 36 games in Swedish
Elite League before leaving to play in NHL... A hustler with or
without the puck... Teammates call him "Hawk."

Year	Club	GP	G	A	Pts.
1983-84	Calgary............	77	30	25	55
1984-85	Calgary............	78	37	35	72
	Totals.............	155	67	60	127

ALLAN MacINNIS 22 6-1 185   **Defenseman**
Has hardest, fastest shot in hockey, according to most goalies...
Blazing shot from blue line or high slot is so hard most goalies
have difficulty catching it or swatting it away with stick, leg pads
or blocking glove... Combines blistering shot with clever play-

making to spark Flames' power play . . . Born July 11, 1963, in Inverness, N.S. . . . Scored 38 goals in 51 games in junior hockey, tying Bobby Orr's Ontario Junior Hockey League scoring record for defensemen . . . Scored 14 goals, 52 assists in second NHL season in 1984–85.

Year	Club	GP	G	A	Pts.
1981-82	Calgary............	2	0	0	0
1982-83	Calgary............	14	1	3	4
1983-84	Calgary............	51	11	34	15
1984-85	Calgary............	67	14	52	66
	Totals............	134	26	89	115

LANNY McDONALD 32 6-0 195   Right Wing

Plagued by injuries last two seasons following spectacular 66-goal season in 1982–83 . . . When he's healthy, he's one of the most dynamic right wings in NHL . . . Has scored 437 goals in NHL career starting with Toronto . . . Easily recognized by his bushy walrus mustache . . . Born Feb. 16, 1953, in Hanna, Alta. . . . Flames hope he stays injury-free this season and regains his goal-scoring touch . . . A class act on and off the ice . . . Won Bill Masterton Memorial Trophy for sprtsmanship and dedication to hockey in 1983 . . . Deeply involved in charity work . . . Does it because he wants to, not just for publicity purposes.

Year	Club	GP	G	A	Pts.
1973-74	Toronto............	70	14	16	30
1974-75	Toronto............	64	17	27	44
1975-76	Toronto............	75	37	56	93
1976-77	Toronto............	80	46	44	90
1977-78	Toronto............	74	47	40	87
1978-79	Toronto............	79	43	42	85
1979-80	Tor-Col............	81	40	35	75
1980-81	Colorado............	80	35	46	81
1981-82	Col-Calg............	71	40	42	82
1982-83	Calgary............	80	66	32	98
1983-84	Calgary............	65	33	33	66
1984-85	Calgary............	43	19	18	37
	Totals............	862	437	431	868

EDDY BEERS 25 6-2 195   Left Wing

Has the size, strength and skill to command respect as a prominent left wing . . . His strongest asset is ability to move to net and create havoc . . . Does an effective job screening goalie . . . Opposing de-

fensemen have trouble forcing him away from net . . . Gets many
goals on rebounds and deflections . . . Born Oct. 12, 1959, in Mer-
ritt, B.C. . . . Not overly fast but is an effective forward because
of physical size and accurate shot . . . Has scored 64 goals in last
two seasons . . . Thirteen of his 28 goals last season were scored
on power plays . . . Scored 50 goals in 42 games in 1981–82 while
playing college hockey at University of Denver.

Year	Club	GP	G	A	Pts.
1981-82	Calgary............	5	1	1	2
1982-83	Calgary............	41	11	15	26
1983-84	Calgary............	73	36	39	75
1984-85	Calgary............	74	28	40	68
	Totals.............	193	76	95	171

DAN QUINN 20 5-10 175   Center

Flames looking for a really big year from talented young center
. . . Has quick hands and feet and finesse moves . . . GM Cliff
Fletcher made smart move selecting Quinn as Flames' No. 1 draft
choice in 1983 . . . Was one of the Ontario Junior Hockey League's
most dangerous scorers in 1982-83, scoring 59 goals, 88 assists,
147 points in 70 games with Belleville Bulls . . . Promoted to NHL
at 18 and scored first goal with 51 seconds remaining in third period of 3-3 tie against Edmonton, Dec. 23, 1983 . . . Born June 1,
1965, in Ottawa . . . Averaged almost a point a game in rookie
season and scored eight points in eight playoff games . . . Showed
flashes of brilliance last season . . . Has played some of his best
games against Stanley Cup champion Edmonton.

Year	Club	GP	G	A	Pts.
1983-84	Calgary............	54	19	33	52
1984-85	Calgary............	74	20	38	58
	Totals.............	128	39	71	110

REJEAN LEMELIN 30 5-11 170   Goaltender

Nicknamed "Reggie" . . . Has gained immense popularity with fans
at Olympic Saddledome . . . Chants of "Reggie!" . . . "Reggie!" . . .

"Reggie!" often heard before and during Flames' games . . . Made it the hard way by struggling in minor leagues for several years before finally getting chance to playing in NHL . . . Born Nov. 19, 1954, in Quebec City, Que. . . . Unseated Don Edwards as Calgary's No. 1 goalie . . . Last season was his best in NHL . . . Compiled 30-12-10 record in 56 games . . . Next win will be his 100th as NHL goalie dating to his days with Atlanta Flames . . . Has 99-57-41 career record . . . Originally property of Philadelphia Flyers . . . Flames signed him as free agent in 1978 . . . Started pro career in 1974 with Philadelphia Firebirds of North American League . . . Makes his home near Philadelphia in South Jersey.

Year	Club	GP	GA	SO	Avg.
1978-79	Atlanta	18	55	0	3.32
1979-80	Atlanta	3	15	0	6.00
1980-81	Calgary	29	88	2	3.24
1981-82	Calgary	34	135	0	4.34
1982-83	Calgary	39	133	0	3.61
1983-84	Calgary	51	150	0	3.50
1984-85	Calgary	56	183	1	3.46
	Totals	230	759	2	3.62

JIM PEPLINSKI 24 6-3 209   **Right Wing**
Not a star but the type of valuable player every team needs . . . Works hard and keeps himself in good physical condition . . . A spirited, enthusiastic athlete . . . Good leader on and off the ice . . . Sets good example for other teammates to follow . . . Born Oct. 24, 1960, in Renfrew, Ont. . . . His best season with Flames was 1981–82 when he scored 30 goals . . . Has the ability to play well with different linemates . . . A versatile player . . . Nicknamed "Pepper" . . . Works as hard defensively as he does offensively . . . A skilled center at winning faceoffs . . . Makes clever passes . . . Excels as penalty-killer.

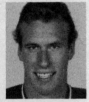

Year	Club	GP	G	A	Pts.
1980-81	Calgary	80	13	25	38
1981-82	Calgary	74	30	37	67
1982-83	Calgary	80	15	26	41
1983-84	Calgary	74	11	22	33
1984-85	Calgary	80	16	29	45
	Totals	388	85	139	224

PAUL BAXTER 29 5-11 194   **Defenseman**
No longer just a ruffian who fights and piles up penalty minutes . . . Has developed into a good defenseman . . . Has learned to play

one-on-one confrontations properly . . . Does a good job blocking shots . . . But don't be fooled . . . He still plays with a mean streak and has a knack for instigating trouble and luring opposing players into taking foolish penalties . . . Born Oct. 25, 1955, in Winnipeg, Man. . . . Began pro career in 1975 with Cleveland Crusaders of WHA . . . Later played for Quebec in WHA and NHL . . . Gained his biggest reputation as a bad man with Pittsburgh . . . Has spent 1,302 minutes in penalty boxes during NHL career, including 409 with Pittsburgh in 1981–82 . . . Has kept penalty minutes total below 200 last two seasons by playing with greater self-control . . . Active in religious work in offseason.

Year	Club	GP	G	A	Pts.
1974-75	Cleveland (WHA)	5	0	0	0
1975-76	Cleveland (WHA)	67	3	7	10
1976-77	Quebec (WHA)	66	6	17	23
1977-78	Quebec (WHA)	76	6	29	35
1978-79	Quebec (WHA)	76	10	36	46
1979-80	Quebec.	61	7	13	20
1980-81	Pittsburgh	51	5	14	19
1981-82	Pittsburgh	76	9	34	43
1982-83	Pittsburgh	75	11	21	32
1983-84	Calgary.	74	7	20	27
1984-85	Calgary.	70	5	14	19
	NHL Totals	407	44	116	160
	WHA Totals	290	25	89	114

COACH BOB JOHNSON: "Badger Bob" . . . Acquired nickname coaching University of Wisconsin . . . Led Badgers to three NCAA championships, 367-175-23 record . . . Chief coaching rival was former Ranger coach Herb Brooks . . . Active for many years in international hockey . . . Coached 1976 U.S. Olympic team and Team USA in 1981 and 1984 Canada Cup . . . Son, Mark Johnson, played for father at Wisconsin, is successful NHL forward with St. Louis . . . Born March 4, 1931, in Minneapolis . . . Started coaching career in 1956 at Minnesota's Warroad High . . . Coached at Colorado College . . . Enthusiastic, positive thinker . . . Has excellent relationship with players . . . Believes hockey should be fun . . . Players respect his coaching methods and personality . . . Has 107-93-40 record since becoming Flames' coach.

MOST COLORFUL PLAYER

Lanny McDonald is one of those players with extraordinary skills who create the impression of being a notch above the norm. His style of play generates excitement among fans when he's on the ice.

Even with a helmet, McDonald is easily recognized, on and off the ice. He's been known throughout his successful NHL career for his walrus mustache as much as he has been known for the No. 9 he wears on his uniform or his goal-scoring ability.

Dating back to their days as the Atlanta Flames, the franchise never has had a player of McDonald's all-around ability and crowd appeal. He's been a colorful right wing since he joined Calgary in 1981 from the old Colorado Rockies. He reached the summit of his career by scoring 66 goals in 1982-83.

ALL-TIME FLAME LEADERS

GOALS: Lanny McDonald, 66, 1982-83
ASSISTS: Kent Nilsson, 82, 1980-81
POINTS: Kent Nilsson, 131, 1980-81
SHUTOUTS: Dan Bouchard, 5, 1973-74
                 Phil Myre, 5, 1974-75

CHICAGO BLACK HAWKS

TEAM DIRECTORY: Pres.: William W. Wirtz; VP: Arthur M. Wirtz Jr.; VP: Tommy Ivan; GM/Coach: Bob Pulford; Co-Coach: Roger Neilson; Dir. Pub. Rel.: Jim DeMaria; Home ice: Chicago Stadium (17,300; 188' × 85'). Colors: Red, black and white. Training camp: Chicago.

SCOUTING REPORT

OFFENSE: If healthy, as good as anybody's in the league, save Edmonton.

The Denis Savard-Steve Larmer-Al Secord line is a top-notch

All-around Denis Savard posted 100 points for third time.

unit. After that, there's a lot of depth, particularly up the middle, and a good mix of checkers and grinders that you can win with.

The only dissenting note was center Tom Lysiak, who had his worst season since coming into the league in 1973. But he rebounded in the playoffs. The Hawks have solid workhorses in Darryl Sutter, Curt Fraser, Billy Gardner and Troy Murray. Ed Olczyk did nothing during his fine rookie year to discourage the notion that he's going to be a star. And in speedy Ken Yaremchuk, Chicago has a potential gamebreaker if coach Bob Pulford can harness the kid.

Injuries and sometimes a refusal to put out for the acid-tongued Orval Tessier ruined the 1983-84 season and took a pretty good chunk out of last year, too. At one point the club's entire left wing—Secord, Sutter and Fraser—was wiped out. The real Hawks showed up in the playoffs, when they devastated Detroit and beat Minnesota, but the club's real problem showed up in the semifinals against Edmonton. And that is . . .

DEFENSE: Exclude Doug Wilson, of course. He might be the best in the league. Wilson was hurt against the Oilers and that didn't help, because the rest of the Hawk defense was pretty well picked apart by the speedy Oilers.

Keith Brown, a high No. 1 pick in 1979, has never lived up to expectations. The Hawks are finding out why Behn Wilson was deemed expendable by Philadelphia; he can't keep the pace demanded by the quick teams.

The undersized Bob Murray, a steady hand here for a decade, is getting a little long on tooth. Hopes that 20-year-old Marc Bergevin and 23-year-old Jerome Dupont will develop had better be realized or the Hawks will remain only the best team of a bad Norris Division lot.

Murray Bannerman, who had established himself as one of the better goalies in the league, did not have a good season last year. The Hawks were overwhelmed by the Oilers, although Bannerman beat them twice at Chicago Stadium. He's pretty good. But is he good enough to take the Hawks to a Stanley Cup?

OUTLOOK: Questions on defense and in goal remain. When push comes to shove, the Hawks are tough enough to hold their own. But when clubs like the Oilers and Flyers begin to skate, Chicago could use a few more legs.

It's a pretty good base, but one or two more players are needed to take the next two steps.

BLACK HAWK ROSTER

No.	Player	Pos.	Ht.	Wt.	Born	1984-85	G	A	Pts.	PIM
2	Marc Bergevin	D	5-11	178	8-11-65/Montreal	Chicago	0	6	6	54
	Randy Boyd	D	6-1	192	5-6-60/Coniston, Ont.	Chicago	0	0	0	6
4	Keith Brown	D	6-1	192	5-60-60/Cornerbrook, Nfld.	Chicago	1	22	23	55
	Bruce Cassidy	D	5-11	176	5-20-65/Ottawa, Ont.	Ottawa	13	27	40	15
25	Jerome Dupont	D	6-3	190	2-21-62/Ottawa, Ont.	Chicago	3	10	13	100
3	Dave Feamster	D	5-11	180	9-10-58/Detroit	Chicago	1	3	4	14
8	Curt Fraser	LW	6-0	200	1-12-58/Winnipeg	Chicago	25	25	50	109
31	Dan Frawley	LW	6-0	170	6-2-62/Sturgeon Falls, Ont.	Chicago	4	3	7	64
14	Bill Gardner	C	5-10	175	3-19-60/Toronto	Chicago	17	34	51	12
10	Jeff Larmer	RW	5-10	172	10-10-62/Peterborough, Ont.	Chicago	0	0	0	0
28	Steve Larmer	RW	5-10	190	6-16-61/Peterborough, Ont.	Chicago	46	40	86	16
29	Steve Ludzik	C	5-11	170	4-3-61/Toronto	Chicago	11	20	31	86
12	Tom Lysiak	C	6-1	196	4-22-53/High Prairie, Alta.	Chicago	16	30	46	13
	Dave Manson	D	6-2	190	1-27-67/Prince Albert, Sask.	Prince Albert	8	30	38	249
7	Tom McMurchy	LW	5-9	165	12-12-63/New Westminster, B.C.	Chicago	1	2	3	13
6	Bob Murray	D	5-10	183	11-26-54/Kingston, Ont.	Chicago	1	2	3	13
19	Troy Murray	C	6-1	195	7-31-62/Edmonton	Chicago	26	40	66	82
5	Jack O'Callahan	D	6-1	185	7-24-57/Charleston, Mass.	Chicago	6	8	14	105
16	Ed Olczyk	LW-C	6-1	195	8-16-66/Chicago	Chicago	20	30	50	67
26	Rick Paterson	C	5-9	187	2-10-58/Kingston, Ont.	Chicago	7	12	19	25
	Wayne Presley	RW	5-11	172	3-23-65/Detroit	Chicago	0	1	1	0
						Kitch.-SSM	30	30	60	91
18	Denis Savard	C	5-10	170	2-2-61/Pt. Gatineau, Que.	Chicago	38	67	105	56
14	Al Secord	LW	6-1	210	9-20-58/Sudbury, Ont.	Chicago	15	11	26	183
27	Darryl Sutter	C	5-11	175	8-19-58/Viking, Alta.	Chicago	20	18	38	12
23	Behn Wilson	D	6-3	210	12-19-58/Kingston, Ont.	Chicago	10	23	33	185
24	Doug Wilson	D	6-1	190	7-5-57/Ottawa, Ont.	Chicago	22	54	76	44
15	Ken Yaremchuk	C	5-11	185	1-1-64/Edmonton	Chicago	10	16	26	16
	Trent Yawney	D	6-3	185	9-29-65/Hudson Bay, Sask.	Saskatoon	16	51	67	158

No.	Player	Pos.	Ht.	Wt.	Born	1984-85	GP	GA	SO	Avg.
30	Murray Bannerman	G	5-11	185	4-27-57/Ft. Frances, Ont.	Chicago	60	215	0	3.83
	Darren Pang	G	5-5	155	2-17-64/Nepean, Ont.	Milwaukee	–	–	–	–
	Jim Ralph	G	5-11	170	5-13-62/Sault Ste. Marie, Ont.	Milwaukee	–	–	–	–

BLACK HAWK PROFILES

DENIS SAVARD 24 5-10 170   Center

Brilliant playmaker and scorer . . . Might be the most exciting player
in the league . . . Incredible free-lance instincts and puck-handling
skills . . . Scored 100 points last year for the third time in his five
NHL seasons. . . . Extremely quick, constantly in motion . . . Yet
some people, including himself, expect still more . . . "I could do
better, I should do better," he says. "Why I don't, I don't know.
I look at Wayne Gretzky and how he does it every night, and I
wonder why I can't be that way. Every night he wants to play a
better game than the night before. I would like to be as consistent
as him. Why I'm not, I don't know." . . . Born Feb. 4, 1961, in
Pte. Gatineau, Que. . . . Considered a blue-chip prospect from his
early teens . . . Center on the Trois Denis line during his years with
the Montreal juniors. He and his linemates, Denis Cyr and Denis
Tremblay, were all born the same day in the same hospital. Cyr,
a draft pick of Calgary, now plays with St. Louis. Tremblay is
out of hockey . . . Third player taken in the 1980 draft with a pick
the Hawks acquired from Quebec for the post-merger rights to
Real Cloutier . . . Has teamed with Al Secord and Steve Larmer
for one of the top scoring lines in hockey . . . One of the smallest
players in the league, but simply too fast and shifty to hit . . . Has
a temper, was fined once for spitting on a referee.

Year	Club	GP	G	A	Pts.
1980-81	Chicago	76	28	47	75
1981-82	Chicago	80	32	87	119
1982-83	Chicago	78	35	85	120
1983-84	Chicago	75	37	57	94
1984-85	Chicago	79	38	67	105
	Totals	388	170	343	513

STEVE LARMER 24 5-10 190   Right Wing

Scored 46 goals last year, the second time in his three NHL seasons
he has passed the 40 mark . . . Excellent finisher for Denis Savard
. . . Always in the right spot at the right time and is able to get his
shot away without giving a goaltender a chance to set up . . . Right
wing with a left-handed shot. . . . Younger brother, Jeff, plays for
the New Jersey Devils . . , Born June 16, 1961, in Peterborough,
Ont. . . . Has always been a gifted goal scorer, but concern about
his skating skills caused him to be passed over until the 120th
pick of the 1980 draft . . . After scoring 38 for the Hawks' farm
club in New Brunswick, he was promoted to the big team for

good in 1982 ... Named Rookie of the Year in the NHL that season
... Durable, has not missed a game in his three seasons ... Had
22 points in 15 playoff games last season ... Quiet, unassuming
personality off the ice.

Year	Club	GP	G	A	Pts.
1980-81	Chicago	4	0	1	1
1981-82	Chicago	3	0	0	0
1982-83	Chicago	80	43	47	90
1983-84	Chicago	80	35	40	75
1984-85	Chicago	80	46	40	86
	Totals	247	124	128	252

DOUG WILSON 28 6-1 190   Defenseman

Winner of the Norris Trophy as the league's best defenseman in
1982. ... May have had an even better season last year ... Strikes
an excellent balance between offense and defense. ... Generally
conceded that he and Calgary's Al MacInnis have the two hardest
shots in the league ... Born July 5, 1957, in Ottawa, where he
had an outstanding junior career ... First-round pick of Chicago
in 1977, it took several seasons for him to begin to reach his
potential ... Admits a more settled lifestyle had a lot to do with
his on-ice maturity ... Credits his wife, Kathy, daughter of a Chicago high school basketball coach, with helping him to grow ...
Another turning point was belated discovery that he suffered from
hypoglycemia (low blood sugar). He adjusted his diet accordingly
... Missed 14 games with a fractured skull in 1983-84 ... Starred
for Team Canada last fall, scoring the tying goal in the classic
3-2 overtime victory over the Soviets ... "A great player and really
a classy guy," Edmonton and Canada coach Glen Sather said ...
Became a father last year.

Year	Club	GP	G	A	Pts.
1977-78	Chicago	77	14	20	34
1978-79	Chicago	56	5	21	26
1979-80	Chicago	73	12	49	61
1980-81	Chicago	76	12	39	51
1981-82	Chicago	76	39	46	85
1982-83	Chicago	74	18	51	69
1983-84	Chicago	66	13	45	58
1984-85	Chicago	78	22	54	76
	Totals	576	135	325	460

TROY MURRAY 23 6-1 195   Center

Blossomed as a scoring threat in his third full NHL season ...
His 26 goals and 40 points were by far his career high ... Added
19 points in 15 playoff games ... Very good defensively, his assignment is often to play against the opposition's top center ... Born

July 31, 1962, in Calgary... Third-round pick in 1980 after a great freshman season at the University of North Dakota... Took time off from school the following year to play for the Canadian National Junior team which beat the Soviets to claim the country's first world championship since the early 1950s... Returned after that tournament to lead the Fighting Sioux to an NCAA championship.

Year	Club	GP	G	A	Pts.
1981-82	Chicago	1	0	0	0
1982-83	Chicago	54	8	8	16
1983-84	Chicago	61	15	15	30
1984-85	Chicago	80	26	40	66
	Totals	196	49	63	112

BILL GARDNER 25 5-10 175   Center

Combines with Denis Savard, Tom Lysiak and Troy Murray to make the Hawks as deep down the middle as any team in the league... Versatile performer who has shown offensive improvement each season... Fine penalty-killer, has played some wing and even pitched in on the power play... "Everything we ask of him he does and does pretty darn well," said former Hawk coach Orval Tessier... Born March 19, 1960, in Toronto... Played junior B hockey as a defenseman on the same team with Wayne Gretzky... Played junior A in Peterborough, where he led the Petes to a berth in the Memorial Cup finals in 1980... Third-round pick in 1979.

Year	Club	GP	G	A	Pts.
1980-81	Chicago	1	0	0	0
1981-82	Chicago	69	8	15	23
1982-83	Chicago	77	15	25	40
1983-84	Chicago	79	27	21	48
1984-85	Chicago	74	17	34	51
	Totals	300	67	95	162

CURT FRASER 27 6-0 200   Left Wing

Hard hit by injuries ever since he came to the Hawks in 1982... Rebounded with a 25-goal, 25-assist season despite missing another seven games last year... Good cornerman with 30-goal ability... Born January 12, 1958, in Cincinnati, but moved to Winnipeg, then North Vancouver, at an early age... Second-round pick of the Canucks in 1978 from the Victoria Cougars... He played in Vancouver three seasons until he was traded for Tony Tanti. Tanti, only 20 at the time, has gone on to become a big scorer for the Canucks and the deal has been widely questioned ... Last year Fraser showed what he could do if healthy.

Year	Club	GP	G	A	Pts.
1978-79	Vancouver	78	16	19	35
1979-80	Vancouver	78	17	25	42
1980-81	Vancouver	77	25	24	49
1981-82	Vancouver	79	28	39	67
1982-83	Van-Chi	74	12	20	32
1983-84	Chicago	29	5	12	17
1984-85	Chicago	73	25	25	50
	Totals	488	128	164	292

ED OLCZYK 19 6-1 195   Right Wing

Hometown boy who made good in his rookie year ... Had 50 points despite missing 10 games and looks like he'll be everything the Hawks expected ... Rugged type with fine skills ... Born August 16, 1966, in Chicago ... A product of Illinois junior programs ... "I was the oddball in school," he said. "Nobody played hockey. But I always wanted to be a Black Hawk." Became a member of the U.S. Olympic team when only 16 years old ... GM Bob Pulford took a paternal interest in the kid and worked hard on the deal that enabled the Hawks to draft him. He wound up giving Los Angeles goalie Bob Janecyk to exchange the sixth pick in the 1984 for the third choice. Pulford also had to give New Jersey, picking second, three players not to take Olczyk ... Playing for the Hawks is a dream come true for the whole family. "I'd dress up as a goalie and I'd sing 'Here Comes the Hawks' and Ed would shoot tennis balls at me," said his mother, Diana ... Played well for Team USA in the Canada Cup.

Year	Club	GP	G	A	Pts.
1984-85	Chicago	70	20	30	50

DARRYL SUTTER 27 5-11 175

Black Hawk captain and leader ... Beset by serious injuries the last two seasons (fractured cheekbone and knee), but when he's in the lineup he makes a big difference ... Missed 21 games last year, but returned to score 19 points in 15 playoff games . . . All the traits that have put five of his brothers in the NHL . . . Second of the brothers to turn professional and had the most difficult route . . . Was the 179th player taken in the 1978 draft . . . Hawks only sent him a form letter inviting him to camp, so he accepted an offer to play in Japan for a year . . . Chicago signed him to play in New Brunswick the following season and Eddie Johnston, his coach there and later coach of the Hawks, pushed for his promotion . . . Born August 19, 1958, in Viking, Alta. . . . Plays at 180, but more like he weighs 210 . . . Very good defensively, excellent at tipping point shots on net.

Year	Club	GP	G	A	Pts.
1979-80	Chicago	8	2	0	2
1980-81	Chicago	76	40	22	62
1981-82	Chicago	40	23	12	35
1982-83	Chicago	80	31	30	61
1983-84	Chicago	59	20	20	40
1984-85	Chicago	49	20	18	38
	Totals	312	136	102	238

MURRAY BANNERMAN 28 5-11 185   Goaltender

Pushed Tony Esposito into retirement when he took over the Hawks' No. 1 goaltending job in 1983-84 . . . Did not generally play as well last season . . . Twice a mid-season All-Star . . . Born April 27, 1957, in Fort Frances, Ont. . . . Vancouver's fifth choice in the 1977 draft but was quickly traded to Chicago for Pit Martin . . . Worked his way up from the low minors . . . Played two years in the AHL at New Brunswick and shared the Hawk goal with Tony Esposito for two seasons . . . Key to the two Hawk wins over Edmonton in last spring's final, but was bombed in the three games at Edmonton.

Year	Club	GP	GA	SO	Avg.
1977-78	Vancouver	1	0	0	0.00
1980-81	Chicago	15	62	0	4.30
1981-82	Chicago	29	116	1	4.17
1982-83	Chicago	41	127	4	3.10
1983-84	Chicago	56	188	2	3.38
1984-85	Chicago	60	215	0	3.83
	Totals	202	708	7	3.63

AL SECORD 27 6-1 210   Left Wing

Another victim of the plague on Black Hawk left wings . . . Secord, who played in only 14 games in 1983-84, missed another 25 last season . . . Had emerged as a 50-goal scorer three years ago when an abdominal pull refused to heal . . . Cast as a tough guy in Boston, he developed rapidly as a player who could put Denis Savard's and Steve Larmer's setups into the net . . . And still as tough as they come . . . Born March 3, 1958, in Sudbury, Ont. . . . Dabbled as an amateur boxer in his teen years . . . "It teaches you discipline," he said . . . He also worked hard at power-skating instruction . . . Never scored more than 32 goals in any of his junior years with St. Catharines . . . No. 1 pick of the Bruins in 1978, scored 23 goals there his second year, but was traded to Chicago for defenseman Mike O'Connell in 1980 . . . "My game has to be physical," he says. "I can't forget what got me here. You've got to be realistic, you can't live in fantasyland. But I also have always wanted to be known as a hockey player, not a fighter."

Year	Club	GP	G	A	Pts.
1978-79	Boston	71	16	7	23
1979-80	Boston	77	23	16	39
1980-81	Bos-Chi	59	13	12	25
1981-82	Chicago	80	44	31	75
1982-83	Chicago	80	54	32	86
1983-84	Chicago	14	4	4	8
1984-85	Chicago	51	15	11	26
	Totals	432	169	113	282

COACH BOB PULFORD: Reluctantly, one of the best coaches in the business . . . When the Hawks' GM fired Orval Tessier last season, it was the third time since coming to Chicago in 1977 that Pully has gone behind the bench . . . Because he hates it doesn't mean he's not good at it . . . Hawks, with several key players returning from injuries, responded with a good stretch drive and playoff victories over Detroit and Minnesota before losing to Edmonton . . . Owner Bill Wirtz wanted Pulford to stay on, so he's worked out an associate coach arrangement with last year's assistant, Roger Neilson. "It's impossible," he said, "to do both jobs well." . . . A stern taskmaster, but not a screamer like Tessier . . . Instills a quiet confidence from behind the bench . . . "A stickler for fundamentals," defenseman Doug Wilson said. "And of course it helps that he's the guy who signs the paychecks, too." . . . Dour, he tries hard with media people he knows, but admits he wouldn't win any personality contests . . . A fine two-way center in his playing days, he played on three Stanley Cup teams in Toronto . . . Finished up in Los Angeles, where he began his coaching career ... Took a veteran Kings team without star talent to a 105-point season in 1974-75 and was named Coach of the Year ... Took over an aging Chicago club far past its best days and has gradually built the Hawks back into contention. High water mark was a 105-point season in 1982-83, but injuries have largely wrecked the last two years ... Born March 31, 1936, in Robinson, Ont.

MOST COLORFUL PLAYER

Save perhaps only Bobby Orr, Bobby Hull was the most exciting player ever to perform in the NHL. He didn't do as many things as well as Gordie Howe and no one has ever had the anticipation, playmaking ability or even close to the statistics of Wayne Gretzky.

But from the time he picked up the puck in his own end and roared towards the goal, no player ever spellbound a home crowd or put fear into the opposition as did The Golden Jet. His shot was absolutely devastating, his effect on audience almost magnetic.

There is no question that had he not jumped to the WHA in 1972 at age 33, Hull would have become the greatest goal scorer in NHL history. In an era that is simply not comparable to today's wide-open style, he scored 610 goals in 15 NHL seasons. Included in his career haul were three scoring titles and two Most Valuable Player awards.

After Hull's defection to start the new league, the Hawks compensated for a time, making it to the Stanley Cup finals the very next season. But the magic that was Chicago Stadium in his heyday was gone. Seats, once impossible to get, began to empty. It took almost a decade before the old barn on North Madison began to fill up again.

ALL-TIME BLACK HAWK LEADERS

GOALS: Bobby Hull, 58, 1968-69
ASSISTS: Denis Savard, 87, 1981-82
POINTS: Denis Savard, 121, 1982-83
SHUTOUTS: Tony Esposito, 15, 1969-70

DETROIT RED WINGS

TEAM DIRECTORY: Owner: Michael Ilitch; GM: Jim Devellano;
Dir. Pub. Rel.: Bill Jamieson; Coach and Asst. GM: Nick Polano.
Home ice: Joe Louis Arena (19,275; 200′ × 85′). Training camp:
Port Huron, Mich.

SCOUTING REPORT

OFFENSE: Almost all the eggs are in one basket. The John
Ogrodnick-Steve Yzerman-Ron Duguay line is one of the league's

Young Steve Yzerman made it two fine years in a row.

best, but the lack of balance, despite coach Nick Polano's periodic efforts to distribute the offense, makes the Wings a very checkable team.

Dwight Foster, a valuable checker and plugger, missed 30 games and that hurt. Kelly Kisio was a nice free-agent find and the Wings think Lane Lambert will develop into a solid, winning winger.

After that, Detroit was toilet-paper thin. That the Wings were ninth in the league last year in goals scored is a tribute only to the one good line. But the Wings signed free-agent left winger Warren Young, who scored 40 goals as a 28-year-old Penguin rookie last season, and he can make a difference.

DEFENSE: Veteran Reed Larson may have had his best season last year. But now Detroit has to replace the retired Brad Park. The future Hall of Famer had slowed considerably, but he was still able to get the puck out of the Wings' zone. There's no visible replacement on the horizon.

GM Jimmy Devellano likes a couple of kids, Larry Trader and Rick Zombo. Whether they will be more than marginal players remains to be seen. Holdovers John Barrett, Colin Campbell and Greg Smith are passable at best.

The goaltending, however, seems to be in reasonably good shape with fiesty Greg Stefan and Corrado Micalef. Stefan is the steadier of the two and the Wings' chief hope in the long, long, rebuilding process.

OUTLOOK: Ogrodnick and Yzerman, two of the best players in the league, will keep the bottom from falling out, but this team is a long, long way from contention.

Devellano never promised a rose garden, but he's heading into his fourth year now. With three drafts behind him, and only really Yzerman to show as a long-term foundation, it's reasonable for owner Mike Ilitch to begin asking some questions about the club's direction.

In his first three years, Devellano picked up just about every veteran he could find to buy some time. Park and Foster were nice additions, but most of these players turned out to be oldies, not goodies. And Devellano really set himself back by trading Murray Craven, a 20-year-old who blossomed at Philadelphia, for an over-the-hill Darryl Sittler. When you're selling your team as a rebuilding one, it's a mistake he couldn't afford to make.

Detroit is a great hockey town and nobody there is expecting miracles. The people will come if they just see a little progress. But the Wings' inept performance in being swept by Chicago in the first round is not what their long-suffering faithful had in mind.

RED WING ROSTER

No.	Player	Pos.	Ht.	Wt.	Born	1984-85	G	A	Pts.	PIM
24	Pierre Aubrey	C	5-10	170	4-15-60/Cape de la Madeline, Que	Detroit	2	2	4	33
						Adirondack	13	10	23	74
3	John Barrett	D	6-1	210	7-1-58/Ottawa, Ont.	Detroit	6	19	25	117
19	Ivan Boldirev	C	6-0	190	8-15-49/Yugoslavia	Detroit	19	30	49	16
	Shawn Burr	C	6-1	180	7-1-66/Sarina, Ont.	Detroit	0	0	0	2
						Adirondack	0	0	0	2
						Kitchener	24	42	66	50
	Colin Campbell	D	5-9	190	1-28-53/London, Ont.	Detroit	1	5	6	124
10	Ron Duguay	RW-C	6-2	210	7-6-57/Sudbury, Ont.	Detroit	38	51	89	51
	Brent Fedyk	RW	6-0	180	3-8-67/Yankton, Sask.	Regina	35	35	70	48
20	Dwight Foster	C-RW	5-11	190	4-2-57/Toronto	Detroit	16	16	32	56
	Jody Gage	RW-LW	5-11	182	11-29-59/Toronto	Adirondack	27	33	60	55
17	Gerard Gallant	RW	5-11	164	9-2-63/Summerside, PEI	Detroit	10	5	15	32
						Adirondack	18	29	47	131
18	Danny Gare	RW	5-9	175	5-14-54/Nelson, B.C.	Detroit	27	29	56	163
	Ed Johnstone	RW	5-9	165	3-2-54/Brandon, Man.	Adirondack	27	28	55	70
	Greg Joly	D	6-1	182	5-30-54/Calgary	Adirondack	9	40	49	111
16	Kelly Kisio		5-9	170	9-1-59/Peace River, Alta.	Detroit	20	41	61	56
26	Joe Kocur	RW	5-11	204	12-21-64/Calgary	Detroit	1	0	1	64
						Adirondack	12	7	19	171
29	Randy Ladouceur	D	6-2	220	6-30-60/Brockville, Ont.	Detroit	3	27	30	108
14	Lane Lambert	RW	6-0	180	11-18-64/Melfort, Sask.	Detroit	14	11	25	104
28	Reed Larson	D	6-0	195	7-30-56/Minneapolis	Detroit	17	45	62	139
15	Claude Loiselle	C	5-11	171	5-29-63/Ottawa, Ont.	Detroit	8	1	9	45
						Adirondack	22	29	51	24
23	Bob Manno	D	6-0	185	10-31-56/Niagara Falls, Ont.	Detroit	10	22	32	32
26	Barry Melrose	D	6-2	205	2-15-56/Kelvington, Sask.	Adirondack	3	13	16	226
25	John Ogrodnick	RW	6-0	190	6-20-59/Edmonton	Detroit	55	50	105	30
	Andre St. Laurent	C	5-10	168	2-16-53/Rouyn, Que.	Adirondack	10	23	33	68
	Brad Smith	C	6-1	195	4-13-58/Windsor, Ont.	Detroit	1	0	1	5
						Adirondack	33	39	72	89
5	Greg Smith	D	6-0	190	7-8-55/Pomoka, Alta.	Detroit	2	18	20	117
2	Larry Trader	D	6-1	197	7-7-63/Barry Bay, Ont.	Detroit	3	7	10	39
						Adirondack	0	4	4	0
15	Paul Woods	C	5-10	172	4-12-55/Hilton, Ont.	Adirondack	2	11	13	8
	Warren Young	LW	6-3	195	1-11-56/Weston, Ont.	Pittsburgh	40	32	72	176
19	Steve Yzerman	C	5-11	170	5-9-63/Cranbrook, B.C.	Detroit	30	59	89	58
11	Rick Zombo	D	6-1	195	5-8-63/Des Plaines, Ill.	Detroit	0	0	0	0
						Adirondack	3	32	35	70

No.	Player	Pos.	Ht.	Wt.	Born		GP	GA	SO	Avg.
35	Ken Holland	G	5-8	160	11-10-55/Vernon, B.C.	Adirondack	43	176	0	4.26
41	Ed Mio	G	5-10	180	1-31-54/Windsor, Ont.	Detroit	7	27	0	4.31
						Adirondack	33	117	2	3.75
1	Corrado Micalef	G	5-8	175	4-20-61/Montreal	Detroit	36	136	0	4.40
						Adirondack	1	2	0	2.00
30	Greg Stefan	G	5-11	180	2-11-61/Brantford, Ont.	Detroit	46	190	0	4.33

RED WING PROFILES

STEVE YZERMAN 20 5-11 170   Center

Proved his excellent rookie year was no accident with 89-point season... Quick, very effective playmaker... "He beats people in one-on-one situations," coach Nick Polano says... Scouts wondered whether he'd be strong enough to play in the league at 18 after being the fourth player taken in the 1983 draft... "The only reason he lasted that long was that his [Peterborough] coach didn't play him enough," GM Jimmy Devellano said. "It was hard to make a comparison on him. We were lucky."... Runnerup to Buffalo's Tom Barrasso for Rookie of the Year... Member of Team Canada for the 1984 Canada Cup... Youngest ever to play in an NHL All-Star Game (18 years, nine months)... Fine student, plans to continue a university education... Born May 9, 1965, in Cranbrook, B.C.... His father is a high-ranking official in social services department of the Canadian government.

Year	Club	GP	G	A	Pts.
1983-84	Detroit	80	39	48	87
1984-85	Detroit	80	30	59	89
	Totals	160	69	107	176

RON DUGUAY 28 6-2 210   Right Wing

Had best of his eight NHL seasons last year, recording 89 points... Fine two-way player, always thought to lack touch around the net, but he did have 38 goals last year... Certainly the most photogenic player in the league, with killer looks and coiffed, curly hair... "Getting him to wear a helmet," says his new wife, Robin, "is a lost cause."... He was never quite the playboy he was portrayed to be in New York, but he kept the photographers busy... Very disappointed to leave the Rangers, who traded him to Detroit in 1983... "But maybe the slower pace has done me some good," he said... Became a father last year... Sold his New York bar... Pretty face seen on product endorsements in the Detroit area... "I really don't see this reputation as a flamboyant guy," Polano says. "He's one of the quietest players I've ever coached. He takes care of himself."... Got into coach Herb Brooks' doghouse in New York and was part of a six-player deal (along with Eddie Mio and Eddie Johnstone) that brought Mark Osborne, Mike Blaisdell and Willie Huber to the Rangers... First-round pick by the Rangers in 1977. "Doogie" was born July 6, 1957, in Sudbury, Ont.

Year	Club	GP	G	A	Pts.
1977-78	New York R	71	20	20	40
1978-79	New York R	79	27	36	63
1979-80	New York R	73	28	22	50
1980-81	New York R	50	17	21	38
1981-82	New York R	72	40	36	76
1982-83	New York R	72	19	25	44
1983-84	Detroit	80	33	47	80
1984-85	Detroit	80	38	51	89
	Totals	577	222	258	480

JOHN OGRODNICK 26 6-0 190   Left Wing

Blossomed into a star last year with his first 100-point season... Arguably, he or Quebec's Michel Goulet is the best left wing in the game...Excellent anticipation, a fine shot, and not a bad checker either...One of the few times the Red Wings have gotten lucky in the draft. Ogrodnick was a fourth-rounder in 1979... Subject of a lot of trade rumors only because he's one of the few Wings opposing GMs consider worth asking about. "I like Detroit," he says. "My wife and I are happy here. I really think this management is going to turn things around."... Still, it's a shame to see his peak years slip by as the Red Wings attempt long-term rebuilding...Durable, has missed only 17 games in five full NHL seasons...Helped New Westminster to two Memorial Cups in his junior days...Enjoys water skating and fishing...Runs two hockey schools in the summer...Born June 20, 1959, in Ottawa...Made first All-Star team.

Year	Club	GP	G	A	Pts.
1979-80	Detroit	41	8	24	32
1980-81	Detroit	80	35	35	70
1981-82	Detroit	80	28	26	54
1982-83	Detroit	80	41	44	85
1983-84	Detroit	64	42	36	78
1984-85	Detroit	79	55	50	105
	Totals	424	209	215	424

GREG STEFAN 24 5-11 180   Goaltender

Feisty young goalie and a pretty good one...Very consistent, which isn't easy on a chronic loser...Keeps the Red Wings in a lot of games...Has been involved in several stick-swinging incidents that have brought league suspensions...Fifth-round choice in 1981 draft, spent less than half a year at Adirondack (AHL) before the desperate Red Wings brought him up...Accomplished golfer . . . Born Feb. 11, 1961, in Brantford, Ont., where he played on several youth teams with Wayne Gretzky.

Year	Club	GP	GA	SO	Avg.
1981-82	Detroit	2	10	0	5.00
1982-83	Detroit	35	139	0	4.52
1983-84	Detroit	50	152	2	3.51
1984-85	Detroit	46	190	0	4.33
	Totals	133	491	2	4.09

REED LARSON 29 6-0 195   Defenseman

One of the hardest shots in the NHL . . . Has never quite achieved star status predicted of him, but the Red Wings have never had much around him to help . . . His 1984-85 season was probably his best. Was a plus-eight last year on a team which scored 43 fewer goals than it gave up . . . Usually a 20-goal scorer and in the 60-70 point range . . . Star at the University of Minnesota under Herb Brooks . . . Had planned on completing four years there, but was suspended following a high-sticking incident and decided to turn pro. "They were trying to make an example of me," he said. "It seemed like a good time. Herbie said, 'Go ahead and sign.'" . . . One of the first Americans to be more than just a fringe NHL player . . . Second-round pick in 1976 . . . He and his wife are very active in groups helping retarded citizens . . . Enjoys the outdoor life . . . Would like to coach when he retires . . . Born July 30, 1956, in Minneapolis.

Year	Club	GP	G	A	Pts.
1976-77	Detroit	14	0	1	1
1977-78	Detroit	75	19	41	60
1978-79	Detroit	79	18	49	67
1979-80	Detroit	80	22	44	66
1980-81	Detroit	78	27	31	58
1981-82	Detroit	80	21	39	60
1982-83	Detroit	80	22	52	74
1983-84	Detroit	78	23	39	62
1984-85	Detroit	77	17	45	62
	Totals	641	169	341	510

WARREN YOUNG 29 6-3 195   Left Wing

Broke in last year as a 28-year-old Penguin rookie, scoring 40 goals and 32 assists . . . Became a free agent July 1, promptly signed with Red Wings and Pittsburgh filed tampering charges . . . Fourth-round pick by California in 1975, kicked around the North Star organization before the Penguins picked him up . . . "All those years I kept wondering, 'Can I play in the NHL?'" he said. "If I had made it and failed, then I'd have quit and not worried. But never getting a chance to know bothered me. It's tough to go through life not knowing." . . . Single. "Can you imagine knocking around the minors that long with a wife and family?" he said . . . Born Jan. 11, 1956, in Toronto.

Year	Club	GP	G	A	Pts.
1981-82	Minnesota	1	0	0	0
1982-83	Minnesota	4	1	1	2
1983-84	Pittsburgh	15	1	7	8
1984-85	Pittsburgh	80	40	32	72
	Totals	100	42	40	82

KELLY KISIO 26 5-9 170   Center

A free-agent bargain . . . A 60-point man for the second consecutive year . . . Overlooked in the draft because of his size . . . Red Wings signed him following the 1979 draft and after finishing up his junior eligibility at Calgary in the Western League, he played two minor-league seasons before signing a contract with Davos of Switzerland . . . Dan Belisle, who had coached Kisio at Dallas of the Central League, recommended the Red Wings take a look when he became Detroit's assistant coach . . . Fourth among NHL rookie scorers in 1983-84 . . . Born Sept. 18, 1959, in Wetaskwin, Alberta, he maintains offseason residence in Red Deer with his wife and two sons.

Year	Club	GP	G	A	Pts.
1983-84	Detroit	70	23	37	60
1984-85	Detroit	75	20	21	41
	Totals	145	43	58	101

DANNY GARE 31 5-9 175   Right Wing

Red Wing captain . . . Bounced back from a disappointing, injury-hampered 1983-84 season (bruised sternum) for a solid 56-point year . . . Slowed down from his big years at Buffalo (two 50-goal seasons), but still a competent performer . . . Buffalo's second-round pick in 1974, he scored a goal in his first NHL game. Undersized, but has always had a lot of heart . . . A Buffalo institution, it was a big shock when Scotty Bowman traded him, Jim Schoenfeld and Derek Smith for Dale McCourt, Mike Foligno and Brent Peterson in December 1981. Gare was coming off a 46-point season and a berth on Team Canada in the 1981 Canada Cup . . . Had a rugged start with the Red Wings as he came down with pneumonia . . . Very active in charity work for sick children

...Born May 14, 1954, in Nelson, B.C.

Year	Club	GP	G	A	Pts.
1974-75	Buffalo	78	31	31	62
1975-76	Buffalo	79	50	23	73
1976-77	Buffalo	35	11	15	26
1977-78	Buffalo	69	39	38	77
1978-79	Buffalo	71	27	40	67
1979-80	Buffalo	76	56	33	89
1980-81	Buffalo	73	46	39	85
1981-82	Buf-Det.	59	20	24	44
1982-83	Detroit	79	26	35	61
1983-84	Detroit	63	13	13	26
1984-85	Detroit	71	27	29	56
	Totals	753	346	320	666

DWIGHT FOSTER 28 5-11 190   Center

Fine comeback story after being purchased from New Jersey in
October 1982...The Bruins had used him as bait for Colorado's
No. 1 pick in 1982 and when he had a miserable season, he became
symbolic of the team's mismanagement...When team moved to
New Jersey, Detroit picked him up for $1 and he was able to start
over again with a lot less pressure on him...Did a fine job as a
checking center as the Red Wings made the playoffs for the first
time since 1977...Missed 30 games last year with a knee injury,
but still scored 32 points and was a plus-12...First-round pick
by the Bruins in 1977, following a 143-point year at Kitchener
...Quickly fell into coach Don Cherry's doghouse...Appeared
to be coming on in his final Boston season, but was having difficulty in contract talks at the time of his trade to the Rockies...
Owns an automotive business in Kitchener. "Dewey" was born
April 2, 1957, in Toronto.

Year	Club	GP	G	A	Pts.
1977-78	Boston	14	2	1	3
1978-79	Boston	44	11	13	24
1979-80	Boston	57	10	28	38
1980-81	Boston	77	24	28	52
1981-82	Colorado	70	12	19	31
1982-83	NJ-Det.	62	17	22	39
1983-84	Detroit	52	9	12	21
1984-85	Detroit	50	16	16	32
	Totals	426	101	159	240

ALL-TIME RED WING LEADERS

GOALS: John Ogrodnick, 55, 1984-85
ASSISTS: Marcel Dionne, 74, 1974-75
POINTS: Marcel Dionne, 121, 1974-75
SHUTOUTS: Terry Sawchuk, 12, 1951-52, 1954-55
              Glenn Hall, 12, 1955-56

COACH HARRY NEALE: Replaced Nick Polano as coach in June after being let go as GM of Vancouver, a job he held for three seasons... Though the Canucks showed improvement after Neale fired coach Bill LaForge in November and Neale went back behind the bench himself, his original decision caused Vancouver ownership to lose confidence in him... Born March 9, 1937, in Sarnia, Ont.... Played junior hockey with the Toronto Marlboros before doing degree work at the University of Toronto and McMaster University... His first coaching job was at Ohio State... With the formation of the World Hockey Assn. in 1972, he was named coach of the Minnesota Fighting Saints... When that franchise folded, he moved on to the New England Whalers before signing with the Canucks in 1978... Groomed for the GM's job from the day he was hired as coach, he succeeded the late Jake Milford on the latter's retirement... A great wit, extremely quotable... "Some of the players aren't too happy with my [hard] practices," he once said. "Well, I'm not to thrilled with their games."... Canucks improved every year of the four he coached them before going upstairs... Track record has been spotty as a GM, but as a coach he has proven capable of pepping up weak clubs.

MOST COLORFUL PLAYER

For 17 seasons, Ted Lindsay was one of the most feared players in the NHL. At 5-8, 163 pounds, a lot of tough guys came bigger, but none was ever more held in more respect.

"By my definition," he once said, "there's a helluva lot more to being tough than getting in a few phony punches where no real punches are tossed. To me, being tough includes wanting to win so badly that you give it all you've got on every shift, going into corners without phoning ahead to see who's there, backing up your mates if they're in trouble and stepping into guys, even if they're bigger than you."

He could play, too. Not only did Lindsay become the NHL's all-time penalty leader at the time of his retirement with 1,808 minutes, but he scored 379 career goals and was named All-Star left wing nine times.

His best years were as a member of the famed Production Line with Gordie Howe and Sid Abel. After being traded to Chicago in 1957 and quitting in 1960, Terrible Ted came back to play one more season with Detroit after three years in retirement.

EDMONTON OILERS

TEAM DIRECTORY: Owner: Peter Pocklington; Pres.-GM-Co-Coach: Glen Sather; Co-Coach: John Muckler; Dir. Player Personnel: Barry Fraser; Dir. Pub. Rel.: Bill Tuele. Home ice: Northlands Coliseum (17,498; 200′ × 85′). Colors: Royal blue, orange and white. Training camp: Edmonton.

SCOUTING REPORT

OFFENSE: Break up the Oilers!

Offensively, there is no NHL team, past or present, which can match the Stanley Cup champions in awesome scoring power. Edmonton has the four highest goal-scoring totals in NHL history—446 (1983-84), 424 (1982-83), 417 (1981-82) and 401 (1984-85). It has the greatest single-season scorer in hockey history, Wayne (The Great) Gretzky. Together, Gretzky and Jari Kurri scored 154 of the Oilers' league-leading 401 last season.

In defenseman Paul Coffey, Edmonton has the best scoring and rushing defenseman since Bobby Orr. In fact, Coffey is a faster skater than Orr.

Edmonton forwards not only have speed, they have size and strength. They can play a straight-ahead attacking game and score. They can use a European weaving, criss-crossing system of offense and score. Joining Gretzky and Kurri as explosive scorers are Mike Krushelnyski, Glenn Anderson, Mark Napier, Mark Messier, Dave Hunter, Willie Lindstrom and rugged Kevin McClelland. Big Dave Semenko is the Oilers' figure of intimidation when a physical style of play is needed.

Edmonton has added another offensive weapon. He's Finland forward Esa Tikkanen, who has the speed and finesse to add more to an already high-scoring offense.

Edmonton had the second best power play in the NHL last season. Glen Sather, the Oilers' GM, head co-coach and team president, is not fully satisfied with his team's power play. He believes Edmonton should score more power-play goals with the talented shooters in its lineup.

DEFENSE: The Oilers are not the best defensive team in the NHL. Because of their high-powered offense, they don't have to be; they have the puck most of the time. But they no longer give up goals as easily as they once did. They became a better defensive team last season as pointedly demonstrated when they whipped the Flyers in the playoff final.

Kurri is one of the league's best defensive forwards, when he

Huddy, Coffey, Kurri have reason to celebrate.

isn't scoring goals. Even Gretzky excels as a defender; he led the NHL with 11 shorthanded goals as a penalty-killer last season. As a team, Edmonton scored 25 shorthanded goals.

Led by Coffey, the Oilers' defense corps is solid; it doesn't turn the puck over with giveaways as much as it once did. Behind Coffey are Charlie Huddy, Randy Gregg, Kevin Lowe, Lee Fogolin and Don Jackson. Jeff Beukeboom, a big rookie defenseman, challenges for a job this season.

Many rival players and coaches rate Grant Fuhr as the best goalie in the NHL. He had an outstanding 1984-85. Andy Moog is recovering from offseason knee surgery. Edmonton should be stronger in goal this season, having acquired veteran Gilles Meloche from Minnesota, one of the leading goalies in the NHL. With Fuhr and Meloche, Edmonton will not lose many games because of poor goaltending.

OUTLOOK: Edmonton has all the ingredients to win its third straight Stanley Cup in 1986.

OILER ROSTER

No.	Player	Pos.	Ht.	Wt.	Born	1984-85	G	A	Pts.	PIM
9	Glenn Anderson	RW	5-11	175	10-2-60/Vancouver	Edmonton	42	39	81	69
	Ken Berry	RW	5-9	170	6-21-60/Vancouver	Nova Scotia	30	27	57	40
	Jeff Beukeboom	D	6-4	208	3-28-65/Ajax, Ont.	Sault Ste. Marie	4	20	24	85
20	Bill Carroll	RW	5-10	180	1-19-59/Toronto	Edmonton	8	9	17	22
7	Paul Coffey	D	6-0	200	6-1-61/Weston, Ont.	Edmonton	37	84	121	97
15	Pat Conacher	C	5-8	185	5-1-59/Edmonton	Nova Scotia	20	45	65	44
14	Ray Cote	C	5-11	160	5-31-61/Pincher Creek, Alta.	Edmonton	0	0	0	2
						Nova Scotia	36	43	79	63
	Tony Currie	C-RW	5-11	166	12-12-57/Sydney, N.S.	Hartford	3	8	11	2
						Nova Scotia	16	31	47	8
	Dale Derkatch	C	5-5	140	10-17-54/Preeceville, Sask.	Regina	4	7	11	0
2	Lee Fogolin	D	6-0	204	2-7-55/Chicago	Edmonton	4	14	18	126
8	Steve Graves	LW	6-0	180	4-7-64/Ottawa, Ont.	Nova Scotia	17	15	32	20
21	Randy Gregg	D	6-4	215	2-19-56/Edmonton	Edmonton	3	20	23	32
99	Wayne Gretzky	C	6-0	170	1-26-61/Brantford, Ont.	Edmonton	73	135	208	52
23	Marc Habscheid	C	5-11	169	3-1-63/Swift Current, Sask.	Edmonton	5	3	8	4
						Nova Scotia	29	29	58	65
22	Charlie Huddy	D	6-0	200	6-2-59/Oshawa, Ont.	Edmonton	7	44	51	46
16	Pat Hughes	RW	6-1	180	3-25-55/Toronto	Edmonton	12	13	25	85
12	Dave Hunter	LW	5-11	195	1-1-58/Petrolia, Ont.	Edmonton	17	19	36	122
29	Don Jackson	D	6-2	210	9-2-56/Minneapolis	Edmonton	3	17	20	141
26	Mike Krushelnyski	LW	6-2	200	4-27-60/Montreal	Edmonton	43	45	88	60
17	Jari Kurri	LW	6-0	195	5-18-60/Finland	Edmonton	71	64	135	30
19	Willy Lindstrom	RW	6-0	180	5-5-51/Sweden	Edmonton	12	20	32	18
4	Kevin Lowe	D	6-2	195	4-15-59/Hawksbury, Ont.	Edmonton	4	22	26	104
8	Dave Lumley	C	6-1	185	9-1-54/Toronto	Hart.-Edm.	9	23	32	111
	Craig MacTavish	C	6-0	185	8-15-58/London, Ont.					
24	Kevin McClelland	RW	6-0	180	7-4-62/Oshawa, Ont.	Edmonton	8	15	23	212
28	Larry Melnyk	D	6-0	193	2-21-60/New Westminster, B.C.	Edmonton	0	11	11	25
						Nova Scotia	2	10	12	97
11	Mark Messier	LW	6-1	207	1-18-61/Edmonton	Edmonton	23	31	54	57
18	Mark Napier	RW	5-10	185	1-28-57/Toronto	Minn.-Edm.	19	44	63	21
	Selmar Odelein	D	6-2	195	4-11-66/Quill Lake, Sask.	Regina	24	35	59	121
5	Jim Playfair	D	6-3	186	5-22-64/Vanderhoff, B.C.	Nova Scotia	0	4	4	107
27	Dave Semenko	LW	6-3	215	7-12-57/Winnipeg	Edmonton	6	12	18	167
5	Steve Smith	D	6-2	200	4-30-63/Scotland	Edmonton	0	0	0	2
						Nova Scotia	2	28	30	161
	Todd Strueby	C	6-1	186	6-15-63/Lanigan, Sask.	Nova Scotia	2	3	5	29
25	Raimo Summenen	RW	5-9	178	3-2-62/Finland	Edmonton	0	4	4	10
						Nova Scotia	20	33	53	2
	Esa Tikkanen	LW	5-11	180	1-25-65/Finland	Finnish Jrs.	–	–	–	–
	Simon Wheeldon	C	5-11	175	8-30-66/Vancouver	Victoria	50	76	126	78

							GP	GA	SO	Avg.
33	Marco Baron	G	5-11	179	4-8-59/Montreal	Edmonton	1	2	0	3.64
						Sher.-N.S.	18	50	0	2.88
31	Grant Fuhr	G	5-10	181	9-28-62/Spruce Grove, Alta.	Edmonton	46	165	1	3.87
27	Gilles Meloche	G	5-9	180	7-12-50/Montreal	Minnesota	32	115	0	3.80
35	Andy Moog	G	5-9	165	2-18-60/Princeton, B.C.	Edmonton	39	111	1	3.30
32	Darryl Reaugh	G	6-4	200	2-13-65/Prince Albert, B.C.	Kamloops	49	170	2	3.71
						Edmonton	1	5	0	5.00
30	Mike Zanier	G	5-11	175	8-22-63/Trail, B.C.	Nova Scotia	44	143	1	3.45
						Edmonton	3	12	0	3.89

OILER PROFILES

WAYNE GRETZKY 24 6-0 170   **Center**

No. 99 . . . The Great Gretzky . . . No player in hockey history has dominated the game in so short a time . . . "He's unbelievable . . . I'm glad I don't have to play against him," says former star Bobby Orr . . . "He'd be great in any era of hockey," says another former star, Gordie Howe . . . Has set more records than any player in hockey . . . Has established and re-established all-time records for most goals (87), most assists (135), most points (212) in single season . . . And he's only 24, with just six years in NHL! . . . Born Jan. 26, 1961, in Brantford, Ont. . . . A magician as passer and playmaking center . . . Led NHL in scoring for sixth consecutive season in 1984-85 . . . Has led NHL in goals four straight seasons, assists six years in a row . . . Playoff MVP when Edmonton won second straight Stanley Cup last season . . . Set playoff scoring record with 17-30-47 in 18 games . . . Has averaged a remarkable 71 goals, 115 assists, 187 points since entering NHL . . . Among all-time leading playoff scorers with 56-100-156 in 70 games . . . Has scored 92 power-play goals, 48 winning goals in career . . . Has won six consecutive Hart Trophies . . . Has 40 shorthanded goals in career, including record 12 in 1983-84 . . . Hockey's highest-paid player with salary estimated near $1 million a year.

Year	Club	GP	G	A	Pts.
1978-79	Ind-Edm (WHA)	80	46	64	110
1979-80	Edmonton.	79	51	86	137
1980-81	Edmonton.	80	55	109	164
1981-82	Edmonton.	80	92	120	212
1982-83	Edmonton.	80	71	125	196
1983-84	Edmonton.	74	87	118	205
1984-85	Edmonton.	80	73	135	208
	NHL Totals	473	429	693	1122
	WHA Totals	80	46	64	110

PAUL COFFEY 24 6-0 200   **Defenseman**

Hockey's most awesome offensive defenseman . . . Finished fifth in NHL scoring last season with 37 goals, 84 assists, 121 points . . . Set playoff scoring record for defensemen with 12 goals, breaking record shared by former All-Stars Bobby Orr and Brad Park . . . Has occasional defensive lapses but players generally regard him as best defenseman in hockey . . . Born June 1, 1961, in Weston, Ont. . . . Has size and speed . . . Almost impossible to stop when he takes off with puck on rink-length rush . . . Threatens to break many of Orr's records as scoring defenseman . . . Often outspoken . . . Claims he was told by his junior hockey coach (former NHL defenseman Rod Seiling) that he'd probably never make it to NHL.

Year	Club	GP	G	A	Pts.
1980-81	Edmonton	74	9	23	32
1981-82	Edmonton	80	29	60	89
1982-83	Edmonton	80	29	67	96
1983-84	Edmonton	80	40	86	126
1984-85	Edmonton	80	37	84	121
	Totals	394	144	320	464

JARI KURRI 25 6-0 190   Right Wing

Flashy Finn forms most dynamic one-two goal-scoring punch as right wing on line with Wayne Gretzky . . . Tied record of 19 goals in playoffs, set in 1975 by Flyers' Reggie Leach in 1975, when Edmonton won second straight Stanley Cup in 1985 . . . Second in NHL scoring behind Gretzky with 71 goals, 135 points . . . His 71 goals are the most ever scored by a right wing . . . Led NHL with 13 game-winning goals . . . Scored on 27.2 percent of his shots, second in NHL to 30.8 scoring percentage by Pittsburgh's Warren Young . . . Born May 18, 1960, in Helsinki, Finland . . . Has speed and deadly shot . . . Does good job when needed as defensive forward.

Year	Club	GP	G	A	Pts.
1980-81	Edmonton	75	32	43	75
1981-82	Edmonton	71	32	54	86
1982-83	Edmonton	80	45	59	104
1983-84	Edmonton	64	52	61	113
1984-85	Edmonton	73	71	64	135
	Totals	363	232	281	513

MARK MESSIER 24 6-1 207   Center-Left Wing

Pound for pound, one of hockey's best all-around players . . . Big, strong, fast . . . A power forward who plays aggressively . . . Excels on offense as well as defensively . . . Injuries kept him from playing in 25 games last season . . . Capable of playing left wing or center . . . Used mostly at center last season . . . One of the best at winning faceoffs . . . Won 26 of 35 faceoffs in one playoff final game against the Flyers . . . Born Jan. 18, 1961, in Edmonton, Alta. . . . Named playoff MVP when Edmonton won first Stanley Cup in 1984 . . . Had 26 points in 19 playoff games that season . . . Good-natured athlete . . . Plays with enthusiasm . . . Twice a 100-point scorer... Good friend of Ken Daneyko, rookie defenseman with New Jersey Devils.

Year	Club	GP	G	A	Pts.
1978-79	Ind-Cin (WHA)	52	1	10	11
1979-80	Edmonton	75	12	21	33
1980-81	Edmonton	72	23	40	63
1981-82	Edmonton	78	50	38	88
1982-83	Edmonton	77	48	58	106
1983-84	Edmonton	73	37	64	101
1984-85	Edmonton	55	23	31	54
	NHL Totals	430	193	252	445
	WHA Totals	52	1	10	11

MIKE KRUSHELNYSKI 25 6-2 200   Left Wing

Third member of explosive line with Wayne Gretzky and Jari Kurri ... Edmonton's fourth-leading scorer... Glen Sather made smart move acquiring him in 1984 trade with Boston... "Special K" turned out to be the missing link Oilers were seeking to play left wing on Gretzky's line... Plays center or left wing... Good at winning faceoffs and often relieves Gretzky of faceoff duties... Born April 27, 1960, in Montreal... Good all-around player... Rugged in corners and near net, yet has many finesse skills... Plays aggressively... Youthful good looks make him popular with young fans.

Year	Club	GP	G	A	Pts.
1981-82	Boston	17	3	3	6
1982-83	Boston	79	23	42	65
1983-84	Boston	66	25	20	45
1984-85	Edmonton	80	43	45	88
	Totals	242	94	110	204

GRANT FUHR 23 5-10 181   Goaltender

May have the fastest reflexes of any goalie in hockey... Seldom beaten on breakaways... Made hockey history by facing two penalty shots in last season's playoff final... He stopped them both ... Has quick hands and stick, and his nimble footwork enables him to make many saves with legs... Can stay up, challenge shooter and make save or make last-second diving, acrobatic save ... Excites fans with bold, daring style... Often skates far out of goal-crease to retrieve puck... Reminds older fans of former Ranger goalie Eddie Giacomin . . . Born Sept. 28, 1962, in Spruce Grove, Alta. . . . Outstanding stick-handler who takes pressure off defensemen by passing puck to forwards . . . Set NHL record for goalie with 14 assists in 1983-84 . . . Has 23 career assists . . . With 97-35-40 record, he needs three wins to reach 100 . . . First black goalie in NHL history.

Year	Club	GP	GA	SO	Avg.
1981-82	Edmonton	48	157	0	3.31
1982-83	Edmonton	32	129	0	4.29
1983-84	Edmonton	45	171	1	3.91
1984-85	Edmonton	46	165	1	3.87
	Totals	171	622	2	3.80

GLENN ANDERSON 25 5-11 175   Right Wing

The list grows longer . . . Still another high-powered Oiler forward . . . Has scored 48, 54, 42 goals in last three seasons . . . Ranks among best, if not the best left wing . . . Slick, quick skater . . . Skilled at slipping past defenders with or without puck to create close-range scoring chances . . . Always on the move . . . Difficult to check . . . Operates well in slot area or from offensive angles in faceoff circles . . . Well-known for ability to pester rival goalies close to net . . . Born Oct. 2, 1960, in Vancouver, B.C. . . . Plays with tenacity and drive . . . Rivals respect his ability but sometimes become annoyed by his persistent, chippy style of play.

Year	Club	GP	G	A	Pts.
1980-81	Edmonton	58	30	23	53
1981-82	Edmonton	80	38	67	105
1982-83	Edmonton	72	48	56	104
1983-84	Edmonton	80	54	45	99
1984-85	Edmonton	80	42	39	81
	Totals	370	212	230	442

GILLES MELOCHE 35 5-9 185   Goaltender

Finally gets big break in 15th NHL season . . . Trade on May 31, 1985, from Minnesota to Stanley Cup champion Edmonton places him on powerhouse team for first time in career . . . Oilers wanted him to work with Grant Fuhr because No. 2 goalie Andy Moog, plagued last season by bad knees, needed offseason surgery . . . Senior goalie in NHL . . . Career record of 236-308-114 doesn't disclose how good he's been . . . Spent first seven full seasons in

NHL with dreadfully weak California Golden Seals and Cleveland Barons ... Often faced barrage of 40 to 50 shots a game playing for weak defensive teams ... Born July 12, 1950, in Montreal ... Exciting goalie to watch ... Master of making seemingly impossible saves ... North Stars taking a chance by giving him up ... Well-respected by players in NHL ... Good puck-handler and passer for goalie ... Has 13 career assists ... Classy guy on and off the ice.

Year	Club	GP	GA	SO	Avg.
1970-71	Chicago	2	6	0	3.00
1971-72	California	56	173	4	3.32
1972-73	California	59	235	1	4.06
1973-74	California	47	198	1	4.24
1974-75	California	47	186	1	4.03
1975-76	California	41	140	1	3.44
1976-77	Cleveland	51	171	2	3.47
1977-78	Cleveland	54	195	1	3.77
1978-79	Minnesota	53	173	2	3.33
1979-80	Minnesota	54	160	1	3.06
1980-81	Minnesota	38	120	2	3.25
1981-82	Minnesota	51	175	1	3.47
1982-83	Minnesota	47	160	1	3.57
1983-84	Minnesota	52	201	2	4.18
1984-85	Minnesota	32	115	0	3.80
	Totals	684	2408	20	3.64

CHARLIE HUDDY 26 6-0 200   Defenseman

Does it all defensively ... Can play role of defensive defenseman or provide offense ... Velocity of his shot from blue line second only to teammate Paul Coffey ... Twenty-goal scorer in 1982-83 ... Collects profusion of assists because of passing skill on high-scoring team ... Annually ranks among the best defensemen in NHL plus-minus ratings ... Born June 2, 1959, in Oshawa, Ont. ... Not flashy but gets the job done ... His skills often are subtle and overlooked by fans ... Led league in plus-minus rating in 1982-83 ... Doesn't make many mistakes in defensive zone ... Takes opposing forwards out of play smartly ... Good shot-blocker.

Year	Club	GP	G	A	Pts.
1980-81	Edmonton	12	2	5	7
1981-82	Edmonton	41	4	11	15
1982-83	Edmonton	76	20	37	57
1983-84	Edmonton	75	8	34	42
1984-85	Edmonton	80	7	44	51
	Totals	284	41	131	172

KEVIN LOWE 26 6-2 195 .   **Defenseman**

Edmonton's first-round draft choice in 1979 . . . A master of the
lost art of effective bodychecking . . . A defensive defenseman whose
role is especially vital to a team which places greater emphasis
on offense . . . Bright, friendly, well-spoken athlete . . . Maintains
good relationship with media . . . His comments to hockey writers
make interesting reading for hockey fans . . . Born April 15, 1959,
in Lachute, Que. . . . Good team leader and smart hockey player
. . . Has cheerful, enthusiastic outlook toward hockey and life . . .
Always plays hard . . . Willing to hit and be hit . . . A defenseman
who excels as a shot-blocker.

Year	Club	GP	G	A	Pts.
1979-80	Edmonton.	64	2	19	21
1980-81	Edmonton.	79	10	24	34
1981-82	Edmonton.	80	9	31	40
1982-83	Edmonton.	80	6	34	40
1983-84	Edmonton.	80	4	42	46
1984-85	Edmonton.	80	4	22	26
	Totals	463	35	172	207

COACH GLEN SATHER: GM and president of Stanley Cup
champion Edmonton . . . Will carry title this
season as co-coach with veteran John Muckler,
who has been Oilers' chief assistant coach and
eventually will become head coach . . . Sather
manages and coaches with same approach he
had as NHL player . . . Fiesty, outspoken and
often accused of being overly cocky . . . No one
can argue with his success . . . Has guided powerful Oilers to two consecutive Stanley Cup championships and
258-150-72 record in six seasons . . . Born Sept. 2, 1943, in High
River, Alta. . . . Scored 80 goals, accumulated 724 penalty minutes
in 10 years as NHL forward . . . Played with Boston, Pittsburgh,
Rangers, St. Louis, Montreal, Minnesota . . . Was an outstanding
penalty-killer and checker . . . Never afraid to fight bigger opponents . . . Nicknamed "Slats" . . . Fiery competitor with a quick wit
and sharp tongue on and off the ice.

MOST COLORFUL PLAYER

Who else but No. 99?

Name a category, and Wayne Gretzky is at the top of the list.

He's only 24 and entering his seventh NHL season but is well on his way to becoming the greatest scorer in hockey history. He is the Rocket Richard, Eddie Shore, Bobby Hull, Phil Esposito of his time.

Gretzky is the greatest drawing attraction in hockey, a sport which sadly lacks genuine superstar athletes whose names become household words. Even non-hockey fans know the name Gretzky. Teams such as Pittsburgh, New Jersey and Vancouver have difficulty selling enough tickets to fill their arenas. But when Gretzky and Edmonton are the opposition, the Penguins, Devils and Canucks play before capacity crowds.

So great are his skills that each game seems to revolve around him. Fans often come only to see No. 99

"Hockey needs more guys like him," says Orr, who did what Gretzky is doing now in the late 1960s and 1970s.

ALL-TIME OILER LEADERS

GOALS: Wayne Gretzky, 92, 1981-82
ASSISTS: Wayne Gretzky, 135, 1984-85
POINTS: Wayne Gretzky, 212, 1981-82
SHUTOUTS: Eddie Mio, 1, 1979-80
Andy Moog, 1, 1982-83, 1983-84, 1984-85
Grant Fuhr, 1, 1983-84, 1984-85

LOS ANGELES KINGS

TEAM DIRECTORY: Chairman: Dr. Jerry Buss; Pres.: Lou Baumeister; GM: Rogie Vachon; Dir. Pub. Rel.: David Courtney; Coach: Pat Quinn. Home ice: The Forum (16,005; 200' × 85'). Colors: Royal blue and gold. Training camp: Victoria, B.C.

SCOUTING REPORT

OFFENSE: There are not many teams with five forwards who score from 46 to 30 goals and from 126 to 83 points in a season. Or who score a collective 56 power-play goals.

The Kings have them in veteran Marcel Dionne, Bernie Nicholls, Dave Taylor, Brian MacLellan and Jim Fox. But after the Big Five, the scoring drops off noticeably. Doug Smith, a promising young forward, scored 21 goals last season. He's capable of scoring 30 or more and could give Los Angeles' strong attack a sixth dangerous scorer.

Veterans Dave (Tiger) Williams, the most penalized player in NHL history, and Terry Ruskowski give the Kings added depth and aggressiveness on the forward line. Phil Sykes scored 17 goals as a rookie last season and is a good defensive forward.

The Kings' offensive game is not a problem. Neither is their power play. Los Angeles led the NHL last season with 89 power-play goals.

DEFENSE: No longer a weak link. Coach Pat Quinn developed the Kings into a good defensive team last season. The Kings took great pride in team defense. The forwards and defensemen worked well as a five-man unit. The fore-checking and back-checking were vastly improved. Forwards made a swift transition from offense to defense and stayed with their men from one end of the ice to the other. The Kings' checking in neutral ice disrupted opponents' rushes.

Los Angeles' penalty-killing was improved. It ranked third in the NHL, allowed the fewest power-play goals-against (54), giving the Kings outstanding special teams (power play, penalty-killing) efficiency.

Mark Hardy emerged as a skilled two-way defenseman. He scored 14 goals, 53 points, and did a solid job defensively. Brian Engblom, Rick Lapointe and Jay Wells were strong defensively. Two rookie defensemen, Craig Redmond and Garry Galley, had outstanding seasons.

The goaltending also is improved. Rookie Bob Janecyk established himself as No. 1 goalie. Another rookie, Darren Eliot, did

Marcel Dionne scored 126—his eighth 100-point year.

a good job as Janecyk's goaltending partner.

Los Angeles had two first-round choices in the 1985 draft, selecting left wing Craig Duncanson and center Dan Gratton.

OUTLOOK: Quinn, GM Rogie Vachon and assistant coach Mike Murphy have developed the Kings into a solid team which plays well defensively and offensively. Last season the Kings had their first winning record in four years. This season they could challenge Calgary and Winnipeg for second or third place in the Smythe Division.

KING ROSTER

No.	Player	Pos.	Ht.	Wt.	Born	1984-85	G	A	Pts.	PIM
16	Marcel Dionne	C	5-8	185	8-3-51/Drummondville, Que.	Los Angeles	46	80	126	46
5	Brian Engblom	D	6-2	200	1-27-57/Winnipeg	Los Angeles	4	19	23	70
15	Darryl Evans	RW	5-8	176	1-12-61/Toronto	Los Angeles	1	0	1	2
						New Haven	22	24	46	12
19	Jim Fox	RW	5-8	183	5-18-60/Coniston, Ont.	Los Angeles	30	53	83	10
3	Garry Galley	D	5-11	190	4-16-63/Ottawa, Ont.	Los Angeles	8	30	38	82
	Dan Gratton	C	6-1	184	12-7-66/Brantford, Ont.	Oshawa	24	48	72	67
21	Anders Hakansson	RW	6-2	192	4-27-56/Sweden	Los Angeles	12	12	24	28
6	Ken Hammond	D	6-1	190	8-22-63/London, Ont.	Los Angeles	1	0	1	0
20	Mark Hardy	D	5-11	195	2-1-59/Switzerland	Los Angeles	14	39	53	97
32	Mike Heidt	D	6-1	193	11-4-63/Calgary	N.S.-N. Haven	1	8	9	16
17	John Paul Kelly	LW	6-1	215	11-15-59/Edmonton	Los Angeles	8	10	18	55
6	Dean Kennedy	D	6-2	195	1-18-63/Redner, Sask.	New Haven	3	14	17	104
28	Rick Lapointe	D	6-2	200	8-2-55/Victoria, B.C.	Los Angeles	4	13	17	46
27	Brian MacLellan	LW	6-3	210	10-27-58/Guelph, Ont.	Los Angeles	31	54	85	53
9	Bernie Nicholls	C	6-0	185	6-24-61/Haliburton, Ont.	Los Angeles	46	54	100	76
	Lyle Phair	LW	6-1	190	— /Pilot Mound, Man.	Mich. St. U.	23	27	50	—
2	Craig Redmond	D	5-10	190	9-22-65/Langley, B.C.	Los Angeles	6	33	39	57
10	Terry Ruskowski	C	5-10	180	12-31-54/Prince Edward, Sask.	Los Angeles	16	33	49	144
	Steve Seguin	RW	6-2	198	4-10-64/Cornwall, Ont.	Los Angeles	0	0	0	9
						New Haven	18	7	25	39
23	Doug Smith	C	5-11	180	5-17-63/Ottawa, Ont.	Los Angeles	21	20	41	14
7	Phil Sykes	LW	6-0	178	5-18-59/Dawson Creek, B.C.	Los Angeles	17	15	32	38
18	Dave Taylor	RW	6-0	195	12-4-55/Sudbury, Ont.	Los Angeles	41	51	92	132
24	Jay Wells	D	6-1	205	5-18-59/Paris, Ont.	Los Angeles	2	9	11	185
26	Brian Wilks	C	5-11	175	2-27-66/N. York, Ont.	Los Angeles	0	0	0	0
						Kitchener	30	63	93	52
22	Tiger Williams	LW	5-11	190	2-3-54/Weyburn, Sask.	Det.-LA	7	11	18	201

No.	Player	Pos.	Ht.	Wt.	Born	1984-85	GP	GA	SO	Avg.
35	Darren Eliot	G	6-1	175	11-26-61/Milton, Ont.	Los Angeles	33	137	0	4.37
1	Bob Janecyk	G	6-1	180	5-18-57/Chicago	Los Angeles	51	183	2	3.66

KING PROFILES

MARCEL DIONNE 34 5-8 185   **Center**
Shows no signs of slowing down...Like Old Man River, he just
keeps rolling along...Eight times a 100-point scorer...Six times
a 50-goal scorer...Kings' veteran center ranks third in career
goals (629) behind Gordie Howe (801) and Phil Esposito (717),
third in career assists (876) behind Howe (1049) and Stan Mikita
(926), third in career points (1505) behind Howe (1850) and Esposito (1590)...Born Aug. 3, 1951, in Drummondville, Que.
...Enters 15th NHL season...Has averaged 107 points a season
...As skilled a playmaker as he is a goal-scorer...Led NHL in
scoring with 137 points in 1979–80...Started NHL career with
Detroit in 1970...An L.A. King for 10 seasons...Nicknamed
"Lou" for his likeness to late comedian Lou Costello..."It's
amazing," said Kings' assistant coach Mike Murphy. "I see no
indication that he's lost any of his ability. Marcel looks like he
can keep on playing at a high level for quite a few more years."

Year	Club	GP	G	A	Pts.
1971-72	Detroit	78	28	49	77
1972-73	Detroit	77	40	50	90
1973-74	Detroit	74	24	54	78
1974-75	Detroit	80	47	74	121
1975-76	Los Angeles	80	40	54	94
1976-77	Los Angeles	80	53	69	122
1977-78	Los Angeles	70	36	43	79
1978-79	Los Angeles	80	59	71	130
1979-80	Los Angeles	80	53	84	137
1980-81	Los Angeles	80	58	77	135
1981-82	Los Angeles	78	50	67	117
1982-83	Los Angeles	80	56	51	107
1983-84	Los Angeles	66	39	53	92
1984-85	Los Angeles	80	46	80	126
	Totals	1083	629	876	1505

BERNIE NICHOLLS 24 6-0 185   **Center**
Became a 100-point scorer last season, his fourth in NHL...Led
Kings with 326 shots on goal...Tall, rangy center with fluid
skating style and better-than-average speed...Has produced 277
points in 251 games since Kings summoned him from New Haven
minor-league team in 1981–82...Emotional, high-strung young
athlete who doesn't hide his emotions on ice...Born June 24,
1961, in Haliburton, Ont....A lot of teams overlooked him in

1980 draft... Kings chose him in fourth round as 73rd player drafted... Runs trapping compound with father in offseason... Grew up rooting for Bobby Orr and Bruins... Flashy, fun-loving athlete who enjoys Los Angeles lifestyle.

Year	Club	GP	G	A	Pts.
1981-82	Los Angeles	22	14	18	32
1982-83	Los Angeles	71	28	22	50
1983-84	Los Angeles	78	41	54	95
1984-85	Los Angeles	80	46	54	100
	Totals	251	129	148	277

DAVE TAYLOR 29 6-0 195   **Right Wing**

Bounced back from injury plagued 1983–84 season with 41 goals, 92 points last season... One of the best all-around right wings in NHL... A proven scorer who is willing to check and hit... Accumulated 132 penalty minutes last season... Starred on Kings' Triple Crown Line with Marcel Dionne and Charlie Simmer until Kings traded Simmer to Boston last year... Born Dec. 4, 1955, in Levack, Ont.... Nicknamed "Stitch"... Twice scored 100 or more points in a season with Kings... Was outstanding hockey player at Clarkson College... One of the league's hardest-hitting forwards.

Year	Club	GP	G	A	Pts.
1977-78	Los Angeles	64	22	21	43
1978-79	Los Angeles	78	43	48	91
1979-80	Los Angeles	61	37	53	90
1980-81	Los Angeles	72	47	65	112
1981-82	Los Angeles	78	39	67	106
1982-83	Los Angeles	46	21	37	58
1983-84	Los Angeles	63	20	49	69
1984-85	Los Angeles	79	41	51	92
	Totals	541	270	391	661

TERRY RUSKOWSKI 30 5-10 180   **Forward**

Teammates call him "Roscoe"... No one ever will accuse him of lack of hustle... Plays a hard-driving brand of hockey... Persistent checker... Fierce competitor with aggressive style of play that often upsets opponents... Replaced Dave Lewis as Kings' captain in 1983-84... Offsets lack of size with hard work and good natural instincts... Eleven-year veteran of pro hockey com-

bat...Had assists totals of 66, 60, 57 while playing in WHA
...One of NHL's most vigorous, aggressive forwards...Born
Dec. 31, 1954, in Prince Albert, Sask....Clever playmaker,
skilled penalty-killer...Doesn't score a lot of goals but collects
numerous assists...Played four years for Chicago before traded
to Los Angeles.

Year	Club	GP	G	A	Pts.
1974-75	Houston (WHA)	71	10	36	46
1975-76	Houston (WHA)	65	14	35	49
1976-77	Houston (WHA)	80	24	60	84
1977-78	Houston (WHA)	78	15	57	72
1978-79	Winnipeg (WHA)	75	20	66	86
1979-80	Chicago	74	15	55	70
1980-81	Chicago	72	8	51	59
1981-82	Chicago	60	7	30	37
1982-83	Chi-LA	76	14	32	46
1983-84	Los Angeles	77	7	25	32
1984-85	Los Angeles	78	16	33	49
	NHL Totals	437	67	226	293
	WHA Totals	369	83	254	337

BRIAN MacLELLAN 26 6-3 210   Left Wing

Big, strong, mobile left wing...Had his best NHL season in
1984–85...Overcame serious medical problems to reach NHL
...Suffered from disease called Legge Perthes as a child...Doctors told him he might never walk correctly as an adult...Recovered from broken neck at 19 when he played junior hockey
...Born Oct. 27, 1958, in Guelph, Ont....Has speed and is
breakaway threat...Also can score effectively on inside shots
because of his size...Kings took a chance and signed him as a
free agent in 1982.

Year	Club	GP	G	A	Pts.
1982-83	Los Angeles	8	0	3	3
1983-84	Los Angeles	72	25	29	54
1984-85	Los Angeles	80	31	54	85
	Totals	160	56	86	142

BRIAN ENGBLOM 30 6-2 200   Defenseman

Kings acquired him Oct. 18, 1983, in trade with Washington for
defenseman Larry Murphy...Started NHL career with Montreal
...Was involved in 1982 trade in which Montreal traded Engblom

and Rod Langway to Washington . . . Born Jan. 27, 1955, in Winnipeg, Man. . . . A defenseman who stays back to protect defensive zone instead of joining attack . . . Good shot-blocker . . . Not a defenseman who has peaks and valleys in his game . . . Good positional player who plays a steady game of defense . . . A good bodychecker who finishes off his checks with authority, taking opponent out of the play.

Year	Club	GP	G	A	Pts.
1977-78	Montreal	28	1	2	3
1978-79	Montreal	62	3	11	14
1979-80	Montreal	70	3	20	23
1980-81	Montreal	80	3	25	28
1981-82	Montreal	76	4	29	33
1982-83	Washington	73	5	22	27
1983-84	Wash-LA	80	2	28	30
1984-85	Los Angeles	79	4	19	23
	Totals	548	25	156	181

JIM FOX 25 5-8 183   Right Wing

Enjoyed his finest season in 1984–85 with 30 goals, 83 points . . . Scoring figures have improved each season since joining Los Angeles in 1980 . . . Plays hard but has knack for avoiding penalties . . . Once played 55 consecutive games without being assessed a penalty . . . Born May 18, 1960, in Coniston, Ont. . . . Hustling player . . . Played in defensive backfield for high-school football team . . . Starred for Ottawa in Ontario Junior Hockey Association . . . Kings claimed him as their first draft choice in 1980.

Year	Club	GP	G	A	Pts.
1980-81	Los Angeles	71	18	25	43
1981-82	Los Angeles	77	30	38	68
1982-83	Los Angeles	77	28	40	68
1983-84	Los Angeles	80	30	42	72
1984-85	Los Angeles	79	30	53	83
	Totals	384	136	198	334

DAVE WILLIAMS 31 5-11 190   Left Wing

Best known as Tiger Williams . . . Most penalized player in NHL history with 3,195 minutes, an average of 290 a season . . . Figure does not include 421 penalty minutes in 75 career playoff games

. . . Has the face of a prize fighter or a character from the old tough-guy Dead End Kids movies . . . Master of physical abuse and attempted intimidation of less physical opponents . . . Born Feb. 3, 1954, in Weyburn, Sask. . . . Veteran left wing started NHL career with Toronto and was traded to Vancouver . . . Canucks traded him to Detroit on Aug. 8, 1984, for Rob McClanahan because of contract dispute . . . Fell into disfavor with Red Wings' GM Jimmy Devellano and was released late in 1984 – 85 . . . Kings signed him to add muscle and hustle to forward line . . . Despite his reputation as fighter, he's a good hockey player . . . Next goal will be 200th of his career.

Year	Club	GP	G	A	Pts.
1974-75	Toronto	42	10	19	29
1975-76	Toronto	78	21	19	40
1976-77	Toronto	77	18	25	43
1977-78	Toronto	78	19	31	50
1978-79	Toronto	77	19	20	39
1979-80	Tor–Van	78	30	23	53
1980-81	Vancouver	77	35	27	62
1981-82	Vancouver	77	17	21	38
1982-83	Vancouver	68	8	13	21
1983-84	Vancouver	67	15	16	31
1984-85	Det-LA	67	7	11	18
	Totals	786	199	225	424

MARK HARDY 26 5-11 195   Defenseman

Set career highs for goals (14), assists (39) and points (53) last season . . . Was defensive partner of Winnipeg's Robert Picard when he played junior hockey in Montreal . . . Only NHL player born in Switzerland . . . Father played hockey in Europe and mother was member of Great Britain's 1952 Olympic figure-skating team . . . Born Feb. 1, 1959, in Semaden, Switzerland . . . Rugged defenseman who dishes out jolting body checks to opposing forwards . . . Learned to skate when he was two years old . . . Because of curly hair, Los Angeles teammates nicknamed him "Harpo."

Year	Club	GP	G	A	Pts.
1979-80	Los Angeles	15	0	1	1
1980-81	Los Angeles	77	5	20	25
1981-82	Los Angeles	77	6	39	45
1982-83	Los Angeles	74	5	34	39
1983-84	Los Angeles	79	8	41	49
1984-85	Los Angeles	78	14	39	53
	Totals	400	38	174	212

BOB JANECYK 28 6-1 180   Goaltender

"Janny" . . . Spent four seasons in Chicago Black Hawks' farm system before finally getting chance for which he was waiting . . . But only played in eight games and Chicago traded him to Kings after 1983–84 season . . . Shared Kings' goaltending with another rookie, Darren Eliot, early last season . . . Eventually became No. 1 goalie and had impressive "rookie" season . . . Had 22-21-8 record, 3.66 goals-against average . . . Born May 18, 1957, in Chicago, Ill. . . . Still trying to sharpen his goaltending to reach high-quality level . . . Sometimes has difficulty with footwork in goal crease . . . Made 48 saves when he beat Buffalo, 4-3, while with Chicago for his first NHL goaltending win on Feb. 29, 1984.

Year	Club	GP	GA	SO	Avg.
1983-84	Chicago	8	28	0	4.08
1984-85	Los Angeles	51	183	2	3.66
	Totals	59	211	2	3.71

COACH PAT QUINN: Known as the Irish Enforcer during nine-year career as rugged NHL defenseman for Toronto, Vancouver, Atlanta . . . Once angered Boston fans by badly beating Bobby Orr in fight at Boston Garden . . . Became Kings' 13th coach in 18 years last season . . . His coaching helped Kings compile best record in eight seasons . . . Born Jan. 29, 1943, in Hamilton, Ont. . . . Had 950 penalty minutes in 606 games as NHL player . . . Coached Flyers from 1978 to 1982 . . . His 1979-80 Flyers set NHL record with remarkable 35-game unbeaten streak en route to 48-12-20 season . . . Winner of Jack Adams Trophy in 1979 as Coach of the Year . . . Flyers were 141-73-48 under his coaching . . . Left coaching to study for law degree . . . Started coaching career with Maine Mariners of American League.

MOST COLORFUL PLAYER

It's not easy for a hockey player to establish identity in California. Too much sun and surf and other outside activities occupy most Californians. Additionally, hockey is a sport foreign to most of them.

Somehow Marcel Dionne has made it big in California.

Even casual sports fans have heard his name for the 10 seasons he's played for the Kings, who rank well below the Dodgers, Rams and college football and basketball in the broad spectrum of California sports interest.

Dionne has gained color and appeal because he is the Kings' most exciting and successful player to watch at the Forum in Inglewood. He's not big or tall, doesn't fit the image of an athlete, but he scores 100 or more points a season, is one of the highest scorers in NHL history and seems to scoot or glide across the ice. In his own sport, he represents to the fans the same qualities O.J. Simpson and Jerry West had in football and basketball, respectively.

ALL-TIME KING LEADERS

GOALS: Marcel Dionne, 59, 1978-79
ASSISTS: Marcel Dionne, 84, 1979-80
POINTS: Marcel Dionne, 137, 1979-80
SHUTOUTS: Rogatien Vachon, 8, 1976-77

MINNESOTA NORTH STARS

TEAM DIRECTORY: Co-Chairmen: George Gund III and Gordon Gund; Pres.: John Karr; GM: Lou Nanne; Dir. Hockey Info.: Dick Dillman; Coach: Lorne Henning. Home ice: Met Center (15,184; 200′ × 85′). Colors: Green, white and gold. Training camp: Bloomington, Minn.

SCOUTING REPORT

OFFENSE: Remember the North Stars, the team that only last November got coach Bill Mahoney fired because it was too offensive-minded? The club that has long been accused of being addicted to goals at the expense of its own end of the ice?

These are the guys who scored only 268 goals last year, tied for the fourth lowest in the league. So who are these North Stars? There have been so many changes over the last three years it's kind of hard to tell. The latest was the acquisition of Kent Nilsson, the multitalented yet recalcitrant Calgary center. The cynics would suggest that the Stars have enough of these kind of offensive-only players already. But the truth is they just didn't score enough goals last year.

To be fair, they had injuries last year. Dino Ciccarelli, the club's top sniper off the wing, left wing Tom McCarthy, a usual 30-goal man, and Craig Hartsburg, the Stars' blue-line catalyst, missed major portions of the season.

There's still a lot of talent here, if it can be formed into some kind of cohesive unit. If Neal Broten, the club's top center, bounces back from a poor season; if Brian Lawton, the first player taken in the 1983 draft begins to live up to his promise; if 21-year-old Brian Bellows, who had a mediocre 62-point season, pushes himself up to next level, and if Ciccarelli and McCarthy are healthy, offense shouldn't be a problem.

DEFENSE: A return to All-Star form by Hartsburg is a must. A healthy Tom Hirsch (he played only 15 games last year) would be a big help. Curt Giles and Gordie Roberts do the job.

GM Lou Nanne thinks he has good ones coming in Randy Velischek and Dan Mandich, another player whose season was ruined by injury. Again, if the Stars are healthier, this could be a pretty good group.

Goaltending, however, remains a question. The North Stars turned back to veteran Gilles Meloche, since traded to Edmonton, in the playoffs. Which leaves Don Beaupre, who, except in flashes, has never come back to his rookie form, and Roland Melanson,

Brian Bellows looks to return to his 1983-84 level.

who was a disappointment after being acquired from the Islanders for a No. 1 draft choice.

OUTLOOK: It's not unreasonable to expect improvement. The division, save Chicago, isn't very strong and it's not hard at all to see the Stars, who finished fourth a year ago, bouncing back

NORTH STAR ROSTER

No.	Player	Pos.	Ht.	Wt.	Born	1984-85	G	A	Pts.	PIM
12	Keith Acton	C	5-8	170	4-15-58/Peterborough, Ont.	Minnesota	20	38	58	90
23	Brian Bellows	RW	5-11	195	9-1-64/St. Catharines, Ont.	Minnesota	26	36	62	72
17	Bo Berglund	RW	5-10	175	4-6-55/Sweden	Que.-Minn.	10	10	20	14
14	Scott Bjugstad	C	6-1	185	6-2-61/New Brighton, Minn.	Minnesota	11	4	15	32
						Springfield	2	3	5	2
7	Neal Broten	C	5-9	160	11-29-59/Roseau, Minn.	Minnesota	19	37	56	39
20	Dino Ciccarelli	C	5-10	180	2-8-60/Sarnia, Ont.	Minnesota	15	17	32	41
29	Tim Coulis	LW	6-0	200	2-24-58/Kenora, Ont.	Minnesota	1	1	2	34
						Springfield	13	17	30	86
2	Curt Giles	D	5-8	180	11-30-58/Humboldt, Minn.	Minnesota	5	25	30	49
21	Dirk Graham	RW	5-11	190	7-29-59/Regina, Sask.	Minnesota	12	11	23	23
						Springfield	20	28	48	41
4	Craig Hartsburg	D	6-1	200	6-29-59/Stratford, Ont.	Minnesota	7	11	18	54
	Tom Hirsch	D	6-4	210	1-27-63/Minneapolis	Minnesota	0	4	4	10
						Springfield	4	5	9	2
	Dave Jensen	D	6-1	190	5-3-61/Minneapolis	Minnesota	0	1	1	4
						Springfield	13	27	40	63
98	Brian Lawton	C	6-0	178	6-29-65/New Brunswick, N.J.	Minnesota	5	6	11	24
						Springfield	14	28	42	37
32	Don Mandich	D	6-3	205	6-12-60/Brantford, Ont.	Minnesota	0	0	0	32
16	Terry Martin	LW	5-11	175	10-25-55/Barrie, Ont.	Minnesota	1	3	4	0
						Nova Scotia	17	11	28	4
9	Dennis Maruk	C	5-8	165	11-17-55/Toronto	Minnesota	19	41	60	56
11	Tom McCarthy	LW	6-2	200	7-31-60/Toronto	Minnesota	16	21	37	36
25	Tony McKegney	LW	6-1	200	2-15-58/Sarnia, Ont.	Que.-Minn.	23	22	45	16
	Kent Nilsson	RW	6-1	195	8-31-55/Sweden	Calgary	37	62	99	14
44	Steve Payne	LW	6-2	210	9-16-58/Toronto	Minnesota	29	22	51	61
24	Willi Plett	RW	6-3	205	6-7-55/Paraguay	Minnesota	14	14	28	157
5	Dave Richter	D	6-5	220	4-8-60/Winnipeg	Minnesota	2	8	10	221
10	Gordie Roberts	D	6-0	195	10-2-57/Detroit	Minnesota	6	36	42	112
3	Bob Rouse	D	6-2	212	6-19-64/Surrey, B.C.	Minnesota	2	9	11	113
						Springfield	0	3	3	6
26	Gord Sherven	RW	6-0	185	8-21-63/Gravelbourg, Sask.	Edm.-Minn.	11	19	30	18
						Nova Scotia	4	5	9	5
28	Harold Snepsts	D	6-3	215	10-24-54/Edmonton	Minnesota	0	7	7	232
	Ken Solheim	RW	6-3	210	3-27-61/Hythe, Alta.	Minnesota	8	10	18	19
						Springfield	6	8	14	0
	Randy Velischek	D	6-1	200	2-10-62/Montreal	Minnesota	4	9	13	26
						Springfield	2	7	9	22

No.	Player	Pos.	Ht.	Wt.	Born		GP	GA	SO	Avg.
33	Don Beaupre	G	5-8	155	9-19-61/Waterloo, Ont.	Minnesota	31	109	1	3.69
	Jon Casey	G	5-9	155	8-29-62/Grand Rapids, Minn.	Baltimore	46	116	4	2.63
1	Roland Melanson	G	5-10	178	6-28-60/Moncton, N.B.	Isl.-Minn.	28	113	0	4.31
	Mike Sands	G	5-9	150	4-6-53/Sudbury, Ont.	Minnesota	3	14	0	6.04
						Springfield	46	140	2	3.24

as high as second place.

Nanne has drawn criticism for his revolving door since this club went to the finals in 1981. But the truth is that most of the players he's traded are no longer in the league and he's made more good moves than bad ones.

If there's fault to be found with Nanne, it's that he's been more talent-conscious in his deals and drafts than he has been in putting together a true team. The North Stars have more than their share of egotists. Either they'll have to grow up or Nanne and new coach Lorne Henning will have to get rid of them for the team to become a real Stanley Cup contender.

NORTH STAR PROFILES

BRIAN BELLOWS 21 5-11 195   Right Wing

One of the most sought-after junior players in history . . . Most scouts say he was the best 17-year-old player they have ever seen . . . Minnesota took him with the second pick of the 1982, after making a deal with the Red Wings for their choice, then giving the Bruins (who took Gord Kluzak first) two players to leave Bellows for them . . . Has he been worth it? Yes and no. After three NHL seasons, he still hasn't scored like expected, but he's one of the better two-way wingers in the league and may yet become dominant . . . Insiders say he has an arrogant attitude and could still use some growing up . . . Miscast as "The Next Wayne Gretzky" as a playmaker, but sometimes you can see a young Gordie Howe . . . Slipped 21 points last year in course of North Stars' miserable season . . . Made the Canadian team for the 1984 Canada Cup, but didn't play much . . . Led Kitchener to the 1982 Memorial Cup championship and was named the tournament's Most Valuable Player . . . Enjoys windsurfing and golf . . . Born Sept. 1, 1964 in St. Catharines, Ont.

Year	Club	GP	G	A	Pts.
1982-83	Minnesota	78	35	30	65
1983-84	Minnesota	78	41	42	83
1984-85	Minnesota	78	26	36	62
	Totals	234	102	108	210

KEITH ACTON 27 5-8 170   Center

Quick, tenacious checker and worker . . . Little guy who tries to play big and is pretty effective at it . . . Acquired from Montreal, along with Mark Napier and a third-round draft choice, for Bobby Smith in 1983. GM Lou Nanne has taken some heat for making too many trades, but this was a good one. Acton, only part of the package, outscored Smith last season . . . Has grown to like it in the Twin Cities despite his initial disappointment with the deal. "The Canadiens were my team," he said. "They represented all my desires. I don't think loyalty is a bad quality but in one afternoon, everything can be taken away." . . . Had an 88-point season and was named for the All-Star Game with the Canadiens in 1981-82, but 50-60 is more his range . . . Nicknamed "Woody", and not because of his facial resemblance to Woody Allen. "It was because at Nova Scotia [Montreal's farm club] I was on the bench, gathering splinters, 95 percent of the time," he said ... 103rd player taken in the 1978 draft ... Story goes that he stuffed weights into his athletic supporter before a junior weigh-in, hoping to cheat his way upwards in the draft ... Born April 15, 1958, in Stouffville, Ont.

Year	Club	GP	G	A	Pts.
1979-80	Montreal...........	2	0	1	1
1980-81	Montreal...........	61	15	24	39
1981-82	Montreal...........	78	36	52	88
1982-83	Montreal...........	78	24	26	50
1983-84	Mont-Minn	71	20	45	65
1984-85	Minnesota	78	20	38	58
	Totals	368	115	186	301

KENT NILSSON 29 6-1 195   Right Wing

Flames' leading scorer for fifth time in six years now starts anew with the North Stars ... Missed achieving third 100-point season by one point in 1984–85 ... Despite success and well-earned reputation as one of NHL's best forwards, name often mentioned in trade rumors, and it finally happened ... Born Aug. 31, 1956, in Nynashamn, Sweden ... Not related to former Ranger star and fellow countryman Ulf Nilsson, with whom he starred in WHA ... Right wing who sometimes plays center ... Finesse player with marvelous passing and scoring skills.... Has accurate wrist shot and backhand shot.

Year	Club	GP	G	A	Pts.
1977-78	Winnipeg (WHA).....	80	42	65	107
1978-79	Winnipeg (WHA).....	78	39	68	107
1979-80	Atlanta	80	40	53	93
1980-81	Calgary.............	80	49	82	131
1981-82	Calgary.............	41	26	29	55
1982-83	Calgary.............	80	46	58	104
1983-84	Calgary.............	67	31	49	80
1984-85	Calgary.............	77	37	62	99
	NHL Totals	425	229	333	562
	WHA Totals	158	81	133	214

DENNIS MARUK 29 5-8 165   Center

North Stars' second-leading scorer with 60 points last season ... Acquired from Washington for a second-round pick in 1984 ... Has always scored, but gotten the reputation of a selfish, all-offense type that you can't win with ... Scored 136 points on the last Washington team not to make the playoffs (1981-82), but reduced ice time in the Caps' new defensive way of looking at things, cut his production to 81 . . . Was a second-round pick of the Oakland Seals in 1975 and played two years in Cleveland when the franchise moved there. The Barons were merged with the North Stars in 1978. Minnesota, suddenly with a glut of centers, moved him to Washington for a No. 1 draft choice. . . . Became the fifth player in NHL history to score 60 goals in one season in 1981-82 . . . Born Nov. 17, 1955, in Toronto.

Year	Club	GP	G	A	Pts.
1975-76	Cleveland	80	30	32	62
1976-77	Cleveland	80	28	50	78
1977-78	Cleveland	76	36	35	71
1978-79	Minn-Wash	76	31	59	90
1979-80	Washington	27	10	17	27
1980-81	Washington	80	50	47	97
1981-82	Washington	80	60	76	136
1982-83	Washington	80	31	50	81
1983-84	Minnesota	71	17	43	60
1984-85	Minnesota	71	19	41	60
	Totals	721	312	450	762

NEAL BROTEN 25 5-9 160   Center

Slumped to 56 points last year, a good place to start looking for reasons in the North Stars' decline . . . Healthy, but just never got it going as regular wingers went down with injuries and lines were juggled all year . . . Skilled, swift playmaker, he broke into the NHL with 98 points in 1981-82 . . . "Outside of Wayne Gretzky," former North Star coach Glen Sonmor said, "I don't know anyone who has better instincts for the game." . . . Third-round choice in 1979 out of the University of Minnesota . . . Winner of the Hobey Baker Award as the NCAA's player of the year in 1981 . . . Member of the 1980 gold-medal U.S. Olympic team . . . Born Nov. 29, 1959, in Roseau, Minn. . . . Older brother of Aaron, who plays for the New Jersey Devils and Paul, a U. of M. player who has been drafted by the Rangers . . . Scored a goal in his first NHL game as a North Star . . . Wife, Sally, is a former rodeo rider.

Year	Club	GP	G	A	Pts.
1980-81	Minnesota	3	2	0	2
1981-82	Minnesota	73	38	59	97
1982-83	Minnesota	79	32	45	77
1983-84	Minnesota	76	28	61	89
1984-85	Minnesota	80	19	37	56
	Totals	311	119	202	321

STEVE PAYNE 27 6-2 210

Strong left wing with a 30-goal touch . . . Somewhat erratic, his goals tend to come in bunches . . . The North Stars' second alltime leading goal scorer behind Bill Goldsworthy . . . Junior linemate of Bobby Smith's at Ottawa, he was the Stars' second-round pick in 1978, the year the North Stars took Smith first overall . . . Scored the overtime winner in the 1984 seventh-game victory over St. Louis in the quarterfinals . . . Born Aug. 16, 1958, in Toronto, where his father was a policeman. "When I was 14, my dad bought me a set of weights," he said. "I always did things to strengthen my wrists from age 10 on up." . . . Very confident attitude. "I've mellowed," he said. "As long as it's light-hearted and not arrogant, it's all right to be cocky." . . . Avid drag-racing fan, would like to some day drive a funny car . . . Married, one son, enjoys hunting . . . Durable, has never missed more than 10 games in any of his six NHL seasons.

Year	Club	GP	G	A	Pts.
1978-79	Minnesota	70	23	17	40
1979-80	Minnesota	80	42	43	85
1981-82	Minnesota	74	33	44	77
1982-83	Minnesota	80	30	39	69
1983-84	Minnesota	78	28	31	59
1984-85	Minnesota	76	29	22	51
	Totals	458	189	196	385

DINO CICCARELLI 25 5-10 180   Right Wing

Gifted goal scorer who missed 29 games last year and suffered his worst NHL season with only 32 points . . . Criticized for his unwillingness to tend to defensive responsibilities and for a selfish attitude . . . Record-setting scorer in junior hockey, was headed towards a certain first-round draft status when he shattered his leg during a practice with the London Knights . . . A metal rod had to be put into his leg and he missed most of the next season . . . Nobody took a chance on him in the six-round draft that year and the North Stars signed him as a free agent. "Actually, it was a clean break when it first happened," he said. "But an infection set in, so they had to operate again." . . . Excellent anticipation, with an ability to get open and to the net that can't be taught . . . Outgoing personality, somewhat the hot dog. "Just looking at him," Pat Quinn said when he coached Philadelphia, "you want to grind him." . . . "Nothing's scary like it is when you think your dreams are over," Dino said. "The scouts used to ask me about the leg and it was sickening the way they'd shake their heads.

Now they shake their heads when they see the game summaries."
...Born Feb. 8, 1960, in Sarnia, Ont.

Year	Club	GP	G	A	Pts.
1980-81	Minnesota	32	18	12	30
1981-82	Minnesota	76	55	52	107
1982-83	Minnesota	77	37	38	75
1983-84	Minnesota	79	38	33	71
1984-85	Minnesota	51	15	17	32
	Totals	315	163	152	315

TONY McKEGNEY 27 6-1 200   Right Wing
Acquired along with Bo Berglund in the January trade that sent
Brad Maxwell and Brent Ashton to Quebec.... It paid off for the
North Stars when McKegney scored eight goals and 14 points in
nine playoff games...The first black player to establish himself
in the NHL...Heard some racial remarks his first year, but never
looked at his color as a barrier to be broken. "If I had my way, I
would like to be remembered as the first [black] to reach prom-
inence," he said. "But it's very seldom that anything is said about
it now. There really are more important things to talk about, aren't
there?"...Born Feb. 15, 1958, in Montreal, was adopted by a
white family when he was 13...Youngest of three brothers. Both
Ian and Mike played in the minor leagues before retiring...
Second-round pick by the Sabres in 1978...Has scored 30 goals
twice and never less than 20 in six full NHL seasons...Bitter
towards Scotty Bowman, who dealt him to Quebec in a five-player
deal in 1983...Keyed Quebec's upset victory over the Sabres in
the next playoffs and crowed about his revenge.

Year	Club	GP	G	A	Pts.
1978-79	Buffalo	52	8	14	22
1979-80	Buffalo	80	23	29	52
1980-81	Buffalo	80	37	32	69
1981-82	Buffalo	73	23	29	52
1982-83	Buffalo	78	36	37	73
1983-84	Quebec	75	24	27	51
1984-85	Que-Min	57	23	22	45
	Totals	495	174	190	364

GORDIE ROBERTS 28 6-0 195   Defenseman
It took a long time for him to live up to expectations..."Everyone
expected too much," said Glen Sonmor, who coached in the WHA
when Roberts broke in there as a much-heralded 17-year-old...
Two years ago, he matured into one of the better defensemen in
the NHL...Quick and a fine skater, his strength is moving the
puck. Now he is much improved defensively. "Ask any defense-

man," he said. "There's a lot of growing pains. You learn by your mistakes. You learn to take advantage of your strong suits and don't do the silly things that get you into trouble."...Born Oct. 2, 1957, in Detroit...Named after Gordie Howe, then later got to play with him in Hartford...Outstanding as a midget in Detroit area programs, one of the first American kids to ever be drafted by a major junior team (Victoria)...Turned pro after only one junior season when the Whalers offered him a five-year deal for $500,000...Acquired by the North Stars for Mike Fidler in 1980...Cross-country skier...Affable, a voracious reader of newspapers...Wife is an interior designer.

Year	Club	GP	G	A	Pts.
1975-76	New England (WHA)	77	3	19	22
1976-77	New England (WHA)	77	13	33	46
1977-78	New England (WHA)	78	15	46	61
1978-79	New England (WHA)	79	11	46	57
1979-80	Hartford	80	8	28	36
1980-81	Hart-Minn.	77	8	42	50
1981-82	Minnesota	79	4	30	34
1982-83	Minnesota	80	3	41	44
1983-84	Minnesota	77	8	45	53
1984-85	Minnesota	78	6	36	42
	NHL Totals	471	37	222	259
	WHA Totals	311	42	144	186

CRAIG HARTSBURG 26 6-1 200   Defenseman

One of the best in the game, when healthy...His career has been set back two seasons in a row with serious injuries. In 1983 it was torn knee ligaments, last season a fractured hip...Returned to play well in the playoffs, scoring eight points in nine games ...Prototype of the offensive defenseman, can control a game... Left his junior team at Sault Ste. Marie at 18 to sign a professional contract with the WHA Birmingham Bulls...The North Stars selected him with the sixth overall pick in the 1979 draft...Three times an All-Star...The North Star captain...Holds the team record by a defenseman for points (77) and assists (60) in one season...Born June 29, 1959, in Stratford, Ont.

Year	Club	GP	G	A	Pts.
1978-79	Birmingham (WHA)	77	9	40	49
1979-80	Minnesota	79	14	30	44
1980-81	Minnesota	74	13	30	43
1981-82	Minnesota	76	17	60	77
1982-83	Minnesota	78	12	50	62
1983-84	Minnesota	26	7	7	14
1984-85	Minnesota	32	7	11	18
	NHL Totals	365	70	188	258
	WHA Totals	77	9	40	49

CURT GILES 26 5-8 180   **Defenseman**

Steady, underrated defenseman ... Bantamweight who plays a lot bigger than his size ... One of the few remaining practitioners of the hip check, which he likes to come across the ice to deliver on unsuspecting opposition forwards ... Hit Philadelphia's Dave Poulin so hard last year the Flyer captain swallowed his tongue ... "An every-nighter," said former Minnesota coach Glen Sonmor. ... Fourth-round pick in 1978 after career at the University of Minnesota-Duluth, where he was twice an All-American ... Called up after only half a season on the Stars' farm club at Oklahoma City ... Named the North Stars' Most Valuable Player in 1980-81 ... One of the few plus players on a poor defensive team last year ... Very popular with his teammates ... Has a degree in secondary education ... Nicknamed "Pengy" for penguin ... Born Nov. 30, 1958, in the Pas, Man.

Year	Club	GP	G	A	Pts.
1979-80	Minnesota	37	2	7	9
1980-81	Minnesota	67	5	22	27
1981-82	Minnesota	74	3	12	15
1982-83	Minnesota	76	2	21	23
1983-84	Minnesota	70	6	22	28
1984-85	Minnesota	77	5	25	30
	Totals	401	23	109	132

COACH LORNE HENNING: Named North Stars' coach in June ... Coached the shared Minnesota-Islander farm team in Springfield last season ... Before that he was an Islander assistant after playing for them for nine years ... "He is bright and inventive and able to relate to the players of this day and age," GM Lou Nanne said ... "He did a fine job in Springfield despite a 36-40-4 record as both the Islanders and North Stars were hard hit by injuries and call-ups ... Turned down the Vancouver coaching job two weeks before signing with Minnesota. "They didn't have the right answers to the questions I asked," he said ... Canucks did not offer him nearly the money that they had other coaching candidates ... Born Feb. 23, 1952, in Estevan, Sask. ... An original Islander, selected in second round of 1972 draft ... Never a great scorer, his forte was checking and especially penalty-killing, but he chipped in three big goals and four assists in the 1980 playoffs, when the Isles won the first of four consecutive Stanley Cups . . . Was on the ice when Bob Nystrom scored overtime goal against the Flyers that meant the first championship . . . Good tennis player.

MOST COLORFUL PLAYER

They invented the cartoon character of the goaltender when they made Gump Worsley.

The roly-poly goalie was one of the best, and most colorful, in NHL history. As he plopped around his crease covering his teammates' blunders, he was the picture of nonchalance. And in truth, the spectre of vulcanized rubber flying at his maskless visage at 90 miles an hour was not nearly as terrifying to Worsley as climbing on an airplane. He often sat in the cockpit just to make sure the pilot was paying close attention.

After ten seasons with the Rangers, then seven (including three Stanley-Cup winning ones) with the Canadiens, The Gumper finished up his career with Minnesota.

He and the Stars' other goaltender, the long, lean, Cesare Maniago, were a Mutt-and-Jeff combination. And an effective one, too, as the Stars never missed getting into the playoffs in five seasons.

Towards the end, they even convinced Worsley to put on a mask. At age 40, it wasn't quite the same, but identification of the man in the Minnesota goal was nonetheless unmistakable. One bellyflop was enough. You knew then it could only be The Gumper. And that reports that he should have quit years before were entirely premature.

ALL-TIME NORTH STAR LEADERS

GOALS: Dino Ciccarelli, 55, 1981-82
ASSISTS: Bobby Smith, 71, 1981-82
POINTS: Bobby Smith, 114, 1981-82
SHUTOUTS: Cesare Maniago, 6, 1967-68

ST. LOUIS BLUES

TEAM DIRECTORY: Chairman-Pres.: Harry Ornest; VP-Dir. Player Personnel: Ronald Caron; Pub. Dir.: Susie Mathieu; Coach: Jacques Demers. Home ice: St. Louis Arena: (17,640; 200' × 85'). Colors: White, blue, gold and red. Training camp: Peoria, Ill.

SCOUTING REPORT

OFFENSE: One line is fine. Bernie Federko pumps away towards 100 points year-in, year-out, Joey Mullen is a 40-goal finisher

If he's healthy, look out for Doug Wickenheiser.

204 THE COMPLETE HANDBOOK OF PRO HOCKEY

and in Brian Sutter the Blues have one of the league's finest cornermen, workers and leaders.

After that, there's a big dropoff in production, so the Blues go with a bunch of sweathogs and play the team concept to the hilt. They probably upgraded themselves by replacing left wing Jorgen Pettersson with Mark Johnson in last February's deal with Hartford. Johnson at least comes to play every night. Doug Gilmour has improved each year and can center a passable second line.

Doug Wickenheiser had emerged as a solid checking winger and 20-goal contributor, but his career is now in jeopardy after suffering serious injuries to both knees during a team prank. The Blues are in big trouble if he can't come back.

After Greg Paslawski, the list of 20-goal scorers, however, runs out. The Blues did acquire a 20-goaler in Mark Hunter from Montreal for draft choices.

DEFENSE: It's hard to figure out how the Blues won a division title last year. After Rob Ramage, who really didn't have a very good season last year, this is a pretty thin group. The hope is that young players like Rik Wilson and Jim Pavese will improve while journeymen like Craig Levie and Tim Bothwell hold things together.

GM Ron Caron has high hopes for Brian Benning, a No. 2 draft pick last year. He's quick and a good playmaker, but on the smallish side.

The goaltending is fair to good. Rick Wamsley's solid play after coming over from Montreal made Liut and his big contract expendable in Caron's eyes. And Greg Millen, who came in the exchange for Liut, is better than he played for the Blues after the deal.

OUTLOOK: The Blues made a little go a long way last year, at least for 60 games. But their lack of depth clearly caught up with them as they faded down the stretch. They managed to hang on for the division title, but were pins waiting to fall to Minnesota in the first round.

Thanks to nice-guy coach Jacques Demers, this is a very harmonious, close-knit group. It's also a small one, however. Owner Harry Ornest defends his roster paring as good business, and that may be true, but a little investment in a farm system could help keep wolves like last April's away from the door. The Blues have the smallest number of players under contract in the league.

Trading away a good No. 1 draft pick for Wamsley last June for a gaggle of second- and third-round picks was an indication that this team is being patched together year-to-year. Caron, who has kept a close eye on the guys he drafted while Montreal's chief

BLUE ROSTER

No.	Player	Pos.	Ht.	Wt.	Born	1984-85	G	A	Pts.	PIM
12	Perry Anderson	LW	6-0	193	10-14-61/Barrie, Ont.	St. Louis	9	9	18	146
6	Dave Barr	C	6-1	185	11-30-60/Edmonton	St. Louis	16	18	34	32
18	Brian Benning	D	6-0	180	6-10-66/Edmonton	St. Louis	0	2	2	0
						Kamloops	3	18	21	26
25	Tim Bothwell	D	6-3	190	5-6-55/Vancouver	St. Louis	4	22	26	62
17	Denis Cyr	RW	5-11	180	2-4-61/Montreal	St. Louis	5	3	8	0
27	Gilbert Delorme	D	6-1	205	11-25-62/Longueuil, Que.	St. Louis	2	12	14	53
23	Luc Dufour	LW	5-11	180	2-13-63/Chicoutimi, Que.	Bos-Que-St. L.	3	6	9	45
24	Bernie Federko	C	6-0	195	5-12-56/Foam Lake, Sask.	St. Louis	30	73	103	27
19	Perry Ganchar	RW	5-9	180	10-28-63/Saskatoon, Sask.	St. Louis	0	2	2	0
18	Doug Gilmour	C	5-11	160	6-25-63/Kingston, Ont.	St. Louis	21	36	57	49
61	Pat Hickey	LW	6-1	190	5-15-53/Brantford, Ont.	St. Louis	10	13	23	32
	Mark Hunter	RW	6-0	194	11-12-62/Petrolia, Ont.	Montreal	21	12	33	123
10	Mark Johnson	RW	5-9	160	9-22-57/Minneapolis	Hart.-St. L.	23	34	57	49
26	Terry Johnson	D	6-3	210	11-28-58/Calgary	St. Louis	0	7	7	120
16	Kevin Levallee	LW	5-8	180	9-16-61/Sudbury, Ont.	St. Louis	15	17	32	8
2	Craig Levie	D	5-11	190	8-17-59/Calgary	St. Louis	6	23	29	33
7	Joe Mullen	RW	5-10	180	2-26-57/New York, N.Y.	St. Louis	40	52	92	6
28	Greg Paslawski	LW	5-11	190	8-25-61/Kindersley, Sask.	St. Louis	22	20	42	23
33	Jim Pavese	D	6-2	204	6-8-62/New York, N.Y.	St. Louis	2	5	7	69
5	Rob Ramage	D	6-2	210	1-11-59/Bryon, Ont.	St. Louis	7	31	38	178
15	Mark Reeds	RW	5-10	188	1-24-60/Burlington, Ont.	St. Louis	9	30	39	25
	Cliff Ronning	C	5-8	157	10-1-65/Vancouver	New Westminster	89	108	197	20
21	Dwight Schofield	D	6-3	195	3-15-56/Waltham, Mass.	St. Louis	1	4	5	184
11	Brian Sutter	LW	5-11	180	10-7-56/Viking, Alta.	St. Louis	37	38	75	121
14	Doug Wickenheiser	C	6-1	190	3-30-61/Regina, Sask.	St. Louis	23	20	43	36
4	Rik Wilson	D	6-0	180	6-17-62/Long Beach, Cal.	St. Louis	8	16	24	39

No.	Player	Pos.	Ht.	Wt.	Born		GP	GA	SO	Avg.
31	Rick Heinz	G	5-10	165	5-30-55/Essex, Ont.	St. Louis	2	3	0	2.57
29	Greg Millen	G	5-9	175	6-25-57/Toronto	Hart-St. L.	54	223	1	4.09
30	Rick Wamsley	G	5-11	185	5-25-59/Simcoe, Ont.	St. Louis	40	126	0	3.26

scout, has been resourceful and has put together a decent team.

But the Blues obviously took advantage of bad years by Chicago and Minnesota to win the division title last season. They are going to be hard-pressed to do it again.

BLUE PROFILES

BRIAN SUTTER 28 5-11 180   **Left Wing**
Oldest of six brothers playing in the NHL . . . One of game's most respected leaders and one of its better players, too . . . Incredibly hard worker . . . Strong, smart, and as evidenced by his scoring at least 30 goals in each of his last five seasons, a pretty good touch around the net . . . "As a coach, I can preach hard work and determination," said Jacques Demers. "But Brian shows them on the ice." . . . Second-round pick by the Blues in 1976 . . . Caught the scouts' eye as the runty, irrepressible left wing on Bryan Trottier's line at Lethbridge . . . Weighed only 160 pounds at the time, still plays a lot bigger than his current 180 . . . All his brothers say they never would have dreamed of playing in the NHL had not Brian shown them how . . . Has built a home in Red Deer, Alta., near his parent's farm in Viking, where he was born Oct. 7, 1956.

Year	Club	GP	G	A	Pts.
1976-77	St Louis	35	4	10	14
1977-78	St Louis	78	9	13	22
1978-79	St Louis	77	41	39	80
1979-80	St Louis	71	23	35	58
1980-81	St Louis	78	35	34	69
1981-82	St Louis	74	39	36	75
1982-83	St Louis	79	46	30	76
1983-84	St Louis	76	32	51	83
1984-85	St Louis	77	37	38	75
	Totals	645	266	286	552

BERNIE FEDERKO 29 6-0 195   **Center**
Led the Blues in scoring last season for the seventh straight time . . . Recorded his third 100-point season in his nine in the NHL . . . Superior playmaker, very deceptive with the puck . . . The Blues' all-time leading scorer . . . Model of consistency, has never scored less than 84 points since his second full season in the league . . . Blues' No. 1 pick in 1976 . . . Born May 12, 1956, in Foam Lake, Sask. . . . Learned to skate on his backyard rink . . . Drives team-

mates to distraction with non-stop chattering . . . Avid golfer, reader and baseball fan.

Year	Club	GP	G	A	Pts.
1976-77	St Louis	31	14	9	23
1977-78	St Louis	72	17	24	41
1978-79	St Louis	74	31	64	95
1979-80	St Louis	79	38	56	94
1980-81	St Louis	78	31	73	104
1981-82	St Louis	74	30	62	92
1982-83	St Louis	75	24	60	84
1983-84	St Louis	79	41	66	107
1984-85	St Louis	76	30	73	103
	Totals	638	256	487	743

JOEY MULLEN 28 5-10 180   Right Wing

Good speed, fine wrist shot and appetite for hard work . . . Another guy termed "too small" for the NHL by the scouts, he has proven himself more than capable . . . Recorded his career high in points last season . . . Until Bobby Carpenter scored 53 last year, Mullen's 41 goals in 1983-84 were the most ever scored by an American-born player . . . Grew up in Hell's Kitchen, on the west side of Manhattan, where he was born Feb. 26, 1957 . . . His first exposure to the sport was on roller skates . . . Dad works at Madison Square Garden and used to drive the Zamboni there . . . Product of the Metropolitan Junior Hockey Association of New York, where he once scored 110 goals in a 45-game season . . . Played four years at Boston College before signing with the Blues as a free agent in 1979 . . . Brother, Brian, plays for the Winnipeg Jets . . . Scored 59 goals in his first pro season at Salt Lake City and had 21 in 27 games the following year when the Blues called him up . . . Averaged better than a point a game in his three-and-a-half NHL seasons.

Year	Club	GP	G	A	Pts.
1981-82	St. Louis	45	25	34	59
1982-83	St. Louis	49	17	30	47
1983-84	St. Louis	80	41	44	85
1984-85	St. Louis	79	40	52	92
	Totals	253	123	160	283

DOUG GILMOUR 22 5-11 160   Center

Gave the Blues some badly-needed offensive balance, enabling Demers to break up the Federko-Mullen-Sutter line . . . Followed his 53-point rookie season with 57 last year . . . Had a fine playoff,

11 points in 11 games, in 1983-84, when the Blues beat Detroit and pushed Minnesota to a seventh-game overtime... Fourth-round pick in 1982, he went on to become the Most Valuable Player in the Ontario Hockey League (at Cornwall) in his final year of junior ... Excellent cook... Married, no kids, but three dogs: a Yorkie, a Boston Terrier and a Boxer... Born June 25, 1963, in Kingston, Ont.

Year	Club	GP	G	A	Pts.
1983-84	St. Louis	80	25	28	53
1984-85	St. Louis	78	21	36	57
	Totals	158	46	64	110

MARK JOHNSON 28 5-9 160   Left Wing

Acquired in late February, along with goalie Greg Millen, in the deal that sent goalie Mike Liut and left wing Jorgen Pettersson to Hartford... After earlier stops in Pittsburgh and Minnesota, he had appeared to have found a home in Hartford with consecutive 69- and 87-point seasons... But an honest player who gave an honest answer, he didn't always espouse the house line that the Whalers are on their way to contention. Thus, he may have been marked for purge by Whalers' Emile Francis... Quick skater, nice playmaker and finisher... A star on the 1980 U.S. Olympic Gold Medal Team (11 points in seven games at Lake Placid)... Third-round choice by the Penguins in the 1977 draft out of the University of Wisconsin, where he played for his father, Bob, now coach of the Calgary Flames... Born Sept. 22, 1957, in Madison, Wis.

Year	Club	GP	G	A	Pts.
1979-80	Pittsburgh	17	3	5	8
1980-81	Pittsburgh	73	10	23	33
1981-82	Pitt-Minn	56	12	13	25
1982-83	Hartford	73	31	38	69
1983-84	Hartford	79	35	52	87
1984-85	Hart-StL	66	23	34	57
	Totals	364	114	165	279

ROB RAMAGE 26 6-2 210   Defenseman

Leader of the Blues' defense... His points fell off drastically from 60 to 38 last year, but the Blues won the division title, so he must have done something right... Voted to the NHL All-Star team for the 1984 game... Still, only in flashes has he lived up to the expectations that made him the first player taken (by Colorado)

in the 1979 draft . . . When the Rockies took him, he had already
played a year of pro hockey with the WHA Birmingham Bulls . . .
A junior teammate of the Flyers' Brad Marsh at London, Ontario
. . . Acquired by the Blues in 1982 for two No. 1 draft choices . . .
Earns credits towards a business degree at Washington University
(in St. Louis) during the offseasons . . . Born Jan. 11, 1959, in
Byron, Ont.

Year	Club	GP	G	A	Pts.
1978-79	Birmingham (WHA) ..	80	12	36	48
1979-80	Colorado	75	8	20	28
1980-81	Colorado	79	20	42	62
1981-82	Colorado	80	13	29	42
1982-83	St. Louis	78	16	35	51
1983-84	St. Louis	80	15	45	60
1984-85	St. Louis	80	7	31	38
	NHL Totals	472	79	202	281
	WHA Totals	80	12	36	48

DOUG WICKENHEISER 24 6-1 195   Center
Career in jeapordy after suffering serious injuries to both knees
during a team prank late last season . . . Took unsuspecting rookie
teammates on a "snipe" hunt (a bird that doesn't exist) and he fell
off a truck . . . Doctors are cautiously optimistic he'll be able to
pick up where he left off . . . Was finally establishing himself as a
solid two-way center after falling victim to unrealistic expectations
in Montreal . . . The Canadiens, with the first pick in the 1980
draft, took Wickenheiser over Denis Savard, a speedy French-
Canadian center who went on to stardom in Chicago . . . "It would
be wrong to blame anyone but me," he said. "I just didn't play
consistently well. I'd have little spurts. I think it would be over-
stating it to say that it was a tremendous relief to get out of
Montreal. I wanted to stay there and live up to the promise everyone says I have. The comparisons to Savard weren't as constant
as a lot of people think." . . . Great final junior season (170 points)
at Regina . . . The move to St. Louis, in the deal that sent him,
Gilbert Delorme and Greg Paslawski from Montreal to the Blues
for Perry Turnbull seemed to take the pressure off. More a blue-
collar player, he fit in well with the Blues' scheme . . . Enjoys
restoring antique cars . . . Born March 30, 1961, in Regina, Sask.

Year	Club	GP	G	A	Pts.
1980-81	Montreal...........	41	7	8	15
1981-82	Montreal...........	56	12	23	35
1982-83	Montreal...........	78	25	30	55
1983-84	Mont-St L..........	73	12	26	38
1984-85	St Louis...........	68	23	20	43
	Totals	316	79	107	186

GREG MILLEN 28 5-9 175   Goaltender

Acquired by the Blues, along with Mark Johnson, in the Mike
Liut deal...Named the Whalers' Most Valuable Player in
1983-84, when he recorded a 3.71 goals-against average in 60 games
for a team that won only 28...One of the few NHL players ever
to take advantage of his free agency. He signed with the Whalers
after his Pittsburgh contract ran out in 1981. The Penguins were
awarded Pat Boutette and Kevin McClelland as compensation
...Very active in the Hartford community and had just signed
a 3-year contract. The trade came as a big shock...Beat Buffalo, 3-1, in his first St. Louis start, but wasn't outstanding
(2-7-1, 3.47 goals-against average) as the Blues faded down the
stretch. "With Greg and Rick Wamsley, we are set in goal for a
long time," GM Ron Caron said...Articulate and honest, he'd
like to be a broadcaster when his playing days are over...
Born June 25, 1957, in Toronto.

Year	Club	GP	GA	SO	Avg.
1978-79	Pittsburgh	28	86	2	3.37
1979-80	Pittsburgh	44	157	2	3.64
1980-81	Pittsburgh	63	258	0	4.16
1981-82	Hartford	55	229	0	4.29
1982-83	Hartford	60	282	1	4.81
1983-84	Hartford	60	221	2	3.70
1984-85	Hart-StL	54	222	1	4.08
	Totals	364	1455	8	4.08

GREG PASLAWSKI 24 5-11 190   Right Wing

Scored 22 goals last year and the Blues think he might get better
...Hard-working, good cornerman and a fine shot...Signed by
the Canadiens as a free agent out of Prince Albert (Tier II) by
then-Montreal chief scout Ron Caron...Caron, who was fired
and surfaced in St. Louis, then acquired Paslawski in the three-
for-one deal that sent Perry Turnbull to Montreal...One of the
very few NHL players who calls himself a basketball fan...Avid
golfer...Born August 25, 1961, in Kindersly, Sask.

Year	Club	GP	G	A	Pts.
1983-84	Mont-St L	60	9	10	19
1984-85	St. Louis	72	22	20	42
	Totals	132	31	30	61

RICK WAMSLEY 26 5-11 185   **Goaltender**
Helped the Blues to the regular-season division title with a
23-12-5 record and 3.26 goals-against average . . . His solid work
was a factor in the trade of Mike Liut to Hartford in February.
The other factor was the huge contract Liut had been given by the
previous Blues' regime . . . Another former Ron Caron Montreal
draft choice whom Caron schemed to bring in after getting the
Blues' job . . . Shared the Montreal goal with Richard Sevigny for
three years, but when he struggled in 1983-84, the Canadiens
turned to rookie Steve Penney for the playoffs . . . Penney was an
unexpected sensation, taking a sub-.500 team to within two games
of berth in the finals, and Wamsley became trade bait . . . Acquired
for the Blues' No. 1 pick in 1984 . . . Originally a fifth-round
choice in 1979 . . . Born May 25, 1959, in Simcol, Ont.

Year	Club	GP	GA	SO	Avg.
1980-81	Montreal	5	8	1	1.90
1981-82	Montreal	38	101	2	2.75
1982-83	Montreal	46	151	0	3.51
1983-84	Montreal	42	144	2	3.70
1984-85	St. Louis	40	126	0	3.26
	Totals	171	530	5	3.10

COACH JACQUES DEMERS: Most often-mentioned candidate

for Coach of the Year until the Blues went into
a late-season swoon and were upset by Minnesota in three straight first-round games . . .
But did a fine job with a team blessed with little
depth . . . Friendly, outgoing, enthusiastic, one
of the few coaches who can be a nice guy to
his players and get away with it . . . "In the
eighties," he says, "athletes dictate if they want
a coach around. If they didn't work for me, I could have been
fired. Unless your name is Scotty Bowman or Al Arbour, that's
the way it is in hockey." . . . After coaching Junior B teams in
Quebec, he broke into professional hockey as director of player
personnel for the WHA Chicago Cougars and also coached WHA
teams at Indianapolis and Chicago . . . Got the Quebec job the last
year the team was in the WHA and stayed on when they joined
the NHL in 1979 . . . After a good start, the Nordiques faded and

Demers, critical of the prima donna personalities of supposed stars the Nordiques have since purged, was fired . . . He stayed on in the organization, coaching the farm club at Fredricton before Caron hired him to coach the Blues in 1983 . . . Born Aug. 26, 1944, in Montreal.

MOST COLORFUL PLAYER

Sutters? Hunters? Nah. Back in 1967, when brothers were really tough, the Plagers came to St. Louis. Fortunately they were finally on the same team, or they probably would have killed each other.

"They still talk about it in Peterborough as the greatest fight they've ever seen," says Bob. "Barc and I started on the ice, kept going in the penalty box, then out in the lobby on the way to dressing rooms. We got dressed and went outside and finished it."

In a sense, they still are. After fighting and defending the Blues to their early expansion success, both Plager brothers remain as symbolic of the franchise as the note on the team's jersey. Barc, after two stints as the team's coach, is now an assistant coach and Bob a special assignment scout.

Bob's wisecracking—"they kick Bob Pulford out of the bars during Happy Hour"—remains a source of joy. And Barc, only by a little the more serious of the two, is an out-and-out inspiration. Early last season Barclay learned his recurring headaches were caused by a brain tumor. Treatments shrunk it, but it remains inoperable. Two months later, Barc donned a toupee (the radiation therapy had caused his hair to fall out) and climbed back behind the bench.

"My wife went to bed with Yul Brynner and woke up with Tom Jones," he said. "I think I've gotta get some glue, so I don't rip it off and throw it across the ice."

"My brother's a battler," Bob says. "I've still got scars and lumps to prove it. If he says he's gonna beat it, he'll beat it."

ALL-TIME BLUE LEADERS

GOALS: Wayne Babych, 54, 1980-81
ASSISTS: Bernie Federko, 73, 1980-81
POINTS: Bernie Federko, 107, 1983-84
SHUTOUTS: Glenn Hall, 8, 1968-69

TORONTO MAPLE LEAFS

TEAM DIRECTORY: Pres.: Harold E. Ballard; Chairman: Paul McNamara; GM: Gerry McNamara; Dir. Pub. Rel.: Gord Stellick; Coach: Dan Maloney. Home ice: Maple Leaf Gardens (16,307; 200′ × 85′). Colors: Blue and white. Training camp: Toronto.

SCOUTING REPORT

OFFENSE: It's a good indication of just how messed up the Leafs are that their leading scorers last year are the players they are most disenchanted with. Rick Vaive, a former 50-goal scorer, slumped to 35 and John Anderson's 32 may have been the least meaningful 32 in the NHL.

The Leafs hope Rick Vaive gets out of his slump.

Bill Derlago scored a point a game, but is an all-offense type who may not fit the definition of a winner. The Leafs' hardest working and most effective forward was probably Miroslav Frycer, who had 55 points in 65 games. Thus it was no accident that Toronto scored the fewest number of goals in the league.

There's going to be some sifting out of roles and bodies this season, so it's hard to tell in which direction the Leafs are going. The status quo might be the best prediction. But if Vaive, their embattled captain, bounces back, if rookie Dan Hodgson makes an impact and if Russ Courtnall, a No. 1 pick in 1983, begins to live up to his promise, the Leafs might score a few more goals.

DEFENSE: With the selection of Wendel Clark, the first player in the entire entry draft, the Leafs have now invested four of the last five No. 1 picks on defensemen. If they don't start showing improvement this season, it's fairly obvious they picked the wrong guys.

Jim Benning went backwards last year, but third-year man Gary Nylund and rookie Al Iafrate were occasionally showing things. Borje Salming plays on, mostly disinterestedly, and Jim Korn, Bob McGill and a cast of thousands are marginal at best. With such a group of maybes and stopgaps, it was remarkable that two teams gave up more goals than the Leafs last year. In Iafrate and Nylund, Toronto might have two cornerstones of a good defense. Then again, it might not.

The one bright spot last season was the play of Calgary castoff Tim Bernhardt in goal. The Leafs began the season with two kids right out of junior, Allan Bester and Ken Wregget, with disastrous results. Both were back riding busses by midseason.

Wregget is considered a pretty good prospect, so it made some sense for the Leafs to go with a tandem of Bernhardt and Wregget this year. But now they've traded for Don Edwards, who was a big bust in Calgary. So who knows? Who ever knows with this crew?

OUTLOOK: Bleak to marginal. After five years of picking near the top of the first round, the Toronto youth movement, which began with the deposing of Darryl Sittler in 1982, is still not showing any results. Maybe you have to get worse before you can get better, but this is ridiculous. The Leafs compiled the worst record in their history last year and the problem is not just talent, but atmosphere.

Owner Harold Ballard has gone to war with just about every good player he's ever had. If GM Gerry McNamara is coming up with young talent, one wonders: where is it? He's now entering

MAPLE LEAF ROSTER

No.	Player	Pos.	Ht.	Wt.	Born	1984-85	G	A	Pts.	PIM
10	John Anderson	RW	5-11	190	3-28-57/Toronto	Toronto	32	31	63	27
3	Jim Benning	D	6-0	185	4-29-63/Edmonton	Toronto	9	35	44	55
23	Jeff Brubaker	LW	6-2	210	2-24-58/Hagerstown, Md.	Toronto	8	4	12	209
	Wendell Clark	D	5-11	190	10-25-66/Kelvington, Sask.	Saskatoon	32	55	87	253
	Rich Costello	RW	6-0	175	6-27-63/Framingham, Mass.	St. Catharines	8	6	14	45
16	Russ Courtnall	C	5-10	165	1-2-63/Duncan, B.C.	Toronto	12	10	22	44
24	Dan Daoust	C	5-11	165	2-29-60/Kirkland Lake, Ont.	Toronto	17	37	54	98
19	Bill Derlago	C	5-10	195	8-25-58/Beulah, Man.	Toronto	31	31	62	21
	Dave Farrish	D	6-1	185	9-1-56/Lucknow, Ont.	St. Catharines	4	12	16	56
14	Miroslav Frycer	C	6-0	200	9-17-59/Czechoslovakia	Toronto	25	30	55	55
9	Stewart Gavin	LW	6-0	180	3-15-60/Ottawa, Ont.	Toronto	12	13	25	38
29	Todd Gill	D	6-1	180	11-9-65/Cardinal, Ont.	Toronto	1	0	1	13
						Windsor	17	40	57	148
	Dan Hodgson	C	5-11	173	8-29-65/Ft. Murray, Alta.	Prince Albert	70	112	182	86
33	Al Iafrate	D	6-3	190	3-21-66/Livonia, Mich.	Toronto	5	16	21	51
18	Peter Ihnacek	C	5-11	182	5-3-57/Czechoslovakia	Toronto	22	22	44	24
12	Jeff Jackson	LW	6-0	193	4-24-65/Chatham, Ont.	Toronto	0	1	1	24
						Hamilton	13	14	27	51
	Fabian Joseph	RW	5-8	165	12-5-65/Sydney, N.S.	Toronto (OHL)	32	43	75	16
26	Bill Kitchen	D	6-1	198	7-16-60/Schoneberg, Ont.	Toronto	1	4	5	27
						St. Catharines	3	7	10	52
20	Jim Korn	D	6-3	210	7-28-57/Hopkins, Minn.	Toronto	5	5	10	171
	Larry Landon	LW	6-0	191	5-54/Niagara Falls, Ont.	Toronto	0	0	0	2
						Sher.-St. C.	28	45	73	10
	Gary Leeman	LW	5-11½	175	2-19-64/Wilcox, Sask.	Toronto	5	26	31	72
						St. Catharines	2	2	4	11
15	Bob McGill	D	6-0	202	4-27-62/Edmonton	Toronto	0	5	5	250
	Craig Muni	D	6-2	201	7-19-62/Toronto	Toronto	0	0	0	6
						St. Catharines	7	17	24	54
2	Gary Nylund	D	6-4	218	10-28-63/Vancouver	Toronto	3	17	20	99
	Fred Perlini	C	6-2	175	4-12-62/Sault Ste. Marie, Ont.	St. Catharines	21	28	49	26
	Cam Plante	D	6-1	195	3-12-64/Brandon, Man.	Toronto	0	0	0	0
						St. Catharines	5	31	36	42
8	Walt Poddubny	C-LW	6-1	203	2-14-60/Thunder Bay, Ont.	Toronto	5	15	20	26
						St. Catharines	5	7	12	10
34	Bill Root	D	6-0	197	9-6-59/Toronto	Toronto	1	1	2	23
						St. Catharines	5	9	14	10
21	Borje Salming	D	6-1	185	4-17-51/Sweden	Toronto	6	33	39	76
	Bill Stewart	D	6-2	180	10-6-57/Toronto	Toronto	0	2	2	32
						St. Catharines	2	5	7	11
32	Ken Strong	RW	5-11	185	5-9-63/Toronto	Toronto	2	0	2	4
						St. Catharines	15	19	34	41
7	Greg Terrion	C	5-11	190	5-2-60/Peterborough, Ont.	Toronto	14	17	31	20
12	Steve Thomas	RW	5-10	180	7-15-63/England	Toronto	1	1	2	2
						St. Catharines	42	48	90	56
22	Rick Vaive	RW	6-0	180	5-14-59/Ottawa, Ont.	Toronto	35	33	68	112
25	Gary Yaremchuk	C	6-0	183	8-15-61/Edmonton	Toronto	1	1	2	16
						St. Catharines	17	47	64	75

No.	Player	Pos.	Ht.	Wt.	Born		GP	GA	SO	Avg.
1	Tim Bernhardt	G	5-9	160	4-19-58/Sarnia, Ont.	Toronto	37	136	9	3.74
						St. Catharines	14	55	0	4.12
31	Alan Bester	G	5-7	150	3-26-64/Hamilton, Ont.	Toronto	15	54	1	4.22
						St. Catharines	30	133	0	4.78
	Bruce Dowie	G	5-8	155	12-9-62/Oakville, Ont.	St. Catharines	10	55	0	5.54
	Don Edwards	G	5-9	160	9-28-55/Hamilton, Ont.	Calgary	34	115	1	4.08
	Rick St. Croix	G	5-9	160	1-3-55/Kenora, Ont.	Toronto	11	54	0	5.16
						St. Catharines	18	92	0	5.13
30	Ken Wregget	G	6-1	185	3-25-64/Medley, Alta.	Toronto	23	103	0	4.84
						St. Catharines	12	48	0	4.19

his fifth season, ample time to put in a foundation. Instead this franchise has become the joke of the league.

In two stretches last season, the Leafs played respectably, particularly away from the sullen Maple Leaf Gardens crowds. Maybe that was the first sign of revival. Maybe it was just a lot of false hope.

LEAF PROFILES

TIM BERNHARDT 27 5-9 160   Goaltender

Calgary organization castoff who turned out to be a huge bargain after being signed as a free agent . . . Key to the Leafs' improved second half . . . The Flames loaned him to the Leafs in 1983 primarily as help for the farm team at St. Catharines . . . Toronto did not offer him a contract when the one with Calgary ran out at the end of last season, so Tim unsuccessfully tried out in Los Angeles before Leafs decided to re-sign him . . . When plan to go with two kids, Ken Wregget and Allan Bester, both right out of junior, bombed and Rick St. Croix was injured, Bernhardt became the No. 1 man . . . Minor-league experience helped mature him . . . Doesn't get rattled, which can be more important than any inherent skill when playing for the Leafs . . . A second-round pick by the Flames in 1978 . . . Born April 19, 1958, in Sarnia, Ont. . . . Never developed as hoped in four minor-league seasons and failed to beat out Daniel Bouchard, Reggie Lemelin, Pat Riggin, and Don Edwards for a job in Calgary . . . Played only five NHL games, in 1982-83, with the Flames before getting his chance in Toronto . . . With acquisition of Edwards from Calgary, Bernhardt is expected to share the job with him this year.

Year	Club	GP	GA	SO	Avg.
1982-83	Calgary............	6	21	0	4.50
1984-85	Toronto............	37	136	0	3.74
	Totals.............	43	157	0	3.83

RICK VAIVE 26 6-0 180   Right Wing

Leaf captain and the team's one legitimate star . . . After three straight 50-goal seasons, slumped to 35 last year . . . Benched twice for failing to follow coach Dan Maloney's practice instructions . . . Handles himself very well off the ice, but has temper problems on it... Argues with officials, bangs his stick on the boards and glass. "It isn't something you can tell yourself not to do, it comes in the heat of the moment," he says. "It's just me."... First-round pick of Vancouver in 1979, traded with Bill Derlago for Tiger Williams and Jerry Butler... Fulfills the tradition (Dave Keon, Darryl Sittler) of the controversial Leaf captain... Great shot off the wing, strong skater, and can body-check... Feeling is that he and Maloney may not be able to co-exist... Usually it's the coach, rather than the star, who eventually goes in these situations. But in this organization, you never know... Born May 14, 1959, in Ottawa.

Year	Club	GP	G	A	Pts.
1979-80	Van-Tor	69	22	15	37
1980-81	Toronto...........	75	33	29	62
1981-82	Toronto...........	77	54	35	89
1982-83	Toronto...........	78	51	28	79
1983-84	Toronto...........	76	52	41	93
1984-85	Toronto...........	72	35	33	68
	Totals.............	447	247	181	428

MIROSLAV FRYCER 26 6-0 200   Right Wing

Defected from Czechoslovakia in April 1980, following the Stastnys to Quebec... Traded to Toronto in March 1982 with a seventh-round choice for Wilf Paiement... Scored 25 goals and 30 assists last year and became perhaps the most consistent player on the team... Missed the final 15 games with a knee injury... Fights a weight problem, had to lose 38 pounds before last season ... Born Sept. 27, 1959, in Ostrava, Czechoslovakia. Name pronounced FREE-cher.

Year	Club	GP	G	A	Pts.
1981-82	Que-Tor	59	24	23	47
1982-83	Toronto...........	67	25	30	55
1983-84	Toronto...........	46	9	16	25
1984-85	Toronto...........	65	25	30	55
	Totals.............	237	83	99	182

BORJE SALMING 34 6-1 185   Defenseman

First European player to make it big in the NHL... Bellwether of the Leaf defense since 1973... Five years removed from his last All-Star season and all the losing appears to have taken its toll on his spirits... Leafs, committed to a youth movement, would move him, but huge contract (two years remaining) is a deterrent in trade talks. Besides, GM Gerry McNamara appears to still want a lot in return... From 1976-79 he was as good a defenseman as there was in the NHL... Six times an All-Star... Agile, seemingly tireless, his willingness to stand up to physical abuse helped blaze a trail for European players... "All the other players had to test us," he once said. "We were just chicken hockey players from Europe. For a couple of years it was chicken this and chicken Swede that."... Pays better attention to his physical conditioning than earlier in his career... Might have a good year left if a contending team would be willing to pry him loose... Plagued by sinus problems throughout his career... Born April 17, 1951, in Karuna, a small mining town in the far north of Sweden.

Year	Club	GP	G	A	Pts.
1973-74	Toronto	76	5	34	39
1974-75	Toronto	60	12	25	37
1975-76	Toronto	78	16	41	57
1976-77	Toronto	76	12	66	78
1977-78	Toronto	80	16	60	76
1978-79	Toronto	78	17	56	73
1979-80	Toronto	74	19	52	71
1980-81	Toronto	72	5	61	66
1981-82	Toronto	69	12	44	56
1982-83	Toronto	69	7	38	45
1983-84	Toronto	68	5	38	43
1984-85	Toronto	73	6	33	39
	Totals	873	132	548	680

DAN DAOUST 25 5-11 165   Center

Honest, smallish player who last year became the team's No. 1 center mostly by default... Undrafted after junior career at Cornwall, Ont., but was signed by Montreal as a free agent... Traded to the Leafs for a third-round draft choice in December 1982 and was a big factor—52 points in 52 games—in sparking the Leafs that year to their highest finish since 1978-79... Named to the All-Rookie team following that year... Gives it what he has, would complement just about any team as a third- or fourth-line center... Born Feb. 29, 1960, in Montreal.

Year	Club	GP	G	A	Pts.
1982-83	Mont-Tor	52	18	34	52
1983-84	Toronto	78	18	56	74
1984-85	Toronto	79	17	37	54
	Totals	209	53	127	180

GARY NYLUND 21 6-4 218   Defenseman

Third player taken in 1982 draft, one of the best talent pools ever
... His development has been held back by two serious operations
to his left knee, but he was able to play 76 games last year...
No question about his attitude, but it's been a very difficult break-
in period playing with a balky knee on a young, bad team... So
far has demonstrated his promise only in flashes, but it's easy to
forget that, entering his fourth season, he's still only 21 years old
..."I don't want to be known as defective merchandise," he has
said. "I don't want anyone to say I could've been great if I hadn't
been injured. I want to give these people their money's worth.
And I'm going to. That's all there is to it."... Irony is that Nylund
and Gord Kluzak, the first player taken in the '82 draft (by Boston),
were two of the most promising junior defensive talents in years
and both have been beset by knee problems... Personable young
man, doesn't appear to have been caught up in the siege mentality
towards the press promoted by the Leaf front office... Might be
a good captain someday... Born Oct. 28, 1963, in Surrey, B.C.,
he had outstanding junior career with the Portland Winter Hawks
... Likes to fish, play the guitar.

Year	Club	GP	G	A	Pts.
1982-83	Toronto............	16	0	3	3
1983-84	Toronto............	47	2	14	16
1984-85	Toronto............	76	3	17	20
	Totals.............	139	5	34	39

RUSS COURTNALL 21 5-10 165   Center

Seventh player taken in the 1983 entry draft... Divided time two
years ago among his junior team at Victoria, the Canadian Olympic
Team and the Leafs... Had 12 points in 14 games that season,
but last year had only 22 in 69 games... Another highly-regarded
junior prospect who is feeling his way with a team that has had
to overdose with youth... Excellent skater, quietly confident, a
little on the smallish side... Older brother Geoff plays with the
Boston Bruins... Born June 2, 1964, in Duncan, B.C.

Year	Club	GP	G	A	Pts.
1983-84	Toronto............	14	3	9	12
1984-85	Toronto............	69	12	10	22
	Totals.............	83	15	19	34

JIM BENNING 22 6-0 185   Defenseman

One of the Leafs' four recent high No. 1 picks... Thrown to the wolves with a regular shift in his rookie 1981-82 season and floundered... "He was under a lot of pressure," said Punch Imlach, the Toronto GM who drafted Benning. "He wouldn't have learned any more going back to junior. Besides, how can you send a kid back to junior who's making $100,000 a year?"... Has made halting progress since... Fine offensive talent as a junior (139 points his final year at Portland) but hasn't done better than 51 points in his four NHL seasons... More of an assist man than a goal-scorer... Strange, bent-over skating style, but good wheels ... Has four hockey-playing younger brothers, including Brian, a second-round pick by St. Louis in 1984... Born April 29, 1963, in Kamloops, B.C., where his dad is a fireman.

Year	Club	GP	G	A	Pts.
1981-82	Toronto............	74	7	24	31
1982-83	Toronto............	74	5	17	22
1983-84	Toronto............	79	12	39	51
1984-85	Toronto............	80	9	35	44
	Totals.............	307	33	115	148

AL IAFRATE 19 6-3 190   Defenseman

Another rushed high No. 1 pick... Taken fourth in 1984, spent the entire season with the Leafs and looked lost most of the time until coming on at the end... Born March 21, 1966, in Dearborn, Mich.... Disappointed as a member of the 1984 U.S. Olympic team, but he's always been put in the position of having to play beyond his years... Bowlegged skating style, he can really move and was playing more aggressively when given a more regular shift down the stretch... Very raw talent, it's going to take some time and some coaching.

Year	Club	GP	G	A	Pts.
1984-85	Toronto............	68	5	16	21

JOHN ANDERSON 28 5-11 190   **Right Wing**

Eight-year veteran who, like Rick Vaive, spent some time in the coach's doghouse last season . . . Still, fell off only five points from the 68 he recorded in 1983-84 . . . First-round pick in 1977 . . . As one of the few Leafs in their prime seasons, he was expected to provide experience and backbone, and has disappointed . . . Opened a chain of fast-food hamburger outlets in Toronto, sold them two years ago, but they still bear his name . . . He's Toronto all the way, born there March 28, 1957.

Year	Club	GP	G	A	Pts.
1977-78	Toronto	17	1	2	3
1978-79	Toronto	71	15	11	26
1979-80	Toronto	74	25	28	53
1980-81	Toronto	75	17	26	43
1981-82	Toronto	69	31	26	57
1982-83	Toronto	80	31	49	80
1983-84	Toronto	73	37	31	68
1984-85	Toronto	75	32	31	63
	Totals	534	189	204	393

DAN HODGSON 20 5-11 173   **Center**

Fourth-round draft choice in 1983 . . . Outstanding junior career at Prince Albert of the Western League . . . Leafs left him in junior to mature and have very high hopes for this kid . . . Scored 182 points last season, second in the WHL . . . Former captain of the Canadian National Jr. Team . . . Didn't go high in the draft because of his size, but very smart with the puck and his speed should be at least adequate for the NHL . . . Born Aug. 29, 1965, in Vermillion, Alta.

GREG TERRION 25 5-11 190   **Center**

Valuable checker and penalty-killer . . . Has been used some on the wing . . . Second-round choice of Los Angeles in 1980, has done a nice job for the Leafs since being picked up in 1982 . . . Honest player, both on the ice and with an opinion . . . Commutes from his home in Marnow, Ont., a rural community 90 minutes from Toronto, where he loves the fishing... Born May 2, 1960, in Peterborough, Ont.

Year	Club	GP	G	A	Pts.
1980-81	Los Angeles	73	12	25	37
1981-82	Los Angeles	61	15	22	37
1982-83	Toronto	74	16	16	32
1983-84	Toronto	79	15	24	39
1984-85	Toronto	72	14	17	31
	Totals	359	72	104	176

BILL DERLAGO 27 5-10 195 Center

Center on the Leafs' No. 1 line... Subject of a lot of trade rumors for years, not the most intense player in the league, but a skilled one... Excellent on faceoffs... First-round pick in 1980 by Vancouver, came to the Leafs along with Rick Vaive in the Tiger Williams-Jerry Butler deal in 1980... Loves to play baseball... Led Leafs to two consecutive NHL Slo-Pitch championships... Born Aug. 25, 1958, in Birtle, Man.

Year	Club	GP	G	A	Pts.
1978-79	Vancouver	9	4	4	8
1979-80	Van-Tor	77	16	27	43
1980-81	Toronto	80	35	39	74
1981-82	Toronto	75	34	50	84
1982-83	Toronto	58	13	24	37
1983-84	Toronto	79	40	20	60
1984-85	Toronto	62	31	31	62
	Totals	440	173	195	368

COACH DAN MALONEY: Hard-nosed and beligerent during his NHL career with Chicago, Los Angeles, Detroit and Toronto, Maloney surprised many with a patient, teaching, approach as a rookie coach... "Like all teams that want to move up the ladder, this team won't improve until it's a fundamentally sound club," he says. "Because that means being strong in all the little things, the parts of the game that have no glamour in them, young players aren't wild about doing them. So it's just a matter of hammering away at them. What we're trying to do is teach a team how to win and it takes a great deal of time and effort." . . . Generally kept his cool despite a negative situation in a demanding press town . . . Succeeded Mike Nykoluk, under whom he had served as assistant coach after finishing his playing career with the Leafs . . . Born Sept. 24, 1950, in Barrie, Ont.

MOST COLORFUL PLAYER

They called Eddie Shack "The Entertainer". They needed a gallon jar of mustard to cover this hot dog.

Shack was certainly not the Leafs' best player during the 60's, when the team won three Stanley Cups, but he was the most fun. A hard-driving winger, but a modest goal scorer, he inspired the catch phrase, "Clear the Track, Here Comes Shack." It was even put to music and became a big seller in Toronto.

When named one of the three stars of the game, Shack didn't just take a polite circle and bow. He did a pirouette. Though he never learned how to read, Shack developed a keen business sense and parlayed a salary which never rose above $50,000 a year into financial security for life.

A big favorite of former Leaf GM Punch Imlach, Shack was one of Imlach's first acquisitions when he became general manager of the expansion Buffalo Sabres in 1970. Since finishing up his NHL career with Pittsburgh, Shack has become a staple at various old-timer games and functions across Canada.

ALL-TIME MAPLE LEAF LEADERS

GOALS: Rick Vaive, 54, 1981-82
ASSISTS: Darryl Sittler, 72, 1977-78
POINTS: Darryl Sittler, 117, 1977-78
SHUTOUTS: Harry Lumley, 13, 1953-54

VANCOUVER CANUCKS

TEAM DIRECTORY: Chairman: Frank A. Griffiths; Asst. to Chairman: Arthur R. Griffiths; GM: Jack Gordon; Dir. Player Personnel: Larry Popein; Dir. Pub. Rel.: Norm Jewison; Coach: Tom Watt. Home ice: Pacific Coliseum (15,613; 200' × 85'). Colors: Black, red and yellow. Training camp: Vancouver.

SCOUTING REPORT

OFFENSE: Before the Canucks can improve their weak offense, they must develop a plan of attack, a system of play which fits the capabilities of their players. They must play better positionally on offense and threaten opponents with more forceful play along the boards and in the corners. They must develop more players willing to take a hit to make a play and who will forecheck to sustain the play in their opponents' end of the ice.

They did none of this effectively last season and the results were obvious. The Canucks scored only 284 goals and ranked a poor 16th in offense. Their power play produced only 61 goals, the fewest in the league, and ranked 19th. Passing and playmaking were not among Vancouver's strong points. And yet the Canucks have some good, fast forwards.

Except for Tony Tanti, the Canucks lack a significant goal-scoring threat. Tanti scored 39 goals in 1984-85. Sweden's Patrik Sundstrom led Vancouver in scoring but only with a low 68 points. Another Swedish forward, Thomas Gradin, scored 64 points. Sundstrom and Gradin are capable of scoring close to 100 points a season, if they have suitable linemates with whom to play.

Stan Smyl is one of the league's better all-around forwards. He works hard and checks hard and does a good job defensively when the opposition has the puck. Other prominent forwards are Cam Neely, Petri Skriko, Mark Kirton, Moe Lemay, Gary Lupul and Taylor Hall, who missed more of last season because of an injury. Veteran center Peter McNab lacks speed but still gets the job done and is an offensive threat close to the net. Another veteran, Al MacAdam, is an effective two-way forward.

DEFENSE: It was worse than the offense last season. Vancouver surrendered 401 goals, most goals-against in the NHL. Its penalty-killing ranked 21st and allowed the most power-play goals in the NHL (89).

J. J. Daigneault, a rookie last season, has great offensive talent but must improve his positional play as a defenseman. Michel Petit is another young defenseman with ability. So is former Ca-

Popular Tony Tanti was the Canucks' top goal-scorer.

nadian Olympic defenseman Doug Lidster. Doug Halward is a
steady veteran defenseman. Rick Lanz and Garth Butcher are
looked upon to contribute more this season. Richard Brodeur and
Frank Caprice, the goalies, need more defensive help than they
received last year.

The Canucks hope 18-year-old right wing Jim Sandlak will be
able to win a job this season. He was their No. 1 choice in the
June draft.

OUTLOOK: The Canucks were a team in chaos last season,
ravaged by early-season injuries and forced to undergo a coaching
change. Fans at Pacific Coliseum booed them and have lost respect
for the team. Attendance is down. The Canucks under Tom Watt
must do something to turn things around this season. It will not
be easy.

CANUCK ROSTER

No.	Player	Pos.	Ht.	Wt.	Born	1984-85	G	A	Pts.	PIM
34	Neil Belland	D	5-11	175	4-3-61/Parry Sound, Ont.	Vancouver	0	6	6	34
						Fredericton	7	34	41	31
29	Jiri Bubla	D	5-11	197	1-27-50/Czechoslovakia	Vancouver	2	15	17	54
5	Garth Butcher	D	6-0	195	10-8-63/Regina, Sask.	Vancouver	3	9	12	152
						Fredericton	1	0	1	11
	Glen Cochrane	D	6-2	189	1-29-58/Cranbrook, B.C.	Philadelphia	0	3	3	100
						Hersey	0	8	8	35
	Craig Coxe	LW	6-4	195	1-21-64/Chula Vista, Cal,	Vancouver	0	0	0	49
						Fredericton	8	7	15	242
15	J.J. Daigneault	D	5-10	185	10-12-65/Montreal	Vancouver	4	23	27	69
19	Ron Delorme	RW	6-2	185	9-3-55/Cochin, Sask.	Vancouver	1	2	3	51
10	Jere Gillis	LW	6-0	190	1-18-57/Bend, Ore.	Vancouver	5	11	16	23
						Fredericton	2	1	3	2
23	Thomas Gradin	C	5-11	170	2-18-56/Sweden	Vancouver	22	42	64	43
28	Taylor Hall	LW	5-11	188	2-20-64/Regina, Sask.	Vancouver	1	4	5	19
2	Doug Halward	D	6-1	197	11-1-55/Toronto	Vancouver	7	27	34	82
6	Bruce Holloway	D	6-0	200	6-27-63/Revelstake, B.C.	Fred.-St. C.	3	4	7	16
						Vancouver	0	0	0	0
16	Mark Kirton	C	5-10	170	2-3-58/Toronto	Vancouver	17	5	22	21
						Fredericton	5	9	14	18
	J.M. Lanthier	D	6-2	195	3-27-63/Montreal	Vancouver	6	4	10	13
						Fredericton	21	21	42	13
4	Rick Lanz	D	6-2	195	9-16-61/Czechoslovakia	Vancouver	2	17	19	69
14	Moe Lemay	C	5-11	185	2-18-62/Saskatoon, Sask.	Vancouver	21	31	52	68
3	Doud Lidster	D	6-1	195	10-18-60/Kamloops, B.C.	Vancouver	6	24	30	55
7	Gary Lupul	C	5-8	175	4-4-59/Powell River, B.C.	Vancouver	12	17	29	82
25	Al MacAdam	LW	6-0	180	3-6-52/Charlottetown, PEI	Vancouver	14	20	34	27
8	Peter McNab	C	6-3	205	5-8-52/Vancouver, B.C.	Vancouver	23	25	48	10
21	Cam Neely	RW	6-1	205	6-6-65/Maple Ridge, B.C.	Vancouver	21	18	39	137
24	Michel Petit	D	6-1	180	2-12-64/St. Maulo, Que.	Vancouver	5	26	31	127
	Jim Sandlak	RW	6-3	204	12-12-66/Kitchener, Ont.	London	40	24	64	128
	Andy Schliebener	D	6-0	180	8-16-62/Ottawa, Ont.	Vancouver	0	0	0	16
						Fredericton	1	11	12	58
26	Petri Skriko	LW	5-10	172	3-12-62/Finland	Vancouver	21	14	35	10
12	Stan Smyl	RW	5-8	185	1-28-58/Clendon, Alta.	Vancouver	27	37	64	100
33	Mike Stevens	RW	5-11	193	12-30-65/Kitchener, Ont.	Vancouver	0	3	3	6
						Kitchener	17	18	35	121
17	Patrik Sundstrom	C	6-0	190	12-14-61/Sweden	Vancouver	25	43	68	46
9	Tony Tanti	C	5-9	185	9-7-63/Toronto	Vancouver	39	20	59	45

No.	Player	Pos.	Ht.	Wt.	Born	1984-85	GP	GA	SO	Avg.
35	Richard Brodeur	G	5-7	175	9-15-52/Montreal	Vancouver	51	228	0	4.67
						Fredericton	4	13	0	3.13
30	Frank Caprice	G	5-9	147	5-2-62/Hamilton, Ont.	Vancouver	28	122	0	4.81
31	John Garrett	G	5-8	175	6-17-51/Toronto	Vancouver	10	44	0	6.49
	Wendell Young	G	5-8	178	8-1-63/Halifax, N.S.	Fredericton	22	83	0	4.01

CANUCK PROFILES

PATRIK SUNDSTROM 23 6-0 190   **Center**
Twin brother of Rangers' forward Peter Sundstrom . . . Led Canucks in scoring last two seasons but production dropped from 38 goals, 91 points in 1983-84 to 25 goals, 68 points last year . . . Playing for weak team often diminishes his exceptional skills . . . Many NHL teams have tried to coax Canucks into trading him . . . Swedish-born center is gifted skater, shooter, passer with finesse skills . . . Born Dec. 14, 1961, in Skelleftea, Sweden . . . Scored one goal, six assists for seven-point game on Feb. 29, 1984, against Pittsburgh . . . Formerly played for Swedish national team.

Year	Club	GP	G	A	Pts.
1982-83	Vancouver	74	23	23	46
1983-84	Vancouver	78	38	53	91
1984-85	Vancouver	71	25	43	68
	Totals	223	86	119	205

STAN SMYL 27 5-8 185   **Right Wing**
Needs seven goals to become 200-goal career scorer . . . Solid as a rock . . . Tough, durable winger who grinds hard and plays with aggressive intensity every game . . . Has 958 penalty minutes in seven seasons with Canucks . . . Nicknamed "Steamer" . . . Best season was 1982-83 when he scored 38 goals, 50 assists, 88 points . . . Born Jan. 28, 1958, in Glendon, Alta. . . . Second in Canucks' career scoring with 476 points . . . Scouts who predicted he was too small to play in NHL were wrong . . . Robust style of play makes him a favorite among Canucks' fans at Pacific Coliseum . . . Never gives up . . . At his best digging for puck in corners or during scrambles in front of net.

Year	Club	GP	G	A	Pts.
1978-79	Vancouver	62	14	24	38
1979-80	Vancouver	77	31	47	78
1980-81	Vancouver	80	25	38	63
1981-82	Vancouver	80	34	44	78
1982-83	Vancouver	74	38	50	88
1983-84	Vancouver	80	24	43	67
1984-85	Vancouver	80	27	37	64
	Totals	533	193	283	476

THOMAS GRADIN 29 5-11 170   Center

Regarded as the most talented player lowly Canucks have had since entering the NHL in 1970-71 . . . Has more assists and points than any player in Canucks' history . . . Ranks fourth in games played . . . Needs four more goals to move ahead of former Canuck Don Lever as Canucks' second-highest goal-scorer . . . Born Feb. 18, 1956, in Solleftea, Sweden . . . Smooth, graceful skater . . . Seldom makes a bad pass . . . Scoring declined last season, partially because Canucks had poor season, a profusion of injuries and underwent coaching change . . . Had to withstand considerable physical abuse from many opposing players when he entered NHL in 1978-79 . . . He was resented at first by some rival players because of his non-physical style of play as European import.

Year	Club	GP	G	A	Pts.
1978-79	Vancouver	76	20	31	51
1979-80	Vancouver	80	30	45	75
1980-81	Vancouver	79	21	48	69
1981-82	Vancouver	76	37	49	86
1982-83	Vancouver	80	32	54	86
1983-84	Vancouver	75	21	57	78
1984-85	Vancouver	76	22	42	64
	Totals	542	183	326	509

TONY TANTI 22 5-9 185   Right Wing

Became an instant hit with Canuck fans in 1983-84 . . . Scored 10 goals in first seven games and 34 points in first 18 games . . . Completed rookie season with 45 goals, 86 points . . . Followed up with 39 goals in 1984-85 . . . Has terrific moves and deadly accurate shot . . . A natural goal-scorer from the day he entered youth hockey . . . Born Sept. 7, 1963, in Toronto . . . Holds Vancouver record for most goals (45), most power-play goals (19) in one season . . . Exciting young player to watch . . . Scored 81 goals, 150 points in 67 games for Oshawa of Ontario Junior League in 1980-81 . . . Chicago drafted him No. 1 in 1981 . . . Canucks made smart move trading Curt Fraser to acquire Tanti on Jan. 6, 1983.

Year	Club	GP	G	A	Pts.
1982-83	Chi-Van	40	9	8	17
1983-84	Vancouver	79	45	41	86
1984-85	Vancouver	68	39	20	59
	Totals	187	93	69	162

PETER McNAB 33 6-3 205   Center

Will not dazzle anyone with speed or fancy footwork but has scored 336 goals in distinguished 12-year NHL career . . . Son of Devils' GM and former NHL player Max McNab . . . Canadian-born but raised in San Diego . . . Did not play outstanding level of hockey as a youngster but still made it as quality NHL player . . . Starred in college hockey at University of Denver . . . Roommate was Devils' forward Rich Preston . . . Born May 8, 1952, in Vancouver, B.C. . . . Was outstanding all-around athlete in high school . . . Could have signed pro baseball contract because of power-hitting skill but lacked speed scouts seek . . . Accurate shooter who uses size to score frequently from close to net . . . Always has played well in playoffs during career with Buffalo and Boston.

Year	Club	GP	G	A	Pts.
1973-74	Buffalo	22	3	6	9
1974-75	Buffalo	53	22	21	43
1975-76	Buffalo	79	24	32	56
1976-77	Boston	80	38	48	86
1977-78	Boston	79	41	39	80
1978-79	Boston	76	35	45	80
1979-80	Boston	74	40	38	78
1980-81	Boston	80	37	46	83
1981-82	Boston	80	36	40	76
1982-83	Boston	74	22	52	74
1983-84	Bos-Van	65	15	22	37
1984-85	Vancouver	75	23	25	48
	Totals	837	336	414	750

MOE LEMAY 23 5-11 185   Left Wing

Last season was his best in NHL . . . Sturdy left wing was low-scoring Canucks' fifth-highest scorer . . . Almost matched his career scoring totals for three seasons in 1984-85 . . . Needed time to develop and win full time job in NHL . . . Born Feb. 18, 1962, in Saskatoon, Sask. . . . Works hard with or without puck . . . Finally showing signs of regaining scoring touch from days in junior hockey . . . Led Ontario Junior League with 68 goals and scored 138 points in 62 games for Ottawa in 1981-82 . . . A streak scorer . . . Needs to become more consistent with his scoring.

Year	Club	GP	G	A	Pts.
1981-82	Vancouver	5	1	2	3
1982-83	Vancouver	44	11	9	20
1983-84	Vancouver	56	12	18	30
1984-85	Vancouver	74	21	31	52
	Totals	179	45	60	105

DOUG HALWARD 28 6-1 197   Defenseman

Started NHL career in 1975-76 with Bruins as No. 1 draft choice
... Not flashy or fancy but gets the job done as defensive defenseman ... Canucks' highest-scoring defenseman with 34 points
last season ... Ten-year NHL veteran achieved career high with
19 goals in 1982-83 ... Nicknamed "Hawk" ... Born Nov. 1, 1955,
in Toronto ... Never lived up to his potential with Boston but
established himself with Los Angeles ... Has played his best hockey
during five seasons as Canuck ... Plays the man well ... An effective bodychecker.

Year	Club	GP	G	A	Pts.
1975-76	Boston	22	1	5	6
1976-77	Boston	18	2	2	4
1977-78	Boston	25	0	2	2
1978-79	Los Angeles	27	1	5	6
1979-80	Los Angeles	63	11	45	56
1980-81	LA-Van	58	4	16	20
1981-82	Vancouver	37	4	13	17
1982-83	Vancouver	75	19	33	52
1983-84	Vancouver	54	7	16	23
1984-85	Vancouver	71	7	27	34
	Totals	510	56	164	220

CAM NEELY 20 6-1 205   Right Wing

Watch out! ... This could be his first big year ... Scored 21 goals
in first full season with Vancouver last season ... Canucks'
No. 1 draft pick, ninth overall selection in 1983 draft ... Has size
and potential to blossom as quality right wing ... Does a good
job defensively ... His minus-10 record was best last season for
defensively poor Canucks ... Born June 6, 1965, in Comox,
B.C.... Was feared scorer in junior hockey ... Scored 73 goals,
141 points as midget league player in 1981-82 ... Was 56-goal,
120-point-scorer in 1982-83 for powerful Portland Winter Hawks
of Western Canada Junior League ... Has the ability to become a
top-grade NHL forward.

Year	Club	GP	G	A	Pts.
1983-84	Vancouver	56	16	15	31
1984-85	Vancouver	72	21	18	39
	Totals	128	37	33	70

RICHARD BRODEUR 33 5-7 175   Goaltender

Little Richard but often plays like King Richard ... Played well
under adverse conditions for defensively weak team last season

. . . Seldom received much support from team with vulnerable defense and forwards who did not excel as backcheckers . . . Six-year WHA veteran with Quebec . . . Master of making the seemingly impossible save . . . Born Sept. 15, 1952, in Longueuil, Que. . . . Overcame serious injuries which could have ended his goaltending career . . . A playoff hero for Canucks in 1982 . . . Made NHL debut in 1979-80 with Islanders . . . Has career goaltending record of 85-110-47 . . . Quickness is his strongest asset as a goalie.

Year	Club	GP	GA	SO	Avg.
1972-73	Quebec (WHA)	24	102	0	4.75
1973-74	Quebec (WHA)	30	89	1	3.32
1974-75	Quebec (WHA)	51	188	0	3.84
1975-76	Quebec (WHA)	69	244	2	3.69
1976-77	Quebec (WHA)	53	167	2	3.45
1977-78	Quebec (WHA)	36	121	0	3.70
1978-79	Quebec (WHA)	42	126	3	3.11
1979-80	New York I	2	6	0	4.50
1980-81	Vancouver	52	177	0	3.51
1981-82	Vancouver	52	168	2	3.35
1982-83	Vancouver	58	208	0	3.79
1983-84	Vancouver	36	141	1	4.02
1984-85	Vancouver	51	228	0	4.67
	NHL Totals	251	928	8	3.86
	WHA Totals	305	1037	8	3.64

JEAN-JACQUES DAIGNEAULT 19 5-10 185   Defenseman
Everyone calls him J.J. . . . Canucks' No. 1 draft selection in 1984 . . . His rookie season was a learning experience . . . Made a lot of mistakes, especially on defense, but displayed flashes of brilliance, notably as offense-oriented defenseman . . . Small but fast . . . Has exceptional skating speed with rapid acceleration . . . Born Oct. 12, 1965, in Montreal . . . Scored 84 points in final junior hockey season . . . Plays with desire and enthusiasm . . . Difficult to check because of his speed . . . Reminds some scouts of Rangers' Reijo Ruotsalainen . . . Must learn to play with greater discipline and control, as well as improving positional play . . . Has great crowd appeal.

Year	Club	GP	G	A	Pts.
1984-85	Vancouver	67	4	23	27

COACH TOM WATT: Takes over as coach of a troubled team
with chance for success this season . . . If any-
one can help improve Canucks, it's Watt . . .
Made NHL coaching debut in 1981-82 with
struggling Winnipeg Jets . . . Named winner of
Jack Adams Trophy as Coach of the Year after
guiding Jets to 33-33-14 record and rise from
21st and last place to 10th in NHL standings
. . . Coached Winnipeg to 33-39-8 record in 1982-
83 . . . Fired as Winnipeg coach on Nov. 23, 1983, after dispute
with GM John Ferguson and Jets in slump with 6-13-2 record . . .
Returned to coaching at University of Toronto . . . Born June 17,
1935, in Toronto . . . First NHL job was in 1980-81 as Canucks'
assistant coach . . . Highly intelligent . . . Innovative coach . . . Au-
thor of two instructional hockey books . . . Active as TV hockey
analyst . . . A teaching coach with background in amateur, college,
international and pro hockey . . . Starting in 1965, compiled 378-
96-29 record in 14 years as University of Toronto coach, winning
20 championships.

MOST COLORFUL PLAYER

One of the Vancouver Canucks' many problems over the years
is that they never have had a truly colorful player with skill and
charisma.

The most colorful player the Canucks have had played for the
team for only five seasons and no longer is a Canuck.

It's a pity. Dave (Tiger) Williams is more than a colorful,
outspoken, controversial player. Although recognized mainly for
fight and penalty minutes, he's a good left wing who has scored
199 goals in his NHL career, starting in 1974 with Toronto and,
after being traded to Vancouver, continuing last season with Detroit
and Los Angeles.

Tiger Williams has charisma. Home fans love him. He's hated
in opponent's arenas. He has the face of a dead-end kid and that's
how he plays hockey. The 5-11, 190-pound Tiger will fight any
opponent at any time—the big and the small. He has more penalty
minutes than any player in NHL history (3,195 in regular-season
play).

"He's a helluva hockey player . . . a good player and a tough
player, my kind of player," says veteran coach Tom McVie.

ALL-TIME CANUCK LEADERS

GOALS: Tony Tanti, 45, 1983-84
ASSISTS: Andre Boudrias, 62, 1974-75
POINTS: Patrik Sundstrom, 91, 1983-84
SHUTOUTS: Gary Smith, 6, 1974-75

Peter McNab is ready for his 13th season.

WINNIPEG JETS

TEAM DIRECTORY: Chairman: Bob Graham; Pres.: Barry Shenkarow; VP-GM: John Ferguson; Dir. Hockey/Media Inf.: Ralph Carter; Dir. Player Personnel: Mike Doran; Coach: Barry Long. Home ice: Winnipeg Arena (15,342; 200' × 95'). Colors: Blue, red and white. Training camp: Winnipeg.

SCOUTING REPORT

OFFENSE: Few NHL teams have the skating speed and passing skill of the Jets. Few teams have a line as good as the combination of Dale Hawerchuk, Paul MacLean and New York City-born Brian Mullen. The Jets' first line scored 126 goals last season. Hawerchuk, a young superstar, scored 53 goals, 130 points. MacLean scored 101 points. If he hadn't been injured, Mullen would have approached the 100-point plateau.

A bit more scoring balance, toughness and size up front and Winnipeg will be more of an offensive threat. The Jets don't go in for an overly complex style of play. They keep it simple with a brisk, drive-for-the-net, move-the-puck-quickly approach.

They have several other quality forwards: hard-driving, hard-hitting, all-purpose Laurie Boschman, breakaway threat Doug Smail, slick, quick Thomas Steen, Scott Arniel, Andrew McBain, Perry Turnbull and Bengt Lundholm.

Winnipeg had the fifth-best power play in the NHL last season. The Jets have two defensemen who provide scoring power: Randy Carlyle, a playmaker and attack-organizer, and David Babych.

DEFENSE: Carlyle, Babych, Dave Ellett, Robert Picard, Tim Watters and Jim Kyte provide coach Barry Long with a well-balanced corps of defensemen. If rookie Bob Dollas develops this season, the Jets will have one of the best defensive units in their division.

The Jets' defensive play still is not up to the level of their offense. Winnipeg must reduce giveaways in its defensive zone, get greater defensive effort from its forwards and improve its 11th-ranked penalty-killing. The power play was burned too often last season, allowing 17 shorthanded goals.

The goaltending is in capable hands with No. 1 goalie Brian Hayward and backup Marc Behrend. Winnipeg has a third goalie with promise, Mark Holden. Hayward, a former college goalie at Cornell, emerged last season as one of the league's best young goalies, playing in 61 of 80 games.

Scoring 135 points, Dale Hawerchuk had his best season.

Winnipeg believes it has a good future prospect in center Ryan Steward, a first-round 1985 draft selection.

OUTLOOK: John Ferguson has redeemed himself as a former Ranger GM. The Rangers fired him just when he was beginning to develop a potentially good young team. Now he has developed Winnipeg into one of the best teams in the NHL. The Jets finished fourth in the NHL last season. They are well-coached, well-disciplined and loom as a threat in the playoffs. Problem is many fans overlook their ability because of the presence of Stanley Cup champion Edmonton in the Smythe Division.

JET ROSTER

No.	Player	Pos.	Ht.	Wt.	Born	1984-85	G	A	Pts.	PIM
11	Scott Arniel	LW	6-1	172	9-17-62/Kingston, Ont.	Winnipeg	22	22	44	81
44	Dave Babych	D	6-1	210	5-23-61/Edmonton	Winnipeg	13	49	62	78
16	Laurie Boschman	C	5-11	175	6-4-60/Karrobert, Man.	Winnipeg	32	44	76	180
4	Wade Campbell	D	6-4	220	2-1-61/Peace River, Alta.	Winnipeg	1	6	7	21
						Sherbrooke	2	6	8	70
8	Randy Carlyle	D	5-10	200	4-19-56/Sudbury, Ont.	Winnipeg	13	38	51	98
5	Bobby Dollas	D	6-2	195	1-31-65/Montreal	Winnipeg	0	0	0	0
						Sherbrooke	1	3	4	4
14	Jordy Douglas	C	6-0	195	1-20-58/Winnipeg	Winnipeg	0	2	2	0
						Sherbrooke	23	21	44	16
26	Murray Eaves	C	5-10	185	5-10-60/Calgary	Winnipeg	0	3	3	2
						Sherbrooke	26	42	68	28
2	Dave Ellett	D	6-1	200	3-30-64/Cleveland	Winnipeg	11	27	38	85
10	Dale Hawerchuk	C	5-11	185	4-4-63/Toronto	Winnipeg	53	77	130	74
6	Jim Kyte	D	6-3	205	3-21-64/Ottawa, Ont.	Winnipeg	0	3	3	111
22	Bengt Lundholm	C	6-0	172	8-4-55/Sweden	Winnipeg	12	18	30	20
15	Paul MacLean	RW	6-0	190	1-15-58/France	Winnipeg	41	60	101	119
20	Andrew McBain	RW	6-1	190	2-18-65/Toronto	Winnipeg	7	15	22	45
19	Brian Mullen	LW	5-10	170	3-16-62/New York, N.Y.	Winnipeg	32	39	71	32
	Jim Nill	D-LW	6-0	186	4-11-58/Hanna, Alta.	Bos.-Winn.	9	17	26	100
3	Robert Picard	D	6-2	205	5-25-57/Montreal	Winnipeg	12	22	34	107
23	Paul Pooley	LW	6-0	175	8-2-60/Exeter, Ont.	Winnipeg	0	2	2	0
						Sherbrooke	18	17	35	16
	Perry Pooley	RW	6-0	175	8-2-60/Exeter, Ont.	Sherbrooke	10	18	28	16
9	Doug Smail	LW	5-9	175	9-2-57/Moose Jaw, Sask.	Winnipeg	31	35	66	45
35	Thomas Steen	C	5-10	195	6-8-60/Sweden	Winnipeg	30	54	84	80
27	Perry Turnbull	LW	6-2	200	3-9-59/Bentley, Alta.	Winnipeg	22	21	43	130
7	Tim Watters	D	5-11	180	7-25-59/Kamloops, B.C.	Winnipeg	2	20	22	74
24	Ron Wilson	LW	5-9	168	5-13-56/Toronto	Winnipeg	10	9	19	31

No.	Player	Pos.	Ht.	Wt.	Born		GP	GA	SO	Avg.
29	Marc Behrand	G	6-1	185	1-11-61/Madison, Wis.	Winnipeg	24	91	1	4.48
						Sherbrooke	7	25	0	3.51
1	Brian Hayward	G	5-10	175	6-25-60/Kingston, Ont.	Winnipeg	61	220	0	3.84
	Mark Holden	G	5-10	165	6-12-57/Weymouth, Mass.	Winnipeg	4	15	0	4.23
	Pokey Reddick	G	5-6	147	10-6-64/Toronto	Sherbrooke	2	7	0	5.68
						Brandon	47	243	0	5.64

JET PROFILES

DALE HAWERCHUK 22 5-11 185   Center
Set personal records for goals (53), assists (77) and points (130) last season...One of hockey's best young centers...Finished third in NHL scoring behind Edmonton's Wayne Gretzky and Jari Kurri in 1984-85...A superstar after only four NHL seasons ...New Jersey Devils' coach Doug Carpenter was not surprised by Hawerchuk's swift rise to stardom..."I could tell he would be a superstar when he was only 15," said Carpenter, who coached Jets' forward in Cornwall of Quebec Junior League...Born April 4, 1963, in Toronto...Winnipeg claimed him as No. 1 choice in 1981 NHL draft...Excels on line with Brian Mullen and Paul MacLean...Injured ribs in playoff last season and was severe loss for Jets.

Year	Club	GP	G	A	Pts.
1981-82	Winnipeg	80	45	58	103
1982-83	Winnipeg	79	40	51	91
1983-84	Winnipeg	80	37	65	102
1984-85	Winnipeg	80	53	77	130
	Totals	319	175	251	426

PAUL MacLEAN 27 6-2 205   Right Wing
Had best pro season in 1984-85...Jets' most accurate shooter, he scored goals on 22 percent of his shots...Has scoring touch with variety of shots...Has fast-breaking moves and drives for openings on net with skill...Uses size well to establish position offensively or battle for puck in corners or along boards...Born March 9, 1958, in Grostenquin, France...Father was stationed in France with Canadian armed forces...Good passer-playmaker ...Important member of Jets' power play...His 119 penalty minutes last season show he does not shy away from rough play.

Year	Club	GP	G	A	Pts.
1980-81	St. Louis	1	0	0	0
1981-82	Winnipeg	74	36	25	61
1982-83	Winnipeg	80	32	44	76
1983-84	Winnipeg	76	40	31	71
1984-85	Winnipeg	79	41	60	101
	Totals	310	149	160	309

THOMAS STEEN 25 5-10 195   Center

Scoring figures last season represent an NHL career high . . . Slick, quick center who can play circling, motion-type European game or straight-ahead NHL style . . . Fast, deceptive skater . . . Good defensive forward skilled at killing penalties . . . Jets' scouts did their homework well . . . Despite being chosen only 103rd in 1979 NHL draft, he has established himself as good NHL player . . . Born June 8, 1960, in Tockmark, Sweden . . . Played in Canada Cup in 1981 and 1984 . . . Needs nine goals to reach 100 for NHL career . . . Collects cars as hobby.

Year	Club	GP	G	A	Pts.
1981-82	Winnipeg	73	15	29	44
1982-83	Winnipeg	75	26	33	59
1983-84	Winnipeg	78	20	45	65
1984-85	Winnipeg	79	30	54	84
	Totals	305	91	161	252

LAURIE BOSCHMAN 25 6-0 185   Center

Toronto Maple Leafs regret trading him to Edmonton . . . Oilers gave up on him too quickly and dealt him to Winnipeg, where he blossomed into quality player two years ago . . . Plays forceful, aggressive game and is willing to fight . . . Has 1,083 career penalty minutes in six NHL seasons . . . Born June 4, 1960, in Major, Sask. . . . Rival players regard him as fierce competitor . . . Plays effectively as center with or without puck . . . Scored 32 goals last season, most in one NHL season . . . Was Maple Leafs' first-round draft pick in 1979 . . . Active in charity work . . . Works in off-season with youth at Christian teen ranch and is involved with Special Olympics.

Year	Club	GP	G	A	Pts.
1979-80	Toronto............	80	16	32	48
1980-81	Toronto............	53	14	19	33
1981-82	Tor-Edm............	65	11	22	33
1982-83	Edm-Winn	74	11	17	28
1983-84	Winnipeg	61	28	46	74
1984-85	Winnipeg	80	32	44	76
	Totals	413	112	180	292

BRIAN MULLEN 23 5-10 180   Left Wing

Born and raised in Hell's Kitchen, New York City . . . Brother of St. Louis' right wing Joe Mullen . . . Like older brother, he followed New York Rangers as a kid and played roller hockey on city streets and in playgrounds . . . Starred in youth hockey in New York Metropolitan Junior Hockey Association . . . Attended University of Wisconsin on hockey scholarship before turning pro with Winnipeg . . . Worked as teenaged stickboy for Rangers at Madison Square Garden . . . Rangers red-faced with embarrassment that they failed to sign him . . . Born March 16, 1962, in New York City . . . Scoring figures have climbed from 50 to 62 to 71 in first three NHL seasons.

Year	Club	GP	G	A	Pts.
1982-83	Winnipeg	80	24	26	50
1983-84	Winnipeg	75	21	41	62
1984-85	Winnipeg	69	32	39	71
	Totals	224	77	106	183

DOUG SMAIL 28 5-9 175   Left Wing

Jets made a wise move signing him as free agent after fine college career at University of North Dakota . . . Helped lead Fighting Sioux to NCAA championship in 1980 . . . Had his best NHL season in 1984-85 with 31 goals, 66 points . . . Has skating speed and uses it well . . . Set NHL record in 1981 for scoring fastest goal from start of game . . . Only five seconds had elapsed when he fired puck into net on Dec. 20, 1981, against St. Louis . . . Born Sept. 2, 1957, in Moose Jaw, Sask. . . . Always a threat to score shorthanded goal when killing penalty.

Year	Club	GP	G	A	Pts.
1980-81	Winnipeg	30	10	8	18
1981-82	Winnipeg	72	17	18	35
1982-83	Winnipeg	80	15	29	44
1983-84	Winnipeg	66	20	17	37
1984-85	Winnipeg	80	31	35	66
	Totals	328	93	107	200

RANDY CARLYLE 29 5-10 200   Defenseman

Fell into disfavor with Pittsburgh after winning Norris Trophy as NHL's most outstanding defenseman in 1981 . . . Had weight problem and play deteriorated . . . Penguins' fans became disturbed by his decline from All-Star status . . . Trade to Winnipeg in 1984 was just what he needed . . . Lost weight, overcame knee injury, regained form as offensive defenseman . . . Born April 19, 1956, in Sudbury, Ont. . . . . "He has a great attitude, has become a team leader since we got him," said Jets' coach Barry Long...Has improved his defensive game, reduced mistakes and still is a scoring threat...At his best directing Jets' power play...Tireless worker who thrives on lots of ice time.

Year	Club	GP	G	A	Pts.
1976-77	Toronto	45	0	5	5
1977-78	Toronto	49	2	11	13
1978-79	Pittsburgh	70	13	34	47
1979-80	Pittsburgh	67	8	28	36
1980-81	Pittsburgh	76	16	67	83
1981-82	Pittsburgh	73	11	64	75
1982-83	Pittsburgh	61	15	41	56
1983-84	Pitt-Winn	55	3	26	29
1984-85	Winnipeg	71	13	38	51
	Totals	567	81	314	395

DAVID BABYCH 24 6-1 210   Defenseman

Did not have an overly consistent 1984-85 season...Some Winnipeg fans booed his play...Despite subpar all-around season, he still led Jets' defensemen in scoring with 62 points...Biggest problem was his play in Jets' defensive zone...Had poor minus-16 record...Brother of Pittsburgh forward Wayne Babych...Born May 23, 1961, in Edmonton, Alta....Was second player chosen in 1980 NHL draft...A hard-hitter on defense...Strongest part of game is generating offense by leading rush and firing shots from blue line...Has good leadership qualities...Skilled at making power play click.

Year	Club	GP	G	A	Pts.
1980-81	Winnipeg	69	6	38	44
1981-82	Winnipeg	79	19	49	68
1982-83	Winnipeg	79	13	61	74
1983-84	Winnipeg	66	18	39	57
1984-85	Winnipeg	78	13	49	62
	Totals	371	69	236	305

BRYAN HAYWARD 25 5-10 175   Goaltender

Established himself as one of NHL's leading goalies last season ...Won No. 1 job from Marc Behrend and responded with 33-17-7 record, 3.84 goals-against average...Placed second in goaltending wins behind Flyers' Pelle Lindbergh, who won 40 games...Played in 61 of Jets' 80 games...Born June 25, 1960, in Georgetown, Ont....Has quick reflexes and plays stand-up style ... Very good at making saves on second and third rebound shots during flurries at net ... Not easily fooled or lured out of position by forwards' dekes ... Starred in college hockey at Cornell ... Jets signed him as a free agent.

Year	Club	GP	GA	SO	Avg.
1982-83	Winnipeg	24	89	1	3.71
1983-84	Winnipeg	28	124	0	4.86
1984-85	Winnipeg	61	220	0	3.84
	Totals	113	433	1	4.05

ROBERT PICARD 28 6-2 205   Defenseman

In many respects, he may have been Winnipeg's most consistent defenseman last season ... Showed flashes of brilliance as Washington's first draft choice in 1977 but until last season never quite reached full potential ... Washington traded him to Toronto, which dealt him to Montreal ... Born May 25, 1957, in Montreal ... Improved his defense play last season ... Still managed to help attack by scoring 12 goals, all in even-strength situations ... Finished season with impressive plus-31 record, best on team.

Year	Club	GP	G	A	Pts.
1977-78	Washington	75	10	27	37
1978-79	Washington	77	21	44	65
1979-80	Washington	78	11	43	54
1980-81	Tor-Mont	67	8	21	29
1981-82	Montreal...........	62	2	26	28
1982-83	Montreal...........	64	7	31	38
1983-84	Mont-Winn	69	6	18	24
1984-85	Winnipeg	78	12	22	34
	Totals	570	77	232	309

COACH BARRY LONG: GM John Ferguson made a smart move when he elevated Long from assistant to head coach Nov. 22, 1983, as successor to Tom Watt ... Guided Jets to 25-25-9 record in remaining 59 games of 1983-84 season ... Established himself as bright young coach last season ... Jets' 45-27-10 record was fourth-best in league, best record since Winnipeg entered NHL six years ago ... Firm but fair coach ... Maintains good relationship with players... Lines of communications always open... Speaks his mind and not afraid to bench player not playing well... Born Jan. 3, 1949, in Brantford, Ont.... Keeps his system of play simple... A pro defenseman for 14 years... Scored 301 points in 666 NHL games... Serious hand injury ended his playing career with Winnipeg... Remained with the Jets as scout... Also played with Los Angeles, Edmonton, Detroit.

Pinpoint shooting Paul MacLean recorded 101 points.

MOST COLORFUL PLAYER

Dale Hawerchuk is easily the most skilled and colorful player to watch since the Winnipeg Jets left the World Hockey Association and entered the NHL in 1979-80.

"Our young superstar," is how GM John Ferguson describes Hawerchuk. "He's still just a kid but he's one of the best players in the league."

Hawerchuk, 22, appeals to fans of all ages for his youthful good looks, pleasing personality and ability to play a hard but clean style of hockey. A center, he excels in all areas of the game.

"The fans love him for the way he plays," says Ferguson. "He's the kind of young player who has the ability to make a team a winner and the personality to give his team a good image that fans like."

ALL-TIME JET LEADERS

GOALS: Bobby Hull, 77, 1974-75
ASSISTS: Ulf Nilsson, 94, 1974-75
POINTS: Bobby Hull, 142, 1974-75
SHUTOUTS: Joe Daley, 5, 1975-76

Capitals' Rod Langway (left) vs. Islanders' Pat Flatley.

Official NHL Statistics

1984–85

FINAL STANDINGS

CLARENCE CAMPBELL CONFERENCE

NORRIS DIVISION

	GP	W	L	T	GF	GA	PTS	PCT
St. Louis	80	37	31	12	299	288	86	.538
Chicago	80	38	35	7	309	299	83	.519
Detroit	80	27	41	12	313	357	66	.413
Minnesota	80	25	43	12	268	321	62	.388
Toronto	80	20	52	8	253	358	48	.300

SMYTHE DIVISION

	GP	W	L	T	GF	GA	PTS	PCT
Edmonton	80	49	20	11	401	298	109	.681
Winnipeg	80	43	27	10	358	332	96	.600
Calgary	80	41	27	12	363	302	94	.588
Los Angeles	80	34	32	14	339	326	82	.513
Vancouver	80	25	46	9	284	401	59	.369

PRINCE OF WALES CONFERENCE

ADAMS DIVISION

	GP	W	L	T	GF	GA	PTS	PCT
Montreal	80	41	27	12	309	262	94	.588
Quebec	80	41	30	9	323	275	91	.569
Buffalo	80	38	28	14	290	237	90	.563
Boston	80	36	34	10	303	287	82	.513
Hartford	80	30	41	9	268	318	69	.431

PATRICK DIVISION

	GP	W	L	T	GF	GA	PTS	PCT
Philadelphia	80	53	20	7	348	241	113	.706
Washington	80	46	25	9	322	240	101	.631
NY Islanders	80	40	34	6	345	312	86	.538
NY Rangers	80	26	44	10	295	345	62	.388
New Jersey	80	22	48	10	264	346	54	.338
Pittsburgh	80	24	51	5	276	385	53	.331

STANLEY CUP: EDMONTON

INDIVIDUAL LEADERS

Goals: Wayne Gretzky, Edmonton, 73
Assists: Wayne Gretzky, Edmonton, 135
Points: Wayne Gretzky, Edmonton, 208
Power-Play Goals: Tim Kerr, Philadelphia, 21
Shorthanded Goals: Wayne Gretzky, Edmonton, 11
Game-Winning Goals: Jari Kurri, Edmonton, 13
Most Goals in One Game: Wayne Gretzky, Edmonton, 5
Shooting Percentage: Warren Young, Pittsburgh, 30.8
Shutouts: Tom Barrasso, Buffalo, 5
Goaltender Wins: Pelle Lindbergh, Philadelphia, 40
Goals-Against Average: Tom Barrasso, Buffalo, 2.66

INDIVIDUAL SCORING LEADERS

PLAYER	TEAM	GP	G	A	PTS	+/−	PIM	PP	SH	GW
Wayne Gretzky	Edmonton	80	73	135	208	98	52	8	11	7
Jari Kurri	Edmonton	73	71	64	135	76	30	14	3	13
Dale Hawerchuk	Winnipeg	80	53	77	130	22	74	17	3	4
Marcel Dionne	Los Angeles	80	46	80	126	11	46	16	1	2
Paul Coffey	Edmonton	80	37	84	121	55	97	12	2	6
Mike Bossy	NY Islanders	76	58	59	117	37	38	14	4	7
John Ogrodnick	Detroit	79	55	50	105	1	30	15	1	6
Denis Savard	Chicago	79	38	67	105	16	56	7	0	1
Bernie Federko	St Louis	76	30	73	103	10−	27	6	0	3
Mike Gartner	Washington	80	50	52	102	17	71	17	0	11
Brent Sutter	NY Islanders	72	42	60	102	42	51	12	0	4
Paul MacLean	Winnipeg	79	41	60	101	5	119	14	0	6
Bernie Nicholls	Los Angeles	80	46	54	100	4−	76	15	0	6
Mario Lemieux	Pittsburgh	73	43	57	100	35−	54	11	0	2
John Tonelli	NY Islanders	80	42	58	100	50	95	8	1	3
Peter Stastny	Quebec	75	32	68	100	23	95	7	1	9
Kent Nilsson	Calgary	77	37	62	99	4−	14	9	3	3
Tim Kerr	Philadelphia	74	54	44	98	29	57	21	0	9
Brian Propp	Philadelphia	76	43	53	96	46	43	12	7	4
Michel Goulet	Quebec	69	55	40	95	10	55	17	0	6
Bob Carpenter	Washington	80	53	42	95	20	87	12	0	7
Dave Taylor	Los Angeles	79	41	51	92	13	132	11	2	6
Joe Mullen	St Louis	79	40	52	92	5	6	13	0	4

PLAYERS BY TEAM

PLAYER	TEAM	GP	G	A	PTS	+/−	PIM	PP	SH	GW
Ray Bourque	Boston	73	20	66	86	30	53	10	1	1
Rick Middleton	Boston	80	30	46	76	2	6	12	3	3
Ken Linseman	Boston	74	25	49	74	22	126	5	1	5
Tom Fergus	Boston	79	30	43	73	14	75	4	0	2
Keith Crowder	Boston	79	32	38	70	31	142	14	0	1
Charlie Simmer	Los Angeles	5	1	0	1	4−	4	0	0	0
	Boston	63	33	30	63	14	35	12	0	5
	Total	68	34	30	64	10	39	12	0	5
Mike O'Connell	Boston	78	15	40	55	3	64	8	0	2
Butch Goring	NY Islanders	29	2	5	7	11−	2	0	1	0
	Boston	39	13	21	34	8−	6	2	2	2
	Total	68	15	26	41	19−	8	2	3	2
Steve Kasper	Boston	77	16	24	40	12−	33	0	5	1
Louis Sleigher	Quebec	6	1	2	3	1−	0	0	0	1
	Boston	70	12	19	31	2−	45	0	0	2
	Total	76	13	21	34	3−	45	0	0	3
Terry O'Reilly	Boston	63	13	17	30	18−	168	0	1	2
Geoff Courtnall	Boston	64	12	16	28	3−	82	0	0	1
Dave Reid	Boston	35	14	13	27	1−	27	2	0	5

Peter Stastny paced Quebec with 100 points.

PLAYER	TEAM	GP	G	A	PTS	+/-	PIM	PP	SH	GW
Morris Lukowich......	Winnipeg	47	5	9	14	13-	31	1	0	2
	Boston	22	5	8	13	7	21	0	0	1
	Total	69	10	17	27	6-	52	1	0	3
Mats Thelin.........	Boston	73	5	13	18	9	78	0	0	2
John Blum	Boston	75	3	13	16	0	263	0	0	0
Mike Milbury	Boston	78	3	13	16	6-	152	0	1	0
Dave Donnelly	Boston	38	6	8	14	1-	46	0	1	1
Barry Pederson	Boston	22	4	8	12	11-	10	0	2	0
Lyndon Byers.......	Boston	33	3	8	11	0	41	0	0	0
Frank Simonetti	Boston	43	1	5	6	1-	26	0	0	0
Nevin Markwart.....	Boston	26	0	4	4	1-	36	0	0	0
Brain Curran	Boston	56	0	1	1	8-	158	0	0	0
Doug Morrison	Boston	1	0	0	0	0	2	0	0	0
Don Sylvestri........	Boston	3	0	0	0	0	2	0	0	0
Greg Johnston	Boston	6	0	0	0	1-	0	0	0	0
Doug Kostynski	Boston	6	0	0	0	0	2	0	0	0
Cleon Daskalakis.....	Boston	8	0	0	0	0	0	0	0	0
Doug Keans.........	Boston	25	0	0	0	0	6	0	0	0
Pete Peeters	Boston	51	0	0	0	0	20	0	0	0
Gil Perreault	Buffalo	78	30	53	83	9	42	10	1	1
Phil Housley	Buffalo	73	16	53	69	15	28	3	0	4
Dave Andreychuk	Buffalo	64	31	30	61	4-	54	14	0	2
Mike Foligno	Buffalo	77	27	29	56	16	154	6	0	6
John Tucker.........	Buffalo	64	22	27	49	6	21	11	0	3
Gilles Hamel	Buffalo	80	18	30	48	3-	36	5	3	4
Paul Cyr...........	Buffalo	71	22	24	46	7-	63	5	0	1
Sean McKenna	Buffalo	65	20	16	36	6-	41	2	0	0
Brent Peterson	Buffalo	74	12	22	34	18	47	2	1	2
Craig Ramsay	Buffalo	79	12	21	33	17	16	0	0	1
Ric Seiling.........	Buffalo	73	16	15	31	30	86	2	3	3
Mike Ramsey........	Buffalo	79	8	22	30	31	102	3	0	2
Mal Davis	Buffalo	47	17	9	26	1	26	5	0	5
Dave Maloney	NY Rangers	16	2	1	3	3	10	0	0	0
	Buffalo	52	1	21	22	20	41	0	0	0
	Total	68	3	22	25	23	51	0	0	0
Lindy Ruff..........	Buffalo	39	13	11	24	1-	45	2	0	2
Hannu Virta	Buffalo	51	1	23	24	2-	16	0	0	0
Bill Hajt	Buffalo	57	5	13	18	32	14	1	1	0
Larry Playfair.......	Buffalo	72	3	14	17	3-	157	0	0	1
Adam Creighton	Buffalo	30	2	8	10	7-	33	1	0	0
Gates Orlando	Buffalo	11	3	6	9	3	6	1	0	0
Dave Fenyves.......	Buffalo	60	1	8	9	0	27	0	0	0
Jerry Korab	Buffalo	25	1	6	7	9-	29	0	0	1
Normand Lacombe	Buffalo	30	2	4	6	3-	25	0	0	0
Timo Jutila	Buffalo	10	1	5	6	5-	13	1	0	0
Tom Barrasso	Buffalo	54	0	6	6	0	41	0	0	0
Jim Schoenfeld	Buffalo	34	0	3	3	0	28	0	0	0
Bob Mongrain	Buffalo	8	1	1	2	1	0	0	0	0
Mike Moller	Buffalo	5	0	2	2	0	0	0	0	0
Jacques Cloutier......	Buffalo	1	0	1	1	0	0	0	0	0
Bob Sauve..........	Buffalo	27	0	1	1	0	4	0	0	0
Claude Verret	Buffalo	3	0	0	0	2-	0	0	0	0
Real Cloutier	Buffalo	4	0	0	0	2-	0	0	0	0

PLAYER	TEAM	GP	G	A	PTS	+/-	PIM	PP	SH	GW
Kent Nilsson	Calgary	77	37	62	99	4-	14	9	3	3
Hakan Loob	Calgary	78	37	35	72	14	14	8	1	5
Carey Wilson	Calgary	74	24	48	72	24	27	4	0	3
Paul Reinhart	Calgary	75	23	46	69	3	18	12	2	5
Eddy Beers	Calgary	74	28	40	68	7	94	13	0	0
Al MacInnis	Calgary	67	14	52	66	7	75	8	0	0
Dan Quinn	Calgary	74	20	38	58	9	22	7	0	3
Richard Kromm	Calgary	73	20	32	52	19	32	1	0	2
Jim Peplinski	Calgary	80	16	29	45	12	111	0	0	1
Colin Patterson	Calgary	57	22	21	43	20	5	3	0	2
Mike Eaves	Calgary	56	14	29	43	14	10	1	2	1
Jamie Macoun	Calgary	70	9	30	39	44	67	0	0	2
Lanny McDonald	Calgary	43	19	18	37	4-	36	9	0	2
Steve Bozek	Calgary	54	13	22	35	11	6	0	0	1
Steve Tambellini	Calgary	47	19	10	29	8	4	1	2	2
Steve Konroyd	Calgary	64	3	23	26	12	73	0	0	0
Tim Hunter	Calgary	71	11	11	22	14	259	1	0	1
Paul Baxter	Calgary	70	5	14	19	39	126	0	0	1
Gino Cavallini	Calgary	27	6	10	16	11	14	1	0	0
Kari Eloranta	Calgary	65	2	11	13	1	39	0	0	0
Doug Risebrough	Calgary	15	7	5	12	10	49	0	1	4
Joel Otto	Calgary	17	4	8	12	3	30	1	0	0
Charles Bourgeois	Calgary	47	2	10	12	14	134	0	0	0
Neil Sheehy	Calgary	31	3	4	7	5	109	0	0	0
Perry Berezan	Calgary	9	3	2	5	5	4	0	0	1
Jim Jackson	Calgary	10	1	4	5	1	0	0	1	1
Yves Courteau	Calgary	14	1	4	5	2	4	0	0	1
Bruce Eakin	Calgary	1	0	0	0	0	0	0	0	0
Don Edwards	Calgary	34	0	0	0	0	4	0	0	0
Reggie Lemelin	Calgary	56	0	0	0	0	4	0	0	0
Denis Savard	Chicago	79	38	67	105	16	56	7	0	1
Steve Larmer	Chicago	80	46	40	86	17	16	14	0	6
Doug Wilson	Chicago	78	22	54	76	23	44	7	0	2
Troy Murray	Chicago	80	26	40	66	16	82	6	4	5
Bill Gardner	Chicago	74	17	34	51	7	12	5	1	1
Curt Fraser	Chicago	73	25	25	50	3	109	4	0	5
Ed Olczyk	Chicago	70	20	30	50	11	67	1	1	2
Tom Lysiak	Chicago	74	16	30	46	16-	13	2	0	4
Bob Murray	Chicago	80	5	38	43	13	56	4	0	1
Darry Sutter	Chicago	49	20	18	38	8	12	2	0	2
Behn Wilson	Chicago	76	10	23	33	5	185	2	0	1
Steve Ludzik	Chicago	79	11	20	31	5	86	0	1	1
Al Secord	Chicago	51	15	11	26	0	193	6	0	2
Ken Yaremchuk	Chicago	63	10	16	26	6-	16	2	0	0
Keith Brown	Chicago	56	1	22	23	2	55	0	0	0
Rick Patterson	Chicago	79	7	12	19	6	25	0	3	1
Jack O'Callahan	Chicago	66	6	8	14	6	105	0	0	1
Jerome Dupont	Chicago	55	3	10	13	5	105	0	0	1
Bob Macmillan	Chicago	36	5	7	12	16-	12	0	0	1
Dan Frawley	Chicago	30	4	3	7	2-	64	0	0	1
Marc Bergevin	Chicago	60	0	6	6	9-	54	0	0	0
Dave Feamster	Chicago	16	1	3	4	5	14	0	0	0
Tom McMurchy	Chicago	15	1	2	3	1-	13	0	0	0
Wayne Presley	Chicago	3	0	1	1	0	0	0	0	0

PLAYER	TEAM	GP	G	A	PTS	+/-	PIM	PP	SH	GW
Murray Bannerman	Chicago	60	0	1	1	0	8	0	0	0
Chris Clifford	Chicago	1	0	0	0	0	0	0	0	0
Darren Pang	Chicago	1	0	0	0	1−	0	0	0	0
Randy Boyd	Chicago	3	0	0	0	0	6	0	0	0
Jeff Larmer	Chicago	7	0	0	0	1	0	0	0	0
Warren Skorodenski	Chicago	27	0	0	0	0	2	0	0	0
John Ogrodnick	Detroit	79	55	50	105	1	30	15	1	6
Ron Duguay	Detroit	80	38	51	89	16−	51	11	3	4
Steve Yzerman	Detroit	80	30	59	89	17−	58	9	0	3
Reed Larson	Detroit	77	17	45	62	7	139	7	0	0
Kelly Kisio	Detroit	75	20	41	61	2	56	5	0	0
Danny Gare	Detroit	71	27	29	56	5	163	3	0	3
Ivan Boldirev	Detroit	75	19	30	49	25−	16	11	0	3
Brad Park	Detroit	67	13	30	43	15−	53	6	0	0
Dwight Foster	Detroit	50	16	16	32	12	56	0	3	0
Bob Manno	Detroit	74	10	22	32	0	32	0	3	1
Randy Ladouceur	Detroit	80	3	27	30	3	108	1	0	1
Darryl Sittler	Detroit	61	11	16	27	10−	37	4	0	2
Lane Lambert	Detroit	69	14	11	25	3−	104	0	0	1
John Barrett	Detroit	71	6	19	25	15−	117	0	0	1
Greg Smith	Detroit	73	2	18	20	26−	117	0	0	0
Gerard Gallant	Detroit	32	6	12	18	9	66	0	0	2
Dave Silk	Boston	29	7	5	12	3	22	0	0	0
	Detroit	12	3	0	3	6−	10	0	0	0
	Total	41	10	5	15	3−	32	0	0	0
Larry Trader	Detroit	40	3	7	10	11	39	1	0	0
Claude Loiselle	Detroit	30	8	1	9	5−	45	0	0	0
Frank Cernik	Detroit	49	5	4	9	7−	13	0	0	0
Colin Campbell	Detroit	57	1	5	6	14−	124	0	0	0
Milan Chalupa	Detroit	14	0	5	5	4	6	0	0	0
Pierre Aubry	Detroit	25	2	2	4	1−	33	0	0	0
Corrado Micalef	Detroit	36	0	3	3	0	6	0	0	0
Greg Stefan	Detroit	46	0	2	2	0	23	0	0	0
Brad Smith	Detroit	1	1	0	1	0	5	0	0	0
Joe Kocur	Detroit	17	1	0	1	4−	64	0	0	0
Rick Zombo	Detroit	1	0	0	0	3−	0	0	0	0
Ed Mio	Detroit	7	0	0	0	0	2	0	0	0
Shawn Burr	Detroit	9	0	0	0	4−	2	0	0	0
Wayne Gretzky	Edmonton	80	73	135	208	98	52	8	11	7
Jari Kurri	Edmonton	73	71	64	135	76	30	14	3	13
Paul Coffey	Edmonton	80	37	84	121	55	97	12	2	6
Mike Krushelnyski	Edmonton	80	43	45	88	56	60	13	0	4
Glenn Anderson	Edmonton	80	42	39	81	24	69	12	1	6
Mark Napier	Minnesota	39	10	18	28	6−	2	3	1	1
	Edmonton	33	9	26	35	12	19	3	0	0
	Total	72	19	44	63	6	21	6	1	1
Mark Messier	Edmonton	55	23	31	54	8	57	4	5	1
Charlie Huddy	Edmonton	80	7	44	51	50	46	3	0	1
Dave Hunter	Edmonton	80	17	19	36	1−	122	1	1	1
Willy Lindstrom	Edmonton	80	12	20	32	5	18	1	0	1
Dave Lumley	Hartford	48	8	20	28	17−	98	1	0	0
	Edmonton	12	1	3	4	1−	13	0	0	0
	Total	60	9	23	32	18−	111	1	0	0

PLAYER	TEAM	GP	G	A	PTS	+/-	PIM	PP	SH	GW
Kevin Lowe	Edmonton	80	4	22	26	9	104	1	0	1
Pat Hughes	Edmonton	73	12	13	25	7-	85	1	1	0
Kevin McClelland	Edmonton	62	8	15	23	11-	205	0	0	3
Randy Gregg	Edmonton	57	3	20	23	27	32	0	0	0
Don Jackson	Edmonton	78	3	17	20	27	141	0	0	0
Dave Semenko	Edmonton	69	6	12	18	5	172	0	0	1
Lee Fogolin	Edmonton	79	4	14	18	16	126	0	1	1
Bill Carroll	Edmonton	65	8	9	17	0	22	0	0	1
Jaroslav Pouzar	Edmonton	33	4	8	12	3	28	0	0	1
Larry Melnyk	Edmonton	28	0	11	11	12	25	0	0	0
Marc Habscheid	Edmonton	26	5	3	8	2-	4	2	0	0
Raimo Summanen	Edmonton	9	0	4	4	1-	0	0	0	0
Grant Fuhr	Edmonton	46	0	3	3	0	6	0	0	0
Marco Baron	Edmonton	1	0	0	0	0	0	0	0	0
Daryl Reaugh	Edmonton	1	0	0	0	0	0	0	0	0
Ray Cote	Edmonton	2	0	0	0	0	2	0	0	0
Steve Smith	Edmonton	2	0	0	0	2-	2	0	0	0
Mike Zanier	Edmonton	3	0	0	0	0	0	0	0	0
Andy Moog	Edmonton	39	0	0	0	0	8	0	0	0
Ron Francis	Hartford	80	24	57	81	23-	66	4	0	1
Sylvain Turgeon	Hartford	64	31	31	62	10-	67	11	0	3
Ray Neufeld	Hartford	76	27	35	62	29-	129	12	0	2
Greg Malone	Hartford	76	22	39	61	16-	67	6	0	4
Risto Siltanen	Hartford	76	12	33	45	24-	30	8	0	2
Kevin Dineen	Hartford	57	25	16	41	6-	120	8	4	2
Torrie Robertson	Hartford	74	11	30	41	13-	337	1	0	3
Bobby Crawford	Hartford	45	14	14	28	3-	8	2	0	0
Ray Ferraro	Hartford	44	11	17	28	1-	40	6	0	2
Joel Quenneville	Hartford	79	6	16	22	15-	96	0	0	0
Dave Tippett	Hartford	80	7	12	19	24-	12	0	0	0
Pat Boutette	Pittsburgh	14	1	3	4	5-	24	0	1	0
	Hartford	33	6	8	14	6-	51	0	0	2
	Total	47	7	11	18	11-	75	0	1	2
Mike Zuke	Hartford	67	4	12	16	4-	12	0	0	1
Paul Fenton	Hartford	33	7	5	12	6	10	0	0	2
Sylvain Cote	Hartford	67	3	9	12	30-	17	1	0	1
Paul MacDermid	Hartford	31	4	7	11	3	29	0	0	0
Mike Crombeen	Hartford	46	4	7	11	0	16	0	1	1
Tony Currie	Hartford	13	3	8	11	4-	2	1	0	0
Mark Fusco	Hartford	63	3	8	11	15-	40	0	0	0
Scot Kleinendorst	Hartford	35	1	8	9	10-	69	0	0	0
Chris Kotsopoulos	Hartford	33	5	3	8	2	53	1	0	0
Ulf Samuelsson	Hartford	41	2	6	8	6-	83	0	0	0
Dean Evason	Washington	15	3	4	7	9	2	0	0	1
	Hartford	2	0	0	0	0	0	0	0	0
	Total	17	3	4	7	9	2	0	0	1
Randy Pierce	Hartford	17	3	2	5	4-	8	0	0	0
Richie Dunn	Hartford	13	1	4	5	3-	2	0	0	0
Jack Brownschidle	Hartford	17	1	4	5	0	5	1	0	0
Mark Paterson	Hartford	13	1	3	4	6-	24	0	0	0
Dave Jensen	Hartford	13	0	4	4	1-	6	0	0	0
Marty Howe	Hartford	19	1	1	2	4-	10	0	0	0

Bernie Nicholls was a 100-pointer for Kings.

PLAYER	TEAM	GP	G	A	PTS	+/-	PIM	PP	SH	GW
Mike Liut	St Louis	32	0	1	1	0	4	0	0	0
	Hartford	13	0	0	0	0	2	0	0	0
	Total	45	0	1	1	0	6	0	0	0
Mike Hoffman	Hartford	1	0	0	0	0	0	0	0	0
Ed Staniowski	Hartford	1	0	0	0	0	0	0	0	0
Steve Weeks	Hartford	23	0	0	0	0	0	0	0	0
Marcel Dionne	Los Angeles	80	46	80	126	11	46	16	1	2
Bernie Nicholls	Los Angeles	80	46	54	100	4−	76	15	0	6
Dave Taylor	Los Angeles	79	41	51	92	13	132	11	2	6
Brian MacLellan	Los Angeles	80	31	54	85	2	53	14	0	3
Jim Fox	Los Angeles	79	30	53	83	4	10	6	0	2
Mark Hardy	Los Angeles	78	14	39	53	20−	97	8	1	2
Terry Ruskowski	Los Angeles	78	16	33	49	2	144	2	0	2
Steve Shutt	Montreal	10	2	0	2	2	9	1	0	0
	Los Angeles	59	16	25	41	16−	10	5	0	1
	Total	69	18	25	43	14−	19	6	0	1
Doug Smith	Los Angeles	62	21	20	41	15−	58	3	1	1
Craig Redmond	Los Angeles	79	6	33	39	8−	57	1	0	0
Garry Galley	Los Angeles	78	8	30	38	3	82	1	1	2
Phil Sykes	Los Angeles	79	17	15	32	18−	38	1	2	2
Anders Hakansson	Los Angeles	73	12	12	24	4−	28	1	1	1
Brian Engblom	Los Angeles	79	4	19	23	2−	70	3	0	0
Bob Miller	Los Angeles	63	4	16	20	17−	35	0	0	0
John Paul Kelly	Los Angeles	73	8	10	18	9−	55	0	0	2
Dave Williams	Detroit	55	3	8	11	16−	158	0	0	0
	Los Angeles	12	4	2	7	0	43	0	0	0
	Total	67	7	11	18	16−	201	0	0	0
Rick Lapointe	Los Angeles	73	4	13	17	10−	46	0	0	1
Carl Mokosak	Los Angeles	30	4	8	12	8−	43	0	0	0
Jay Wells	Los Angeles	77	2	9	11	4	185	0	0	0
Russ Anderson	Los Angeles	14	1	1	2	2−	20	0	0	0
Bob Janecyk	Los Angeles	51	0	2	2	0	27	0	0	0
Ken Hammond	Los Angeles	3	1	0	1	2	0	0	0	1
Daryl Evans	Los Angeles	7	1	0	1	2	2	0	0	0
Bill O'Dwyer	Los Angeles	13	1	0	1	0	15	0	0	0
Brian Wilks	Los Angeles	2	0	0	0	1−	0	0	0	0
Steve Seguin	Los Angeles	5	0	0	0	5−	9	0	0	0
Darren Eliot	Los Angeles	33	0	0	0	0	0	0	0	0
Brian Bellows	Minnesota	78	26	36	62	18−	72	8	1	3
Dennis Maruk	Minnesota	71	19	41	60	2−	56	5	0	3
Keith Acton	Minnesota	78	20	38	58	3−	90	4	0	3
Neal Broten	Minnesota	80	19	37	56	18−	39	5	1	1
Steve Payne	Minnesota	76	29	22	51	14−	61	14	0	4
Tony McKegney	Quebec	30	12	9	21	2	12	1	3	1
	Minnesota	27	11	13	24	9	4	2	0	1
	Total	57	23	22	45	11	16	3	3	2
Gordie Roberts	Minnesota	78	6	36	42	12−	112	1	0	0
Tom McCarthy	Minnesota	44	16	21	37	3	36	6	0	1
Dino Ciccarelli	Minnesota	51	15	17	32	10−	41	5	0	0
Gord Sherven	Edmonton	37	9	7	16	2−	10	1	0	1
	Minnesota	32	2	12	14	3	8	0	0	1
	Total	69	11	19	30	1	18	1	0	2
Curt Giles	Minnesota	77	5	25	30	3	49	3	0	0

PLAYER	TEAM	GP	G	A	PTS	+/-	PIM	PP	SH	GW
Willi Plett	Minnesota	47	14	14	28	4	157	1	0	1
Dirk Graham	Minnesota	36	12	11	23	15-	23	3	0	1
Bo Berglund	Quebec	12	4	1	5	2	6	0	0	1
	Minnesota	33	6	9	15	3-	8	1	0	1
	Total	45	10	10	20	1-	14	1	0	2
Ken Solheim	Minnesota	55	8	10	18	15-	19	4	0	1
Craig Hartsburg	Minnesota	32	7	11	18	5-	54	1	1	1
Scott Bjugstad	Minnesota	72	11	4	15	21-	32	1	0	1
Randy Velischek	Minnesota	52	4	9	13	7	26	0	0	0
Ron Wilson	Minnesota	13	4	8	12	1-	2	0	0	0
Brian Lawton	Minnesota	40	5	6	11	2-	24	1	0	1
Bob Rouse	Minnesota	63	2	9	11	14-	113	0	0	0
Dave Richter	Minnesota	55	2	8	10	3	221	0	0	0
Paul Holmgren	Minnesota	16	4	3	7	4-	38	2	0	0
Harold Snepsts	Minnesota	71	0	7	7	19-	232	0	0	0
Tim Trimper	Minnesota	20	1	4	5	9-	15	0	0	0
Terry Martin	Edmonton	4	0	2	2	3	0	0	0	0
	Minnesota	7	1	1	2	0	0	0	0	0
	Total	11	1	3	4	3	0	0	0	0
Tom Hirsch	Minnesota	15	0	4	4	13-	10	0	0	0
Jim Archibald	Minnesota	4	1	2	3	0	11	0	0	0
Tim Coulis	Minnesota	7	1	1	2	1-	34	0	0	0
David Jensen	Minnesota	5	0	1	1	5-	4	0	0	0
Don Biggs	Minnesota	1	0	0	0	0	0	0	0	0
John Markell	Minnesota	1	0	0	0	0	0	0	0	0
Mike Sands	Minnesota	3	0	0	0	0	2	0	0	0
Chris Pryor	Minnesota	4	0	0	0	2-	16	0	0	0
Dan Mandich	Minnesota	10	0	0	0	3-	32	0	0	0
Roland Melanson	NY Islanders	8	0	0	0	0	0	0	0	0
	Minnesota	20	0	0	0	0	9	0	0	0
	Total	28	0	0	0	0	9	0	0	0
Gilles Meloche	Minnesota	32	0	0	0	0	2	0	0	0
Don Beaupre	Minnesota	31	0	0	0	0	4	0	0	0
Mats Naslund	Montreal	80	42	37	79	19	14	9	2	8
Mario Tremblay	Montreal	75	31	35	66	21	120	14	0	6
Chris Chelios	Montreal	74	9	55	64	11	87	2	1	0
Guy Carbonneau	Montreal	79	23	34	57	28	43	0	4	2
Pierre Mondou	Montreal	67	18	39	57	15	21	2	0	2
Bobby Smith	Montreal	65	16	40	56	9-	59	8	0	1
Larry Robinson	Montreal	76	14	33	47	32	44	6	0	3
Tom Kurvers	Montreal	75	10	35	45	2-	30	6	1	3
Mike McPhee	Montreal	70	17	22	39	1	120	0	0	2
Ryan Walter	Montreal	72	19	19	38	18-	59	11	0	0
Chris Nilan	Montreal	77	21	16	37	3	358	1	0	2
Mark Hunter	Montreal	72	21	12	33	13-	123	6	0	3
Bob Gainey	Montreal	79	19	13	32	13	40	0	3	3
Petr Svoboda	Montreal	73	4	27	31	16	65	0	0	1
Ron Flockhart	Pittsburgh	12	0	5	5	4	4	0	0	0
	Montreal	42	10	12	22	3	14	1	0	2
	Total	54	10	17	27	7	18	1	0	2
Alfie Turcotte	Montreal	53	8	16	24	1-	35	3	0	1
Lucien Deblois	Montreal	51	12	11	23	9	20	4	1	2
Craig Ludwig	Montreal	72	5	14	19	5	90	1	0	0

PLAYER	TEAM	GP	G	A	PTS	+/-	PIM	PP	SH	GW
Rick Green	Montreal	77	1	18	19	11–	30	1	0	0
Guy Lafleur	Montreal	19	2	3	5	3–	10	0	0	0
Serge Boisvert	Montreal	14	2	2	4	3–	0	0	0	0
John Newberry	Montreal	16	0	4	4	3	6	0	0	0
Kent Carlson	Montreal	18	1	1	2	1	33	0	0	0
Steve Rooney	Montreal	3	1	0	1	1–	7	1	0	0
Claude Lemieux	Montreal	1	0	1	1	1	7	0	0	0
Thomas Rundqvist	Montreal	2	0	1	1	1	0	0	0	0
Ric Nattress	Montreal	5	0	1	1	2–	2	0	0	0
Jeff Teal	Montreal	6	0	1	1	0	0	0	0	0
Steve Penny	Montreal	54	0	1	1	0	10	0	0	0
Stephane Richer	Montreal	1	0	0	0	0	0	0	0	0
Patrick Roy	Montreal	1	0	0	0	0	0	0	0	0
Doug Soetaert	Montreal	28	0	0	0	0	4	0	0	0
Mel Bridgman	New Jersey	80	22	39	61	16–	105	5	3	3
Aaron Broten	New Jersey	80	22	35	57	18–	38	10	0	2
Dave Pichette	New Jersey	71	17	40	57	20–	41	8	0	2
Kirk Muller	New Jersey	80	17	37	54	31–	69	9	1	0
Tim Higgins	New Jersey	71	19	29	48	10–	30	5	0	2
Paul Gagne	New Jersey	79	24	19	43	11–	28	3	0	1
Doug Sulliman	New Jersey	57	22	16	38	11–	4	6	0	1
Pat Verbeek	New Jersey	78	15	18	33	24–	162	5	1	1
John MacLean	New Jersey	61	13	20	33	11–	44	1	0	4
Bruce Driver	New Jersey	67	9	23	32	22–	36	3	1	0
Jan Ludvig	New Jersey	74	12	19	31	19–	53	3	0	1
Rick Meagher	New Jersey	71	11	20	31	13–	22	1	1	1
Uli Hiemer	New Jersey	53	5	24	29	14–	70	3	0	0
Rich Preston	New Jersey	75	12	15	27	24–	26	1	0	1
Joe Cirella	New Jersey	66	6	18	24	45–	143	2	0	0
Greg Adams	New Jersey	36	12	9	21	14–	14	5	0	0
Phil Russell	New Jersey	66	4	16	20	14–	110	0	1	0
Don Lever	New Jersey	67	10	8	18	29–	31	0	1	1
Dave Lewis	New Jersey	74	3	9	12	29–	78	0	0	2
Rocky Trottier	New Jersey	33	5	3	8	3–	2	0	0	0
Bob Lorimer	New Jersey	46	2	6	8	6	35	0	0	0
Bob Hoffmeyer	New Jersey	37	1	6	7	15–	65	0	0	0
Gary McAdam	New Jersey	4	1	1	2	0	0	0	0	0
Rich Chernomaz	New Jersey	3	0	2	2	2	2	0	0	0
Mitch Wilson	New Jersey	9	0	2	2	1	21	0	0	0
Hannu Kamppuri	New Jersey	13	0	1	1	0	2	0	0	0
Ken Daneyko	New Jersey	1	0	0	0	1–	10	0	0	0
Alan Hepple	New Jersey	1	0	0	0	2–	0	0	0	0
Ron Low	New Jersey	26	0	0	0	0	21	0	0	0
Glenn Resch	New Jersey	51	0	0	0	0	6	0	0	0
Mike Bossy	NY Islanders	76	58	59	117	37	38	14	4	7
Brent Sutter	NY Islanders	72	42	60	102	42	51	12	0	4
John Tonelli	NY Islanders	80	42	58	100	50	95	8	1	3
Denis Potvin	NY Islanders	77	17	51	68	36	96	6	0	1
Bryan Trottier	NY Islanders	68	28	31	59	5	47	4	5	3
Pat LaFontaine	NY Islanders	67	19	35	54	9	32	1	0	1
Patrick Flatley	NY Islanders	78	20	31	51	8–	106	2	0	4
Tomas Jonsson	NY Islanders	69	16	34	50	1–	58	8	0	4

PLAYER	TEAM	GP	G	A	PTS	+/-	PIM	PP	SH	GW
Duane Sutter	NY Islanders	78	17	24	41	12-	174	1	0	1
Greg Gilbert	NY Islanders	58	13	25	38	4-	36	2	0	2
Paul Boutilier	NY Islanders	78	12	23	35	0	90	2	1	3
Clark Gillies	NY Islanders	54	15	17	32	0	73	5	0	2
Stefan Persson	NY Islanders	54	3	19	22	8	30	3	0	0
Bob Bourne	NY Islanders	44	8	12	20	8-	51	1	0	1
Anders Kallur	NY Islanders	51	10	8	18	9-	26	0	2	2
Gord Dineen	NY Islanders	48	1	12	13	10	89	0	0	0
Dave Langevin	NY Islanders	56	0	13	13	6-	35	0	0	0
Roger Kortko	NY Islanders	27	2	9	11	3-	9	1	0	0
Gerald Diduck	NY Islanders	65	2	8	10	2	80	0	0	0
Gord Lane	NY Islanders	57	1	8	9	10	83	0	0	0
Ken Morrow	NY Islanders	15	1	7	8	5	14	0	0	0
Bob Nystrom	NY Islanders	36	2	5	7	6	58	0	0	0
Mats Hallin	NY Islanders	38	5	0	5	7-	50	0	0	1
Scott Howson	NY Islanders	8	4	1	5	4	2	1	0	0
Alan Kerr	NY Islanders	19	3	1	4	7-	24	0	0	0
Dale Henry	NY Islanders	16	2	1	3	1	19	0	0	1
Ken Leiter	NY Islanders	5	0	2	2	0	2	0	0	0
Ron Handy	NY Islanders	10	0	2	2	1-	0	0	0	0
Kelly Hrudey	NY Islanders	41	0	1	1	0	17	0	0	0
Vern Smith	NY Islanders	1	0	0	0	0	0	0	0	0
Mark Hamway	NY Islanders	2	0	0	0	0	0	0	0	0
Billy Smith	NY Islanders	37	0	0	0	0	25	0	0	0
Reijo Ruotsalainen	NY Rangers	80	28	45	73	27-	32	10	0	2
Mike Rogers	NY Rangers	78	26	38	64	25-	24	5	1	1
Pierre Larouche	NY Rangers	65	24	36	60	17-	8	5	0	3
Tomas Sandstrom	NY Rangers	74	29	30	59	3	51	5	0	3
Anders Hedberg	NY Rangers	64	20	31	51	15-	10	9	0	2
Ron Greschner	NY Rangers	48	16	29	45	19-	42	8	0	2
Mark Pavelich	NY Rangers	48	14	31	45	1	29	6	0	3
Peter Sundstrom	NY Rangers	76	18	26	44	26-	34	0	2	2
James Patrick	NY Rangers	75	8	28	36	17-	71	4	1	1
Steve Patrick	Buffalo	14	2	2	4	3-	4	0	0	0
	NY Rangers	43	11	18	29	5-	63	4	0	0
	Total	57	13	20	33	8-	67	4	0	0
Jan Erixon	NY Rangers	66	7	22	29	11-	33	0	1	0
George McPhee	NY Rangers	49	12	15	27	9-	139	1	0	1
Don Maloney	NY Rangers	37	11	16	27	9-	32	5	0	0
Barry Beck	NY Rangers	56	7	19	26	11-	65	2	2	0
Mike Allison	NY Rangers	31	9	15	24	0	17	2	0	1
Grant Ledyard	NY Rangers	42	8	12	20	8	53	1	0	1
Robbie Ftorek	NY Rangers	48	9	10	19	7-	35	0	1	1
Bob Brooke	NY Rangers	72	7	9	16	18-	79	0	0	2
Willie Huber	NY Rangers	49	3	11	14	20-	55	1	0	0
Jim Wiemer	Buffalo	10	3	2	5	5-	4	2	0	0
	NY Rangers	22	4	3	7	10-	30	2	0	0
	Total	32	7	5	12	15-	34	4	0	0
Dave Gagner	NY Rangers	38	6	6	12	16-	16	0	1	0
Chris Kontos	NY Rangers	28	4	8	12	12-	24	1	0	0
Tom Laidlaw	NY Rangers	61	1	11	12	12-	52	0	0	0
Nick Fotiu	NY Rangers	46	4	7	11	7-	54	0	0	1
Mark Osborne	NY Rangers	23	4	4	8	2-	33	0	0	0

PLAYER	TEAM	GP	G	A	PTS	+/−	PIM	PP	SH	GW
Andre Dore	NY Rangers	25	0	7	7	2−	35	0	0	0
Randy Heath	NY Rangers	12	2	3	5	1−	15	1	0	0
Steve Richmond	NY Rangers	34	0	5	5	16−	90	0	0	0
John Vanbiesbrouck	NY Rangers	42	0	5	5	0	17	0	0	0
Kelly Miller	NY Rangers	5	0	2	2	2−	2	0	0	0
Mike Blaisdell	NY Rangers	12	1	0	1	4−	11	0	0	0
Larry Patey	NY Rangers	7	0	1	1	6−	12	0	0	0
Simo Saarinen	NY Rangers	8	0	0	0	4−	8	0	0	0
Glen Hanlon	NY Rangers	44	0	0	0	0	4	0	0	0
Tim Kerr	Philadelphia	74	54	44	98	29	57	21	0	9
Brian Propp	Philadelphia	76	43	53	96	46	43	12	7	4
Dave Poulin	Philadelphia	73	30	44	74	43	59	1	4	5
Ilkka Sinisalo	Philadelphia	70	36	37	73	32	16	7	1	8
Murray Craven	Philadelphia	80	26	35	61	45	30	2	2	5
Peter Zezel	Philadelphia	65	15	46	61	22	26	8	0	2
Mark Howe	Philadelphia	73	18	39	57	51	31	3	2	1
Ron Sutter	Philadelphia	73	16	29	45	13	94	2	0	5
Brad McCrimmon	Philadelphia	66	8	35	43	52	81	1	0	1
Lindsay Carson	Philadelphia	77	20	19	39	0	123	1	0	1
Derrick Smith	Philadelphia	77	17	22	39	28	31	0	1	4
Rick Tocchet	Philadelphia	75	14	25	39	6	181	0	0	0
Thomas Eriksson	Philadelphia	72	10	29	39	24	36	4	1	1
Doug Crossman	Philadelphia	80	4	33	37	31	65	1	1	1
Len Hachborn	Philadelphia	40	5	17	22	16	23	0	0	0
Brad Marsh	Philadelphia	77	2	18	20	42	91	0	0	0
Miroslav Dvorak	Philadelphia	47	3	14	17	12	4	0	1	1
Todd Bergen	Philadelphia	14	11	5	16	9	4	3	0	3
Rich Sutter	Philadelphia	56	6	10	16	0	89	0	0	0
Dave Brown	Philadelphia	57	3	6	9	3−	165	0	0	1
Tim Young	Philadelphia	20	2	6	8	2	12	0	0	1
Ed Hospodar	Philadelphia	50	3	4	7	7	130	0	0	0
Glen Cochrane	Philadelphia	18	0	3	3	4−	100	0	0	0
Ray Allison	Philadelphia	11	1	1	2	3	2	0	0	0
Ross Fitzpatrick	Philadelphia	5	1	0	1	3−	0	1	0	0
Paul Guay	Philadelphia	2	0	1	1	2	0	0	0	0
Bob Froese	Philadelphia	17	0	1	1	0	2	0	0	0
Darren Jensen	Philadelphia	1	0	0	0	0	0	0	0	0
Mike Stothers	Philadelphia	1	0	0	0	1−	0	0	0	0
Steve Smith	Philadelphia	2	0	0	0	2	7	0	0	0
Joe Paterson	Philadelphia	6	0	0	0	1−	31	0	0	0
Pelle Lindbergh	Philadelphia	65	0	0	0	0	4	0	0	0
Mario Lemieux	Pittsburgh	73	43	57	100	35−	54	11	0	2
Warren Young	Pittsburgh	80	40	32	72	20−	174	9	0	3
Doug Shedden	Pittsburgh	80	35	32	67	51−	30	12	0	3
Mike Bullard	Pittsburgh	68	32	31	63	43−	75	14	0	3
John Chabot	Montreal	10	1	6	7	3	2	0	0	0
	Pittsburgh	67	8	45	53	37−	12	2	1	2
	Total	77	9	51	60	34−	14	2	1	2
Wayne Babych	Pittsburgh	65	20	34	54	7−	35	3	0	3
Moe Mantha	Pittsburgh	71	11	40	51	35−	54	3	0	1
Doug Bodger	Pittsburgh	65	5	26	31	24−	67	3	0	1

PLAYER	TEAM	GP	G	A	PTS	+/−	PIM	PP	SH	GW
Andy Brickley	Pittsburgh	45	7	15	22	14 −	10	1	0	1
Randy Hillier	Pittsburgh	45	2	19	21	12 −	56	1	0	1
Mitch Lamoureux	Pittsburgh	62	11	8	19	9 −	53	0	2	0
Gary Rissling	Pittsburgh	56	10	9	19	6 −	209	0	0	0
Kevin McCarthy	Pittsburgh	64	9	10	19	20 −	30	0	1	0
Troy Loney	Pittsburgh	46	10	8	18	11 −	59	1	0	1
Dave Hannan	Pittsburgh	30	6	7	13	8 −	43	0	1	1
Bruce Crowder	Pittsburgh	26	4	7	11	9 −	23	0	0	0
Joe McDonnell	Pittsburgh	40	2	9	11	19 −	20	2	0	0
Rod Buskas	Pittsburgh	69	2	7	9	21 −	191	0	0	0
Todd Charlesworth	Pittsburgh	67	1	8	9	23 −	31	0	0	1
Roger Belanger	Pittsburgh	44	3	5	8	13 −	32	0	0	0
Wally Weir	Hartford	34	2	3	5	7 −	56	0	0	0
	Pittsburgh	14	0	3	3	1	34	0	0	0
	Total	48	2	6	8	6 −	90	0	0	0
Bryan Maxwell	Pittsburgh	44	0	8	8	23 −	57	0	0	0
Jim McGeough	Washington	11	3	0	3	0	12	0	0	0
	Pittsburgh	14	0	4	4	4 −	4	0	0	0
	Total	25	3	4	7	4 −	16	0	0	0
Greg Fox	Pittsburgh	26	2	5	7	6 −	26	0	0	0
Arto Javanainen	Pittsburgh	14	4	1	5	1	2	0	0	0
Jim Hamilton	Pittsburgh	11	2	1	3	6 −	0	0	0	0
Steve Gatzos	Pittsburgh	6	0	2	2	6 −	2	0	0	0
Rick Kehoe	Pittsburgh	6	0	2	2	0	0	0	0	0
Greg Hotham	Pittsburgh	11	0	2	2	3 −	4	0	0	0
Bob Errey	Pittsburgh	16	0	2	2	8 −	7	0	0	0
Michel Dion	Pittsburgh	10	0	1	1	0	0	0	0	0
Bob Geale	Pittsburgh	1	0	0	0	1 −	2	0	0	0
Tom O'Regan	Pittsburgh	1	0	0	0	1 −	0	0	0	0
Petteri Lehto	Pittsburgh	6	0	0	0	4 −	4	0	0	0
Mike Rowe	Pittsburgh	6	0	0	0	7 −	7	0	0	0
Brian Ford	Pittsburgh	8	0	0	0	0	0	0	0	0
Marty McSorley	Pittsburgh	15	0	0	0	3 −	15	0	0	0
Roberto Romano	Pittsburgh	31	0	0	0	0	2	0	0	0
Denis Herron	Pittsburgh	42	0	0	0	0	4	0	0	0
Peter Stastny	Quebec	75	32	68	100	23	95	7	1	9
Michel Goulet	Quebec	69	55	40	95	10	55	17	0	6
Anton Stastny	Quebec	79	38	42	80	18	30	9	0	3
Dale Hunter	Quebec	80	20	52	72	23	209	3	3	3
Brent Ashton	Minnesota	29	4	7	11	1	15	0	0	0
	Quebec	49	27	24	51	18	38	6	1	2
	Total	78	31	31	62	19	53	6	1	2
Wilf Paiement	Quebec	68	23	28	51	12	165	2	1	4
Mario Marois	Quebec	76	6	37	43	2	91	2	0	0
Paul Gillis	Quebec	77	14	28	42	12	168	0	0	3
J.F. Sauve	Quebec	64	13	29	42	11	21	8	0	1
Brad Maxwell	Minnesota	18	3	7	10	8 −	53	1	0	0
	Quebec	50	7	24	31	22	119	1	0	1
	Total	68	10	31	41	14	172	2	0	1
Bruce Bell	Quebec	75	6	31	37	32	44	2	0	1
Alain Cote	Quebec	80	13	22	35	12	31	1	1	0
Randy Moller	Quebec	79	7	22	29	29	120	0	0	0
Alain Lemieux	St. Louis	19	4	2	6	2	0	0	0	1
	Quebec	30	11	11	22	1 −	12	2	0	2
	Total	49	15	13	28	1	12	2	0	3

PLAYER	TEAM	GP	G	A	PTS	+/−	PIM	PP	SH	GW
Pat Price...........	Quebec	68	1	26	27	17	118	0	0	0
Normand Rochefort....	Quebec	73	3	21	24	12	74	1	0	1
Marian Stastny.......	Quebec	50	7	14	21	1	4	0	0	1
Andre Savard.........	Quebec	35	9	10	19	3−	8	1	1	1
Mark Kumpel.........	Quebec	42	8	7	15	4	26	1	0	0
Jean Marc Gaulin	Quebec	22	3	3	6	2	8	0	0	0
Jimmy Mann.........	Quebec	25	0	4	4	3	54	0	0	0
Peter Loob	Quebec	8	1	2	3	5	0	0	0	0
Blake Wesley........	Quebec	21	0	2	2	2−	28	0	0	0
Daniel Bouchard......	Quebec	29	0	2	2	0	2	0	0	0
Wayne Groulx	Quebec	1	0	0	0	0	0	0	0	0
Claude Julien	Quebec	1	0	0	0	0	0	0	0	0
Ed Lee	Quebec	2	0	0	0	4−	5	0	0	0
Roger Hagglund	Quebec	3	0	0	0	0	0	0	0	0
Yvon Vautour........	Quebec	5	0	0	0	0	2	0	0	0
Dave Shaw	Quebec	14	0	0	0	5−	11	0	0	0
Richard Sevigny	Quebec	20	0	0	0	0	8	0	0	0
Gord Donnelly	Quebec	22	0	0	0	1	33	0	0	0
Mario Gosselin.......	Quebec	36	0	0	0	0	2	0	0	0
Bernie Federko	St. Louis	76	30	73	103	10−	27	6	0	3
Joe Mullen	St. Louis	79	40	52	92	5	6	13	0	4
Brian Sutter.........	St. Louis	77	37	37	74	11	121	14	0	7
Mark Johnson	Hartford	49	19	28	47	24−	21	10	0	2
	St. Louis	17	4	6	10	2−	2	2	0	0
	Total	66	23	34	57	26−	23	12	0	2
Doug Gilmour	St. Louis	78	21	36	57	3	49	3	1	3
Jorgen Pettersson.....	St. Louis	75	23	32	55	8	20	8	0	3
Doug Wickenheiser	St. Louis	68	23	20	43	9	36	1	2	3
Greg Paslawski.......	St. Louis	72	22	20	42	6	21	7	0	2
Mark Reeds.........	St. Louis	80	9	30	39	8	25	0	1	4
Rob Ramage	St. Louis	80	7	31	38	7−	178	1	0	0
Dave Barr	St. Louis	75	16	18	34	5	32	2	0	1
Kevin Lavallee	St. Louis	38	15	17	32	2	8	2	0	1
Craig Levie	St. Louis	61	6	23	29	2	33	2	0	1
Tim Bothwell	St. Louis	79	4	22	26	27	62	1	0	0
Rik Wilson	St. Louis	51	8	16	24	14	39	3	0	0
Pat Hickey..........	St. Louis	57	10	13	23	4−	32	0	3	1
Perry Anderson	St. Louis	71	9	9	18	2	146	0	0	1
Gilbert Delorme	St. Louis	74	2	12	14	7	53	1	0	0
Luc Dufour	Quebec	30	2	3	5	5−	27	0	0	0
	St. Louis	23	1	3	4	8−	18	0	0	0
	Total	53	3	6	9	13−	45	0	0	0
Denis Cyr	St. Louis	9	5	3	8	1	0	0	0	1
Jim Pavese	St. Louis	51	2	5	7	4−	69	0	0	1
Terry Johnson	St. Louis	74	0	7	7	13	120	0	0	0
Dwight Schofield	St. Louis	43	1	4	5	4−	184	0	0	0
Brian Benning	St. Louis	4	0	2	2	6−	0	0	0	0
Perry Ganchar	St. Louis	7	0	2	2	0	0	0	0	0
Rick Wamsley	St. Louis	40	0	1	1	0	0	0	0	0
Rick Heinz..........	St. Louis	2	0	0	0	0	0	0	0	0
Greg Millen.........	Hartford	44	0	0	0	0	4	0	0	0
	St. Louis	10	0	0	0	0	0	0	0	0
	Total	54	0	0	0	0	4	0	0	0

PLAYER	TEAM	GP	G	A	PTS	+/-	PIM	PP	SH	GW
Rick Vaive	Toronto	72	35	33	68	26-	112	13	0	2
John Anderson	Toronto	75	32	31	63	20-	27	14	1	5
Bill Derlago	Toronto	62	31	31	62	15-	21	7	5	4
Miroslav Frycer	Toronto	65	25	30	55	7-	55	5	0	1
Dan Daoust	Toronto	79	17	37	54	26-	98	1	3	2
Peter Ihnacak	Toronto	70	22	22	44	26-	24	8	0	1
Jim Benning	Toronto	80	9	35	44	39-	55	6	0	2
Borje Salming	Toronto	73	6	33	39	26-	76	3	0	0
Greg Terrion	Toronto	72	14	17	31	15-	20	1	4	0
Gary Leeman	Toronto	53	5	26	31	12-	72	3	0	0
Stewart Gavin	Toronto	73	12	13	25	22-	38	0	0	0
Russ Courtnall	Toronto	69	12	10	22	23-	44	0	2	1
Al Iafrate	Toronto	68	5	16	21	19-	51	3	0	0
Walt Poddubny	Toronto	32	5	15	20	1	26	1	0	0
Gary Nylund	Toronto	76	3	17	20	37-	99	0	0	1
Jeff Brubaker	Toronto	68	8	4	12	18-	209	2	0	1
Jim Korn	Toronto	41	5	5	10	17-	171	2	0	0
Bill Kitchen	Toronto	29	1	4	5	6-	27	0	0	0
Bob McGill	Toronto	72	0	5	5	0	250	0	0	0
Ken Strong	Toronto	11	2	0	2	3-	4	0	0	0
Gary Yaremchuk	Toronto	12	1	1	2	7-	16	0	0	0
Steve Thomas	Toronto	18	1	1	2	13-	2	0	0	0
Bill Root	Toronto	35	1	1	2	25-	23	0	0	0
Gaston Gingras	Toronto	5	0	2	2	7-	0	0	0	0
Bill Stewart	Toronto	27	0	2	2	3-	32	0	0	0
Tim Bernhardt	Toronto	37	0	2	2	0	4	0	0	0
Todd Gill	Toronto	10	1	0	1	1-	13	0	0	0
Allan Bester	Toronto	15	0	1	1	0	4	0	0	0
Jeff Jackson	Toronto	17	0	1	1	4-	24	0	0	0
Ken Wregget	Toronto	23	0	1	1	0	10	0	0	0
Wes Jarvis	Toronto	26	0	1	1	6-	2	0	0	0
Greg Britz	Toronto	1	0	0	0	0	2	0	0	0
Basil McRae	Toronto	1	0	0	0	0	0	0	0	0
Cam Plante	Toronto	2	0	0	0	0	0	0	0	0
Leigh Verstraete	Toronto	2	0	0	0	0	0	0	0	0
Derek Laxdal	Toronto	3	0	0	0	1-	6	0	0	0
Larry Landon	Toronto	7	0	0	0	4-	2	0	0	0
Craig Muni	Toronto	8	0	0	0	0	0	0	0	0
Rick St. Croix	Toronto	11	0	0	0	0	0	0	0	0
Patrik Sundstrom	Vancouver	71	25	43	68	17-	46	5	0	2
Stan Smyl	Vancouver	80	27	37	64	18-	100	6	2	1
Thomas Gradin	Vancouver	76	22	42	64	22-	43	3	0	3
Tony Tanti	Vancouver	68	39	20	59	21-	45	14	0	4
Moe Lemay	Vancouver	74	21	31	52	11-	68	4	1	2
Peter McNab	Vancouver	75	23	25	48	20-	10	9	0	1
Cam Neely	Vancouver	72	21	18	39	26-	137	4	0	1
Petri Skriko	Vancouver	72	21	14	35	26-	10	3	0	2
Al MacAdam	Vancouver	80	14	20	34	29-	27	0	2	2
Doug Halward	Vancouver	71	7	27	34	42-	82	2	1	0
Michel Petit	Vancouver	69	5	26	31	26-	127	1	1	1
Doug Lidster	Vancouver	78	6	24	30	11-	55	2	0	0
Gary Lupul	Vancouver	66	12	17	29	15-	82	2	0	2
J.J. Daigneault	Vancouver	67	4	23	27	14-	69	2	0	0

PLAYER	TEAM	GP	G	A	PTS	+/−	PIM	PP	SH	GW
Mark Kirton	Vancouver	62	17	5	22	22−	21	2	0	0
Rick Lanz	Vancouver	57	2	17	19	22−	69	2	0	0
Jiri Bubla	Vancouver	56	2	15	17	15−	54	0	0	0
Jere Gillis	Vancouver	37	5	11	16	7−	23	0	0	1
Garth Butcher	Vancouver	75	3	9	12	31−	152	0	0	1
Jean-Marc Lanthier	Vancouver	27	6	4	10	16−	13	2	0	1
Neil Belland	Vancouver	13	0	6	6	4−	6	0	0	0
Taylor Hall	Vancouver	7	1	4	5	0	19	0	0	0
Ron Delorme	Vancouver	31	1	2	3	8−	51	0	0	0
Mike Stevens	Vancouver	6	0	3	3	2−	6	0	0	0
Frank Caprice	Vancouver	28	0	2	2	0	0	0	0	0
Grant Martin	Vancouver	12	0	1	1	8−	39	0	0	0
Richard Brodeur	Vancouver	51	0	1	1	0	4	0	0	0
Marc Crawford	Vancouver	1	0	0	0	4−	4	0	0	0
Bruce Holloway	Vancouver	2	0	0	0	1−	0	0	0	0
Dave Morrison	Vancouver	8	0	0	0	6−	0	0	0	0
Craig Coxe	Vancouver	9	0	0	0	5−	49	0	0	0
John Garrett	Vancouver	10	0	0	0	0	14	0	0	0
Andy Schliebener	Vancouver	11	0	0	0	11−	16	0	0	0
Greg Adams	Washington	51	6	12	18	8	72	0	0	1
Lou Franceschetti	Washington	22	4	7	11	1	45	0	0	1
Peter Andersson	Washington	57	0	10	10	5	21	0	0	0
Paul Gardner	Washington	12	2	4	6	1−	6	2	0	0
Glen Currie	Washington	44	1	5	6	2	19	0	0	0
Timo Blomqvist	Washington	53	1	4	5	11	51	0	0	0
Andre Hidi	Washington	6	2	1	3	2	9	1	0	0
Dave Shand	Washington	13	1	1	2	1	34	0	0	0
Kevin Hatcher	Washington	2	1	0	1	1	0	0	1	0
Mikko Leinonen	Washington	3	0	1	1	1	2	0	0	0
Bob Mason	Washington	12	0	1	1	0	0	0	0	0
Pat Riggin	Washington	57	0	1	1	0	2	0	0	0
Al Jensen	Washington	14	0	0	0	0	6	0	0	0
Mike Gartner	Washington	80	50	52	102	17	71	17	0	11
Bob Carpenter	Washington	80	53	42	95	20	87	12	0	7
Dave Christian	Washington	80	26	43	69	20	14	5	0	2
Scott Stevens	Washington	80	21	44	65	19	221	16	0	5
Larry Murphy	Washington	79	13	42	55	21	51	3	0	0
Craig Laughlin	Washington	78	16	34	50	12	38	5	0	3
Alan Haworth	Washington	76	23	26	49	19	48	4	0	2
Bengt Gustafsson	Washington	51	14	29	43	13	8	6	1	3
Gaetan Duchesne	Washington	67	15	23	38	16	32	0	1	1
Mike McEwen	Washington	56	11	27	38	22	42	4	0	3
Doug Jarvis	Washington	80	9	28	37	19	32	1	1	1
Bob Gould	Washington	78	14	19	33	10	69	0	1	3
Bryan Erickson	Washington	57	15	13	28	11	23	1	0	1
Rod Langway	Washington	79	4	22	26	35	54	0	0	1
Gary Sampson	Washington	46	10	15	25	20	13	0	1	0
Darren Veitch	Washington	75	3	18	21	31	37	2	0	0
Mark Taylor	Pittsburgh	47	7	10	17	7−	19	0	1	1
	Washington	9	1	1	2	1−	2	0	0	0
	Total	56	8	11	19	8−	21	0	1	1

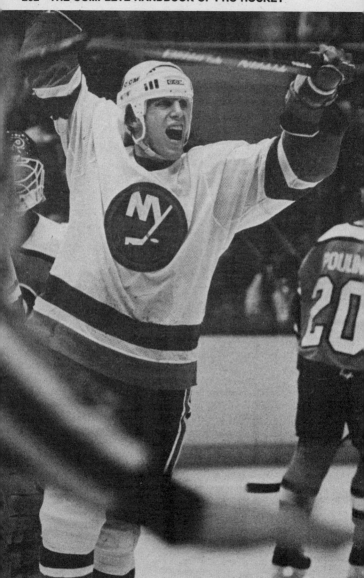

This is after Mike Bossy scored 50th goal last year.

PLAYER	TEAM	GP	G	A	PTS	+/−	PIM	PP	SH	GW
Dale Hawerchuk	Winnipeg	80	53	77	130	22	74	17	3	4
Paul MacLean	Winnipeg	79	41	60	101	5	119	14	0	6
Thomas Steen	Winnipeg	79	30	54	84	1−	80	7	2	4
Laurie Boschman	Winnipeg	80	32	44	76	8−	180	5	2	4
Brian Mullen	Winnipeg	69	32	39	71	15	32	8	0	4
Doug Smail	Winnipeg	80	31	35	66	12	45	0	3	5
Dave Babych	Winnipeg	78	13	49	62	16−	78	6	0	1
Randy Carlyle	Winnipeg	71	13	38	51	23	98	6	0	2
Scott Arniel	Winnipeg	79	22	22	44	7	81	3	0	3
Perry Turnbull	Winnipeg	66	22	21	43	9	130	2	0	1
Dave Ellett	Winnipeg	80	11	27	38	20	85	3	0	0
Robert Picard	Winnipeg	78	12	22	34	31	107	0	0	3
Bengt Lundholm	Winnipeg	78	12	18	30	8	20	1	0	1
Jim Nill	Boston	49	1	9	10	11−	62	0	0	0
	Winnipeg	20	8	8	16	2	38	1	0	1
	Total	69	9	17	26	9−	100	1	0	1
Andrew McBain	Winnipeg	77	7	15	22	2−	45	0	0	0
Tim Watters	Winnipeg	63	2	20	22	20	74	0	0	1
Ron Wilson	Winnipeg	75	10	9	19	8−	31	1	1	1
Wade Campbell	Winnipeg	40	1	6	7	1	21	0	1	0
Brian Hayward	Winnipeg	61	0	4	4	0	10	0	0	0
Murray Eaves	Winnipeg	3	0	3	3	3	0	0	0	0
Jim Kyte	Winnipeg	71	0	3	3	26−	111	0	0	0
Jordy Douglas	Winnipeg	7	0	2	2	6−	0	0	0	0
Paul Pooley	Winnipeg	12	0	2	2	1	0	0	0	0
Tom Martin	Winnipeg	8	1	0	1	1	42	0	0	0
Mark Holden	Winnipeg	4	0	1	1	0	0	0	0	0
Peter Taglianetti	Winnipeg	1	0	0	0	1	0	0	0	0
Dan McFall	Winnipeg	2	0	0	0	3−	0	0	0	0
Bobby Dollas	Winnipeg	9	0	0	0	3	0	0	0	0
Marc Behrend	Winnipeg	23	0	0	0	0	0	0	0	0

GOALTENDERS' RECORDS

ALL GOALS AGAINST A TEAM IN ANY GAME ARE CHARGED TO THE INDIVIDUAL GOALTENDER OF THAT GAME FOR PURPOSES OF AWARDING THE BILL JENNINGS TROPHY.

WON-LOST-TIED RECORD IS BASED ON WHICH GOALTENDER WAS PLAYING WHEN WINNING OR TYING GOAL WAS SCORED.

CODE: GPI—GAMES PLAYED IN. MINS—MINUTES PLAYED. AVG—60-MINUTE AVERAGE. EN—EMPTY-NET GOALS (NOT COUNTED IN PERSONAL AVERAGES BUT INCLUDED IN TEAM TOTALS). SO—SHUTOUTS. GA—GOALS-AGAINST. SA—SHOTS AGAINST.

GOALTENDERS	TEAM	GPI	MINS	AVG	W	L	T	EN	SO	GA	SA
Tom Barrasso	Buffalo	54	3248	2.66	25	18	10	4	5	144	1274
Bob Sauve	Buffalo	27	1564	3.22	13	10	3	1	0	84	581
Jacques Cloutier	Buffalo	1	65	3.69	0	0	1	0	0	4	37
BUFFALO	**TOTALS**	80	4877	2.92	38	28	14		5	237	1892
Al Jensen	Washington	14	803	2.54	10	3	1	1	1	34	295
Bob Mason	Washington	12	661	2.81	8	2	1	0	1	31	291
Pat Riggin	Washington	57	3388	2.98	28	20	7	6	2	168	1478
WASHINGTON	**TOTALS**	80	4852	2.97	46	25	9		4	240	2064
Bob Froese	Philadelphia	17	923	2.41	13	2	0	0	1	37	427
Pelle Lindbergh	Philadelphia	65	3858	3.02	40	17	7	3	2	194	1929
Darren Jensen	Philadelphia	1	60	7.00	0	1	0	0	0	7	30
PHILADELPHIA	**TOTALS**	80	4841	2.99	53	20	7		3	241	2386
Patrick Roy	Montreal	1	20	.00	1	0	0	0	0	0	2
Steve Penney	Montreal	54	3252	3.08	26	18	8	3	1	167	1344
Doug Soetaert	Montreal	28	1606	3.40	14	9	4	1	0	91	622
MONTREAL	**TOTALS**	80	4878	3.22	41	27	12		1	262	1968
Mario Gosselin	Quebec	36	2020	3.30	19	11	3	0	1	111	887
Richard Sevigny	Quebec	20	1104	3.37	10	6	2	0	1	62	491
Daniel Bouchard	Quebec	29	1738	3.49	12	13	4	1	0	101	824
QUEBEC	**TOTALS**	80	4862	3.39	41	30	9		2	275	2202
Doug Keans	Boston	25	1497	3.29	16	6	3	0	1	82	669
Pete Peeters	Boston	51	2975	3.47	19	26	4	3	1	172	1307
Don Sylvestri	Boston	3	102	3.53	0	0	2	0	0	6	52
Cleon Daskalakis	Boston	8	289	4.98	1	2	1	0	0	24	141
BOSTON	**TOTALS**	80	4863	3.54	36	34	10		2	287	2169
Rick Heinz	St. Louis	2	70	2.57	0	0	0	0	0	3	26
Rick Wamsley	St. Louis	40	2319	3.26	23	12	5	3	0	126	1094
Greg Millen	St. Louis	10	607	3.46	2	7	1	2	0	35	271
Mike Liut	St. Louis	32	1869	3.82	12	12	6	0	1	119	992
ST. LOUIS	**TOTALS**	80	4865	3.55	37	31	12		1	288	2383

The puck eyes New Jersey's Glenn Resch.

GOALTENDERS	TEAM	GPI	MINS	AVG	W	L	T	EN	SO	GA	SA
Andy Moog	Edmonton	39	2019	3.30	22	9	3	1	1	111	1050
Marco Baron	Edmonton	1	33	3.64	0	1	0	0	0	2	9
Grant Fuhr	Edmonton	46	2559	3.87	26	8	7	1	1	165	1426
Mike Zanier	Edmonton	3	185	3.89	1	1	1	0	0	12	100
Daryl Reaugh	Edmonton	1	60	5.00	0	1	0	1	0	5	35
EDMONTON	**TOTALS**	80	4856	3.68	49	20	11		3	298	2620

FUHR AND MOOG SHARED SHUTOUT VS. QUEBEC, JAN. 8

GOALTENDERS	TEAM	GPI	MINS	AVG	W	L	T	EN	SO	GA	SA
Chris Clifford	Chicago	1	20	.00	0	0	0	0	0	0	8
Warren Skorodenski	Chicago	27	1396	3.22	11	9	3	2	2	75	775
Murray Bannerman	Chicago	60	3371	3.83	27	25	4	3	0	215	1847
Darren Pang	Chicago	1	60	4.00	0	1	0	0	0	4	22
CHICAGO	**TOTALS**	80	4847	3.70	38	35	7		2	299	2652

GOALTENDERS	TEAM	GPI	MINS	AVG	W	L	T	EN	SO	GA	SA
Reggie Lemelin	Calgary	56	3176	3.46	30	12	10	3	1	183	1638
Don Edwards	Calgary	34	1691	4.08	11	15	2	1	1	115	858
CALGARY	**TOTALS**	80	4867	3.72	41	27	12		2	302	2496

GOALTENDERS	TEAM	GPI	MINS	AVG	W	L	T	EN	SO	GA	SA
Kelly Hrudey	NY Islanders	41	2335	3.62	19	17	3	2	2	141	1234
Billy Smith	NY Islanders	37	2090	3.82	18	14	3	1	0	133	1100
Roland Melanson	NY Islanders	8	425	4.94	3	3	0	0	0	35	257
ISLANDERS	**TOTALS**	80	4850	3.86	40	34	6		2	312	2591

GOALTENDERS	TEAM	GPI	MINS	AVG	W	L	T	EN	SO	GA	SA
Mike Liut	Hartford	13	791	2.88	5	7	1	0	1	38	419
Ed Staniowski	Hartford	1	20	3.00	0	0	0	0	0	1	10
Steve Weeks	Hartford	23	1397	3.91	9	12	2	0	2	91	700
Greg Millen	Hartford	44	2659	4.22	16	22	6	1	1	187	1288
HARTFORD	**TOTALS**	80	4867	3.92	30	41	9		4	318	2417

GOALTENDERS	TEAM	GPI	MINS	AVG	W	L	T	EN	SO	GA	SA
Don Beaupre	Minnesota	31	1770	3.69	10	17	3	3	1	109	934
Gilles Meloche	Minnesota	32	1817	3.80	10	13	6	1	0	115	949
Roland Melanson	Minnesota	20	1142	4.10	5	10	3	1	0	78	587
Mike Sands	Minnesota	3	139	6.04	0	3	0	0	0	14	88
MINNESOTA	**TOTALS**	80	4868	3.96	25	43	12		1	321	2558

GOALTENDERS	TEAM	GPI	MINS	AVG	W	L	T	EN	SO	GA	SA
Bob Janecyk	Los Angeles	51	3002	3.66	22	21	8	4	2	183	1483
Darren Eliot	Los Angeles	33	1882	4.37	12	11	6	2	0	137	944
LOS ANGELES	**TOTALS**	80	4884	4.00	34	32	14		2	326	2427

GOALTENDERS	TEAM	GPI	MINS	AVG	W	L	T	EN	SO	GA	SA
Brian Hayward	Winnipeg	63	3481	3.86	33	17	8	5	0	224	1814
Mark Holden	Winnipeg	4	213	4.23	2	0	0	0	0	15	104
Marc Behrend	Winnipeg	23	1173	4.45	8	10	2	1	1	87	624
WINNIPEG	**TOTALS**	80	4867	4.09	43	27	10		1	332	2542

GOALTENDERS	TEAM	GPI	MINS	AVG	W	L	T	EN	SO	GA	SA
Glen Hanlon	NY Rangers	44	2510	4.18	14	20	7	1	0	175	1439
John Vanbiesbrouck	NY Rangers	42	2358	4.22	12	24	3	3	1	166	1346
NY RANGERS	**TOTALS**	80	4868	4.25	26	44	10		1	345	2785

GOALTENDERS	TEAM	GPI	MINS	AVG	W	L	T	EN	SO	GA	SA
Ron Low	New Jersey	26	1326	3.85	6	11	4	1	1	85	628
Glenn Resch	New Jersey	51	2884	4.16	15	27	5	4	0	200	1401
Hannu Kamppuri	New Jersey	13	645	5.02	1	10	1	2	0	54	351
NEW JERSEY	**TOTALS**	80	4855	4.28	22	48	10		1	346	2380

Montreal's Steve Penney was 3.08 in first full season.

GOALTENDERS	TEAM	GPI	MINS	AVG	W	L	T	EN	SO	GA	SA
Ed Mio	Detroit	7	376	4.31	1	3	2	1	0	27	174
Greg Stefan	Detroit	46	2635	4.33	21	19	3	1	0	190	1361
Corrado Micalef	Detroit	36	1856	4.40	5	19	7	2	0	136	986
DETROIT	**TOTALS**	80	4867	4.40	27	41	12		0	357	2521
Tim Bernhardt	Toronto	37	2182	3.74	13	19	4	2	0	136	1106
Allan Bester	Toronto	15	767	4.22	3	9	1	3	1	54	430
Ken Wregget	Toronto	23	1278	4.84	2	15	3	4	0	103	752
Rick St. Croix	Toronto	11	628	5.16	2	9	0	0	0	54	314
TORONTO	**TOTALS**	80	4858	4.40	20	52	8		1	356	2604
Roberto Romano	Pittsburgh	31	1629	4.42	9	17	2	1	1	120	974
Denis Herron	Pittsburgh	42	2193	4.65	10	22	3	2	1	170	1362
Michel Dion	Pittsburgh	10	553	4.67	3	6	0	1	0	43	316
Brian Ford	Pittsburgh	8	457	6.30	2	6	0	0	0	48	292
PITTSBURGH	**TOTALS**	80	4832	4.78	24	51	5		2	385	2944
Richard Brodeur	Vancouver	51	2930	4.67	16	27	6	4	0	228	1574
Frank Caprice	Vancouver	28	1523	4.81	8	14	3	3	0	122	818
John Garrett	Vancouver	10	407	6.49	1	5	0	0	0	44	243
VANCOUVER	**TOTALS**	80	4860	4.95	25	46	9		0	401	2635

All-Time NHL Records

Game

MOST GOALS: 7, Joe Malone, Quebec Bulldogs, Jan. 31, 1920 vs. Toronto St. Pats; (Modern) 6, Syd Howe, Detroit Red Wings, Feb. 3, 1944 vs. New York Rangers; 6, Red Berenson, St. Louis Blues, Nov. 7, 1968 vs. Philadelphia Flyers; 6, Darryl Sittler, Toronto Maple Leafs, Feb. 7, 1976 vs. Boston Bruins

MOST ASSISTS: 7, Bill Taylor, Detroit Red Wings, Mar. 16, 1947 vs. Chicago Black Hawks; Wayne Gretzky, Edmonton, Feb. 15, 1980 vs. Washington Capitals

MOST POINTS: 10, Darryl Sittler, Toronto Maple Leafs, Feb. 7, 1976 vs. Boston Bruins (six goals, four assists)

MOST PENALTY MINUTES: 67, Randy Holt, Los Angeles Kings, Mar. 11, 1979 vs. Philadelphia Flyers

Season

MOST GOALS: 92, Wayne Gretzky, Edmonton Oilers, 1981-82

MOST ASSISTS: 135, Wayne Gretzky, Edmonton Oilers, 1984-85

MOST POINTS: 212, Wayne Gretzky, Edmonton Oilers, 1981-82

MOST SHUTOUTS: 22, George Hainsworth, Montreal Canadiens, 1928-29; (Modern) 15, Tony Esposito, Chicago Black Hawks, 1969-70

MOST PENALTY MINUTES: 472, Dave Schultz, Philadelphia Flyers, 1974-75

MOST POINTS BY A ROOKIE: 109, Peter Stastny, Quebec, 1980-81

MOST ASSISTS BY A GOALIE: 8, Mike Palmateer, Washington Capitals, 1980-81

Career

MOST SEASONS: 26, Gordie Howe, Detroit Red Wings, Hartford Whalers, 1946-47 to 1970-71, 1979-80

MOST GAMES: 1,767, Gordie Howe, Detroit Red Wings, Hartford Whalers

MOST GOALS: 801, Gordie Howe, Detroit Red Wings, Hartford Whalers

MOST POINTS: 1,850, Gordie Howe, Detroit Red Wings, Hartford Whalers

MOST PENALTY MINUTES: 2,994, Dave Williams, Toronto, Vancouver, 1974-84

There's no way to stop record-setting Wayne Gretzky.

MOST SHUTOUTS: 103, Terry Sawchuk, Detroit, Boston, Toronto, Los Angeles, New York Rangers

MOST CONSECUTIVE GAMES: 914, Garry Unger, Toronto, Detroit, St. Louis, Atlanta, Feb. 24, 1968 through Dec. 21, 1979

NHL Trophy Winners

HART MEMORIAL TROPHY

Awarded to the league's Most Valuable Player. Selected in a vote of hockey writers and broadcasters in each of the 21 NHL cities. The award was presented by the National Hockey League in 1960 after the original Hart Trophy was retired to the Hockey Hall of Fame. The original Hart Trophy was donated in 1923 by Dr. David A. Hart, father of Cecil Hart, former manager-coach of the Montreal Canadiens.

1923-24 Frank Nighbor, Ottawa	1954-55 Ted Kennedy, Toronto
1924-25 Billy Burch, Hamilton	1955-56 Jean Beliveau, Montreal
1925-26 Nels Stewart, Montreal M.	1956-57 Gordie Howe, Detroit
1926-27 Herb Gardiner, Montreal C.	1957-58 Gordie Howe, Detroit
1927-28 Howie Morenz, Montreal C.	1958-59 Andy Bathgate, New York R.
1928-29 Roy Worters, New York A.	1959-60 Gordie Howe, Detroit
1929-30 Nels Stewart, Montreal M.	1960-61 Bernie Geoffrion, Montreal
1930-31 Howie Morenz, Montreal C.	1961-62 Jacques Plante, Montreal
1931-32 Howie Morenz, Montreal C.	1962-63 Gordie Howe, Detroit
1932-33 Eddie Shore, Boston	1963-64 Jean Beliveau, Montreal
1933-34 Aurel Joliat, Montreal C.	1964-65 Bobby Hull, Chicago
1934-35 Eddie Shore, Boston	1965-66 Bobby Hull, Chicago
1935-36 Eddie Shore, Boston	1966-67 Stan Mikita, Chicago
1936-37 Babe Siebert, Montreal C.	1967-68 Stan Mikita, Chicago
1937-38 Eddie Shore, Boston	1968-69 Phil Esposito, Boston
1938-39 Toe Blake, Montreal C.	1969-70 Bobby Orr, Boston
1939-40 Eddie Goodfellow, Detroit	1970-71 Bobby Orr, Boston
1940-41 Bill Cowley, Boston	1971-72 Bobby Orr, Boston
1941-42 Tommy Anderson, New York A.	1972-73 Bobby Clarke, Philadelphia
1942-43 Bill Cowley, Boston	1973-74 Phil Esposito, Boston
1943-44 Babe Pratt, Toronto	1974-75 Bobby Clarke, Philadelphia
1944-45 Elmer Lach, Montreal C.	1975-76 Bobby Clarke, Philadelphia
1945-46 Max Bentley, Chicago	1976-77 Guy Lafleur, Montreal
1946-47 Maurice Richard, Montreal	1977-78 Guy Lafleur, Montreal
1947-48 Buddy O'Conner, New York R.	1978-79 Bryan Trottier, New York I.
1948-49 Sid Abel, Detroit	1979-80 Wayne Gretzky, Edmonton
1949-50 Charlie Rayner, New York R.	1980-81 Wayne Gretzky, Edmonton
1950-51 Milt Schmidt, Boston	1981-82 Wayne Gretzky, Edmonton
1951-52 Gordie Howe, Detroit	1982-83 Wayne Gretzky, Edmonton
1952-53 Gordie Howe, Detroit	1983-84 Wayne Gretzky, Edmonton
1953-54 Al Rollins, Chicago	1984-85 Wayne Gretzky, Edmonton

VEZINA TROPHY

Awarded to the goalie voted most valuable by the Professional Hockey Writers' Association. Up until the 1981-82 season, the trophy was awarded to the goalie or goalies for the team which gives up the fewest goals during the regular season.

The trophy was presented to the NHL in 1926-27 by the owners of the Montreal Canadiens in memory of Georges Vezina, former Canadien goalie.

1926-27 George Hainsworth, Montreal C.	1963-64 Charlie Hodge, Montreal
1927-28 George Hainsworth, Montreal C.	1964-65 Terry Sawchuk, Toronto
1928-29 George Hainsworth, Montreal C.	Johnny Bower, Toronto
1929-30 Tiny Thompson, Boston	1965-66 Lorne Worsley, Montreal
1930-31 Roy Worters, New York A.	Charlie Hodge, Montreal
1931-32 Charlie Gardiner, Chicago	1966-67 Glenn Hall, Chicago
1932-33 Tiny Thompson, Boston	Denis DeJordy, Chicago
1933-34 Charlie Gardiner, Chicago	1967-68 Lorne Worsley, Montreal
1934-35 Lorne Chabot, Chicago	Rogatien Vachon, Montreal
1935-36 Tiny Thompson, Boston	1968-69 Glenn Hall, St. Louis
1936-37 Normie Smith, Detroit	Jacques Plante, St. Louis
1937-38 Tiny Thompson, Boston	1969-70 Tony Esposito, Chicago
1938-39 Frank Brimsek, Boston	1970-71 Ed Giacomin, New York R.
1939-40 Davey Kerr, New York R.	Gilles Villemure, New York R.
1940-41 Turk Broda, Toronto	1971-72 Tony Esposito, Chicago
1941-42 Frank Brimsek, Boston	Gary Smith, Chicago
1942-43 Johnny Mowers, Detroit	1972-73 Ken Dryden, Montreal
1943-44 Bill Durnan, Montreal	1973-74 Bernie Parent, Philadelphia
1944-45 Bill Durnan, Montreal	Tony Esposito, Chicago
1945-46 Bill Durnan, Montreal	1974-75 Bernie Parent, Philadelphia
1946-47 Bill Durnan, Montreal	1975-76 Ken Dryden, Montreal
1947-48 Turk Broda, Toronto	1976-77 Ken Dryden, Montreal
1948-49 Bill Durnan, Montreal	Michel Larocque, Montreal
1949-50 Bill Durnan, Montreal	1977-78 Ken Dryden, Montreal
1950-51 Al Rollins, Toronto	Michel Larocque, Montreal
1951-52 Terry Sawchuk, Detroit	1978-79 Ken Dryden, Montreal
1952-53 Terry Sawchuk, Detroit	Michel Larocque, Montreal
1953-54 Harry Lumley, Toronto	1979-80 Bob Sauve, Buffalo
1954-55 Terry Sawchuk, Detroit	Don Edwards, Buffalo
1955-56 Jacques Plante, Montreal	1980-81 Richard Sevigny, Montreal
1956-57 Jacques Plante, Montreal	Denis Herron, Montreal
1957-58 Jacques Plante, Montreal	Michel Larocque, Montreal
1958-59 Jacques Plante, Montreal	1981-82 Billy Smith, New York I.
1959-60 Jacques Plante, Montreal	1982-83 Pete Peeters, Boston
1960-61 Johnny Bower, Toronto	1983-84 Tom Barrasso, Buffalo
1961-62 Jacques Plante, Montreal	1984-85 Pelle Lindbergh, Philadelphia
1962-63 Glenn Hall, Chicago	

ART ROSS TROPHY

Awarded to the player who compiles the highest number of scoring points during the regular season.

If players are tied for the lead, the trophy is awarded to the one with the most goals. If still tied, it is given to the player with the fewer number of games played. If these do not break the deadlock, the trophy is presented to the player who scored his first goal of the season at the earliest date.

The trophy was presented by Art Ross, the former manager-coach of the Boston Bruins, to the NHL in 1947.

Season	Player and Clubs	Games Played	Goals	Assists	Points
1917-18	Joe Malone, Mtl. Canadiens	20	44	–	44
1918-19	Newsy Lalonde, Mtl. Canadiens	17	23	9	32
1919-20	Joe Malone, Quebec	24	39	9	48
1920-21	Newsy Lalonde, Mtl. Canadiens	24	33	8	41
1921-22	Punch Broadbent, Ottawa	24	32	14	46
1922-23	Babe Dye, Toronto	22	26	11	37
1923-24	Cy Denneny, Ottawa	21	22	1	23
1924-25	Babe Dye, Toronto	29	38	6	44
1925-26	Nels Stewart, Montreal	36	34	8	42
1926-27	Bill Cook, N.Y. Rangers	44	33	4	37
1927-28	Howie Morenz, Mtl. Canadiens	43	33	18	51
1928-29	Ace Bailey, Toronto	44	22	10	32
1929-30	Cooney Weiland, Boston	44	43	30	73
1930-31	Howie Morenz, Mtl. Canadiens	39	28	23	51
1931-32	Harvey Jackson, Toronto	48	28	25	53
1932-33	Bill Cook, N.Y. Rangers	48	28	22	50
1933-34	Charlie Conacher, Toronto	42	32	20	52
1934-35	Charlie Conacher, Toronto	48	36	21	57
1935-36	Dave Schriner, N.Y. Americans	48	19	26	45
1936-37	Dave Schriner, N.Y. Americans	48	21	25	46
1937-38	Gordie Drillon, Toronto	48	26	26	52
1938-39	Toe Blake, Mtl. Canadiens	48	24	23	47
1939-40	Milt Schmidt, Boston	48	22	30	52
1940-41	Bill Cowley, Boston	46	17	45	62
1941-42	Bryan Hextall, N.Y. Rangers	48	24	32	56
1942-43	Doug Bentley, Chicago	50	33	40	73
1943-44	Herbie Cain, Boston	48	36	46	82
1944-45	Elmer Lach, Montreal	50	26	54	80
1945-46	Max Bentley, Chicago	47	31	30	61
1946-47	Max Bentley, Chicago	60	29	43	72
1947-48	Elmer Lach, Montreal	60	30	31	61
1948-49	Roy Conacher, Chicago	60	26	42	68
1949-50	Ted Lindsay, Detroit	69	23	55	78
1950-51	Gordie Howe, Detroit	70	43	43	86
1951-52	Gordie Howe, Detroit	70	47	39	86
1952-53	Gordie Howe, Detroit	70	49	46	95

Season	Player and Clubs	Games Played	Goals	Assists	Points
1953-54	Gordie Howe, Detroit	70	33	48	81
1954-55	Bernie Geoffrion, Montreal	70	38	37	75
1955-56	Jean Beliveau, Montreal	70	47	41	88
1956-57	Gordie Howe, Detroit	70	44	45	89
1957-58	Dickie Moore, Montreal	70	36	48	84
1958-59	Dickie Moore, Montreal	70	41	55	96
1959-60	Bobby Hull, Chicago	70	39	42	81
1960-61	Bernie Geoffrion, Montreal	64	50	45	95
1961-62	Bobby Hull, Chicago	70	50	34	84
1962-63	Gordie Howe, Detroit	70	38	48	86
1963-64	Stan Mikita, Chicago	70	39	50	89
1964-65	Stan Mikita, Chicago	70	28	59	87
1965-66	Bobby Hull, Chicago	65	54	43	97
1966-67	Stan Mikita, Chicago	70	35	62	97
1967-68	Stan Mikita, Chicago	72	40	47	87
1968-69	Phil Esposito, Boston	74	49	77	126
1969-70	Bobby Orr, Boston	76	33	87	120
1970-71	Phil Esposito, Boston	78	76	76	152
1971-72	Phil Esposito, Boston	76	66	67	133
1972-73	Phil Esposito, Boston	78	55	75	130
1973-74	Phil Esposito, Boston	78	68	77	145
1974-75	Bobby Orr, Boston	80	46	89	135
1975-76	Guy Lafleur, Montreal	80	56	69	125
1976-77	Guy Lafleur, Montreal	80	56	80	136
1977-78	Guy Lafleur, Montreal	78	60	72	132
1978-79	Bryan Trottier, New York I.	76	47	87	134
1979-80	Marcel Dionne, Los Angeles	80	53	84	137
1980-81	Wayne Gretzky, Edmonton	80	55	109	164
1981-82	Wayne Gretzky, Edmonton	80	92	120	212
1982-83	Wayne Gretzky, Edmonton	80	71	125	196
1983-84	Wayne Gretzky, Edmonton	74	87	118	205
1984-85	Wayne Gretzky, Edmonton	80	73	135	208

JACK ADAMS AWARD

Awarded by the National Hockey League Broadcasters' Association to the "NHL coach adjudged to have contributed the most to his team's success." It is presented in memory of the late Jack Adams, longtime coach and general manager of the Detroit Red Wings.

1973-74 Fred Shero, Philadelphia
1974-75 Bob Pulford, Los Angeles
1975-76 Don Cherry, Boston
1976-77 Scotty Bowman, Montreal
1977-78 Bobby Kromm, Detroit
1978-79 Al Arbour, New York I.

1979-80 Pat Quinn, Philadelphia
1980-81 Red Berenson, St. Louis
1981-82 Tom Watt, Winnipeg
1982-83 Orval Tessier, Chicago
1983-84 Bryan Murray, Washington
1984-85 Mike Keenan, Philadelphia

FRANK J. SELKE TROPHY

Awarded to the forward "who best excels in the defensive aspects of the game."

The trophy was presented to the NHL in 1977 by the Board of Governors in honor of Frank J. Selke, a "Builder" member of the Hall of Fame who spent more than 60 years in the game as coach, manager and front-office executive.

1977-78 Bob Gainey, Montreal	1981-82 Steve Kasper, Boston
1978-79 Bob Gainey, Montreal	1982-83 Bobby Clarke, Philadelphia
1979-80 Bob Gainey, Montreal	1983-84 Doug Jarvis, Washington
1980-81 Bob Gainey, Montreal	1984-85 Craig Ramsey, Buffalo

WILLIAM M. JENNINGS AWARD

Awarded to the goalie or goalies for the team which gives up the fewest goals during the regular season. To be eligible, a goalie must play at least 25 games.

The trophy was presented to the NHL in 1982 in memory of William M. Jennings, an architect of the league's expansion from six teams to the present 21.

1981-82 Denis Herron, Montreal	1983-84 Al Jensen, Washington
Rick Wamsley, Montreal	Pat Riggin, Washington
1982-83 Billy Smith, New York I.	1984-85 Tom Barrasso, Buffalo
Roland Melanson, New York I.	Bob Suave, Buffalo

BILL MASTERTON TROPHY

Awarded by the Professional Hockey Writers' Association to "the NHL player who exemplifies the qualities of preseverance, sportsmanship and dedication to hockey." Named for the late Minnesota North Star player.

1967-68 Claude Provost, Montreal	1976-77 Ed Westfall, New York I.
1968-69 Ted Hampson, Oakland	1977-78 Butch Goring, Los Angeles
1969-70 Pit Martin, Chicago	1978-79 Serge Savard, Montreal
1970-71 Jean Ratelle, New York R.	1979-80 Al MacAdam, Minnesota
1971-72 Bobby Clarke, Philadelphia	1980-81 Blake Dunlop, St. Louis
1972-73 Lowell MacDonald, Pittsburgh	1981-82 Glenn Resch, Colorado
1973-74 Henri Richard, Montreal	1982-83 Lanny McDonald, Calgary
1974-75 Don Luce, Buffalo	1983-84 Brad Park, Detroit
1975-76 Rod Gilbert, New York R.	1984-85 Anders Hedberg, New York R.

JAMES NORRIS MEMORIAL TROPHY

Awarded to the league's best defenseman. Selected by a vote of hockey writers and broadcasters in each of the 21 NHL cities.

It was presented in 1953 by the four children of the late James Norris Sr., in memory of the former owner-president of the Detroit Red Wings.

1953-54 Red Kelly, Detroit
1954-55 Doug Harvey, Montreal
1955-56 Doug Harvey, Montreal
1956-57 Doug Harvey, Montreal
1957-58 Doug Harvey, Montreal
1958-59 Tom Johnson, Montreal
1959-60 Doug Harvey, Montreal
1960-61 Doug Harvey, Montreal
1961-62 Doug Harvey, New York R.
1962-63 Pierre Pilote, Chicago
1963-64 Pierre Pilote, Chicago
1964-65 Pierre Pilote, Chicago
1965-66 Jacques Laperriere, Montreal
1966-67 Harry Howell, New York R.
1967-68 Bobby Orr, Boston
1968-69 Bobby Orr, Boston

1969-70 Bobby Orr, Boston
1970-71 Bobby Orr, Boston
1971-72 Bobby Orr, Boston
1972-73 Bobby Orr, Boston
1973-74 Bobby Orr, Boston
1974-75 Bobby Orr, Boston
1975-76 Denis Potvin, New York I.
1976-77 Larry Robinson, Montreal
1977-78 Denis Potvin, New York I.
1978-79 Denis Potvin, New York I.
1979-80 Larry Robinson, Montreal
1980-81 Randy Carlyle, Pittsburgh
1981-82 Doug Wilson, Chicago
1982-83 Rod Langway, Washington
1983-84 Rod Langway, Washington
1984-85 Paul Coffey, Edmonton

CONN SMYTHE TROPHY

Awarded to the Most Valuable Player in the Stanley Cup play-offs. Selected in a vote of the League Governors.

The trophy was presented by Maple Leaf Gardens Ltd. in 1964 to honor the former coach, manager, president and owner of the Toronto Maple Leafs.

1964-65 Jean Beliveau, Montreal
1965-66 Roger Crozier, Detroit
1966-67 Dave Keon, Toronto
1967-68 Glenn Hall, St. Louis
1968-69 Serge Savard, Montreal
1969-70 Bobby Orr, Boston
1970-71 Ken Dryden, Montreal
1971-72 Bobby Orr, Boston
1972-73 Yvan Cournoyer, Montreal
1973-74 Bernie Parent, Philadelphia
1974-75 Bernie Parent, Philadelphia

1975-76 Reggie Leach, Philadelphia
1976-77 Guy Lafleur, Montreal
1977-78 Larry Robinson, Montreal
1978-79 Bob Gainey, Montreal
1979-80 Bryan Trottier, New York I.
1980-81 Butch Goring, New York I.
1981-82 Mike Bossy, New York I.
1982-83 Billy Smith, New York.
1983-84 Mark Messier, Edmonton
1984-85 Wayne Gretzky, Edmonton

CALDER MEMORIAL TROPHY

Awarded to the league's outstanding rookie. Selected by a vote of hockey writers and broadcasters in each of the 21 NHL cities. It was originated in 1937 by Frank Calder, first president of the NHL. After his death in 1943, the league presented the Calder Memorial Trophy in his memory.

To be eligible to receive the trophy, a player cannot have participated in more than 20 games in any preceding season or in six or more games in each of any two preceding seasons.

Prior to 1936-37, top rookies were named but there was no trophy.

1932-33 Carl Voss, Detroit
1933-34 Russ Blinco, Montreal M.
1934-35 Dave Schriner, New York A.
1935-36 Mike Karakas, Chicago
1936-37 Syl Apps, Toronto
1937-38 Cully Dahlstrom, Chicago
1938-39 Frank Brimsek, Boston
1939-40 Kilby MacDonald, New York R.
1940-41 Johnny Quilty, Montreal C.
1941-42 Grant Warwick, New York R.
1942-43 Gaye Stewart, Toronto
1943-44 Gus Bodnar, Toronto
1944-45 Frank McCool, Toronto
1945-46 Edgar Laprade, New York R.
1946-47 Howie Meeker, Toronto
1947-48 Jim McFadden, Detroit
1948-49 Pentti Lund, New York R.
1949-50 Jack Gelineau, Boston
1950-51 Terry Sawchuk, Detroit
1951-52 Bernie Geoffrion, Montreal
1952-53 Lorne Worsley, New York R.
1953-54 Camille Henry, New York R.
1954-55 Ed Litzenberger, Chicago
1955-56 Glenn Hall, Detroit
1956-57 Larry Regan, Boston
1957-58 Frank Mahovlich, Toronto
1958-59 Ralph Backstrom, Montreal

1959-60 Bill Hay, Chicago
1960-61 Dave Keon, Toronto
1961-62 Bobby Rousseau, Montreal
1962-63 Kent Douglas, Toronto
1963-64 Jacques Laperriere, Montreal
1964-65 Roger Crozier, Detroit
1965-66 Brit Selby
1966-67 Bobby Orr, Boston
1967-68 Derek Sanderson, Boston
1968-69 Danny Grant, Minnesota
1969-70 Tony Esposito
1970-71 Gil Perreault, Buffalo
1971-72 Ken Dryden, Montreal
1972-73 Steve Vickers, New York R.
1973-74 Denis Potvin, New York I.
1974-75 Eric Vail, Atlanta
1975-76 Bryan Trottier, New York I.
1976-77 Willi Plett, Atlanta
1977-78 Mike Bossy, New York I.
1978-79 Bobby Smith, Minnesota
1979-80 Ray Bourque, Boston
1980-81 Peter Stastny, Quebec
1981-82 Dale Hawerchuk, Winnipeg
1982-83 Steve Larmer, Chicago
1983-84 Tom Barrasso, Buffalo
1984-85 Mario Lemieux, Pittsburgh

LADY BYNG TROPHY

Awarded to the player combining the highest type of sportsmanship and gentlemanly conduct plus a high standard of playing ability. Selected by a vote of hockey writers and broadcasters in the 21 NHL cities.

Lady Byng, the wife of the Governor-General of Canada in 1925, presented the trophy to the NHL during that year.

1924-25 Frank Nighbor, Ottawa
1925-26 Frank Nighbor, Ottawa
1926-27 Billy Burch, New York A.
1927-28 Frank Boucher, New York R.
1928-29 Frank Boucher, New York R.
1929-30 Frank Boucher, New York R.
1930-31 Frank Boucher, New York R.
1931-32 Joe Primeau, Toronto
1932-33 Frank Boucher, New York R.
1933-34 Frank Boucher, New York R.
1934-35 Frank Boucher, New York R.
1935-36 Doc Romnes, Chicago
1936-37 Marty Barry, Detroit
1937-38 Gordie Drillon, Toronto
1938-39 Clint Smith, New York R.
1939-40 Bobby Bauer, Boston
1940-41 Bobby Bauer, Boston
1941-42 Syl Apps, Toronto
1942-43 Max Bentley, Chicago
1943-44 Clint Smith, Chicago
1944-45 Bill Mosienko, Chicago
1945-46 Toe Blake, Montreal
1946-47 Bobby Bauer, Boston
1947-48 Buddy O'Connor, New York R.
1948-49 Bill Quackenbush, Detroit
1949-50 Edgar Laprade, New York R.
1950-51 Red Kelly, Detroit
1951-52 Sid Smith, Toronto
1952-53 Red Kelly, Detroit
1953-54 Red Kelly, Detroit
1954-55 Sid Smith, Toronto

1955-56 Earl Reibel, Detroit
1956-57 Andy Hebenton, New York R.
1957-58 Camille Henry, New York R.
1958-59 Alex Delvecchio, Detroit
1959-60 Don McKenney, Boston
1960-61 Red Kelly, Toronto
1961-62 Dave Keon, Toronto
1962-63 Dave Keon, Toronto
1963-64 Ken Wharram, Chicago
1964-65 Bobby Hull, Chicago
1965-66 Alex Delvecchio, Detroit
1966-67 Stan Mikita, Chicago
1967-68 Stan Mikita, Chicago
1968-69 Alex Delvecchio, Detroit
1969-70 Phil Goyette, St. Louis
1970-71 Johnny Bucyk, Boston
1971-72 Jean Ratelle, New York R.
1972-73 Gil Perreault, Buffalo
1973-74 John Bucyk, Boston
1974-75 Marcel Dionne, Detroit
1975-76 Jean Ratelle, New York R.
1976-77 Marcel Dionne, Los Angeles
1977-78 Butch Goring, Los Angeles
1978-79 Bob MacMillan, Atlanta
1979-80 Wayne Gretzky, Edmonton
1980-81 Rick Kehoe, Pittsburgh
1981-82 Rick Middleton, Boston
1982-83 Mike Bossy, New York I.
1983-84 Mike Bossy, New York I.
1984-85 Jari Kurri, Edmonton

STANLEY CUP WINNERS

Season	Champions	Coach
1892-93	Montreal A.A.A.	
1894-95	Montreal Victorias	Mike Grant*
1895-96	Winnipeg Victorias	
1896-97	Montreal Victorias	Mike Grant*
1897-98	Montreal Victorias	F. Richardson
1898-99	Montreal Shamrocks	H. J. Trihey*
1899-00	Montreal Shamrocks	H. J. Trihey*
1900-01	Winnipeg Victorias	
1901-02	Montreal A.A.A.	R. R. Boon*
1902-03	Ottawa Silver Seven	A. T. Smith
1903-04	Ottawa Silver Seven	A. T. Smith
1904-05	Ottawa Silver Seven	A. T. Smith
1905-06	Montreal Wanderers	
1906-07	Kenora Thistles (January)	Tommy Phillips*
1906-07	Montreal Wanderers (March)	Cecil Blachford
1907-08	Montreal Wanderers	Cecil Blachford
1908-09	Ottawa Senators	Bruce Stuart*
1909-10	Montreal Wanderers	Pud Glass*
1910-11	Ottawa Senators	Bruce Stuart*
1911-12	Quebec Bulldogs	C. Nolan
** 1912-13	Quebec Bulldogs	Joe Marlowe*
1913-14	Toronto Blue Shirts	Scotty Davidson*
1914-15	Vancouver Millionaires	Frank Patrick
1915-16	Montreal Canadiens	George Kennedy
1916-17	Seattle Metropolitans	Pete Muldoon
1917-18	Toronto Arenas	Dick Carroll
*** 1918-19	No decision.	
1919-20	Ottawa Senators	Pete Green
1920-21	Ottawa Senators	Pete Green
1921-22	Toronto St. Pats	Eddie Powers
1922-23	Ottawa Senators	Pete Green
1923-24	Montreal Canadiens	Leo Dandurand
1924-25	Victoria Cougars	Lester Patrick
1925-26	Montreal Maroons	Eddie Gerard
1926-27	Ottawa Senators	Dave Gill
1927-28	New York Rangers	Lester Patrick
1928-29	Boston Bruins	Cy Denneny
1929-30	Montreal Canadiens	Cecil Hart

* In the early years the teams were frequently run by the Captain.
** Victoria defeated Quebec in challenge series. No official recognition.
*** In the spring of 1919 the Montreal Canadiens traveled to Seattle to meet Seattle, PCHL champions. After five games had been played—teams were tied at 2 wins each and 1 tie—the series was called off by the local Department of Health because of the influenza epidemic and the death from influenza of Joe Hall.

The Flyers and Oilers battle for the Cup in 1984-85.

Season	Champions	Coach
1930-31	Montreal Canadiens	Cecil Hart
1931-32	Toronto Maple Leafs	Dick Irvin
1932-33	New York Rangers	Lester Patrick
1933-34	Chicago Black Hawks	Tommy Gorman
1934-35	Montreal Maroons	Tommy Gorman
1935-36	Detroit Red Wings	Jack Adams
1936-37	Detroit Red Wings	Jack Adams
1937-38	Chicago Black Hawks	Bill Stewart
1938-39	Boston Bruins	Art Ross
1939-40	New York Rangers	Frank Boucher
1940-41	Boston Bruins	Cooney Weiland
1941-42	Toronto Maple Leafs	Hap Day
1942-43	Detroit Red Wings	Jack Adams
1943-44	Montreal Canadiens	Dick Irvin
1944-45	Toronto Maple Leafs	Hap Day
1945-46	Montreal Canadiens	Dick Irvin
1946-47	Toronto Maple Leafs	Hap Day
1947-48	Toronto Maple Leafs	Hap Day
1948-49	Toronto Maple Leafs	Hap Day
1949-50	Detroit Red Wings	Tommy Ivan

Season	Champions	Coach
1950-51	Toronto Maple Leafs	Joe Primeau
1951-52	Detroit Red Wings	Tommy Ivan
1952-53	Montreal Canadiens	Dick Irvin
1953-54	Detroit Red Wings	Tommy Ivan
1954-55	Detroit Red Wings	Jimmy Skinner
1955-56	Montreal Canadiens	Toe Blake
1956-57	Montreal Canadiens	Toe Blake
1957-58	Montreal Canadiens	Toe Blake
1958-59	Montreal Canadiens	Toe Blake
1959-60	Montreal Canadiens	Toe Blake
1960-61	Chicago Black Hawks	Rudy Pilous
1961-62	Toronto Maple Leafs	Punch Imlach
1962-63	Toronto Maple Leafs	Punch Imlach
1963-64	Toronto Maple Leafs	Punch Imlach
1964-65	Montreal Canadiens	Toe Blake
1965-66	Montreal Canadiens	Toe Blake
1966-67	Toronto Maple Leafs	Punch Imlach
1967-68	Montreal Canadiens	Toe Blake
1968-69	Montreal Canadiens	Claude Ruel
1969-70	Boston Bruins	Harry Sinden
1970-71	Montreal Canadiens	Al MacNeil
1971-72	Boston Bruins	Tom Johnson
1972-73	Montreal Canadiens	Scotty Bowman
1973-74	Philadelphia Flyers	Fred Shero
1974-75	Philadelphia Flyers	Fred Shero
1975-76	Montreal Canadiens	Scotty Bowman
1976-77	Montreal Canadiens	Scotty Bowman
1977-78	Montreal Canadiens	Scotty Bowman
1978-79	Montreal Canadiens	Scotty Bowman
1979-80	New York Islanders	Al Arbour
1980-81	New York Islanders	Al Arbour
1981-82	New York Islanders	Al Arbour
1982-83	New York Islanders	Al Arbour
1983-84	Edmonton Oilers	Glen Sather
1984-85	Edmonton Oilers	Glen Sather

NHL TV/Radio Roundup

"Hockey Night in Canada" (CBC) in English and French (French TV Network) will again carry NHL games on Saturday night. On Friday nights there will be "NHL on CTV." In the U.S. a national cable TV package will consist of 30-to-33 regular-season games plus all playoff games. The carrier was undetermined at press time.

BOSTON BRUINS

Bruins' games are carried over WSBK-TV (Channel 38), with Fred Cusick and John Peirson at the mike. Bob Wilson and Johnny Bucyk handle the radio calls on WPLM (1390).

BUFFALO SABRES

Plans were uncertain at press time.

CALGARY FLAMES

Flames' games can be found on CFAC-TV (Channels 2 and 7), with Ed Whalen and John Davidson describing the action. Peter Maher and Doug Barkley are the radio voices on CHQR (810).

CHICAGO BLACK HAWKS

Plans were uncertain at press time.

DETROIT RED WINGS

Bruce Martyn does the play-by-play and Sid Abel the color for the Red Wings on WXON (Channel 20) and WJR radio (760).

EDMONTON OILERS

The Oilers are heard on CFRN radio (1260), with Rod Phillips and Ken Brown doing the honors. The television outlets are CITV (Channel 13), with Bruce Buchanan announcing, and CBXT (Channel 5).

HARTFORD WHALERS

Whalers' games are carried over WTIC radio (1080) and WVIT-TV (Channel 30). Cable TV station Sportschannel also carries Whaler games. Chuck Kaiton handles radio play-by-play and Rick Peckman handles TV and cable play-by-play.

LOS ANGELES KINGS

Bob Miller and Nick Nickson handle Kings' action on the club's own cable network (channel undesignated at press time) and on KLAC radio (570).

MINNESOTA NORTH STARS

The Stars shine on KITN-TV (Channel 29), with Frank Mazzocco and Roger Buxton. Al Shaver and Russ Small are on radio at KSTP (1500).

MONTREAL CANADIENS

The Canadiens are covered in English on CBMT (Channel 6) and French on CBFT (Channel 2) and CFMT (Channel 10). Dick Irvin handles telecasts in English while Lionel Duval, Rene Lecavalier, Jacques Moreau, Bert Raymond and Gilles Tremblay say it in French. English language radio broadcasts are carried on CBM (940) and CFCF (600), with Irvin and Ron Reusch, and Richard Garneau teams with Duval to provide French radio coverage on CBF (690).

NEW JERSEY DEVILS

TV arrangements were uncertain at press time. Larry Hirsch and Fred Shero are on WMCA radio (570).

NEW YORK ISLANDERS

Islander outlets are WOR-TV (Channel 9), SportsChannel and WOR radio (710). Jiggs McDonald and Eddie Westfall call the shots on TV while Barry Landers (play-by-play) and Jean Potvin (color) handle radio. Stan Fischler serves as host of pregame and postgame shows for all home games as well as between-period interviews.

NEW YORK RANGERS

Sam Rosen, Phil Esposito and Bruce Beck handle Ranger telecasts on WOR-TV (Channel 9). Marv Albert and Sal Messina are the voices of the Rangers on WNBC radio (660).

PHILADELPHIA FLYERS

Gene Hart and Bobby Taylor cover the Flyers on WIP radio (610) and WTAF-TV (Channel 29).

PITTSBURGH PENGUINS

Penguin games can be heard on KDKA (1020) and seen on WPGH-TV (Channel 53), with Mike Lange and Paul Steigerwald.

QUEBEC NORDIQUES
The Nordiques are carried on CHRC radio (800), with Alain Crete and Andre Belisle and CFCM-TV (Channel 4), with Claude Bedard and Andre Cote.

ST. LOUIS BLUES
Dan Kelly is the anchor man for Blues' games on KDNL-TV (Channel 30) and KMOX radio (1120).

TORONTO MAPLE LEAFS
Dave Hodge, Jim Hughson, Bob Cole and Joe Bowen cover the Maple Leafs on CBLT-TV (Channel 5) and CHCH-TV (Channel 11) and a radio network.

VANCOUVER CANUCKS
All games are carried on CKNW radio (980), with Jim Robson doing the play-by-play. Robson calls the action on CBC (Channel 2) and Bernie Pascall is on CHAN-TV (Channel 8).

WASHINGTON CAPITALS
Ron Weber covers Capital games on WTOP radio (1500). The TV voices on WDCA (Channel 20) are Mike Fornes, play-by-play, and Al Koken, analyst.

WINNIPEG JETS
Jets' games are carried on CKY radio (580), with Ken Nicholson and Curt Keilback. TV arrangements were still to be made at press time.

Official 1985–86 NHL Schedule

SUBJECT TO CHANGE   *Afternoon Game

Thur Oct 10
Tor at Bos
Hart at Buff
Mont at Pitt
Chi at Que
Wash at NYR
NJ at Phil
Minn at Det
Winn at Edm
Van at LA

Fri Oct 11
Winn at Calg

Sat Oct 12
Bos at Det
NYR at Hart
Buff at Minn
Chi at Mont
Que at Tor
NYI at LA
Wash at NJ
Phil at Pitt
StL at Van

Sun Oct 13
Mont at Bos
Que at Winn
NJ at NYR
Phil at Wash
Tor at Chi
StL at Edm
Calg at LA

Mon Oct 14
Det at Buff
NYI at Van

Tues Oct 15
Hart at Que
Minn at Pitt

Wed Oct 16
Bos at Van
Buff at Mont
NYI at Edm
NYR at LA
Pitt at Chi
Wash at Tor
Winn at Det
StL at Calg

Thur Oct 17
Hart at NJ
Que at Phil
Det at Minn

Fri Oct 18
Bos at Edm
Wash at Buff
LA at Van

Sat Oct 19
Bos at Calg
Mont at Hart
Buff at Wash
Pitt at Que
NYR at NYI
NJ at StL
Minn at Phil
Winn at Tor
Chi at Det

Sun Oct 20
Van at NYR
Phil at Chi
Calg at Winn
Edm at LA

Mon Oct 21
Que at Mont

Tues Oct 22
Bos at LA
Van at NYI
StL at Minn

Wed Oct 23
Hart at Chi
Mont at Buff
NJ at NYR
Pitt at Tor
Wash at Calg
Van at Det
Minn at StL

Thur Oct 24
Hart at Phil
Que at NYI
Chi at NJ
Tor at Pitt

Fri Oct 25
Van at Buff
LA at NYR
Wash at Winn
Calg at Edm

Sat Oct 26
Hart at Mont
Que at Pitt

NYI at StL
LA at NJ
Minn at Tor
Det at Calg

Sun Oct 27
Bos at NYR
Minn at Buff
Van at Phil
Wash at Chi
Det at Winn

Mon Oct 28
Edm at Calg

Tues Oct 29
Bos at NJ
Hart at Pitt
Mont at Que
LA at NYI
StL at Wash

Wed Oct 30
Que at Hart
Buff at Calg
Phil at Mont
Pitt at Det
Tor at Van
Chi at Minn
Winn at Edm

Thur Oct 31
LA at Bos
Det at NJ

Fri Nov 1
Buff at Edm
NYI at Wash

Sat Nov 2
Chi at Bos
LA at Hart
Buff at Van
Pitt at Mont
Phil at Que
Wash at NYI
NYR at NJ
Tor at Calg
Det at StL
Winn at Minn

Sun Nov 3
LA at Phil
Tor at Edm
StL at Winn

Tues Nov 5
Bos at Que
Mont at Hart
Calg at NYI
Chi at Wash
Edm at Van

Wed Nov 6
Winn at Buff
Mont at Minn
NYI at Tor
Phil at NYR
Calg at NJ
Wash at Pitt
StL at Det
Edm at LA

Thur Nov 7
Hart at Bos
Chi at Phil

Fri Nov 8
StL at Buff
NYR at Winn
Pitt at NJ
Tor at Det
Van at Edm

Sat. Nov 9
Bos at Phil
Hart at Que
Mont at LA
NJ at NYI
NYR at Minn
Chi at Pitt
Calg at Wash
StL at Tor
Van at Winn

Sun Nov 10
Minn at Bos
Calg at Buff

Mon Nov 11
Chi at NYR
Det at Van

Tues Nov 12
Mont at NYI
Edm at Wash
Tor at StL

Wed Nov 13
Bos at Buff
Minn at Hart

Mont at NYR
Que at Chi
Pitt at Van
Det at LA
Winn at Calg

Thur Nov 14
Bos at Tor
Que at StL
Edm at Phil

Fri Nov 15
NJ at NYR
Van at Wash

Sat Nov 16
Wash at Bos
Phil at Hart
Buff at Que
NYR at Mont
Edm at NYI
NJ at Calg
Pitt at LA
Chi at Tor
Det at Minn
Van at StL

Sun Nov 17
Tor at Buff
NYI at Phil
Edm at NYR
Minn at Chi
Calg at Winn

Mon Nov 18
Bos at Mont

Tues Nov 19
Buff at Hart
Edm at Que
Phil at NYI
NJ at LA
Pitt at Wash
Van at Det
Minn at Calg

Wed Nov 20
Edm at Mont
Tor at NYR
Wash at Phil
Van at Chi
StL at Winn

Thur Nov 21
NYI at Bos

Hart at Phil
LA at Det
StL at Minn

Fri Nov 22
Que at Buff
NJ at Van
Winn at Pitt

Sat Nov 23
*Phil at Bos
Winn at Hart
Calg at Mont
Que at Wash
NYR at NYI
NJ at Edm
Det at Tor
Chi at StL
LA at Minn

Sun Nov 24
NYI at NYR
Pitt at Phil
LA at Chi

Mon Nov 25
Minn at Buff

Mon Nov 26
Calg at Que
Winn at NJ
Tor at StL
Chi at Van

Wed Nov 27
Hart at LA
Buff at Det
Mont at Wash
NYI at Minn
Calg at NYR
Winn at Phil
Tor at Pitt
Van at Edm

Thur Nov 28
Que at Bos

Fri Nov 29
Hart at Van
Mont at Buff
NYI at Winn
NYR at Wash
Phil at Minn
StL at Det

Sat Nov 30
Bos at Que
Hart at Edm
Buff at Tor
Det at Mont
NYI at Calg
NYR at Pitt
Wash at NJ
Chi at LA
Minn at StL

Sun Dec 1
NJ at Bos
Phil at Winn
Calg at Edm

Mon Dec 2
Van at Mont
Pitt at NYR

Tues Dec 3
Winn at NYI
Phil at Det
Chi at Minn
Edm at LA

Wed Dec 4
Hart at Calg
Buff at StL
Van at Que
Winn at NYR
NJ at Tor
Det at Pitt

Thur Dec 5
Mont at Bos
Tor at Phil
StL at Wash
LA at Edm

Fri Dec 6
Pitt at Buff
NYI at Que
Van at NJ
Chi at Calg

Sat Dec 7
Bos at Hart
Mont at Tor
Que at NYI
*NYR at Phil
NJ at Pitt
Van at Wash
Det at StL
Minn at Edm
LA at Winn

Sun Dec 8
Buff at Bos
Phil at NYR
Chi at Edm
LA at Winn

Mon Dec 9
NJ at Minn

Tues Dec 10
Bos at Phil
Buff at Que
Pitt at NYI
Tor at Wash
Edm at StL
LA at Calg

Wed Dec 11
Mont at Hart
NYI at Pitt

NYR at NJ
StL at Tor
Minn at Det
Edm at Chi
Winn at Van

Thur Dec 12
Que at Bos
Mont at Phil
LA at Calg

Fri Dec 13
Hart at Buff
Edm at Winn

Sat Dec 14
*NYR at Bos
Pitt at Hart
Chi at Mont
NJ at Que
StL at NYI
Phil at Det
Wash at LA
*Tor at Minn
Calg at Van

Sun Dec 15
Que at Buff
Pitt at NYR
StL at NJ
Tor at Winn
Det at Chi
Van at Edm

Mon Dec 16
Hart at Mont

Tues Dec 17
Buff at NYI
Phil at NJ
Calg at Pitt
Wash at Van
Det at Minn
Winn at StL

Wed Dec 18
Calg at Hart
Buff at NYR
Que at Mont
Wash at Edm
Tor at LA
Winn at Chi

Thur Dec 19
Hart at Bos
Mont at Que
NJ at Phil
Pitt at Minn

Fri Dec 20
NYI at NYR
Wash at Winn
Tor at Van
Calg at StL
LA at Edm

Sat Dec 21
*Minn at Bos
NJ at Hart
Buff at Mont
NYR at NYI
Phil at Pitt
Chi at Det
Van at LA

Sun Dec 22
Bos at Buff
*Wash at Que
Minn at NJ
Pitt at Phil
Calg at Chi
Winn at Edm

Mon Dec 23
NYI at Hart
Det at NYR
Winn at Van

Thur Dec 26
Bos at Pitt
Hart at NYI
NYR at Buff
Que at Wash
Tor at Det
Chi at StL
Minn at Winn

Fri Dec 27
Mont at NJ
Phil at Calg
Edm at Van

Sat Dec 28
Bos at StL
Hart at Tor
NJ at Mont
Det at Que
NYI at Pitt
*NYR at Minn
Chi at Wash
Winn at LA

Sun Dec 29
Bos at Chi
Det at Hart
NYI at Buff
Wash at NYR
Phil at Edm

Mon Dec 30
Phil at Van
Winn at LA

Tues Dec 31
Bos at Buff
Hart at Que
NYI at Det
Pitt at StL
Calg at Minn

Wed Jan 1
Mont at Tor

*NYR at Wash
Pitt at Chi

Thur Jan 2
Bos at NYI
Que at Hart
Buff at Det
Phil at LA
Van at Minn
Edm at Calg

Fri Jan 3
Mont at Winn
Wash at NJ

Sat Jan 4
Buff at Bos
Hart at Edm
Mont at Calg
Que at Det
Chi at NYI
NYR at Pitt
NJ at Wash
Phil at StL
LA at Tor

Sun Jan 5
LA at Buff
Que at NYR
Det at Tor
Minn at Chi
Van at Winn
Calg at Edm

Mon Jan 6
StL at Mont
NJ at Pitt

Tues Jan 7
Hart at Calg
StL at Que
Minn at NYI
Det at Wash
Van at Winn

Wed Jan 8
Bos at Mont
NJ at Chi
LA at Pitt
Edm at Tor

Thur Jan 9
StL at Bos
Pitt at NYI
Wash at Phil
Van at Calg

Fri Jan 10
Hart at Van
Tor at Buff
Mont at NYR
Edm at Que
Chi at Det
LA at Minn

Sat Jan 11
*Winn at Bos
Edm at Mont
Que at Tor
Det at NYI
*Phil at NJ
Wash at Minn
LA at StL

Sun Jan 12
Hart at Chi
StL at NYR
Calg at Phil

Mon Jan 13
Edm at Bos
Buff at Pitt
Det at Tor

Tues Jan 14
Winn at Que
NYR at Van
NJ at Pitt
Calg at Wash
Chi at Minn

Wed Jan 15
Edm at Hart
Buff at Chi
Winn at Mont
NYI at Pitt
NYR at LA
NJ at Det
Tor at StL

Thur Jan 16
Calg at Bos
StL at Minn

Fri Jan 17
Que at Hart
Mont at Buff
NYI at Phil
Wash at NJ
Chi at Winn
LA at Van

Sat Jan 18
Hart at Que
NYI at Mont
NYR at Edm
Phil at Wash
Pitt at StL
Minn at Tor
*Calg at Det
Van at LA

Sun Jan 19
Bos at Winn
Buff at NJ
Minn at Pitt
Calg at Tor
Det at Chi

Mon Jan 20
Hart at NYR
Mont at Que

Tues Jan 21
Phil at NYI
NJ at Van
Minn at Wash
StL at LA

Wed Jan 22
Bos at Det
Winn at Buff
Mont at Chi
NYR at Tor
NJ at Calg
Pitt at Edm

Thur Jan 23
Winn at Bos
Tor at Hart
Mont at Minn
Que at NYR
Det at Phil
StL at LA

Fri Jan 24
Chi at Buff
NYI at Wash
NJ at Edm
Pitt at Van

Sat Jan 25
*Det at Bos
Winn at Hart
Buff at Que
Tor at Mont
Chi at NYI
Phil at StL
Pitt at Calg
Wash at Minn
LA at Edm

Mon Jan 27
Hart at Bos
Buff at Mont
NYR at Que
NJ at Minn
Edm at Chi
LA at Calg

Tues Jan 28
Tor at NYI
Phil at Pitt
Wash at Det

Wed Jan 29
Bos at Hart
Buff at Minn
Que at Mont
NYR at Chi
Pitt at NJ
Wash at Tor
Edm at StL
Minn at LA
Calg at Van

Thur Jan 30
Phil at NYI

Fri Jan 31
NYR at Buff
StL at Det
Minn at Van
Calg at Edm

Sat Feb 1
Bos at Mont
NYR at Hart
Phil at Que
Pitt at NYI
NJ at Wash
Chi at Tor
Det at StL
LA at Winn
Edm at Calg

Sun Feb 2
Pitt at Bos
Wash at Hart
Que at Buff
NYI at NJ
*Tor at Chi
LA at Winn

Tues Feb 4
All-Star Game
at Hart

Wed Feb 5
Mont at Que
NYI at Chi
NYR at StL

Thur Feb 6
Buff at Bos
Hart at Det
Edm at NJ
StL at Phil
Tor at Minn
LA at Calg

Fri Feb 7
Mont at Wash
Winn at Van

Sat Feb 8
*NYR at Bos
Buff at Hart
Mont at Det
*Chi at Que
NYI at LA
NJ at Pitt
*Minn at Phil
Edm at Wash
StL at Tor

Sun Feb 9
*Que at Bos
NJ at Hart
Edm at Buff
*Phil at Chi

Winn at Van
Calg at LA

Mon Feb 10
Minn at Mont

Tues Feb 11
Bos at Chi
Hart at StL
Van at NYI
Minn at Tor
Edm at Det

Wed Feb 12
Phil at Buff
Que at LA
Van at NYR
Wash at Pitt
Winn at Calg

Thur Feb 13
Mont at NJ
NYI at Minn
Tor at Chi
Minn at StL

Fri Feb 14
Hart at Winn
Buff at Calg
Que at Edm
NYR at Det

Sat Feb 15
Bos at StL
Hart at Minn
Phil at Mont
NJ at NYI
Van at Pitt
Wash at LA
Chi at Tor

Sun Feb 16
Bos at Minn
Buff at Edm
Que at Calg
Det at NYR
Pitt at NJ
Van at Tor
*StL at Chi

Mon Feb 17
LA at Mont
*Winn at Phil

Tues Feb 18
Bos at Calg
Van at Hart
LA at Que
Wash at NYI
Det at StL

Wed Feb 19
Hart at Buff
Wash at Mont
Winn at Pitt

Tor at Edm
Minn at Chi

Thur Feb 20
Que at NYI
StL at NYR
LA at Phil
Tor at Calg

Fri Feb 21
NYI at Buff
Que at Minn
Pitt at Det
Chi at Winn
Calg at Van

Sat Feb 22
Bos at Edm
Hart at Mont
Det at NYI
*LA at NJ
*Wash at Phil
StL at Pitt

Sun Feb 23
Bos at Van
StL at Hart
Wash at Buff
*Que at Winn
*Tor at Minn
*Calg at Chi

Mon Feb 24
Mont at Edm
Minn at NYR
LA at Pitt

Tues Feb 25
Bos at Que
NYR at Tor
Det at Wash
Calg at StL

Wed Feb 26
Minn at Hart
Buff at Pitt
Mont at Van
NYI at NJ
Edm at Winn

Thur Feb 27
Wash at Bos
Pitt at NYR
Phil at Calg
Chi at LA

Fri Feb 28
Que at Buff
NYI at Winn
Phil at Van
Tor at Det

Sat Mar 1
*NJ at Bos
Hart at Pitt
Buff at Que

Mont at LA
NYI at Minn
NYR at Wash
Det at Tor
Chi at StL
Van at Calg

Sun Mar 2
Bos at Hart
Wash at NYR
Winn at NJ
Phil at Edm
*StL at Chi
Calg at LA

Mon Mar 3
Winn at Tor
Minn at Det

Tues Mar 4
Buff at Phil
Mont at NYI
StL at Que
NJ at Wash
Pitt at Calg
Edm at Van

Wed Mar 5
Buff at Hart
NYR at Winn
Tor at Minn
Det at Chi
LA at Edm

Thur Mar 6
Que at Bos
StL at Mont
NYR at Calg
Det at NJ
Tor at Phil
LA at Van

Fri Mar 7
Hart at Buff
Pitt at Edm

Sat Mar 8
Bos at Mont
Que at Hart
Wash at NYI
*Phil at NJ
Chi at Tor
Van at StL
*Winn at Minn

Sun Mar 9
NJ at Buff
*NYI at Wash
Phil at NYR
*Pitt at Winn
*Calg at Det
*StL at Chi
*Edm at LA

Mon Mar 10
Hart at Mont

Tues Mar 11
Buff at StL
Van at Que
Calg at NYI
NYR at NJ
Pitt at Wash
Edm at Minn

Wed Mar 12
Bos at Pitt
Buff at Chi
Van at Mont
Calg at NYR
Det at LA
Edm at Winn

Thur Mar 13
Mont at Bos
NYI at Hart
Tor at NJ
Wash at Phil
Minn at StL

Fri Mar 14
Calg at Que
Det at Edm

Sat Mar 15
*Van at Bos
Chi at Hart
Buff at LA
Calg at Mont
Minn at Que
NJ at NYI
NYR at Pitt
Phil at Tor
Wash at StL

Sun Mar 16
NYI at NYR
NJ at Phil
*Det at Winn
*Van at Chi

Mon Mar 17
Que at Mont
Wash at Pitt
LA at Tor
StL at Minn

Tues Mar 18
Hart at Det
NYR at NYI
LA at Wash
Winn at Edm

Wed Mar 19
Hart at StL
Buff at Van
Mont at Winn
Tor at Que
Pitt at NJ
Minn at Calg

Thur Mar 20
LA at Bos

NYI at Tor
Pitt at Phil
StL at Det

Fri Mar 21
NJ at Buff
Winn at Wash
Minn at Edm
Van at Calg

Sat Mar 22
*NYI at Bos
LA at Hart
Mont at StL
Pitt at Que
*NYR at Phil
NJ at Tor
*Chi at Det
Minn at Van

Sun Mar 23
Bos at Hart
LA at Buff
Chi at NYR
*Phil at Wash
*Calg at Winn

Mon Mar 24
Que at Minn
Van at Winn

Tues Mar 25
Bos at Wash
StL at NYI
NYR at NJ
Edm at Det

Wed Mar 26
Mont at Hart
Que at Van
Edm at Pitt
Minn at Tor
Det at Chi
Calg at LA

Thur Mar 27
Mont at Bos
Buff at Phil
StL at NJ

Fri Mar 28
NYI at Wash
Edm at NYR
Winn at Calg
LA at Van

Sat Mar 29
*Buff at Bos
Wash at Hart
Pitt at Mont
Que at LA
Edm at NYI
NYR at Phil
*Chi at NJ
StL at Tor
*Minn at Det

Sun Mar 30
Bos at Buff
Tor at Chi
Calg at Van

Mon Mar 31
NJ at NYR
Winn at LA

Tues Apr 1
Buff at Hart
Det at Que
NYI at Wash
Pitt at Wash
Tor at StL
Chi at Minn
Van at Calg

Wed Apr 2
Det at Mont
NYI at Pitt
Phil at NYR
Que at NJ
Minn at Chi
Winn at LA
Van at Edm

Thur Apr 3
Tor at Bos
Hart at Wash

Fri Apr 4
Mont at Buff
Edm at Calg

Sat Apr 5
Bos at Que
Tor at Hart
Buff at Mont
NJ at NYI
NYR at Wash
Phil at Pitt
Det at Minn
Chi at StL
Van at LA

Sun Apr 6
Hart at Bos
*NYI at NJ
Pitt at NYR
Wash at Phil
Tor at Det
*StL at Chi
*Calg at Winn
Edm at Van

THE COMPLETE ENCYCLOPEDIA OF
HOCKEY

EDITED BY ZANDER HOLLANDER
AND HAL BOCK

All the vital facts, figures and drama in this revised, updated third edition:

Illustrated with more than 200 historic photos, this mammoth work contains:

- Lifetime year-by-year records of more than 3,000 NHL players
- Reviews of every NHL season • Profiles of the greatest players
- Hockey Hall of Fame • NHL and Stanley Cup all-time records
- Official Rules • Color photo insert

"A valuable and welcome addition to the reference library of any hockey collector, fan or journalist."
> —From the foreword by John A. Ziegler, Jr.
> President, NHL

"An outstanding reference book."
> —American Library Association

"A great book about a great game."
> —Bill Chadwick, Member of the Hall of Fame

An Associated Features Book

NAL Hardcover (0453-00449-0) $24.95 U.S. only